Charles Edward Yate

Northern Afghanistan

Or, Letters from the Afghan Boundary Commission

Charles Edward Yate

Northern Afghanistan
Or, Letters from the Afghan Boundary Commission

ISBN/EAN: 9783744764933

Printed in Europe, USA, Canada, Australia, Japan

Cover: Foto ©ninafisch / pixelio.de

More available books at **www.hansebooks.com**

NORTHERN AFGHANISTAN

OR

LETTERS FROM THE

AFGHAN BOUNDARY COMMISSION

BY

MAJOR C. E. YATE, C.S.I., C.M.G.
BOMBAY STAFF CORPS, F.R.G.S.

WITH ROUTE MAPS

WILLIAM BLACKWOOD AND SONS
EDINBURGH AND LONDON
MDCCCLXXXVIII

All Rights reserved

PREFACE.

THESE letters, written at different times from the Afghan Boundary Commission, are now published in a connected form as a sequel to my brother Captain A. C. Yate's book, entitled 'England and Russia Face to Face in Asia.'

Commencing at the time when the question of peace or war between England and Russia hung in the balance, the letters describe the sojourn of the British Commission around Herat during the summer of 1885; the subsequent meeting of the joint British and Russian Commissions in November of that year, and the progress of the demarcation of the frontier up to the time of their separation in September 1886; the return of the British Commission through Kabul to India in October 1886; the negotiations at St Petersburg during the summer of 1887; the final settlement and demarcation of the frontier during the winter of 1887, and return through Russian Trans-Caspian territory in February 1888; with a general description of the various points of interest connected with the frontier, as well as of the people and the country traversed, and a few notes on the difference between British and Russian military systems in the East.

The sketch-map of Afghanistan, for which I am indebted to Major Gore, R.E., shows the routes traversed by the Boundary Commission during 1884, 1885, and 1886. The second map, taken from the Blue-Books, illustrates on a larger scale the various points of interest connected with the settlement of the frontier.

CHAS. E. YATE.

LONDON, 12th *April* 1888.

CONTENTS.

CHAP.		PAGE
I.	THE HIGHLANDS OF THE PAROPAMISUS,	1
II.	PREPARATIONS FOR WAR,	11
III.	HERAT AND ITS ANTIQUITIES,	23
IV.	THE SIGNING OF THE PROTOCOL—PEACE DECLARED,	43
V.	LIFE AT KUHSAN—REDUCTION OF THE ESCORT,	50
VI.	FINAL VISIT TO HERAT,	61
VII.	THE MEETING OF THE JOINT COMMISSIONS,	70
VIII.	ACROSS BADGHIS,	88
IX.	CHRISTMAS AT MARUCHAK,	107
X.	WINTER-QUARTERS AT CHAHAR SHAMBA,	120
XI.	MARUCHAK AGAIN,	159
XII.	THE HERAT FRONTIER,	173
XIII.	A SNOWSTORM IN THE CHUL,	199
XIV.	DELAYS IN THE NEGOTIATIONS—RETURN TO CHAHAR SHAMBA,	209
XV.	BALA MURGHAB,	213
XVI.	THE MARCH TO THE OXUS,	226
XVII.	MORE RUSSIAN DELAYS—THE KHOJAH SALIH QUESTION AND THE BANKS OF THE OXUS,	240
XVIII.	AFGHAN TURKISTAN—KILIF TO BALKH,	250

CONTENTS.

XIX.	SUMMER-QUARTERS AT SHADIAN,	261
XX.	VISIT TO MAZAR-I-SHARIF,	272
XXI.	COSSACK AND SEPOY,	286
XXII.	THE DEPARTURE OF THE JOINT COMMISSIONS—TASHKURGHAN AND HAIBAK,	314
XXIII.	OVER THE HINDU KUSH,	325
XXIV.	THE MAIMANAH AND ANDKHUI FRONTIER,	334
XXV.	THE COMMISSION AT KABUL,	353
XXVI.	RECEPTION AT LAHORE,	371
XXVII.	NEGOTIATIONS AT ST PETERSBURG—FINAL SETTLEMENT,	378
XXVIII.	COMPLETION OF THE DEMARCATION, AND RETURN THROUGH TRANS-CASPIA,	384
INDEX,		421

PLAN OF BALKH, ... *To face p.* 256
MAP OF THE NORTH-WEST FRONTIER OF AFGHANISTAN,
In pocket at end.
SKETCH-MAP OF PARTS OF AFGHANISTAN, . . " "

NORTHERN AFGHANISTAN.

CHAPTER I.

THE HIGHLANDS OF THE PAROPAMISUS.

CAMP TAGOU ROBAT, 1*st July* 1885.

AFTER the hurricane, which nearly tore our tents to ribbons, at Sinjao, on the 16th and 17th June, no time was lost by Colonel Ridgeway in getting us into more sheltered quarters, and on the 19th we started for the Karukh valley, lying north-east of Herat. Our marches were :—

		Miles.
19th.	Gondou-Bala, ...	10
20th.	Deh Shaikh, ...	7
21st.	Deh Moghul, ...	8
22d.	Mach Gandak, ...	12

At this latter place we halted on a grassy sward, on the banks of the Karukh stream. Our route had led us across the drainage of the country below the main range, and between that and the low range of hills that lies immediately over Herat to the north, thus avoiding the Herat valley, although so close to the city itself. On the morning of the 20th, a small party of us, consisting of Colonel Ridgeway, Major Rind, Dr Charles, Lieutenant Drummond, and myself, striking off to the right of the line of march, followed a track down the bed of the stream through the low hills till we came to the hill at the mouth of the Kamar Kalagh gorge immediately overlooking Herat, from the top of which we had a capital bird's-eye view of the city. The north wall immediately faced us, with the lofty tesselated pillars and buildings of the Musalla between us and the north gate. The citadel was clearly visible, while the immense height of the walls, or rather of the mounds on which the walls are built, was shown by the lowness of the city inside. The roofs of the houses and the *chaharsu* or central dome, with a few trees here and there, were all that was visible, and with that we had to be content for the present. The wind was so boisterous on the top of these hills that we were not sorry to get shelter from it in the gorge below, and turning our horses' heads northwards again, we rejoined the camp for breakfast at Deh Moghul. The next day's march to Mach Gandak was the prettiest we had had for some time. Our road led across a series of small ridges dividing a succession of little valleys one from the other, with the high range of mountains in the background, from which all these little valleys came radiating down. The villages were all separate little fortlets, with nothing visible but four square walls, too high even to allow of the domes forming the roof of the houses inside to be seen. The crops for the most part were nearly ripe, and the fortlets and orchards scattered about all gave an interest to the scene. At Mach Gandak we found Captains Maitland, Talbot, and Griesbach awaiting our arrival, on their return from a tour in the Dawandah range, which bounds the Karukh valley on the east, dividing it from Obeh and the upper waters of the Hari Rud. We all enjoyed the treat of being encamped once more on a grassy sward, free from the wind and dust that made our lives such a burden to us in the Sinjao valley. The cavalry horses, too, and especially the grass-cutters, must have revelled in the change; but, alas! though political officers and camp quartermasters may propose, the doctors dispose, and before many days had elapsed the fiat went forth that the ground was damp and unhealthy, and a further move was advisable. Owing to the quantity of cultivation about, the only other site available was a bare stony bit of plateau covered with thistles, and the change was looked forward to with anything but pleasure. However, as everything was quiet in Herat, and there was no news of any Russian movements on the frontier, or any apparent cause for special anxiety, Colonel Ridgeway determined to go out and see for himself some of the sites for a summer camp farther up the valley lately visited by Captains Maitland and Griesbach. Accordingly a small party of us, consisting of Colonel Ridgeway, Major Bax, Major Rind, and myself, started on the 27th, and passing through Karukh, camped some 16 miles up the valley. Karukh is a large straggling village inhabited by all classes of Afghans, Jamshidis, and Tajiks. Our road, which led through the lower part of the village, ran along a narrow lane between the walls, sometimes of houses and sometimes of gardens. The men were noticeable as all wearing white turbans, a peculiarity which I at first set down as due to the sanctity of the place; but on further inquiry I found it is the common habit of the people here, whether of Afghan or Aimak origin. The Jamshidis settled hereabouts differ materially both in dress and habit from their wilder and more independent brethren of Kushk and Bala Murghab,—the result, I presume, of two or three generations of settled life. I noticed, too, that they were much more sparing of their salutations to us than their brethren across the mountains.

On the 28th we made an excursion to a place called Jauz-i-kili, lying immediately under the Dawandah range.

Following up the valley of the Malimar stream, an affluent of the Karukh, we eventually, after a ride of some two and a half hours, found ourselves in the uplands, resting under the shade of some fine old clumps of apricot-trees. The only available site for a camp we found was under cultivation, not to mention the fact that the road up was hardly passable for our baggage-camels; so we had to decide against the place. The air was delicious, and the first thing that brought home to us how much we had risen was the sight of the apricots on the trees above us—little green things about the size of marbles; whereas in the gardens at Mach Gandak and Karukh the apricot season was all but over. The only habitations in the place were two or three black *kibitkas*. An old man welcomed us pleasantly. He described himself as a Badghisi, or, as he pronounced it, Baighisi, though what that was he could not say, except that they were originally of Arab descent. Possibly they peopled Badghis in olden times before driven out by Turkoman raids. Now, he said, they only numbered about a thousand families all told, and these were all scattered. He had fifteen families with him cultivating the ground we saw, but all except two or three were away with their flocks at their *ailagh* or summer-quarters, still higher up in the hills; while in the winter they went down and pitched in the valley below. This seems to be the life of the generality of the people in these parts. They have no houses or settled homes, but are known everywhere by the name of "Siah Khana," from their tents, made of a black blanket sort of material, in which they live both summer and winter.

On the 29th we marched across the Karukh valley, and up to our present quarters in the Tagou Robat on the main range of the Paropamisus, above the Zarmast pass; and here in all probability we shall remain. The valley where we crossed it was only some 2 or 3 miles broad and quite uncultivated, though some 4 miles higher up we could see the village of Nourozabad; and again, near the head of the valley, where the Dawandah and the main range meet at the Kotal-i-Aokhurak, the little village of Badantoo was visible, with its green crops covering the lower slopes of the Dawandah range—all apparently well watered from the still unmelted patches of snow on the heights above.

There are two passes leading up the main range on the northern side of the valley: the Armalik—from a little village of that name at its mouth—and the Zarmast, both meeting at the top. We ascended by the Armalik, a rough but pretty pass, the road following the course of a clear rippling stream, the water beautifully cool, and the banks lined with willows, hawthorn, and white brier. At the top the ascent was steep, almost too much so for the few camels we had with us, but the scenery and air were delicious. Here we came upon a flock of ibex, but they were too quick for us, and though one of our party tried a shot at them, he was fain to acknowledge that an ibex running up a hill at 400 yards was too much for him. Tagou Robat is a sort of hollow at the top of the range between the Armalik and Zarmast *kotals* on the south, and the Kashka *kotal* on the north, and so named from a small brick *robat*, or shelter-house, on the banks of the stream, which here runs down a gorge to the west and falls into the Kushk river below. While the tents were being pitched I tried my luck with the rod, and soon found that the stream was full of fish,—of what sort I cannot say, but they took a fly well, and were very good eating.

The Zarmast pass, which I examined the next day, was found to be much more open than the Armalik, though steeper, but without the trees, rocks, and banks of the latter so fatal to the baggage-animals; and as there appeared to be no great difficulty in getting the baggage up, it was soon decided to make this our summer-quarters—at any rate for the present—and orders were sent for the camp to march up accordingly.

The 1st of July we devoted to a trip to Naratu, a curious old fort on a scarped hill some 12 miles to the north. Our road led over the Band-i-Kashka, and then wound along the hillsides for some miles, finally descending into a sort of valley or plateau to the old fort called Kilah-i-Aman Beg, after the Dehzingeh Hazarah who built it, not far from the *ziarat* of Kwajah Dehistan. Dehistan is one of the cities of Badghis mentioned by Ebn Haukel, the Arab geographer of the tenth century, but I did not notice any particularly ancient-looking remains about. Naratu itself is a scarped hill, precipitous on all sides except at one narrow point on the east, connecting it with a long low ridge, which forms the only entrance. The sides are everywhere so steep that it is most difficult to get up; and although the path to the one entrance wound all round the south-eastern side of the hill, even then it was too steep for our horses, and we had to dismount and lead them up. The old gateway forming the eastern end of the hill must have been a massive bit of masonry in its day; but now it is all in ruins, and we had some difficulty in picking our way through to the old stone archway that once formed the inner gate. The scarp is surmounted with the ruins of a massive wall of stone and mortar all round, but even without this wall the precipitous face of rock must have made the place wellnigh impregnable. The western and southern faces were the strongest, owing to the unbroken nature of the scarp. The north side has two scarps, and each of these was fortified. At the north-west corner is a second small fortification on the lower scarp, called the Kilah-i-Dukhtar, and the wall was continued eastwards along the top of this lower scarp nearly up to the gateway at the eastern end. On this lower ledge there is a spring of water issuing from under the limestone rock of the upper scarp—the only natural supply of water that we

saw in the place. There are several reservoirs on the face
of the hill, some even now holding water; and in addition
to these, we saw several wells cut down through the solid
rock, which may have touched some hidden spring below.
In one we could just distinguish some arches, evidently
betokening a large reservoir 20 or 30 feet below, but apparently now dry. As this shaft was sunk in a great mass
of rock without any apparent drainage to it, it could not
have been intended for the storage of rain-water, and probably tapped the sources of the spring on the northern face.
No one here can tell us the origin of the fort. The only
tradition concerning it is that it was built by Naraiman; but
who Naraiman was is not known, nor even the history of
his daughter, who gave her name to the fortification on the
north-west corner.

The great attraction of the place in these days is the
ziarat or shrine of Imam Ali Asgar, the grandson of Hazrat
Ali. This *ziarat* occupies the centre of the hill, and is enclosed by walls some 15 or 20 yards square, and overshadowed
by pear-trees, the fruit of which, I noticed, was only just
formed. These trees are covered with bits of rags, the offerings of thousands of pilgrims, and one old trunk bristles with
pegs of wood stuck into it in all directions, as well as with
bits of stone. Above the grove are the usual poles with
red and white flags, surmounted with tin hands, the meaning
of which, as a symbol, I have never been able to fathom.
At the *ziarat* we found a curious unkempt old Fakir or religious mendicant, who, when we entered, was busy ladling
a bowl of milk into a skin; but directly he saw us, he rushed
out and insisted on shaking hands in the warmest manner,
and eventually produced his store of bread and divided it
amongst us. The view from the top of the hill was very fine:
on every side vast grassy uplands covered with clusters of
kibitkas, the summer homes of the Kilah-i-Nau Hazarahs.
The country was covered with their flocks and herds grazing in

all directions; and as every hollow has its spring or rill of water, there are plenty of places for the owners to camp at. The hill tops and sides have a sprinkling of juniper-trees, though we looked in vain for those forests of pine which we had been led to expect.

The country to the west of our camp along the road to Kushk is much the same. The road runs along the stream for some distance, and then turns up across the hills amongst beautiful scenery, passing close to a hamlet of Hazarahs. Imagine some eight or ten *kibitkas* clustered on a little plateau above the stream; a short distance off, gradually working their way home for the night, a couple of flocks averaging a thousand head or more apiece; on another hill a lot of black cattle, and above them again a herd of camels —all wandering where they like. The great peculiarity of the camels of these parts is, that they always seem to affect the highest points of the hills, and one often sees them in the distance on the sky-line roaming about far above all other domestic animals.

All the hillsides here have at some time or other been terraced out with enormous labour, but who the labourers were who can tell? The Hazarahs and Jamshidis who now divide the northern slopes of these hills between them, seem to use them solely as summer grazing-grounds; and I have seen few signs of cultivation. No one lives up here in the winter now; but I cannot help thinking that at some time these hills had their regular population, else whence all these signs of former cultivation? Our camp here now stands at a height of some 6000 feet above sea-level, in the most perfect climate, clear, dry, and cool, and unequalled, so far as I know, by any hill station in India. No fogs, no rains, and sheltered from the wind; the thermometer in my tent, as I write now at noon, marking only 70°, and the hills, or rather downs, around covered with grass, and rideable in almost any direction. A perfect sanitarium, some will say, for our troops when we garrison Herat. Others, alas! say, Too late! too late! The Russians will have Herat, and we cannot prevent them. Not so, I trust. Not content with the admission that Afghanistan is beyond the sphere of Russian influence, we shall soon, I hope, lay down the dictum that not only is Afghanistan within the sphere of British influence, but that it is an integral portion of the British Indian Empire, and that we mean to maintain that empire in its integrity.

3d July.

The main camp arrived this morning at the foot of the hills, and we expect them up here to-morrow. The situation is central, being about equidistant from Herat and Bala Murghab, so that we get all news of importance without loss of time, and we are also within easy reach of both Kushk and Kilah-i-Nau. It is a great comfort to be away from villages and cultivation, where there is always the danger of some quarrel over a restless grass-cutter or a stray mule; whereas here not only is the supply of grass inexhaustible, the hills for miles around being covered knee-deep with a luxuriant crop of pure rye-grass, but whatever population there is, is exceedingly friendly to us—indeed so much so, that the Hazarah chief of Kilah-i-Nau sent a message to Colonel Ridgeway asking him to take up his residence amongst them.

The chief news from the frontier relates to the sickness of the Russian troops at Panjdeh, and to the arrival of some new Russian General, who was received at Panjdeh with a salute and much distinction. The Sarik Turkomans at Panjdeh are said to be much dissatisfied with Russian rule, and to talk of migrating south *en masse* to escape it. The Afghan troops have not advanced beyond Bala Murghab, as any fresh occupation of Maruchak might only lead to fresh excitement. Sirdar Mahomed Aslam Khan is with the Afghans at Bala Murghab. Mr Merk and Dr Owen returned a few days ago from a trip to Kushk, which they found nearly empty, almost the entire population having moved off to their summer-quarters in the hills. Captain Gore and Dr Aitchison are still in the neighbourhood of Mashhad, while Dr Weir is with Mr Finn on a tour along the Perso-Russian frontier. Captains Maitland and the Hon. M. G. Talbot leave shortly for Obeh, and Captain Peacocke and myself for Kilah-i-Nau, whence we hope to have the chance of exploring and surveying some of the hitherto unknown Firozkohi and Taimani country. The heat and want of water in the desert will be so great for the next two months, that it is not considered probable that we shall commence the demarcation of the frontier before September, supposing that the negotiations are brought to a successful conclusion in the meantime.

CHAPTER II.

PREPARATIONS FOR WAR.

CAMP, ROZABAGH, 21st *July* 1885.

WHEN last I wrote, the main camp was just arriving at Tagou Robat, and we were all congratulating ourselves on the prospect of spending our hot weather in that glorious climate, little thinking that ten days hence would see us all on the march down again. But so it was. The cavalry arrived up on the 4th, and the infantry and remainder of the camp on the 5th, and we all settled down to what we thought were to be our summer-quarters. No difficulty was experienced in bringing the heavy baggage up the Zarmast pass, despite its steep ascent and the fact that the Zarmast is the most difficult pass in the whole of the Paropamisus range. There will be no difficulty, therefore, in turning the place into the sanitarium it is evidently meant for, when the proper time comes. Our time at Tagou Robat was pleasantly occupied, by some in long afternoon rides over the hills, and by others in fishing and in proposals for picnics to Naratu and other places in the neighbourhood, never destined to come off. One party, consisting of Major Meiklejohn, Captain Durand, and Dr Charles, did indeed make good their visit to Naratu on the 10th, but others put off the trip till the morrow, and when the morrow came, half the camp was wending its way down the hill. I must not forget to mention the cordial welcome we always received in the Hazarah hamlets when riding about the hills. Whenever I felt doubtful about the road and went up to the nearest cluster of *kibitkas* to ask my way, the whole hamlet, young and old, generally turned out with words of welcome and desire to be of service. The Hazarahs were much more genial in this respect than the Ghilzai and Mishwani Nomads, who were interspersed and scattered about amongst them. Curiously enough, these people live all about the hills, within hail almost of each other, and yet neither can talk the other's language, and, so far as one can judge, they have little or no intercourse with each other. All the Afghans in the Herat valley talk Persian fluently, but these Nomads seem to stick to their native Pushtoo despite all surroundings. We always found them civil, but all their energies were generally devoted to selling us a pair of old *kurjins* or some bit of carpet; in fact, wherever you meet a Mishwani, he is pretty sure to have something to sell you.

It is astonishing what a number of these Nomads are supported in these hills at this time of the year. To the west of the Hazarahs come the Jamshidis—the Tagou-i-Jawal at the head of the Kushk river being the recognised boundary between the lands occupied by the two races; while Sirdar Sher Ahmed Khan, who went along the foot of the hills exploring the direct road above Kushk to the Ardewan pass, reports that the whole country to the west of the Jamshidis, again, is covered with the black tents of Nomads from the Herat valley, while almost all the Afghan cavalry are grazing their horses opposite the Baba pass, and yet the pasturage is so luxuriant that there is room for thousands more. However, we were not to add to the number for long. On the 10th the fiat went forth that we were to march down to the Tunian ford, some 20 miles east of Herat, cross the Hari Rud there, and march round to the south-west of the city. Application was received from the Afghan authorities for the services of officers to advise the governor regarding the fortifications of Herat, and next morning Captain Peacocke and myself were on our way there. Rumour at the same time was busy with the report of fresh Russian reinforcements at Zulfikar, and as the papers all tell us that this and Maruchak are the two points that the Amir insists upon, and that we therefore insist upon for him, we can hardly suppose that the Russians would bring down fresh troops to Zulfikar if they had any intention of evacuating it again shortly after. However, nothing further has been heard of the reinforcements, and we can only trust, for their sake, that they are not having the same unhealthy and uncomfortable time of it as their brethren at Pul-i-Khishti. We certainly have had the pull of the Russians in the way of climate and health. While they have been sweltering in the heat of the desert and decimated by sickness, we have been revelling in a climate where the thermometer rarely exceeded 75° in our tents by day, and where we sat down to dinner at night in our *cardigans*, or greatcoats, with hardly a man sick in hospital. Even here in the plains of the Herat valley the heat is nothing to complain of. If the thermometer does go up to 95°, and sometimes even to 100°, in our tents, still the breeze is always cool and the night just pleasant. In fact, we find a greatcoat most comforting before marching in the early dawn. Yet this is the hottest month in the year. Certainly no climate that I know of in India can hold a candle to that of Herat at this season of the year, and were the latter a British station with regular houses, &c., it would be one of the healthiest and pleasantest of our possessions.

It had been intended, on leaving Tagou Robat, to march the camp across the Karukh valley, and cross over the Bund-i-Khinjak at the southern end of the Dawandah range on to Tuuian, thereby avoiding the dense cultivation near Karukh. Ressaldar-Major Muhammad Husain, of the

7th Bengal Cavalry, who was sent on ahead to reconnoitre, however, reported the road unfit for camels, and so we stuck to our old road *viâ* Karukh and Mach Gandak. Karukh is the seat of the Shaikh-ul-Islam, one of the most powerful divines of the Herat district. Here we found the reverend old gentleman passing the last weary days of the Ramzan fast under the cool shade of a huge grove of pine-trees. Despite the heat in the rays of the sun outside, the soughing of the pine-branches overhead tended of itself to minimise the pangs of any unassuageable thirst; and I must say the pine-grove looked as pleasant a place to pass the Ramzan in as any that I have seen in the country about. In the absence of Dr Aitchison at Turbat-i-Shaikh Jam, I did not ascertain what species of pine these were; but they were fine strong trees, some 70 or 80 feet in height—a living proof of how much might be done in the way of arboriculture in this country under proper supervision. The trees are said to be 120 years old, having been planted by the present Shaikh-ul-Islam's father, who was the first to acquire possession of this plot of land, in the midst of which his remains now lie entombed in a huge *ziarat*. The camp halted a day on purpose to allow Dr Owen to operate on the eye of the Shaikh-ul-Islam. But professional jealousy, or political intrigue, or something, intervened; and before the appointed time, the private *hakim* of Kazi Saad-ud-Din, the Amir's representative, had carried the day and persuaded the old gentleman not to undergo the operation.

At Tunian the Hari Rud was found to be easily fordable, the water less than 2 feet in depth with a good bottom. The right bank is scarped by the water when in flood, and is some 20 feet in height; but the left bank lies low, with a wide expanse of grassy sward, where the cavalry fed themselves with ease for some days.

Here Captain Peacocke and myself rejoined from our visit to Herat. We had had a busy time of it there, thoroughly examining the works inside and outside the city, and were most civilly and hospitably received and entertained. We were met on arrival some 4 miles outside the city by Rustam Khan, the brother of the Sipah Salar, or commander-in-chief, and escorted by him and a regiment of Kabul cavalry to the quarters assigned to us in the garden of Shahzadah Kasim, on the north-east side of the city. The morning of the next day was spent in an inspection of the outside of the city; and the evening of the inside. Visits were also paid to the governor and the commander-in-chief; at the latter's house the Naib Salar and General Ghaus-ud-Din Khan were both present. The names of both these officers will be remembered as the commanders of the Afghan troops at Panjdeh, and their cordial greeting was proof of itself that all rumour of any ill feeling against the British officers there on account of the Afghan defeat was devoid of foundation. The Naib Salar was looking thin and ill, having only just recovered from the effects of his wound —a bullet through the thigh; but General Ghaus-ud-Din was as hale and hearty and ready for a fight as ever, and came down to the garden with Rustam Khan on purpose to escort us over the fortifications.

Of these works I can enter into no detail here. Suffice it to say that we spent five days in Herat, and met with the greatest civility throughout. The population of the place are only too anxious for the British to come; while as for the soldiers, so far from entertaining any ill feeling against the British, they are only longing for their aid in the coming struggle, and would be the first to welcome their advent. The religious element, too, is notoriously in favour of the British alliance; so much so, that it is said that when the Governor some short time ago referred the question as to whether the alliance and co-operation of the British would in any way detract from the merit of an Afghan *ghaza*, or crusade, against the Russians, the question was met by a most decided negative—and not only by a negative, but by strong advice in addition to secure British co-operation. This dictum, too, was given by Umar Jan Sahibzadah, now without doubt the most influential priest in Herat. I well remember this man at the time he came to Kandahar with Sirdar Abdullah Khan Nasiri as the envoy of Sirdar Ayub Khan from Herat—an austere, thin-featured man, who had more to do in raising Zemindawar against us at the time of Maiwand than any other person, and who even then was one of the most influential and fanatical priests of the day. To have him on our side is indeed a change of the cards.

From Tunian the Mission marched quietly down the Herat valley, which here is seen in its greatest fertility. I shall not easily forget the view I had of it on the evening of the 19th, when I rode out with Major Bax and Captain Griesbach to a small mound near our camp at Kurt, called Tepe Ghar, or the cave-mound. Standing on the top of the mound, we could not but admire the beauty and fertility of the scene. Away on the other side of the valley the walls of Herat stood out, backed by the tall minarets of the Musalla—the latter, alas! destined soon to be demolished. The Amir's orders for the demolition of both the Musalla and the still older Madrasah close by are being rapidly carried into effect, and a few days, or at most weeks, will see the last of this famous relic of bygone grandeur. The rooms and habitations have mostly disappeared, but the massive arches, some 80 feet in height, the still higher minarets, and the large dome, all of which bear traces of the beautiful tile-work with which they were covered, attest its former magnificence.

In the centre of the valley the waters of the Hari Rud glistened in the setting sun; while on every side, interspersed amongst the numerous villages and orchards, were lying the heaps of freshly cut corn, waiting to be threshed. The irrigation-works are certainly one of the wonders of this country. The valley here is a perfect network of canals and *juis*, as they are called, varying in size from some 30 feet in breadth and 2 in depth to the smallest cut of barely a foot in breadth. The annual labour expended in the repair alone of the canals is very great; but for all that, the people apparently prefer canals to any system of well irrigation, which is here unknown.

To-day the main camp is halting at Chahgazak, some 20 miles to the south of Herat; while Colonel Sir West Ridgeway, with Major Holdich, Captains Durand, Peacocke, Heath, and Griesbach, Dr Owen, Kazi Mahomed Aslam, and myself are at Rozabagh, a large village about 6 miles south of the city, where Sir West Ridgeway meets the governor of Herat to discuss the situation.

Captain Cotton and Captain de Laessoe, with Ressaldar-Major Muhammad Husain, have just returned from a trip farther up the valley, where they have been prospecting for sites for a camp to which to move the Mission when the present arrangements with the governor of Herat have been concluded. Captains Maitland and the Hon. M. G. Talbot are still away exploring and surveying the upper waters of the Hari Rud, somewhere about Daulatyar. Captain Gore is on his way back from Mashhad, and Mr Finn, Lieutenant Yate, and Dr Weir are still travelling along the Persian frontier. The native *attachés* are nearly all away too. Sirdar Muhammad Aslam Khan is still at Bala Murghab, doing capital work in controlling the relations of the Afghan troops there with the Russians at Pul-i-Khishti. Subadar Muhammad Husain, of the 2d Sikhs, is similarly employed on the western portion of the frontier. Ressaldar-Major Bahawaldin Khan, of the Central India Horse, is away on treasure-convoy duty at Mashhad; while Mirza Ghulam Ahmad and Khan Baba Khan are located at Mashhad and Turbat-i-Shaikh Jam respectively.

To-morrow morning Major Holdich, Captains Durand and Peacocke, and Kazi Muhammad Aslam Khan proceed to Herat to set the works on the fortification going without further loss of time, rejoining Sir West Ridgeway at Rozabagh a day or two hence. It is now hoped that the Amir's local officials will cease all petty obstruction and put their shoulders to the wheel, recognising at last that the Amir's interests are in reality bound up with those of the British Government.

The Amir's proclamation with the salute of 101 guns and general illumination of the city in honour of his appointment as a G.C.S.I. seems to have occasioned an extraordinary and most unexpected excitement amongst the Heratis. The rumour has gone abroad that the British Government has given Hindustan to the Amir in exchange for Kandahar and Herat, and nothing will persuade the villagers that the British are not shortly to take possession of Herat. The wish is evidently the father of the thought, and the eager manner in which the rumour has been credited and insisted upon may of itself very possibly have frightened the Amir's officials, who are probably the only people in the province to whom a British occupation would be unpalatable.

There is no particular news of any Russian advance, with the exception of the move forward of 100 Cossacks from Pul-i-Khishti up the Kushk valley to Chaman-i-Bed. Various Panjdeh Turkomans who were arrested by the Russians a short time ago, on the charge of being supposed to be friendly to the British, have, it is said, been released again, but the Sariks are still groaning under Russian rule. We have no very recent news from Turkistan, but everything is supposed to be quite quiet there, despite the rumours current some little time ago regarding the imprisonment of Abdullah Khan Tohki, the governor of Badakshan, by Sirdar Ishak Khan.

10th August 1885.

Our camp at Rozabagh was broken up on the 28th ult., when Sir West Ridgeway returned to the main camp at Chah Gazak, but only for a couple of days. On the 30th, with the cavalry escort, and accompanied by Captain Peacocke, Mr Merk, Captain Griesbach, Dr Owen, and myself, he marched northwards again, while the Heavy camp and the Infantry Escort at the same time moved westwards to a more elevated site in the Doshakh range, conveniently situated in case of any emergency. Here Dr Aitchison and Captain Gore rejoined after their long absence in Persia, the former having completed and carefully stored his botanical collections in the Mission House at Mashhad, out of harm's way, and the latter having not only fixed the longitude of Mashhad telegraphically with Teheran, but having completed the survey of a great portion of North-Eastern Khorasan in addition. Mr Finn not being at all in good health, Captain de Laessoe was sent off to assist or relieve him of his work along the Persian frontier. When last heard of, the party were at Kuchan, whence Lieutenant Yate was starting for Astrabad on return to India, crossing the Caspian to Baku, and thence visiting Batoum, Sebastopol, Constantinople, Athens, and Cairo *en route*. In the meantime Captain Cotton had been out on a trip with Ressaldar-Major Muhammad Husain, of the 7th Bengal Cavalry, across the Persian frontier, round by Charakhs and Yezdan, both Persian frontier stations. The country in that direction is very arid and the water often brackish.

On the 2d August, Major Bax, Captain Peacocke, and myself started on a fresh visit to Herat to report progress on the fortification works. On nearing the city on the morning of the 3d, we were met by Rustam Khan, the brother of the Sipah Salar, and learned that we had been expected by another road, and that the old Khalifah of Awalwali, a large shrine some 2 miles north-west of the city, had prepared tea and sweetmeats all ready for us, which unfortunately we had thus missed, and the good priest consequently had all his trouble for nothing. Three days were spent in the city in a thorough superintendence of all the works, which were being pushed on as rapidly as possible. Everything was thrown open for our inspection without the slightest hesitation—store-houses, magazines, and all. The Amir's letter informing the people that he was sending his own son with reinforcements had considerably inspirited the Afghan troops; and were the Amir really to send his son, or even any member of his family, to Herat, the troops would know that he was in earnest in the defence, and that is the one thing they require to know. The present Sipah Salar, being only the son of a Kafir slave-girl, is a man of no position or influence, and the men can hardly be expected to fight so loyally for him as they would for a member of their own Royal Family. I can only hope that the Amir will carry out his promise, and that without the least loss of time.

The houses in Herat are all low, and no buildings of two and three storeys in height—like the Wali's and Sir Oliver St John's residences at Kandahar, for instance—were noticeable. The Herat bazaar, too, is a very poor affair—far larger than that of Kandahar, in so far that the four main streets converging from the various gates to the *chaharsu* in the centre are all roofed throughout, but that is all. The shops are almost all shut—a few in the centre, close to the *chaharsu*, being all that remain. Everything about Herat, in fact, betokens the poverty of the people, and that is easily accounted for when one thinks of the number of sieges that this unfortunate city has undergone, and the number of times that it has changed hands, not to mention the time after time that it has been plundered by the troops of various rival chiefs. The Heratis have certainly had a very hard time of it at the hands of their Afghan masters, and no wonder now that they long for a change. The idea is still prevalent that the British Government is going to take over the country, and the people look anxiously for our coming, hoping for us to save them from the Russians. The treatment the Turkoman women are getting at the hands of the Russian soldiers is being everywhere spread about the country, and is causing considerable consternation amongst the people. With us they know that their womenkind are safe, and the steady discipline and good conduct of our troops during the last Afghan war is now bearing good fruit in bringing the sympathies of the people on our side.

Captain Durand, during his visit to Herat, took some capital sketches of the place; and he, again, was followed by Captain Griesbach, who succeeded in taking several good photographs of both the city and its surroundings. To talk, though, of Herat under present circumstances as a city, is a misnomer. The citizen is only conspicuous by his absence. The entire number of families in Herat is probably under 2000, and as many of these as possible are clearing out. At any rate, hardly any but soldiers are to be seen about the place. In former sieges, generally the greater part of the population of the valley flocked into the city for protection; but now, in the face of a Russian advance, the desire of every one is to get themselves and their families away out of the city to some far-off place in the districts, where they will be safer from molestation. The position of the unfortunate Herati during a siege, with the Russians outside and the Afghans in, would certainly be far from pleasant, and the farther they get away the better. Nothing can be more marked than the difference between the Herati and the Afghan. The former is far quieter and more subdued in manner—a cultivator, as a rule, pure and simple, rarely or never armed, nor apparently trained to the use of arms. Even the local sowars, when called out on duty, have scarcely a weapon amongst them, and when they do possess one, it is of the oldest and rottenest description; whereas the Kabulis swagger about armed to the teeth, with knives half as long as themselves, and weapons of every sort and shape. Despite all this swagger, though, the attitude of the Kabuli soldier towards the British is remarkably friendly. He still confidently hopes for the aid of the British soldier in the coming struggle; and though, of course, there may be some who pray fanatically for preservation from all unbelievers alike, yet they are few and far between, and the feeling of the mass towards us is one of hope and dependence.

Captains Maitland and the Hon. M. G. Talbot returned on the 8th from their interesting tour up the valley of the Hari Rud, having been able to get as far as Daulatyar, and having explored much hitherto entirely unknown country. The wildest fastnesses of the Firozkohi and the Taimani lie in these upper waters of the Hari Rud, but the Taimanis were found to be a quiet, inoffensive set of people, while the Firozkohis, who had some row on amongst themselves, had all moved away from their ordinary habitations on the Hari Rud, and gone off in a body north to the upper valley of the Murghab, only a few thieves being left in the country, but these did not trouble the British camp. Curiously enough, the Afghan soldiers going to and from Kabul on leave all came to the British camp for protection along the way, and even the supposed fierce and fanatical Zamindawari is said to have done the same—a striking example of the widespread confidence in our power of protection.

The weather lately has been terribly hot and dusty. With the thermometer up to 100° in our tents, and the dust pouring in through every opening, we have often wished ourselves back again on the grassy slopes of the Tagou Robat. However, the present uncertainty surely cannot go on for ever, and something will be decided before long. Once we know what it is we have to do, we shall buckle to in earnest to do it; and we only trust that our future fate, whatever it may be, may redound to the credit of our country.

CHAPTER III.

HERAT AND ITS ANTIQUITIES.

CAMP SANGBAST, 30*th August* 1885.

MATTERS here are much in the same position as when last I wrote. The Heavy camp and Infantry Escort are still encamped in the midst of the Doshakh range, where they enjoy a climate much more free from wind than we get here down in the Herat valley. The wind has been terrible for the last fortnight. Night and day it has raged unceasingly, and our tents are almost in ribbons—so bad, indeed, that Major Bax reported that if we did not soon get into some more sheltered spot, his men would hardly have a tent left amongst them. Fortunately, the last few days the wind has lulled, for all our efforts have failed to find a sheltered spot, and indeed I do not suppose there is such a place anywhere south of the hills. Lieutenants Drummond and Wright have searched in vain amongst the nooks and corners in the northern end of the Doshakh hills, but the ravines there are all too small for such a camp as ours, and, with the exception of bringing us back glowing accounts of the picturesque charms of Robat-i-Pai, a holy nook up in the hills possessing the mark of the Prophet's footsteps, nothing has resulted. So, till the times have changed or the political horizon has cleared, we must just face the wind as best we can. The heat has decreased of late, which is something, and the thermometer now rarely rises much above 90° in our tents.

Everything has been so quiet of late on the frontier, that we were somewhat surprised on the 14th to hear that a collision of some sort had occurred between the Russian and Afghan pickets at Kara Tepe. This is the Afghan frontier-post on the banks of the river Kushk, some 19 miles above Chaman-i-Bed, which, with Islim, marks the Russian frontier in that direction. Some Afghans—so they at least report—patrolled as far as the Russian border at Islim, but on their return were followed back by a Russian patrol. The Kara Tepe picket, seeing their own patrol pursued, as they thought, by the Russians, at once turned out, and the result was that one of the Russians—the officer or non-commissioned officer in command, so it is said—was shot. The Afghan story is, that the man in front was loading the rifle slung on his back, and that it went off by accident and wounded the man behind him. The Russian story we have not heard; but so far, the Afghan version has not been contradicted. The wounded man was taken in by the Afghans and tended at Kara Tepe till a day or two after, when a party of twenty Russians came down from Islim and carried him off on a bed. The Russians, of course, in this case were quite in the wrong, having had no business to cross the frontier line and push up to Kara Tepe, which is some 15 miles within Afghan territory; but Russian ideas of right and wrong in these parts are very vague, and the incident only shows how easily a collision can at any time be brought about. Though nothing further has happened, still the incident seems to have had some effect on the local Afghan authorities, waking them up to the fact that the present state of inaction along the frontier might at any moment develop into one of hostile advance, and inducing them to infuse even fresh energy into the works on the Herat defences.

There is no doubt in the Amir's endeavours to imbue his people with the idea of the earnestness of his preparations. Large quantities of grain are ordered to be stored in the city, sufficient for a siege of many months' duration, and the strictest orders have been issued to the governor on the subject of the fortifications. When a petition a short time ago was submitted to him by the Heratis, praying that the graves on a certain mound inconveniently near the city might not be disturbed, the Amir replied at once, pointing out to them how ill advised they had been to listen to such ideas; that all his energies were being devoted to save them and their families from foreign invasion, and that nothing must be allowed to stand in the way of any necessary precautions. As it happened, the destruction of these graves might have been the cause of much religious ill feeling had not the governor, by a good deal of tact, succeeded in calming the people's fears.

On the 18th instant Major Holdich, Captains Maitland, Peacocke, Gore, Talbot, and myself, visited Herat to inspect and report upon the progress of the works, and spent three busy days there, examining the place thoroughly, inside and out.

Herat is an interesting but not an inviting-looking city; few Eastern cities are. All who remember Kandahar will know what Herat is like: the same square mud-built fort, with this exception—that whereas Kandahar is simply surrounded by walls, Herat is surrounded by an enormous mound or rampart of earth, on the top of which the walls are built. The city, like Kandahar, is divided into four quarters by the four principal streets, which run straight inwards from the entrance-gate to the old citadel on the north, and from the Irak, Kandahar, and Kushk gates on the west, south, and east respectively. These four main streets meet in the centre of the city under a large central dome called the *chaharsu*. All the trade of the city is comprised in these four streets, and, with the exception of a few odd fruit-stalls here and there, there are no shops worth speaking of anywhere else. These four streets are roofed with wooden beams, covered with matting and earth during almost their entire length, from the gateways to the *chaharsu*—the central portion adjoining the *chaharsu* being alone roofed over with regular brick domes. At present not half the shops are occupied, and only those in the immediate neighbourhood of the *chaharsu* are open.

The most prominent place in the city is the old citadel, standing on a height of its own, slightly back from the main northern rampart, and towering over the rest of the city. The walls are mostly of brick, and apparently are of great age, as Ebn Haukel, describing this citadel, says: "Herat has a castle with ditches. This castle is situated in the centre of the town, and is fortified with very strong walls." The ditches we found mostly filled up; the castle no longer stands in the centre of the town; and the strong walls, instead of a place of refuge, would probably be the most dangerous of all under a modern bombardment. Still, the citadel as it stands forms a cool and pleasant residence for the local commander-in-chief. The inhabited portion is some 110 yards in length by 60 in breadth, and is a lofty building supported by four bastions along its face, and with the entrance-gate facing the main street down to the *chaharsu*. From the Sipah Salar's rooms on the northern face, a capital view is obtained of the country beyond. Immediately below, some 80 feet down, is the new citadel—an open space used generally as a parade-ground for the troops in garrison; and away beyond that again, the buildings and minarets of the Musalla, with a stretch of open and gradually rising country up to the hills beyond.

The northern face has two gates, known respectively as the Malik and the Kutabchak — the bastions round the former bearing the mark of many a shot. The road through the Kandahar gate on the south leads straight away through suburbs to the Pul-i-Malun, the old bridge across the Hari

Rud on the highroad to Kandahar. Only about half of the original bridge now remains; and though the main channel of the river is every year turned under the arches still standing at the conclusion of the spring floods, yet for several months of the year there is a long stretch of water to be waded through—though I am told the flood is seldom so high as to render it impassable for many days at a time. Some twenty-five or twenty-seven arches, all told, are now standing. Some of these are broken through, but still passable, except towards the northern end, where the main channel of the river has cut a couple of arches clean away. Only three or four small blocks of masonry, sticking up in the shingle-bed of the river on the southern bank, show how far the bridge originally extended.

The western face of the city is the least populated of all, and the houses on this side are practically nothing but a mass of ruins. The gateway, situated like the others halfway between the two corner bastions, is known as the Irak gate, and also, like the others, has a *ziarat* out in front of it. How a *ziarat* came to be planted opposite almost each of the gates, I do not know; but so it is.

The eastern gate is known indifferently as the Kushk or Khush gate. It appears, though, from Ebn Haukel, that Khushk is the correct spelling, and that of the various gates mentioned by him, this is the only one that has in any way retained its ancient name.

The only building in the city noticeable by its size and height above the uniform dead level of mud-domes is the Juma Musjid—a large, lofty, arched structure in the north-eastern portion of the city. Ebn Haukel says: "In all Khorasan and Mawar-ul-nahr there is not any place which has a finer or more capacious mosque than Heri or Herat. Next to it we may rank the mosque at Balkh, and after that the mosque of Sistan." Now, whether this is the original mosque referred to or not, it is impossible to say. Mirza

Khalil, our Persian writer, searched carefully for me for any evidence of the age of the building; but the only thing he could find was an inscription engraved on the arch of the Mehrab, or prayer niche, on a marble slab set up by Sultan Abu Saiad in A.H. 866 (A.D. 1462) to record the abolition of some oppressive tax.

The governor's residence—known as the Chahar Bagh—is also in the north-eastern quarter of the city, some little way to the west of the Juma Musjid. The entrance, as in all Afghan houses, is down a low dirty passage, leading out of a narrow lane; immediately at the end of the passage is a large stable courtyard, but turning sharp to the left down another dark passage, the visitor is astonished to find himself in a large open court some 80 yards by 60—the walls around all coloured, and the ground laid out in walks and flower-beds, with a tank and fountain in the centre. Rooms open off this courtyard to the north and south—used mostly, I believe, for the transaction of business. The governor generally receives his visitors in a room to the south, situated a little back from, and slightly elevated above, the level of the courtyard, and entered through a narrow passage at the side. To the south-east of this courtyard, again, lies what is called the New Palace; a smaller courtyard, but with the walls of the rooms surrounding it highly coloured and ornamented with gilt moulding and decorations, though otherwise undistinguishable externally from the buildings around it. The European visitor has so few chances of seeing the inside of the houses in Herat—or, in fact, in any Eastern city—that it is difficult to form an opinion of their comfort; but from all accounts, there is little wealth or display. The city has been subjected to so many sieges, and has suffered so badly at the hands of its various rulers, that its wealth has long since gone. The total population at the last census some years ago was only 1700 families; and though it is said that there are now some 2000 families in the city, I doubt if the actual population amounts to 10,000 souls all told.

There are many small courtyards and gardens scattered about the city, full of mulberry and other trees; but most of them look sadly out of repair. Water is brought into the city through a siphon from the canals; and in addition to the sixteen large reservoirs and to the many private tanks and the various running channels all over the city, most of the houses have a private well of their own. Water is procurable at a short depth everywhere in the city—though, curiously enough, the water in some of the wells is slightly brackish, and in others perfectly good.

The city lies low, in a sort of hollow, surrounded by the great rampart of earth on which the walls are built. Everything is built of mud, and there is no such thing as stonework, and very little brickwork, in the place. The streets, with the exception of the four main thoroughfares centring on the *chaharsu*, are simply dirty crooked lanes winding about amongst interminable lines of dead mud-walls, with here and there a low dark doorway marking the entrance to somebody's house—the passage descending generally a step or two, and turning off sharp at right angles to prevent any glimpse from outside of what goes on within. Of citizens scarcely a soul is to be seen—nothing but soldiers lounging about. The greater part of the houses in the city are uninhabited, and mostly in ruins; and were it not for the Kabul garrison, the place would almost be like a city of the dead.

The troops are quartered in barrack squares—generally a double row of domed rooms opening inwards into the square, some 50 or 60 yards across, with a gateway at either end. A great deal could be, and is even now being, done to improve the city. A good wide road has been cleared all round inside the walls, many ruins are being pulled down and spaces cleared; and were only a little trouble taken to plant trees and keep the ground clean and in good order Herat would hardly know itself again.

The objects of interest outside the city are almost entirely confined to *ziarats*, or shrines, and holy places of sorts. Amongst these, of course, the buildings of the Musalla on the north face of the city stood pre-eminent; but being now in course of demolition, under orders from the Amir, nothing but the tradition of their beauty will remain for future generations.

The Musalla consists in reality of the remains of three buildings running north-east and south-west, and covering a space of nearly 600 yards from end to end. Of the eastern building—known generally, I believe, as the Madrasah or College—nothing but two high arches facing each other and four minarets remain. The arches must be from 60 to 80 feet in height, and are covered with the remains of what was once fine tile or mosaic work of beautiful and artistic designs—now, of course, much defaced. The tiles on the minaret have mostly been worn off by stress of weather, but inside the arches the beautiful mosaic-work is still in many places almost perfect—sufficient to give one an idea of the splendour of the building when new. The minarets of this Madrasah appear taller than the rest, and must be between 120 and 150 feet in height. There is a tradition that the building included two colleges—called in Turki the Kosh Madrasah, or the Pair of Colleges—and that they were built by Shah Rukh Mirza, who died ruler of Herat, if I remember right, in A.D. 1446. Just to the west of the present archway lies a large handsome black marble slab, well carved in Arabic, but not easily decipherable. I was told it was the tombstone of Baikrar, son of Umar Shaikh, the son of Amir Taimur; though I believe the only really legible part of the inscription was the date of death— A.H. 843, or A.D. 1440. Between the Madrasah and the Musalla, 100 yards or so from each, is a domed building commonly called the tomb of Shah Rukh. This was formerly covered with blue tiles and scrolls of text from the Koran, but is much weatherworn. It is faced on the east by another archway and one solitary minaret. Within the dome there are six tombstones, finely carved and engraved, to the memory of the following :—

1. Baisanghor, son of Shah Rukh, son of Taimur; dated A.H. 836 – A.D. 1433.

2. Sultan Ahmad, son of Abdul Latif, son of Sultan Ubed, son of Shah Rukh; dated A.H. 848 – A.D. 1445.

3. Gohar Shad; dated A.H. 861 – A.D. 1457.

4. Allah ud Dowlah, son of Baisanghor, son of Shah Rukh; dated A.H. 863 – A.D. 1459.

5. Ibrahim Sultan, son of Allah u'd Dowlah, son of Baisanghor, son of Shah Rukh, son of Amir Taimur; dated A.H. 863 – A.D. 1459.

6. Shah Rukh Sultan, son of Sultan Abu Saiad, son of Sultan Muhammad, son of Miran Shah, son of Amir Taimur; dated A.H. 898 – A.D. 1493.

It appears, therefore, that after all this building is not the mausoleum of the great Shah Rukh, the son of Amir Taimur, as is popularly supposed, but of some other Shah Rukh—a great-great-grandson of Taimur's—who was buried here last of all, and thus probably gave his name to the building forty-seven years after the death of his great namesake.

Gohar Shad is said to have been the wife of Shah Rukh and a sister of Kara Yusuf Turkoman, and the founder of the Gohar Shad Musjid in Mashhad. "The college of Gohar Shad Begum, her tomb and her grand mosque," are mentioned amongst the sights of Herat seen by the Emperor Baber in 1506; but where the college was that bore her name I did not hear, neither did I find any trace in Herat of her mosque. Her tombstone alone remains, and that is overturned, uncared for, and half buried in rubbish.

To the west of the tomb of Shah Rukh stands the Musalla—a huge massive building of burnt brick, almost entirely faced at one time with tiles and mosaic-work, all the various patterns of which are beautifully fitted together in minute pieces set in gypsum plaster. Musalla means, I believe, a place of prayer; and doubtless, on this account, the walls were covered with the numerous texts in tile-work that now ornament them. The main building consists of a lofty dome some 75 feet in diameter, with a smaller dome behind it, and any number of rooms and buildings around it. The entrance to this dome is through a lofty archway on the east, some 80 feet in height, the face of which is entirely covered with tile-work and huge inscriptions in gilt; while above the archway is a lot of curious little rooms and passages, the use of which I cannot tell. To the east of this arch is a large courtyard some 80 yards square, surrounded with corridors and rooms several storeys in height—all covered with tile-work. The main entrance of all is on the eastern side of this court, through another huge archway, also some 80 feet in height; but though the inside of the arch is all lined with tiles, or rather mosaic-work in regular patterns, the outside is bare, and looks as if it had never been finished. Four minarets, some 120 feet in height, form the four corners of the building: a good deal of the tile-work has been worn off by the weather—especially towards the north, the side of the prevailing winds; but when new, they must have been marvellously handsome. It is hoped that they may be preserved from the general demolition. The rooms, it is said, were built for the accommodation of students, but where they all came from it is hard to tell.

To the east of these buildings, and almost due north of the citadel, is a long mound, evidently at some time or other part of the rampart of the city wall. At what date the city was contracted within its present limits I could not ascertain; but from the fact that Ebn Haukel distinctly describes the citadel as standing in the centre of the town, whereas it is now on the northern face, I can only conclude that the walls extended up to this mound so late as the tenth century. The mound is now known by the name of Tal-i-Bhangian, or the Mound of the Bhang-eaters—the people given to the consumption of this drug being said to have formerly made use of this mound for their orgies. Before that, again, they say it was called the Mound of Holy Men, from the number of the latter who were buried in it. Certainly the mound is one mass of graves; and at one place on the northern side the workmen, in digging out foundations for the new fortifications, found a large stone chamber full of human bones, but with nothing in it to show who the people buried there were. No coins were found, or anything else, to give an idea of the age or customs of the people who raised the mound. But one of the two *ziarats* on the top of the mound takes us back to the early days of Mahomadanism, as the inscription round the pedestal of the tombstone enshrined therein gives the name of Abdullah, son of Maavia, son of Jafir, son of Abu Talib, who was the father of Ali, the son-in-law of the Prophet. The date of death, however, is not given—only a statement to the effect that the building was erected by Shaikh Bayazid, son of Ali Mashrif, in A.H. 865 = A.D. 1461. The second shrine—known as the Ziarat-i-Shahzadah Kasim—is apparently of later but uncertain age, as on one side of the tombstone Abul Kasim, son of Jafir, is said to have died in A.H. 994 = A.D. 1586, and on the other in A.H. 897 = A.D. 1493; while the other tombstones lying about are said to have been brought from other places, and are of little interest.

Next to the Musalla, the prettiest and most famous shrine in the neighbourhood is Gazargah—the residence of the Mir of Gazargah, one of the richest and most influential divines in the Herat province. Gazargah lies up at the foot of the hills some 2 miles to the north-east of the city. The shrine is distinguishable from afar by the huge lofty square-topped mass of building over a high arch—the usual feature of all sacred buildings in this part of the world. The shrine is well worth a visit, if only to see the simple yet handsome tomb of the Amir Dost Muhammad, and the handsome carved marble-work on the tomb of the saint, Kwajah Abdullah Ansari. Passing first through a large walled garden of pine and mulberry trees, the visitor comes to an octagonal-shaped domed building, full of little rooms and three-cornered recesses, two or three storeys in height, all opening inwards— built apparently as a cool breezy place in which to pass the heat of the summer days. Beyond this, again, is the main enclosure of the *ziarat*, now a deserted and dilapidated-looking place. Everything wears a look of decay: the unkept courtyard, the broken tile-work on the archway and entrance to the shrine, and general want of repair visible everywhere, betoken a great falling off from former prosperity. The entrance to the shrine lies through a doorway under a high arched vestibule, crossing a long covered corridor, paved with slabs of white marble worn and polished into the most dangerous state of slipperiness by, I presume, the feet of countless pilgrims. Round about this door sit *moollas*, beggars, and pilgrims of sorts, in addition to all the blind *hafizes* or reciters of the Koran, and showmen generally of the place. It is astonishing how these blind men know every tomb and the history of the people in each. In front of the entrance, looking inwards, but now half buried in the ground, is a carved figure in white marble of some long thin animal, said to be a tiger—though what a tiger is the emblem of, in such a place, I cannot say. Passing through the entrance, one emerges into a square court surrounded by high walls and little rooms, with a lofty wall and half-domed portico at the eastern end. The tile-work on this wall has been handsome, but is now much out of repair. The tomb of the saint—a mound some 10 yards long and 6 feet high, and covered with stone—stands immediately in front of this recess. The tomb of Amir Dost Muhammad lies close by to the north; and the remainder of the court, as also the little rooms around, are filled with graves as close as they can be packed.

The great feature of the place is the headstone of white marble at the grave of the saint, which stands some 14 or 15 feet in height, and is most exquisitely carved throughout. This stone is a beautiful piece of work, as not only is the carving of the inscription well done, but the whole design and proportions of the stone are beautiful. From the Arabic inscription carved in the Khaṭṭ-i-śulś character on the headstone, it would appear that the present building was erected by Shah Rukh Mirza, the son of Taimur Lang, in the year A.H. 859, or A.D. 1455. This date, though, is nine years, I think, subsequent to the death of Shah Rukh; but still he may have commenced the work. The whole of the Arabic inscription, however, could not be deciphered; and though there is no mistake about the date 859, possibly it might not refer to Shah Rukh. The full name of the saint is given as Abu Ismail Khwajah Abdullah Ansari, and the date of his death is recorded separately on a corner of the stone, and in a different character, by a Persian quatrain, in which the word *Fát*, by the Abjad reckoning, gives the year A.H. 481, or A.D. 1089. On one side of the grave there is an inscription recorded by Hasan, son of Husain Shamlu, in A.H. 1049, or A.D. 1640; and round the balustrade there is another, but without date.

Amir Dost Muhammad's tombstone is a plain, simple, but handsome block of pure white marble, some 8 feet in length by 1½ or 2 feet in breadth, finely carved, and surrounded by a white marble balustrade. At the head and foot of the grave stand pieces of white marble, in imitation, but a very poor imitation, of the head- and foot-stones of the saint's shrine: they are dwarfed and quite lost in comparison with the original stones.

Inside the portico there are some twenty or thirty tombstones, but none were found of any very great age: the oldest, apparently, was one of black marble, beautifully engraved in Arabic, and bearing the date A.H. 865 = A.D. 1461, but without any name. Four or five other similar tombstones had both names and dates obliterated. Two others bore the names of Rustam Muhammad Khan and Muhammad Amin Khan, both described as descendants of Changiz Khan, and dated respectively, according to the Abjad reckoning, A.H. 1053 and 1076 = A.D. 1643 and 1666; a third, to Muhammad Iwaz Khan, simply described as a son of the third Khan, is dated A.H. 1067 = A.D. 1656; while a fourth, to Shahzadah Masa'ud, is as late as A.H. 1256 = A.D. 1840.

In the courtyard we noticed two older tombstones with Arabic inscriptions — one to Sultan Mahmud, dated A.H. 761 = A.D. 1360, and the other to Ustad Muhammad Khwajah, dated A.H. 842 = A.D. 1438; but anything like a really careful examination would have taken a very much longer time than Mirza Khalil and myself had at our disposal.

Not only is the courtyard packed full of graves, but every little room and enclosure round it is the same. One particularly fine black marble stone marks the grave of the mother of some monarch. No name is given—presumably it was not the custom at that time to inscribe the name of any woman on her tombstone; but the title "Mahd-i-Uliya"—lit., eminent cradle—gives the clue to her royal position. The date of her death is given in a Persian hemistich, the translation of which is: "The place of descent of the light of pardon from the kindness of the incomparable and eternal God." The first word, which gives the date, has been misspelt Mahbit instead of Mahbit, probably on purpose. As it stands, by the Abjad reckoning the date of her death is A.H. 866 = A.D. 1462; and that is probably more contemporary with the tombs around than A.H. 475 = A.D. 1083, which would have been the date had the word been spelt correctly. None of the tombstones that we noticed were much more than 400 years old.

At the entrance to the courtyard there is a large curious circular font or bowl made of white marble, and used, so far as I could make out, to mix sherbet in for the pilgrims visiting the shrine. Outside is the covered reservoir, locally said to have been built by a daughter of Shah Rukh; but the inscription, on being deciphered, showed that it was originally built by Shah Rukh himself, but fell into disrepair, and was restored in the year A.H. 1100 = A.D. 1689, by some lady of royal descent whose name is not given.

The Mutawali, or superintendent of the endowment of this shrine, is Mir Mortaza, in whose family the office has regularly descended for generations. His son, Muhammad Umar Jan, is a man of some thirty-five years of age, and is married to a daughter of the late Amir Sher Ali, a sister of Sirdar Ayub Khan.

A mile or more to the north of the city there is a domed building covered with the remains of old tile-work, and with a hole in the centre of the floor—giving access, apparently, to some underground chamber, now mostly filled up. Tradition declares that there used to be a passage from this chamber right into the citadel; but the appearance of the building would seem to show that it was erected as a mausoleum. If there are any tombstones in it, they are buried in rubbish; but some five or six are lying about a little way off, both of black and white marble—some inscribed in Arabic, and others in the Persian Nastalik character, though only one of them could be deciphered: that was to Amir Jalalu'din, and dated A.H. 847 = A.D. 1444. There is another stone bearing the name of Amir Jalalu'din in the Ziarat-i-Shahzadah Kasim, and I heard of a third between Gazargah and the canal, dated A.H. 858 = A.D. 1455; but who all these Amir Jalalu'dins were, could not be ascertained.

To the west of this domed building with the underground chamber, there are various other shrines and tombs of holy men—so holy, in fact, that access to some of them by Shiahs was even forbidden by their Sunni guardians. One of these, called the tomb of Moulana Jami Sha'ir, is probably the place referred to by the Emperor Baber as "the mausoleum and tomb of Moulana Abdul Rahman Jam"; while the "Takht" of Shaikh Zainu'din referred to in the same memoirs lies close by. Curiously enough, the determination of the date of the latter's death, as rendered by the Abjad reckoning of the last clause of the Persian inscription on the pillar at the head of the grave, proved such a puzzle that no two of the experts to whom I showed it could agree in their interpretation of it. The translation of the inscription is something to the following effect: " Shaikh Zainu'din, Imam and Leader of men of Religion. The Axis of the World. The Threshold of Forgiveness. The Relation of Truth, who rose from the Earth below to the Heaven above, and on whose skirt there was no dust. His age was eighty-one, and the time of his death was also that number, with one year added to the calculation."

The Abjad reckoning is a system of denoting dates by giving certain numerical values to the different letters of the alphabet; and this very inscription has been variously calculated for me as A.H. 202, A.H. 621, A.H. 741, and A.H. 832 = A.D. 818, A.D. 1224, A.D. 1341, and A.D. 1429: which is correct I know not.

Another noted Herat shrine is the Ziarat-i-Awalwali, as it is called, some 2 miles to the north-west of the city. The original tombstone has disappeared; but from an inscription on a slab let into the wall above the door, it appears that the building in reality contains the tomb of Sultan Abul Walid Ahmad, the son of Abul Raza Abulah Hanafi of Azadan of Herat, who died in A.H. 232 = A.D. 847, and that the present building—a lofty arched portico, with the usual doméd enclosure behind—was erected by Sultan Husain Mirza, who reigned at Herat, I believe, from A.D. 1487 to 1505. The building is of plain brick, and unadorned outside, though there is some good mosaic-work inside. The garden in front has been allowed to go to ruin, and nothing remains at present but some large pine-trees. Baber mentions the building under the name of "Balmeri, which was originally called Abul Walid."

Another large and similar shrine—known as the Ziarat-i-Sultan Mir Shahid—lies to the south-west of the city, close to the Burj-i-Khakistar bastion. The tomb lies in the centre of the lofty domed room behind the entrance-portico, and is surmounted by flags of various colours—the poles of which are tipped with the figure of an open hand. No special meaning is attached to this symbol, so far as the *moollahs* could tell me—all they knew being a tradition to the effect that the standards presented by the Prophet to his people were surmounted by a hand, and that the custom has been thus continued.

To show how little the Heratis know of the history of their own shrines, I may mention that I was assured that the Sultan Mir Shahid buried here was the ruler of Herat when the city was besieged and captured by the famous Hataku Khan, son of Tuleh Khan, and grandson of Changiz Khan, after his capture of Baghdad about the year 1253; that he fell in the defence, and thus earned the title of Shahid, or martyr. By having the tombstone cleaned, however, and the Arabic inscription deciphered, it appeared that the name of the saint was Abdullah ul Wahid, son of Zaid, son of Ali (the son-in-law of the Prophet), son of Abu Talib; that he was born in A.H. 35 or A.H. 37 (= A.D. 656 or A.D. 658), and died in A.H. 88 (= A.D. 707) in the lifetime of his father; that his tomb was discovered in A.H. 320 (= A.D. 932) in the time of Ali ibn Hasan (an Imam, I believe, of the Zaidi sect), son of Shaikh Hasan il Basreh; and that the present building was erected by Shah Sultan Husain in A.H. 890 (= A.D. 1485). The tombstone was so blackened by lamp-oil, that I do not suppose it had been deciphered for ages—so long, in fact, that the identity of the saint had been quite forgotten. In the same building there is another tombstone to the memory of Jafir Abu Ishak, who died in A.H. 289 = A.D. 902.

In addition to the small shrines at each of the city gates, there is one called the Ziarat-i-Khojah Ali Bafar immediately adjoining the powder-mill to the north-east of the city, and another, called the Ziarat-i-Khwajah Tak, adjoining the graveyard used for the burial of Kabulis on the mound to the south-east of the city. But it is needless for me to recapitulate all the shrines. *Ziarats* swarm here all over the country. Every graveyard has its *ziarat*, or rather every *ziarat* has its graveyard. Only one point calls for notice, and that is the talent displayed by the masons of Herat in the carving of the marble tombstones so much in use. Considering that no stonework whatever is used in building, the workmanship displayed in the carving of these stones redounds much to the credit of the artificers. The white marble comes, I believe, from the upper portion of the Hari Rud valley, in the direction of Obeh; while the Sang-i-Musa, or the black marble as I have called it, is brought, if I remember right, all the way from Shah Maksud, in the hills north of Kandahar.

The fruit of Herat is hardly as good as that of Kandahar. Certainly I have tasted here some most luscious nectarines, such as I do not remember to have seen at Kandahar. The peaches here, too, are magnificent to look at—a good deal larger than a ball of soap, for instance, and in fact almost as big as a cricket-ball; but somehow we never get them properly ripe. They have always been so bruised and have become so rotten by the time they reached our camp, that it was impossible to enjoy them. Both nectarines and peaches, too, seem to be grown in very small quantities, and are more a sample of what might be grown than a stern reality. The grapes here, also, have few varieties; and the curious thing about them is, that the grapes on each bunch are never of one uniform size. A bunch of small grapes, either red or white, always has in it a certain proportion of large grapes full of seeds, while the small ones have none at all. The amount of grapes that can be purchased for a copper is something marvellous: so cheap are they, in fact, that the poorest *sais* in camp can always command either a bunch of grapes or a melon, whichever he prefers.

Many are the rumours and hopes and fears now current amongst the native followers in our camp regarding our return to India. It is now exactly a year since we started, and every now and again my servants come up to me and ask in a hopeless sort of way if they will ever see their fathers and mothers again. I can promise nothing. I can only appeal to their reason and say to them, " Think of all the correspondence, negotiation, and delay that goes on between two petty native States in India regarding half a mile of boundary. What must it be when two great Powers like England and Russia commence to negotiate about an entire frontier?" This convinces them. They see the argument, I really believe, and settle down to their work more firmly convinced than ever that they will see their fathers and mothers no more.

On the 23d, Sir West Ridgeway, accompanied by Major Holdich, Captains Gore and Talbot, and Mr Merk, started for the Infantry camp, where they still are, leaving us quite a small party here—viz., Major Bax, Captains Maitland, Peacocke, and Heath, Lieutenants Drummond and Wright, and Dr Owen and myself. Sirdar Muhammad Aslam Khan has just arrived from Bala Murghab, where his place has been taken by Sirdar Sher Ahmed Khan, and proceeds to Mashhad almost directly on treasure-convoy duty. The health of the men keeps wonderfully good,—we have hardly a man in hospital.

Dr Aitchison and Captain Griesbach are away on a botanical and geological tour in Khorasan. Captain de Laessoe is at Mashhad, and Mr Finn and Dr Weir still somewhere in the neighbourhood of Astrabad.

The Survey officers are all busy working up the results of their late surveys—Captain Gore that of Khorasan, and Captain Talbot of the upper valley of the Hari Rud. Surveyors Heera Singh and Muhammad Sharif have also brought back some capital maps of the Taimani country and of the hitherto unexplored districts in the neighbourhood of Taiwara and Ghor, which will be a valuable contribution to the results of the Mission. I fear, though, little more can be done in the way of exploration and survey till the present unsettled state of affairs comes to an end.

CHAPTER IV.

THE SIGNING OF THE PROTOCOL—PEACE DECLARED.

CAMP ROBAT-I-AFGHAN, 14*th Sept.* 1885.

AT last we have heard some definite news, and we now know that peace is declared. The protocol has been signed, and the Commissions are to meet at Zulfikar within the next two months. Glad, indeed, must the Afghan authorities be to think that their rule at Herat is to be granted a fresh lease of life, and still more glad are all our men and followers to think that at last there is a chance of getting back to their wives and families. Only the other day, the sight of a fresh consignment of warm clothing filled the hearts of the followers with blank despair. The Sirkar would never give us a fresh issue of warm clothing, argued they, unless it is their intention to keep us here another winter; and they shuddered at the thought. Many were the longing glances cast at a few lucky men going down to Quetta with a *kafila* of ponies to bring up some stores, and many were the harrowing stories of starving children told that day, in the vain hope of getting permission to accompany that convoy. Now all is hope again. Something has been settled; something has to be done, and all are ready to be up and doing. It is not only the inaction, but the uncertainty and want of some object in life, that has told so heavily on us all during the past five months of weary waiting; and now all are anxious to be at work again. The only fear is that the demarcation of the frontier will not be commenced soon enough to allow of our completing it in time to cross the passes this year; but as long as we have work before us, we are content to leave the future to take care of itself.

The camp will probably shortly be on the move down the valley in the direction of Kuhsan, where we shall be conveniently situated, both with regard to the telegraph office at Mashhad and to Zulfikar. The Russians, it is presumed, will now withdraw their troops from the Zulfikar pass, which they have so long held, in spite of all promises to the contrary; and when the Commission meets, the Afghan Irregular Horse will probably occupy their place. At present the Russians have got a force of about a thousand men, including Cossacks, artillery, and infantry, in the Zulfikar pass, and have had all along; whereas the only Afghans in the neighbourhood are a few cavalry patrols watching the passes, and there is not an Afghan Regular nearer than Herat, despite the alarmist telegrams that were published by the Russians to the contrary when moving more troops up to Zulfikar some little time ago. The Infantry camp will probably move up, and rejoin us at Kuhsan; and once again we shall all be collected together on the same camping-ground where we joined Sir Peter Lumsden just ten months ago, little thinking then what was before us.

The temperature has changed wonderfully during the last few days, and the hot weather of these parts, such as it is, has come and gone. The mornings are cool and fresh, and the nights so cold that two, and even three, blankets are none too much—the thermometer going down as low as 41° at night, and rarely rising above 88° by day. There are no rains here as in India. There were some clouds about a few days ago, and some rain fell in the hills, but it was only an occasional shower; all the rain, as a rule, falls in the spring. The year is divided into four seasons, as in England—not into three, as in India—and the autumn is now coming on apace, and very soon the trees will be casting their leaves, and the country assuming its wintry garb.

The sand-grouse are now appearing in regular flocks, and even duck are beginning to show up again : another month and I have no doubt the latter will be swarming along the river. Last year, when we marched up in November, the river was full of all sorts of wild fowl; but the long marches and terribly cold wind that here beset us put a stop to almost all *shikar*. Now we are already looking forward to a 1st of October amongst the pheasants in the bed of the river below Kuhsan, where by all accounts they swarm. Here there are none, but Toman Agha is said to be full of them. Our old haunts on the Murghab at Karawul Khana and Maruchak are said to be as full of pheasants as ever again, and Sirdar Muhammad Aslam Khan, who visited Maruchak not long ago, said that he found some seventy or eighty pheasants in the old fort alone. The ditch was full of pigs and the old ruins of pheasants, and yet only five months ago this fort was the home of some 200 or 300 Afghan Khasadars,—a sure sign of the small impression their short residence there has made. The large black-breasted sand-grouse we found breeding all over the plains in May and June. A little hollow scratched in the ground by the side of a tuft of wormwood scrub was all the nest they made, and now the young birds are flying about, and are uncommonly good to eat.

Just where we are now encamped on a large rushy common, there is little to shoot but plover; even pigeons are scarce. The nearer one gets to Herat, though, the thicker the pigeons become, and the villages round about the city simply swarm with them. The fields are alive with flocks of them; but woe to the man who shoots them, as they are all considered private property and a regular source of income. The round towers at the corners of the villages are generally made into pigeon-houses, in addition to the regular square-built pigeon-towers that one sees dotted about the country. The birds have to be fed throughout the winter, and if not fed in one tower, they go off to another where they are fed; and it is the object of every owner to tempt as many birds as he can to take up their residence in his particular tower for the breeding-season in the spring. A large tower, it is said, will produce as much as 15 *kharwars* (1 *kharwar* = 10 maunds Indian) of manure in a year, and the ordinary round bastion-shaped tower at the corner of a village at least 6 or 7 *kharwars*—each *kharwar* selling at the rate of 15 *krans* or 6 rupees. The Amir Sher Ali's Kabuli troops were much disliked, I am told, on account of their pigeon-shooting propensities, but no complaints have reached me regarding the present garrison on this score.

We have had no news lately of any fresh movement of Russian troops along the frontier, and probably all their energies will be directed now to the housing of those already on the frontier for the winter. The Turkoman *kibitka* is the warmest and most comfortable habitation possible, and will doubtless be largely requisitioned for their use. Our own men can bear full testimony to their comfort in cold weather, and I only trust that we shall find ourselves as well housed this year as we were last, should it be our fate to spend another winter up here. Our tents, after all they have gone through, are little calculated to bear the stress of fresh winter-storms, and we have no longer Panjdeh to draw on for *kibitkas*.

From Panjdeh there is little news. The Russians are still encamped at Kizil Tepe, and have hitherto so far observed the neutrality of Panjdeh, that they have not allowed their troops to cross the Kushk and enter the habitations. A Sarik to whom I was talking the other day amused me by his contempt of the Russian currency. Not like us, he said, who paid for our supplies in solid cash,—the Russians had not a coin amongst them. Their

SIGNING OF THE PROTOCOL—PEACE DECLARED. 47

only money was paper, and paper he seemed to think of small account. The paper rouble here goes by the name of *manat*, and though it ought to be worth 3½ *krans*, it actually is only worth 3 *krans* (2½ *krans* = one rupee).

I have been rather amused, too, of late, to see some of the extracts from Indian native papers extolling Russian rule as evidenced by their promotion of native officers to high commands—as, for instance, of Ali Khan to be governor of Merv, and the late Iwaz Khan to be *hakim* of Panjdeh. Could the editors of those native papers see the real state of affairs, they would probably tell a very different tale. No revenue is at present taken from either Merv or Panjdeh, and will not be taken, I believe, for the next seven years; but supposing revenue were taken, the entire population of Merv and Yulatan combined does not come up to 50,000 houses, and the revenue at the outside would hardly amount to Rs. 80,000 — a charge not equal to that of the smallest *tahsil* in our districts. Ali Khan is a man who has been educated at St Petersburg, and, though a Mussalman, is a European officer; and yet, despite the high-sounding title of Governor of Merv, his pay, I am told, is only Rs. 300 a-month, equal to that of the lowest grade of Extra Assistant Commissioner in the British service, and he is the one man in the Russian service who has risen to such a high position, while we have hundreds in the British service, some of them drawing double and treble his pay, with far greater charges and responsibilities. Again, take Husain Khan, the present, or Iwaz Khan, the late, governor of Panjdeh: their pay was fixed at Rs. 120 a-month, not even equal to that of an officiating *tahsildar* in our service. Panjdeh is simply a settlement of some 9000 houses, paying no revenue at present, and at the best with only a revenue of some Rs. 15,000 or Rs. 16,000. I should be very sorry for the Indian *tahsildar* who changed his lot with Husain Khan to become *hakim* of Panjdeh. The *tahsildar* in our service has a career of promotion before him. Husain Khan has no hopes of promotion, and in all probability will be thrust aside as soon as his day is over.

Of our life in camp I have little news to tell. The Infantry Escort and Heavy camp, comprising Major Meiklejohn, Major Rind, Captain Durand, Captain Cotton, Lieutenant Rawlins, and Dr Charles, are still encamped at Kiliki, in the Doshakh range. Captain Gore is away again surveying on the Persian frontier. Sir West Ridgeway and Major Holdich returned to the Cavalry camp here on the 9th; and Captain Talbot and Mr Merk have started off again on a trip to the Taimani country, to the south-east of Herat, hitherto utterly unexplored. Major Holdich, Captain Peacocke, Captain Heath, and myself, start to-morrow on a fresh visit to Herat to inspect the progress of the fortifications. Major Bax and Lieutenant Wright are away on a trip to Mashhad, having taken advantage of the escort of a convoy proceeding to Mashhad for treasure under the charge of Sirdar Muhammad Aslam Khan. Sirdar Sher Ahmed Khan is still at Bala Murghab, and Kazi Muhammad Aslam at Herat. Subadar Muhammad Husain accompanies Captain Talbot to the Taimani country, and possibly up to Balkh. Mr Finn and Dr Weir have completed their trip along the Persian frontier, and the former has now rejoined his own appointment as consul at Resht. Jemadar Amir Muhammad, of the 11th Bengal Lancers, who has been out prospecting the country north of the passes, reports that the Afghan cavalry horses have eaten up all the grass at the Band-i-Baba, but that there is still a good supply to the north of the Ardewan pass. The weather is getting so cool now, though, that we no longer hanker after summer-quarters.

A convoy of some thousands of breech-loading rifles has been sent down from Kabul to Herat by the Amir for the armament of the troops in garrison there—a most welcome addition to their strength. The heavy guns, too, from

Chaman, are well on their way past Girishk, the number of yokes of bullocks said to have been requisitioned to drag them being something fabulous.

Rumour has it that there is a great scarcity of grain in Kandahar this year, but I do not know with what truth. Here, in the Herat district, the supply is plentiful; but the villagers are all unwilling to sell, still firmly adhering to the belief that a British force is coming up, and that they will get better prices hereafter. I only hope that they will.

CHAPTER V.

LIFE AT KUHSAN—REDUCTION OF THE ESCORT.

CAMP KUHSAN, 28*th September* 1885.

ALL the Mission is now once more concentrated at Kuhsan, in readiness to meet the Russians on their arrival. Ten months ago we all met here once before, fully expecting then as now to meet the Russians without further delay, and knowing just as little then as we do now what is before us. Now, as then, our minds are occupied with the thought of how we can best entertain the Russian Commission, and this time we can but trust our preparations will not be all in vain.

The weather has become much cooler since last I wrote, and is even cold in fact. Flannel and serge have taken the place of *khaki* in the day-time, and greatcoats are even coming into use again for dinner. The way in which the cold wind finds one out through all the partitions of a tent is something only to be learnt by experience. Indian tents are a poor protection against the winds of these parts. My own tent, for instance, a small Kashmir Swiss cottage, has the *kanats* laced on to the fly, and is also laced up at the corners. In India I should not notice that it was not all one piece; here, unless I sew the divisions all up, I am reminded of it every minute. Even as I now write, the paper I am writing on is being blown all over the tent, and I have to put on my thickest coat to keep warm. Luckily we have an unlimited supply of wood close to hand in the jungle in the bed of the river, and I see our men busy carrying in great logs in all directions.

Nothing has been settled yet regarding our winter-quarters: our plans even are not yet fixed; but it is certain that the whole of the frontier cannot be demarcated this autumn, and that we must make up our minds to winter somewhere here. Captains Peacocke, Heath, and myself start to-morrow to inspect and report upon the suitability of the old *robats* or caravanserais here and at Kafir Kilah for winter-quarters, but it is doubtful if they will be found large enough to house the entire Mission. Last year the men were most comfortably housed in the Turkoman felt *kibitkas*; but now, alas! we have no longer the Turkomans to draw upon, and this year the Panjdeh *kibitkas* are destined to house the Russian, not the British, soldier.

Kuhsan, I should mention, is the last inhabited place in this the north-west corner of Afghanistan. Kafir Kilah, some 8 miles beyond, is not a village, simply a frontier post on the Persian border guarding the highroad to Mashhad. Toman Agha, about 12 miles lower down the river, is entirely uninhabited, and so is all the country down to Zulfikar, some 60 miles beyond.

We have not heard yet that the Russian troops have evacuated the Zulfikar pass, of which they have held possession so long, but presumably they will do so before the Commissioners meet. The Escort on either side is to be limited to 100 men; consequently the bulk of our small party will have to remain here, or in some other equally convenient place, during the demarcation.

Sir West Ridgeway starts for Mashhad early next month, in order to be close to the telegraph office, and thus avoid all unnecessary delay in the final arrangements.

Captains Maitland and the Hon. M. Talbot are to meet at Daulatyar on the 6th, and proceed together on a surveying tour up to Bamian and Balkh; with them also is

Subadar Muhammad Husain of the 2d Sikhs, who, being the son of a Hazarah chief himself, will be of much assistance in traversing the Hazarahjat and the country of the Shaikh Ali Hazarahs beyond.

Talking of the Hazarahjat, Ibrahim Khan, the Assistant District Superintendent of Police at Peshawar, our last joined native *attaché*, tells us that the road from Kabul through the Hazarahjat is now in first-rate order; and the fact that a large camel convoy of breech-loading rifles and ammunition has just come through by that road from Kabul, is proof of itself that the road is passable for anything but wheeled artillery.

CAMP KUHSAN, 12*th October* 1885.

Sir West Ridgeway left us on the 1st and arrived at Mashhad on the 7th, where the final arrangements regarding the meeting of the Commissions are being settled. The telegraph line, though, between Teheran and Mashhad, is down again as usual, we hear, and this will delay work considerably. Dr Owen and Captain de Laessoe are with Sir West Ridgeway at Mashhad, also Mirza Hasan Ali Khan. We in camp here are principally concerned in finding some suitable position for our winter-quarters, in case we have to pass the winter in the Herat valley. The winter hereabouts is said to be much colder than at Bala Murghab, where we wintered last year, and the wind very severe. At Bala Murghab we enjoyed a dry still cold, which invigorated and did not distress us. Here, they say, the wind blows in a perfect hurricane up the valley for on an average of about two days in the week; and when we think of what we suffered from the wind the day we first arrived here in November last, we have some idea of what we may have to endure in January and February next. If we have to stay here, the first thing to see to is the supply of wood, and to get this we must be somewhere at this the western end of the Herat valley. Higher up the river the jungle in the river-bed ceases, whereas here the supply is unlimited, and to be had in any quantity simply for the cutting—in fact, without cutting, as the drift-wood alone will last us yet many a day. Ghorian has been proposed as a good site, but there seems to be some objection on the part of the Amir's officials to our wintering there, and the supply of wood is short. However, Major Holdich, Major Meiklejohn, Mr Merk, and Lieutenant Drummond start to-day to inspect it on their way to Herat, and the question of its suitability or otherwise will soon be settled. The present idea is that Kuhsan promises best, as there are a lot of walled fields around the village, which would of themselves give a certain amount of shelter from the wind, and in which, with the help of the wood close at hand, the men might be able to hut themselves without much difficulty.

The Kuhsan *robat* is very dilapidated, but with some repair might take in a couple of hundred men or so, and the remainder would have to hut themselves around. The Kafir Kilah *robat* is better, but it is out of the way. These *robats* are all large buildings of burnt bricks, some 60 or 70 yards square, with a double row of domed corridors all round, and an open courtyard in the centre. In olden days this must have given grand shelter; now they are mostly in ruins. Khush *robat*, I remember, was exceptionally large, and looked big enough at first sight to shelter a brigade, but the accumulated filth of ages made it quite unfit for habitation.

There is a ruined old place called the Citadel here, surrounded by a moat and garrisoned by a company of Khasadars or Afghan irregulars; but it is all in ruins, and very dirty, and not enough shelter even for the hundred men now in it. These Khasadars are all men from the Logar valley, pleasant and civil when we visit them, and with the same innate craving that I have noticed amongst the Afghan troops elsewhere for some sort of uniform. Time after time has the Afghan sepoy expressed to me his wish that the Amir would give him a uniform; and the wish, I must say, does honour to the man, and shows that he has some real soldierly feeling in him. Happy is the Afghan who can swagger about in the British soldier's red tunic, and marvellous is the variety of counties one sees on the shoulders of the soldiers in Herat. Where they all get the tunics from is the mystery, as I believe all these red coats are the private property of the men themselves, not served out by the Amir. The demand for them is doubtless very brisk on the frontier—something like the demand round our camp here for ammunition-boots. Why the Afghans of all ranks have such a fancy for ammunition-boots I cannot say; but so it is, and half the men one meets are wearing them. A boot that in India costs about Rs. 4 or 5, is sold here easily for Rs. 10 and even Rs. 12; and a large trade could be done in them at that price, I have little doubt.

Well, to return to the Khasadars in the Kuhsan fort. When Majors Bax, Meiklejohn, and Rind, Dr Charles, and myself were inspecting the old fort a few nights ago, the Sad Bashi or commandant turned out a guard of honour that showed to the full the different ideas of the men regarding uniform. Each man had got himself up in his best, and never shall I forget one man, apparently a would-be Highlander, who grinned with delight whenever his get-up attracted attention. His kilt consisted of a piece of the checked cloth in red-and-blue squares woven hereabouts, put round his waist like a towel, over a pair of loose, baggy, white trousers; a *barak* coat, if I remember right; and a hat that was the pride of his life—something like a broken mushroom-shaped topee covered with bright red cloth, and with a white band round it. He was a cheery, good-tempered fellow, and long may he live to wear it. Poor Khasadars! they have a hard time of it quartered indefinitely in some out-of-the-way place like this, far from their homes, without the slightest chance of relief. There are fifty more in the *robat* at Kafir Kilah, some 6 miles farther on, watching the highroad through there to Mashhad. The Persian border commences at a small *nullah* some few miles beyond, and the strictest watch is kept on all passers-by, and all suspicious characters are arrested. The Afghan authorities are most particular, and no one is allowed to cross the frontier who cannot satisfactorily account for himself. All sorts of people, I believe, turn up—German-speaking Jews, Persian-speaking Turks, and many others, all generally on the search, they say, for some long-lost relation who was heard of last in Herat, but all equally ignorant of their relation's present whereabouts. Some doubtless get through, but the majority, I fancy, are stopped and turned back.

At Kafir Kilah, in addition to the great big *robat*, there are the remains of the old fort that gives the name to the place. Who the Kafir was that built the fort I cannot say, but nothing now remains except a flat-topped mound some 100 yards in length and slightly less in breadth, with the remains of bastions at the angles, and covered as usual with broken pottery and porcelain of fine make and design. From the inscription carved on some small marble-slabs in the wall over the doorway, it would appear that the *robat* was built in the year A.H. 1037, or A.D. 1628.

Many were the hopes indulged that a 1st of October at Toman Agha would produce a good bag of pheasants; but, alas! all were doomed to disappointment. Captains Durand, Peacocke, and Heath, Lieutenant Rawlins and myself, were all out there, but to little purpose: the jungle was so thick that it was impossible to get through it, and the pheasants, if they were there, were safe inside it. Curiously enough, few hens or young birds were seen. Old cocks were found here and there on the edge of the jungle, and a few hens, but only one or two young birds, and they were very small—hardly bigger than partridges. Possibly the hens are still with their broods in the thick jungle. Large flocks of " coolen," or *kulang* as they are here called, are daily seen wending their way south, doubtless on the road to India, with now and then a flock of pelicans in their wake, while the duck are getting more and more plentiful every day. *Chakor* swarm in the river-bed, and afford capital shooting. A pack of a hundred or more will be seen darting off into the jungle, and once marked down, can be put up a few at a time, giving grand sport. Partridge for breakfast is therefore a regular standing dish now in camp. We get two kinds of sand-grouse,—the common imperial or black-breasted grouse, and a white-breasted pintail variety slightly smaller: the former, though, are the best eating, and the young birds excellent.

Captains Maitland and the Hon. M. G. Talbot are now past Daulatyar, and well away on their journey through the Hazarahjat to Bamian and Balkh, a grand trip through utterly unexplored country. Mr Merk left Captain Talbot in the Taimani country, and rejoined camp on the 1st, after a pleasant three weeks' outing through country hitherto visited only by Ferrier, and his account of it seems to have been incorrectly recorded. On the 4th, Major Bax and Lieutenant Wright arrived back from Mashhad, where they spent a pleasant week, and were most hospitably entertained, —Nawab Mirza Hasan Ali Khan's Persian cook having amply demonstrated the merits of Persian cookery. The Prince Governor of Mashhad entertained them and Dr Aitchison at dinner. Asaf-ud-Daulah, the Governor-General of Khorasan, also received them most cordially, and not only entertained them with an endless variety of chocolates and sherbets at his reception, but held a review of all the Persian troops in Mashhad in their honour. Some 1500 cavalry and about 1000 infantry, all told, marched past,—the cavalry all irregulars, with the exception of one regiment of Khorasanis. All Mashhad was at the review, and all the Persians turned out in full dress. At the special request of the Asaf-ud-

Daulah, the treasure-guard of twenty-five men of the 11th Bengal Lancers, under Ressaldar Muhammad Akram Khan, then in Mashhad, also paraded and marched past, and went through the lance exercise, a charge, and a few other manœuvres, which elicited great commendation. We can only trust that it is not the last time that British troops will parade with the Persian in friendly rivalry, or with the Afghan either. Major Bax and Lieutenant Wright returned *via* Turbat-i-Haidari and Khaf, thus seeing a good bit of new country.

Captains Durand and Peacocke and Lieutenant Rawlins are away examining the road through the Nihalsheni pass, through which the Demarcation party expect to march very shortly on their way to meet the Russian Commission at Zulfikar. Captain Peacocke proceeds direct through the Ardewan pass to meet Major Holdich at Herat, for probably a final inspection of the fortifications. The works now in progress are mostly completed, and the construction of the remainder will depend a good deal on the future policy of the Government.

CAMP KUHSAN, 27*th October* 1885.

Sir West Ridgeway returned from Mashhad yesterday, and the uncertainty in which we have all been kept for the past fortnight is now partially put at rest by the final orders regarding the reduction of the Mission. The Escort of the Demarcation party, not to exceed in number 100 men for duty, as agreed upon by the two Governments at home, will be furnished by the 11th Bengal Lancers under the command of Major Bax and Lieutenant Drummond. Another party of some 60 men of the 20th Panjab Infantry may also possibly remain under the command of Captain Cotton to escort the treasure and surplus stores to our winter-quarters at Maimanah, Shibarghan, Balkh, or whatever place may eventually be fixed upon.

All the rest of the Escort return to India, but by what

route is not yet settled. Various routes are open—viz., through Seistan and Baluchistan, down to Gwadar; or across the desert to Nushki, by the road we came this time last year; or direct down the highroad through Farah, Girishk, and Kandahar; or finally, through Bamian and Kabul, or rather Ghorband and Charikar, to Peshawar. What the decision of Government will be is yet unknown. Several officers will also return, and the Mission will be reduced as much as possible with regard to the work that still lies before it.

A Committee composed of Major Bax, Major Rind, and myself, has been busy for some days past considering what reductions could best be carried out, and everything has been arranged so far as is possible without final orders on the subject.

The camp has been very quiet of late, and there has been little to talk about beyond reductions, with the exception of the experiences of the various members out pig-sticking. Pig, I may mention, swarm in the thick tamarisk-jungle of the river-bed, and some were seen daily by those out shooting. At last it was determined to try if, after all, numbers could not succeed in driving them out into the open. The first attempt was made one afternoon by a beat up the river. The men of the 20th Panjab Infantry, with every huge Afghan and every other sort of dog that could be mustered in camp—and their name is legion—turning out to beat. One pig was eventually driven out and run for some distance; but the great feature of the day's sport was the charge of a whole sounder of pig across the river right into the main body of the hunt. Some pig had been run and lost, and almost all, both horse- and foot-men, had collected on the banks of the river preparatory to a fresh start, when, all of a sudden, a hoorush was heard, and a whole sounder swept down the opposite bank pursued by one or two stray horsemen, and, boldly plunging into the river, swam straight for the assembled crowd. Such a gallop and such a rush there was along the bank to meet them, and then a curious sight was seen. On the top of the bank were officers and sowars on horseback, some with spears and swords, some with revolvers, sepoys with sticks and stones, orderlies with guns and rifles, *dooliwalas* and followers of every description, and dogs of every breed, and yet, nothing daunted, on came the pig, swimming gallantly, and headed by a fine old boar, whose wicked little eyes and glistening tusks were about the only part of him visible, and not paying the slightest attention to the discharge of rifles, revolvers, or stones. The Commissariat Babu, I may mention, figured prominently with a revolver on horseback. Up came the pig to the bank, the old boar made straight for the nearest dog, rolled him over, and charging right into the middle of the crowd, went through them all, and vanished unscathed into the jungle behind, followed by the whole of his family. When all had gone and we looked round to count the spoil, nothing remained but a poor little pig shot by an orderly with his officer's rifle. So much for the Herati pig.

The second day down the river afforded a run and a kill; but the jungle was too thick to get the pig thoroughly out, and the best fun was the new experience we had of shooting pheasants off horseback.

Orders have already been issued to stock the road from here *viâ* Bala Murghab and Maimanah to Balkh with supplies, and Sirdar Sher Ahmed Khan goes on to Maimanah in advance to prepare the way. Sirdar Muhammad Ishak Khan and the Wali of Maimanah both wrote some time ago to say that they had received orders from the Amir to prepare for our arrival, and asking what amount of supplies we should require. Our party this winter will be a difficult one to feed, owing to the large number of Persian mules we have, in addition to all our Indian animals. The daily consumption of barley is consequently a serious item; but so long as we get into winter-quarters in time to collect sufficient grain before the severe weather sets in, we shall have no particular difficulty in feeding ourselves. Afghan Turkistan is an unknown country to us as yet, and we are all anxious for a new field.

There is no particular news from the border, with the exception that the Russian troops have evacuated Panjdeh, and have gone back to Aimakjar and Hazrat Imam, lower down the Murghab, and half-way to Merv. The climate and ground are said to be better there, and the troops will probably be permanently located at those places in preference to Panjdeh. There is no news of the withdrawal of the Russian troops at present in occupation of the Zulfikar pass, but as the Escorts are to be limited to 100 men a side, it is presumed they will be withdrawn before the Commissions meet. Major Durand, Captain Peacocke, and Lieutenant Rawlins, when out the other day, fixed the marches for the Demarcation party down along the Hari Rud valley from here to Zulfikar, and found a good site for the camp a little to the south of the pass, where the party will wait for Sir West Ridgeway to rejoin them from Herat. It is not known yet on what day the Russian Commissioner will arrive; but the two months allowed by the protocol expire on the 10th November, and it is hoped he will be up to date.

CHAPTER VI.

FINAL VISIT TO HERAT.

CAMP KAREZ ELIAS, 8*th November* 1885.

THE principal event of the last ten days has been the visit of Sir West Ridgeway to Herat to inspect the fortifications. The Afghan authorities have hitherto invariably opposed any visit of the Commissioner to Herat, either fearing that such a visit would make the people think that the province was after all to be really ceded to the British Government, or for some other inscrutable reason best known to themselves; but the Government of India, taking matters into their own hands, soon impressed on the Amir the necessity of issuing special orders for the reception of Sir West Ridgeway with all honours. The time was short, and a visit to Herat, just when the Commission had to be starting for Zulfikar, very inconvenient; but all details for future arrangements having been settled during the short stay at Kuhsan on the 27th and 28th ultimo, Sir West marched for Herat on the morning of the 29th, leaving orders for the Demarcation party, consisting of Majors Bax, Holdich, and Durand, Captain Gore, Lieutenant Drummond, Ressaldar-Major Sirdar Muhammad Aslam Khan, and the escort of 100 lances of the 11th Bengal Lancers, to march from Kuhsan on the 1st, and halt at Karez Elias, the most advanced Afghan frontier-post, some 10 miles above Zulfikar, while the remainder of the camp was to march on the 2d to

Mamezak, a village some 25 miles west of Herat, and then, as soon as the winter clothing, &c., was complete, proceed to Balkh, preparatory to a return to India *viâ* the Shaikh Ali Hazarah country and the Ghorband pass to Charikar, and thence down to Peshawar.

This was the route selected by the Amir for the return of the Mission, and was said by him to be open all the year round. The latter point appeared at the time rather doubtful; but to be prepared against all eventualities, Captain Maitland was directed by Sir West Ridgeway, when starting for Bamian nearly two months ago, to send on Subadar Muhammad Husain Khan, of the 2d Sikhs, from Bamian to explore that road; and on his report the further march of the party beyond Balkh would probably have depended. A party of sixty men of the 20th Panjab Infantry, under Captain Cotton, was to be left at Maimanah with stores and treasure, to await the arrival of the Demarcation party, when the settlement of the first portion of the frontier from Zulfikar to Maruchak had been completed. These arrangements, though, were all subsequently upset by special orders from the Government of India, countermanding the return of the party by the Ghorband route, and now the main camp is halted at Mamezak pending further orders.

Our party to Herat with Sir West Ridgeway consisted of Captains Peacocke, Cotton, Griesbach, and De Laessoe, Mr Merk, Drs Owen and Charles, Lieutenants Wright, Rawlins, and Galindo, and myself, and an escort of half a troop of the 11th Bengal Lancers. We marched the first day 22 miles to Rozanak, 25 miles the second day to Sangbast, and 18 miles into Herat the third day, the 31st October. All sorts of difficulties regarding the Commissioner's reception were raised by the Afghan authorities, as usual; but Sir West stood firm, and eventually all went off well.

The first man to greet us as we neared the city was Ressaldar-Major Bahaudin Khan, of the Central India

Horse, who for some little time past has been acting as British Agent in Herat. Shortly afterwards, Rustam Ali Khan, the Sipah Salar's brother, appeared, and then, about 2 miles from the city, we were met by the Naib-ul-Hukumat, as the governor is styled, with all his following. We proceeded, escorted by him through the villages, till, emerging into open ground on the north-west of the city, we found a guard of honour of Afghan troops, consisting of a squadron of cavalry, a battery of artillery, and a battalion of infantry, drawn up in line, who presented arms and fired a salute as we passed.

The Bagh-i-Karta, a garden to the south-east of the city, across the Karobar *nullah*, was set apart for the Commissioner's use, and we all were encamped outside, as there was no room for tents within. The ride round the outside of the city to our quarters was a sight alone sufficient of itself to impress the new-comer with a sense of the strength of the place. The scarped ditch and the huge rampart, with its three lines of musketry-fire, one above the other, not to mention the outworks and redoubts, made one naturally feel that one would be sorry to have to assault such a place, and to express a hope that it may never be our fate to have to do so. We may legitimately hope to have a share in the defence, if the city is ever attacked, but never, I trust, will we allow it to fall into other hands, and so have to retake it.

The 1st inst. was mostly taken up with ceremonial visits. In the morning Sir West Ridgeway, accompanied by all the British and Native officers, paid his visit to the governor and the Sipah Salar, or commander-in-chief—to the former in his residence in the Chahar Bagh, and the latter in the old citadel, both of which places I have already described in former letters. The ceremonial at each was the same—the trays of fruit and sweetmeats, the little cups of green tea handed round, and the usual giving of presents. The governor presented various webs of *kurk* and *barak*, the warm goat and camel-hair cloth of the country, with a few furs and silks, and a Turkoman horse and carpet, the latter of which was subsequently packed up for transmission to his Excellency the Viceroy. The Sipah Salar in his turn also presented a Turkoman horse and some more *kurk* and *barak*. At the governor's were assembled all the local chiefs and celebrities,—amongst them Ambia Khan, the chief of the Taimanis, the Nizam-u'-Doulah, chief of the Hazarahs, Yalantush Khan, Jamshidi, the late governor of Panjdeh, who behaved so well at the time of the Russian attack, and who himself had his horse shot and a bullet through his coat early that same morning. At the Sipah Salar's we found Generals Ghaus-ud-din and Allah Dad Khan, with various other brigadiers of artillery and colonels of regiments.

In the afternoon, return visits were paid by the governor and Sipah Salar, when the same formalities were gone through again; all the Afghan chiefs and officers were duly presented, and the usual presents, consisting of rifles, guns, pistols, watches, and a horse, were given in return. Glad enough we were when all ceremonial was at an end.

Almost the whole of the 2d was spent by Sir West Ridgeway in the inspection of the fortifications. The Afghans and Heratis have, without doubt, proved themselves good workmen, and the way in which they have carried out Captain Peacocke's instructions shows what good material they have amongst them. There is every hope now that Herat will shortly be a really very strong place of defence, and long may it remain the bulwark of the British Indian Empire.

On the morning of the 3d we said good-bye to all returning to join the main camp at Mamezak, and started off across Badghis to join the Demarcation party near Zulfikar. Our party consisted of Sir West Ridgeway, Captains Peacocke and De Laessoe, Mr Merk, Dr Owen, Kazi Muhammad

Aslam Khan, and myself, and our route was as follows :—

		Miles.
3d.	Kilah Mambar Bashi, on the Sinjou stream,	20
4th.	Sang Kotal,	17
5th.	Kara Bagh,	16
6th.	Gulran,	13
7th.	Kizil Bulak,	20
8th.	Karez Elias,	12

This route, I think, has already been mostly described; suffice it to say, that during the first two marches, while on the south side of the mountains, we were much struck by the amount of fresh land taken up for cultivation since our last visit in the summer. Then the land was all waste: now, we found fresh little irrigation-channels cut in all directions, and men ploughing in almost every available spot; the road, too, formerly a mere track, now a well-marked path,—all signs of increased prosperity. There is not a doubt but that the money brought into the country by the presence of the Commission, and the expenditure on the fortifications, has given a great stimulus to trade of all sorts; and when so much can be done by the presence of a mere Mission, what could not be done with a British occupation?

As we marched out of Herat our road led us through the Musalla, the tall minarets of which are now alone standing; the rest is simply a mass of *débris*, which a perfect army of donkeys is engaged in clearing away. Riding up the Kamar Kalagh gorge, through the low hills to the north of the city, we passed an Afghan regiment at target practice. The practice, though, was hardly in accord with our theories on the subject. First of all, the butts, instead of being on the level, were well up the hillside; secondly, the targets were only scarped banks of earth, coloured white, with a red patch in the centre, corresponding, I presume, to our bull's-eye; and thirdly, there were no markers, and no one knew where his bullet hit. The men were marched out from the ranks in squads of four, who all knelt or sat on the ground and fired one after the other, and then got up and gave place to another four. I sadly fear the Amir has not yet instituted such a thing as a prize for musketry, and marksmen, I should say, are quite unknown; yet the material that these regiments are formed of is splendid, and under British officers would be fit for anything. The Afghan soldier, as a rule, is very poor, and cannot afford to join the cavalry; but I hope yet to see the day when the restrictions placed by the present Amir on his men enlisting in India will be abolished, and our frontier infantry regiments full of the men such as I have seen around me in Herat. So long as we have to campaign in countries like Afghanistan, so long must we get men able to stand the climate. The Afghan soldier is a sturdy fellow, who takes naturally to ammunition-boots, stockings, and *puttees*, wears any amount of warm clothes when he can get them, and is never so happy as in a British red tunic. The ordinary Hindustani in Afghanistan is out of place. His feet cannot accommodate themselves to boots, and in cold and wet he is next to useless. He will take off his clothes to cook, and will divest himself of his trousers and go about with bare legs on the slightest provocation, and then neglect to put them on again at sundown, and next day finds himself ill in hospital. The wonderfully good health that all our men and followers on the Mission have enjoyed may be safely put down to the selection of so many Pathans for the escort, and to the liberality of Government, and stringent orders regarding the wearing of warm clothing by the others. For months past the daily number of men in hospital has only been about three or four; and this, out of a camp of some 1200 souls, speaks for itself—a striking contrast to the sickness and mortality reported amongst the Russians. The liberality of the Government of India in the way of free issues of warm clothing has amply repaid itself, and will, I trust, form a precedent for future expeditions. Nothing in India can compare for warmth with the *barak* cloth made in the Herat districts, with which our men are now all clothed. The blanketing coats and trousers served out to us on leaving India were no protection at all against the real cold of these parts, and wore out in no time; whereas the *barak* suit made here costs little more, wears double and treble the time, and keeps out the cold in a manner that no other cloth that I know of can equal. The supply of *barak* unfortunately would not equal the demand, had we any great number of men to clothe; but with an ensured demand there is little doubt but that the supply would be largely increased, and I can think of nothing better than the establishment of a regular Government agency in Herat for the purchase of *barak* for the clothing required to be kept in stock for the equipment of the first army-corps that may be ordered on service up here. The troops like *barak* clothing and look well in it, and any little extra cost in the price is more than covered by the money which was wasted in the issue to our men, with the so-called Indian-made warm clothing, of flannel waist-belts and chest-protectors, neither of which were appreciated or understood, and were rarely or never worn, whereas a double-breasted *barak* coat answers every purpose.

At Sang Kotal we camped for the night at the southern side of the hills, and crossed the pass the next morning. The rise from the south is very gradual and the ascent trifling; but there is a short but steep descent on the northern side, and then the road winds gradually out on to the downs of Badghis—the last hill, as a matter of course, being crowned by the usual Turkoman watch-tower, now fortunately no longer required. Much has been written about the fertility of Badghis, yet I could not but be surprised at the amount of water we saw, whilst the ruins of old forts, old *karezes*, and old irrigation-channels show how well cultivated this district was in olden days. Now all is a waste. We have ridden across it from south-west to north-east, and with the exception of the Afghan outposts and a few shepherds, there is not a human being to be seen. Imagine a succession of rolling downs of alluvial soil, covered in most places at this time of the year with dried grass, large leafy sorts of thistles, and perfect forests of asafœtida plants; the hollows, where there is water, full of thick reeds and bulrushes, and every few miles or so a mound marking the site of some old fort. An old ruined *robat* or caravanserai half-way between Sang Kotal and Kara Bagh, called Robat-i-Sargardan, and another at Gulran, show of themselves what traffic there used to be along this road. Kara Bagh, with its mound marking the site of the old fort with a well at the top, has already been described. At Gulran there is the ruin of an old mud-fort, the ditch of which is some 150 yards square, with an outer line of walls, now simply a mound, 30 feet above it, and the old keep, a square building about 30 yards across, above that again in the centre of all. Who it belonged to who can tell? Captain de Laessoe tried his best to decipher some of the inscriptions on the tombstones at the Ziarat-i-Baba Furk, a few miles west of Kara Bagh, but the graves appeared to be mostly those of Persians. The number of graveyards all over these downs is extraordinary, and shows how thickly populated the country must have been. Even at Kizil Bulak, so named from a small spring which bubbles up at the foot of some reddish-coloured rocks, and loses itself again within 100 yards, there is still the inevitable graveyard on the top of the mounds above. To the north of Kizil Bulak the character of the country changes from the rolling downs to rocky scarps, all facing west towards the Hari Rud, and covered every here and there with pistachio-trees, or rather bushes, for they are rarely more than 15 feet in height. Curiously enough, some large hawk chooses these small trees in which to build a huge nest of twigs and branches—a great mass of sticks two and three feet in diameter, visible from any distance—and yet I have never been able to find out for certain what the bird is. We passed several of these old nests by the roadside on the march to Kizil Bulak; and as I myself saw them here early last spring, before the birds had begun to build, I can only conclude they are the relics of olden days, when these downs knew not the sight of man.

The weather for our march has been splendid, slightly better than we expected; but still I have worn a waistcoat and a *cardigan* all day in the sun under my coat without feeling it at all too hot. The air on the downs is fresh and clear, and in the shade of a tent simply delicious. Not that it is always so; in many places we saw the marks of perfect hurricanes of wind, in huge masses of sticks and stalks, of thistles and shrubs of all kinds, which had evidently been blown for miles across the downs, gathering bulk as they went, like a snowball, till finally brought to rest at the bottom of some hollow. At other places, for some 200 or 300 yards in width, a clean sweep had been made of the asafœtida-stalks, which were all lying flat on the ground with their heads to the south. Talking of asafœtida, I should mention that we found some hundreds of *powindahs*, the camel-carriers of Afghanistan, encamped outside the Kandahar gate at Herat, all engaged, they told us, in the transport of asafœtida to India for sale. Were the trade properly fostered, there is little doubt that it would be highly remunerative. Now I must close. A letter has just been received by Sir West Ridgeway from Colonel Kuhlberg, the Russian Commissioner, stating simply that he will be up to time. According to our reading, time is up on the 10th; but so far as we know, the Russian troops have not yet evacuated the Zulfikar pass— an essential preliminary to peaceful negotiations. However, I will be able to tell more on this subject in my next.

CHAPTER VII.

THE MEETING OF THE JOINT COMMISSIONS.

CAMP ZULFIKAR, 10*th November* 1885.

THE Commissioners have met at last, though not the Commissions, and we have now a prospect of some work before us once more.

We arrived here to-day from Karez Elias; and our Russian interpreter, an Armenian from Tabriz, named Ananiantz, who has joined us from the British Legation at Teheran, was at once sent over to the Russian camp, and returned with the news that the Commissioner himself had arrived, but that the other members of the Commission would not be here for some days. Sir West Ridgeway, on hearing this, rode over to the Russian camp to pay Colonel Kuhlberg a private visit; and thus I can tell you the Commissioners have met, but not the Commissions. M. Lessar arrived in the course of the afternoon, and the remaining members, it is supposed, will turn up shortly.

We are now a party of fourteen, all told, in camp—namely, Sir West Ridgeway, Majors Bax, Holdich, and Durand; Captains Peacocke, Gore, and De Laessoe; Mr Merk, Dr Owen, and Lieutenant Drummond; Ressaldar-Majors Sirdar Muhammad Aslam Khan, Kazi Muhammad Aslam Khan, Khan Baba Khan, and myself. Mr Merk and Khan Baba Khan leave in a day or two to join the main camp at Mamezak, where the remainder of the Mission are still await-

THE MEETING OF THE JOINT COMMISSIONS. 71

ing final orders regarding the route they are to take on their return to India.

My last letter told of our arrival at Karez Elias on our return from Herat. Karez Elias, hitherto important only as the most advanced post in Afghan occupation, is simply a little hollow in a ravine, with a small marsh at the bottom of it—the site, I presume, of some ancient *karez*. Our supplies are stored at Ab-i-Charmi—three wells of fresh water some three miles to the east; another depot is at Gulran, and a third at Maruchak; and the task of collecting all these supplies in such a country as this, without a habitation within 60 miles, has been no slight joke. Our camp, much as it has been reduced, still numbers some 600 men, including servants, Persian muleteers, and everybody, with nearly 900 animals, horses, ponies, and mules. We are all equipped with mule-carriage; and pleasant though it is to have our baggage up so quickly, still the feeding of so many mules is a serious drain on the commissariat. The big Persian mules all take their four *seers* of barley apiece every day, and cannot do with less, their owners say, despite the idea we have that the mule is a hardy animal that can pick up a livelihood anywhere, like a donkey on thistles, and thrive on it too. Camel-carriage, though very cumbersome, is doubtless much more suited to this country. Camel-grazing is procurable everywhere; and if ever we have a campaign in these parts, there is no doubt but that the mule-carriage will have to be limited strictly to the movable column, leaving the baggage of the remainder and all stores to be brought up on camels, owing to the difficulty that will be experienced in providing grain. Here, with us, camels have to be employed in bringing up the grain with which to feed the mules—a thing that would be next to impossible were we on active service. The supply of camels seems almost unlimited, and we are inundated with offers of camels for hire from all quarters. The liberal hire that had to be given when the Mission was started from Quetta has drawn men from all sides in the hopes of employment; and we have now a mixture of Persian, Afghan, Seistani, Herati, Turkoman, and Usbeg camel-men about our camp, one and all willing to engage to bring just as many more camels as ever we want. Alas for their hopes! we are reducing, not increasing, our numbers. Our pay may have been high, as local rates go, but still it has had a capital effect on the country generally, and no doubt greatly added to the difficulties the Russians experienced in procuring transport at the time when war seemed imminent. Everything now is so quiet and friendly that we can hardly believe that scarcely three months have elapsed since war seemed merely a question of hours, or that our thoughts, now centred on entertaining our Russian guests, were then solely bent on defending Herat to the best of our power against their assault.

On arrival at Karez Elias on the 8th, we found that Major Holdich and Captain Gore were both away in the hills fixing their points for the survey before them, and they were fortunate in having a clear day. Yesterday and to-day have been both raw cold days, with a bitter north wind, and the clouds hugging the tops of the hills in a persistent manner that put all hopes of survey work out of the question. A change of the wind to the south, though, bids fair to put all clear again.

Yesterday, Major Durand, Captains Peacocke and De Laessoe, and Ressaldar-Major Sirdar Muhammad Aslam Khan, with the camp colour-party, moved on to Zulfikar, to open communications with the Russians and select our camping-ground. On arrival they rode up to the Russian camp, and found no one there but a couple of Cossack officers with a small party of Cossacks and some five-and-twenty infantry. Neither of these officers could speak either French or German, or anything but Russian, and communication could only be carried on through a Turki interpreter of theirs who spoke a little Persian. Colonel Kuhlberg had not arrived, but was expected, they said, though they knew nothing of his movements. The Russians, men and officers, were all living in huts, sunk some four feet into the ground, slightly walled round at the top, and roofed with reeds plastered over with mud, sloping on either side from a ridge-pole in the centre. There was not a tent in the whole camp. The Russian soldiers are described as diminutive little fellows, who came popping up out of these holes of huts, most of them badly dressed, but very respectful and careful about saluting. The Russian officers invited our party into an empty hut, and were kind in offering anything they had that could be of use. A site for the camp was afterwards selected near the river, about a mile south of the Russians, into which we all marched this afternoon: the day was so cold and cloudy that we did not start till 10 A.M.

11th November 1885.

The Commission is now engaged on its first meeting here in our mess-tent. But to continue the narrative from yesterday. Sir West Ridgeway, on arrival at the Russian camp, was met by Colonel Kuhlberg, who came out to meet him directly he heard who was coming, and received him most civilly, while, to make up for the want of ceremony at meeting, a Cossack guard of honour was waiting to salute him on his departure. M. Lessar had also just arrived, having ridden in from Pul-i-Khatun, but was not well and did not appear. Colonel Kuhlberg readily accepted Sir West's invitation to dinner, and we all had an opportunity of thus pleasantly making each other's acquaintance. English was spoken at dinner throughout, and Colonel Kuhlberg seems quite at home in it He told us that his party would number fifteen officers altogether, besides subordinates, and that he had with him 140 men of his escort, besides irregulars, postal sowars, &c. No objection, of course, is raised to this on either side, as we have the same difficulty to contend with; and were our escort to be cut down to 100 lances all told, including non-commissioned officers, trumpeters, farriers, orderlies, police, and everybody, the sentry-duty would be so heavy that the poor men would hardly get a single night in bed. As it is, we have only 94 men for duty. In addition to our escort, there is also Kazi Saad-ud-Din and all his Afghan sowars to be counted in too, a goodly band of themselves, but necessary for postal and other arrangements. Seven of the fifteen Russian officers are said by Colonel Kuhlberg to be topographers, trained in the School of Survey in Tiflis, to which he himself belongs, and every preparation has been made by him for a large-scale survey of the whole frontier. He talked of wintering at Panjdeh, but nothing is settled on that point yet.

This afternoon, just after the meeting of the Commission had broken up, and Colonel Kuhlberg and M. Lessar had ridden away, a grass-cutter was brought in bitten in the arm and scratched about the side by what he declared was a tiger, which had attacked him while cutting grass in the tamarisk jungle in the river-bed close by. Some twenty or thirty sowars soon turned out, and we beat the jungle, but with no result beyond finding the fresh tracks of some panthers. Tigers are here, we know, as we have seen their tracks, and not long ago Captain Griesbach saw one cross the road just in front of him when riding along near here; but the grass-cutter's wounds are clearly due to a panther.

I should mention that the first arrival of the Cossacks in camp to-day caused the greatest interest amongst our men. No sooner had Colonel Kuhlberg disappeared into the tent and our guard of honour was dismissed, than the four Cossack orderlies who came with him were taken off to tea by the men of the 11th Bengal Lancers, who keenly enjoyed the sight of a new face. The Cossacks are little bits of chaps, with long loose coats almost down to their heels, and with a

Berdan rifle, almost as long as themselves, slung across their shoulders, wrapped in a coarse black-felt cover. Their horses are small, sturdy, shaggy-looking ponies, and very diminutive beside the horses of the 11th Bengal Lancers. Their accoutrements generally are of the simplest, and their saddles are a sight that our men cannot get over at all. Imagine a great flat cushion or pad on the top of the horse, with a high flat wooden knob at the pommel and cantle, between which the rider has to balance himself as best he can, for I will defy any one to find anything in their saddles to grip with his knees. The stirrups are of brass, and circular at the bottom, with a round disc like a huge wad-punch underneath. What the origin of this was no one can tell, but presumably it is the relic of some ancient custom now perpetuated by regulation.

12th November 1885.

The first stone of the Afghan frontier-pillars has now been laid, and there is every hope that the work will progress apace. This morning at 9 A.M. Sir West Ridgeway and Major Durand, our Assistant Commissioner, with Colonel Kuhlberg and M. Lessar, rode down the Hari Rud valley to the point about a mile and a half to the north of the mouth of the pass, and fixed the site of the first pillar as near as possible on the spot laid down for the boundary in the Protocol. Kazi Saad-ud-Din, the Amir's representative, at once set his men to work, and the pillar will probably be finished to-day.

The Zulfikar pass is not a pass through any range of mountains, as might be supposed, but simply a gorge or break in the line of high cliffs that bounds the valley of the Hari Rud on the east almost all the way up from Pul-i-Khatun to Karez Elias, a distance of some 40 miles. Through the whole of this, the Zulfikar pass is the only practicable communication between the road along the valley of the river below and the country above. A fresh means of access can be obtained some 10 miles to the north of Zulfikar, but the road there will require a good deal of work to make it practicable, and the loss of the ready-made road at Zulfikar must be very inconvenient, to say the least of it, to the Russians: no wonder they wished to retain it. The possession of Zulfikar would have just nicely rounded off the Russian frontier, and have given them the site for a good frontier-post, with direct lateral communication between their main lines of advance up the valleys of the Hari Rud and the Kushk. By the loss of Zulfikar they are at present practically cut off from all lateral communication with the Hari Rud anywhere south of Pul-i-Khatun, nearly 30 miles to the north.

Camp Zulfikar, 20th November 1885.

My last letter told of the successful laying of the foundation-stone of the first boundary pillar on the banks of the Hari Rud, a mile and a half north of Zulfikar, or, more correctly speaking, of an old tower on a mound opposite the mouth of the Zulfikar pass. Little more could be done beyond that till the ground was surveyed, and the line traced in the Russian map, and agreed upon in the Protocol, identified; consequently the brunt of the work fell next on Major Holdich and Captain Gore. The Russian large-scale map of the pass having been accepted by the Commission, they have had simply to test the main points and see that the line is correctly laid down, without going into that minute detail which would have detained the Commission at Zulfikar for long.

On the evening of the 12th the majority of the Russian Commission arrived, and when some of us rode over on the afternoon of the 13th to call on its members, we found some twenty *kibitkas* pitched on what was the old Russian parade-ground, and the Commission fairly established therein.

On the 14th, Colonel Kuhlberg came over with a kind invitation for us all to dine at his camp that evening. We little expected the grand reception that was in store for us. A double row of bonfires, kept alight by the Russian infantry soldiers, lighted our way up to a big reed-hut, in which we were received by Colonel Kuhlberg and all his officers, arrayed in full dress and decorations galore. The reed-hut had been decorated out of all recognition. The walls were covered with green leaves and ornamented with Cossack knives and swords, the roof covered with canvas, and the poles supporting the roof draped with white-red cloth and ornamented with bayonets, the sockets of which formed candlesticks. At the centre table Colonel Kuhlberg, M. Lessar, and Captains Gideonoff and Komaroff entertained Sir West Ridgeway, Majors Bax, Holdich, and Durand, and myself. The rest of the party split up amongst five tables. One novel feature of the entertainment to us was the sideboard, covered with the *zakuska*, in the shape of anchovies and caviare, and other little appetisers of a like nature, to which we were all bid before sitting down to dinner, and where we soon learnt to take a glass of *vodka* in the place of our usual sherry and bitters. From the ready manner in which we all seem to take to this little relish before dinner, I can only wonder that the custom has never found its way into England or India. The dinner was capital, our hosts most pleasant, and we were soon on the best of terms possible with our new acquaintances. Even those who knew no common language were all talking in some sort of jargon before the evening was out. Commencing on port with the soup, we ran through Madeira, claret, and Caucasian wine with the joints, and finished up with champagne and jam, by which time the most shy of men in an unknown tongue could at any rate summon up courage to clink his glass with his neighbour's and drink to his very good health.

A Cossack guard outside sang beautifully in chorus the whole evening through—a real treat to us, who have heard no music or singing since we left India fifteen months ago. The Cossacks here, I believe, are the 4th squadron of the Kubanski Regiment, and are light blithe-looking little fellows, clad, when in full dress, in long black coats with red shoulder-straps. Each carries a whip—an article not forming a portion of the equipment of our cavalry soldiers; and it is most amusing to see each man swing himself into his saddle, and at once turn round and bring his whip down across his pony's flank, and go off at full gallop in a cloud of dust, so different from the more stately regulation of our men.

The 15th and 16th were occupied mostly by meetings of the Commission and by interchange of visits with the Russian officers. Major Durand is the British and Captain Gideonoff the Russian Assistant Commissioner, M. Lessar attending on the part of the Russian Foreign Office.

The entire Russian Commission, so far as we know at present, is, I believe, composed of the following officers:—

Colonel Kuhlberg, Colonel of the Staff, Commissioner.

Captain Gideonoff, Staff and Astronomical Survey, Assistant Commissioner.

Court Councillor Lessar, Agent on the part of the Russian Foreign Office.

Captain Komaroff, Commanding the Escort.

Dr Semmer, in medical charge.

Captain Kondratenko, Topographer.

Captain Tchaplanski, Topographer.

Lieutenant Gorokh, Russian Sappers, Treasury and Commissariat Officer.

Titulary Councillor Ilyin, Topographer.

Titulary Councillor Tolmatchoff, Topographer.

Titulary Councillor Swetowidoff, Topographer.

M. Mirzaeff, Interpreter.

M. Mehemetoff, Interpreter.

Cossack Captain Varenik, Escort.

Cossack Lieutenant Kiachko, Escort.
Cossack Sub-Lieutenant Winnikoff, Escort.

None of the topographers speak anything but Russian, but the doctor speaks German, the Cossack lieutenant French, and the interpreter Mirzaeff Persian; so that, as none of us can speak either Russian or Turki, our conversation is mostly limited with all but the four seniors and these latter three. Colonel Kuhlberg and M. Lessar both speak English well; Captain Komaroff speaks German, French, and a little English; and Captain Gideonoff a little French. Our knowledge of oriental languages seems to surprise the Russians, as, so far as I can gather, none of them as a rule acquire the languages of the people under them, work being always carried on through interpreters, as their policy is to make the people talk Russian.

On the 16th, Sir West Ridgeway entertained the whole of the Russian Commission, and we did our best to show how well we appreciated the preparations they had made for us by decorating our mess-tent to the best of our power in their honour in return. With the help of the cavalry lances, swords, bits and chains, and a muster of all the best felts and carpets in camp, our *shamianah* and mess-tent looked quite gay, and, with the addition of a guard of honour of the 11th Bengal Lancers outside, and one or two more of them and a man of the 20th Panjab Infantry inside, I may add, very picturesque—at least that was the verdict of our Russian guests. We sat down a party of thirty-one altogether, sixteen of the Russians, as above, and fifteen of ourselves—viz., Sir West Ridgeway, Majors Bax, Holdich, and Durand; Captains Gore, Peacocke, and De Laessoe; Mr Merk, Dr Owen, Lieutenant Drummond, Nawab Mirza Hasan Ali Khan, Sirdar Muhammad Aslam Khan, Kazi Muhammad Aslam Khan, Khan Baba Khan, and myself. We had no band or singing to offer our guests, not even the *sarnais* of the 20th Panjab Infantry, which have charmed the savage hearts in our camp all these months, and which now, alas! just at the time when we would fain have shown what our Afreedi warriors can do, are doomed to reduction and return to India.

It would have been a grand *finale* could we have given our guests a Katak dance, and shown the Cossacks, who seem so fond of flourishing their swords and knives, what our men can do in that line; but protocols and orders of Government cutting down the Escort have left us without even that resource; while as to singing, the *dooliwalas*, I think, possess the only talent in the camp. The Russians, we hear, had a band of no less than thirty-five men all told off in readiness to accompany General Zelenoy last year, had he come; but unfortunately, we were not allowed such a luxury, despite the kindness of Colonel Prinsep and the officers of the 11th Bengal Lancers in offering theirs. However, although we could not return the compliment in music, we did our best to show the Cossacks how we appreciated their singing for us two nights before. While we were at dinner inside, Sergeants Manley and Brown and the men of the cavalry took good care of the Cossacks without. A cloth was spread round one of the big bonfires lighted by the men of the cavalry in front of the tent to illuminate the scene and show our guests the way; and there the fun was fast and furious, despite all restrictions of language. Colonel Kuhlberg arrived escorted by about half a troop of Cossacks headed by a man with a large green flag—the squadron colour, I presume—and these men were all set down to a good supper of bread and meat. The bread, it is said, they particularly relished, so different from their own dry black bread; and in fact, as I heard it expressed, the Cossacks ate it like so much plum-cake. The Sikhs were all ready to join in when the brandy came round, and when Lieutenant Drummond and the Cossack lieutenant went out shortly after, they found all as merry as possible. One Cossack

THE MEETING OF THE JOINT COMMISSIONS. 81

under-officer even knew some two words of English, and jumping up, drank to the health of "Victoria," an example that was instantly followed by all the rest. Lieutenant Drummond drank to the health of the Cossacks, and to his astonishment found himself at once hoisted up on their shoulders. Sergeant Manley and the Sikhs at once followed suit with the Cossack lieutenant, and neither was let down again till the Cossacks had sung a whole chorus around them—an honour, so Colonel Kuhlberg said, that fell to the lot of few, and then only on special occasions. Inside we were nearly as merry. When the wine came round after dinner, Sir West Ridgeway proposed the health of the Emperor, to which Colonel Kuhlberg at once responded by proposing the health of the Queen.

Kazi Saad-ud-Din and the governor of Herat are both encamped here with us. Both exchanged visits on arrival with Colonel Kuhlberg, who received them both with his usual courtesy, Mr Merk acting as interpreter each time. They both take an energetic part in the proceedings.

The plans for future progress have been so far settled that the morning of the 18th saw several of us on the move. Captain Peacocke started with three Russian topographers to survey the country east of Maruchak. This portion was reconnoitred by Captain Peacocke last year, but under the greatest difficulties, the snowstorms for days together quite obscuring all his points, and the cold being so intense that hardly a watch in his camp could be kept going, thus rendering his traverse exceedingly difficult. As it is, even now, with the fine weather that we may look for up to Christmas, this is still the most difficult portion of the whole frontier to survey, as the survey officers can only give three points trigonometrically fixed to work upon—a small number on which to found the topographical survey of such a stretch of country. The zone to be surveyed is the country north of the Kaisar Rud and west of the Andkhui river, and this the Russians

F

will divide into three sections, each topographer taking one. It is very unfortunate that our survey party should be so short-handed, but it cannot be helped. Captain the Hon. M. Talbot is away at Bamian, where, we hear, he hopes to connect his survey with those done at Kabul during the last war. He will then bring the survey up to Balkh and the frontier from there. Being entirely alone, with not even a sub-surveyor to help him, the opportunity of getting much of the country topographically surveyed is lost, as one officer can do comparatively little of the latter when he has to carry on his triangulation at one and the same time. Sub-Surveyor Heera Singh is busy carrying a survey through the Firozkohi country up to Maimanah, and will not join us till too late to be of much help this year, while Imam Sharif is away joining the surveys of this summer to the south of Herat on to those formerly done at Kandahar. Major Holdich, Captain Gore, and Sub-Surveyor Ata Muhammad, the only ones of the party left, are all now away with another party of Russian topographers surveying the country from Zulfikar to Chaman-i-Bed. This survey is expected to be completed in time for the Commissioners to commence the demarcation on the 26th instant, on which date Sir West Ridgeway, accompanied by Majors Holdich and Durand, Captains Gore and De Laessoe, Dr Owen, Nawab Mirza Hasan Ali Khan, Kazi Muhammad Aslam Khan, and myself, with a light camp move along the line of the frontier with the Russian Commission. The remainder of the camp, under the command of Major Bax, with Lieutenant Drummond and Sirdar Muhammad Aslam Khan, march round *viâ* Gulran in seven marches to Chaman-i-Bed, in time to meet the Commissioners there on arrival. It is impossible for the whole camp to march together along the frontier owing to the want of water. As it is, at the first camp at the head of the Zulfikar pass there is no water at all, and the only supply will be what can be taken there in camel

THE MEETING OF THE JOINT COMMISSIONS. 83

pakhals, while at other places the supply will be very limited.

Final orders have at last been issued for the return march of the party now at Mamezak to India. The route to be followed is practically the same as that we all marched up by last year, with this difference, that instead of risking the crossing of the Helmand at Chahar Burjak, the party will probably march round the Seistan lakes, and thus avoid the river altogether. The Helmand very possibly may be found at its usual level and easily fordable; but still there is always the chance of a winter flood, and it has been thought best to avoid the risk of a detention on the banks of the river in a place where it might not be easy to find further supplies at hand.

The party returning to India is comprised as follows:—
Major Meiklejohn, 20th Panjab Infantry, in command.
Major Rind, Commissariat Transport and Treasury Officer.
Captain Heath, Lieutenant Wright, and 88 rank and file
    of the 11th Bengal Lancers.
Lieutenant Rawlins and 164 rank and file of the 20th
    Panjab Infantry.
Dr Charles and the Military Hospital.
Lieutenant Galindo, 14th Hussars, Intelligence Department.
Conductor Lyttle, Mr Wilson, with Commissariat, Transport, and other details.
Mr Merk, Political Officer, and Native *Attachés*; Ressaldar-Major Muhammad Husain Khan, 7th Bengal Cavalry; Ressaldar-Major Baha-u'-din Khan, Central India Horse; Mirza Muhammad Taki Khan and Khan Baba Khan.

Mr Merk and Ressaldar-Major Baha-u'-din Khan, having seen the party safe to the Helmand, return and rejoin the Commissioner's camp; a political officer from the Baluchistan agency being sent out to meet the party at

Khwajah Ali, and take them across the desert to Nushki and Quetta.

I give the route laid down for the march, as it can now be followed in the latest edition of the Turkistan map, viz.:—

		Miles.
Nov. 28. Mamezak (25 miles west of Herat) to Deh Afghan,		8
,, 29. Pahra,		13
,, 30. Chah Gazak,		11
Dec. 1. Half-way to Sher Baksh,		19
,, 2. Sher Baksh,		18½
,, 3. Sarmandal,		22
,, 4. Halt.		
,, 5. Karez Dasht,		10
,, 6. Sangbur,		23
,, 7. Zigin,		17
,, 8. Gang,		23
,, 9. Kin,		21
,, 10. Kushk Rud,		11
,, 11. Lash Jowain,		21
,, 12. Halt.		
,, 13. Silgan,		18
,, 14. Half-way to Boli,		14
,, 15. Boli,		14
,, 16. Nasirabad,		14
,, 17. Halt.		
,, 18. Halt.		
,, 19. Wasilan,		12
,, 20. Burj-i-Alam Khan,		7
,, 21. Gor-i-Haji,		18
,, 22. Dah Dehli,		12
,, 23. Chahar Burjak,		21
,, 24. Khwajah,		18½
,, 25. Rudbar,		19½
,, 26. Halt.		
,, 27. Landi Baraich,		12½
,, 28. Khwajah Ali,		17

and Quetta, about 20th January 1886.

A camel sowar postal-line will be established from Quetta *viâ* Nushki to meet the party at Nasirabad, and in the meantime postal communication will be kept open with them from the Commissioner's camp by a line of Afghan sowars from Herat.

A farewell order has just been issued by Sir West Ridgeway, specially thanking Majors Rind and Meiklejohn, and notifying his appreciation of the thorough manner in which the men of both the 11th Bengal Lancers and the 20th Panjab Infantry have done their duty, even under the most trying circumstances; finally adding, that "their conduct and their invariably cheerful discharge of their duties have raised the name of the British army in Afghanistan, and the people of the country have learnt that their presence amongst them is an unmixed advantage."

The return party have some long marches before them, necessitated by the want of water on the road, but the sturdy sepoys of the 20th Panjab Infantry think little of that now. Our only regret is that the party should have to go, and that we should have to lose them—a regret shared equally by all.

Captain Cotton and his sixty men, with treasure and stores, are now on their march *viâ* Kushk to Chahar Shumba, where we join them after the completion of the boundary settlement up to Maruchak. The weather keeps cloudy and comparatively warm, the thermometer ranging from $62°$ by day to about $38°$ by night; and we can only hope that with so many of us on the march, and so much surveying to be done, we shall not have a burst of wet weather.

Our last discovery is the existence of a couple of shops, kept by a Greek and an Armenian respectively, in the Russian camp, with a varied assortment of goods, including a consignment of Caucasian wines which are all new to our taste. I fancy, though, that some liquors of a stronger nature must also be kept there, to judge from the attraction which that neighbourhood evidently possesses for some of our followers. An English-speaking commissariat sergeant has also turned up in the Russian camp, who gave a grand dinner to-day to Sergeants Manley and Brown, an entertainment which the latter and Duffadar Mir Baz, of the 11th

Bengal Lancers, are going to return when the two camps next meet again at Chaman-i-Bed. Duffadar Mir Baz is a fine specimen of the Indian soldier, and plays a prominent part in all our camp arrangements. He it is who, armed with what he calls his compass, lays out our camp and sees that our tent-pegs are properly dressed in line, takes particular care of the flagstaff, and, in fact, is the camp quartermaster's general factotum. Having spent some months in England as orderly to Sirdar Muhammad Afzul Khan, he is quite prepared to join in any dinner-party, and no doubt will make a capital host.

Talking of entertainments, I must not forget to tell of the dinner-party given the night before last by our native *attachés*, Sirdar Muhammad Aslam Khan, Kazi Muhammad Aslam Khan, and Khan Baba Khan, to their brother Mussulmans in the Russian service, Mirzaeff and Mehemetoff. The latter, a Lesghin from Daghestan, is strict, and takes no wine; but not so the former, a Russianised Persian, who readily fraternised over the champagne at dinner on the 16th with his friends around. How or why he comes to be named officially as Mirzaeff, I cannot quite understand. To the best of my belief, the Russian officers call him Nazar Beg. He himself says his name is Sherif, that his father's name was Hasan, and that he is called after his grandfather, whose name was Mirza. Why he should be styled Mirzaeff any more than Hasaneff, I have no idea. Similarly, Mehemetoff is known as Zachariah Beg. Possibly his grandfather was a Mehemet something. Whether or no, Zachariah Beg seems to love a good fight. Commencing life amongst a corps comprised of about a hundred cadets from Daghestani families of position, he spent four years in St Petersburg in some sort of body-guard duty about the late Emperor's Court. Returning at the end of his time with the rank of lieutenant and a decoration, he was a volunteer at Geok Tepe, where, rushing forward too soon, he was blown up in the explosion of one of the mines, and was taken out for dead some three hours afterwards, but recovered. He served also as a volunteer through the Turkish war at Kars and in Asia Minor, and now boasts of a row of some half-dozen decorations on his breast. The Caucasian dress which he wears is certainly very striking. Imagine a sort of pink-coloured silk waistcoat with high collar bound with gold-lace, buttoned tight up at the throat, and over this a long black coat fitting tight round the body, but with loose flowing skirts almost down to his heels, the usual row of silver-topped cartridge-cases across each breast, with a huge double-edged knife slung in front, and a curved sword with embossed silver scabbard at his side, long boots, and black breeches, and there you have the Lesghin. If they are all as handy with their knives as our friend here seems to be, no wonder they were a difficult race to conquer. The Caucasians, however, seem to be much split up amongst themselves. There are so many different tribes and people in the country, that they say they have no less than forty-five languages, and a village on one side of a valley often has an entirely different language from that spoken in the village on the other side. In one village will be found fine men and handsome women, and in the next a dirty ugly lot, of an entirely different race. However, to return to our dinner. The table was laid in the mess *shamianah*, and the party consisted of seven—the three hosts, the two Russian guests, and Mr Merk and myself; and a merry evening we had of it, too. The conversation, of course, was entirely in Persian; but unfortunately, the Lesghin could talk nothing but Russian or Turki, and consequently all his ideas had to be translated by his Persian friend, helped on by a few odd words in Turki which the speaker's energy and gesticulation made comprehensible to all.

CHAPTER VIII.

ACROSS BADGHIS.

CAMP, HAUZ-I-KHAN, *4th December* 1885.

I HAVE already telegraphed the successful settlement of the frontier from Zulfikar to Hauz-i-Khan, and that the Commissions are now halting here pending the completion of the survey of the country on to Maruchak, a further distance of some 40 miles as the crow flies. Hauz-i-Khan lies some 70 miles almost due east of Zulfikar, but the boundary laid down in the Protocol trends considerably to the south, and the line actually demarcated is some 95 miles in length instead of 70. The main portion of the camp left Zulfikar on the 21st November, under the command of Major Bax, and marched round by the following route, as it was impossible to provide water for all along the actual frontier line—viz., Zulfikar to

	Miles.
Karez Elias,	12
Kizil Bulak,	12
Gulran,	20
Tutachi,	16
Bank of the Moghor stream,	14
Kara Tepe,	14
Chaman-i-Bed,	16
Hauz-i-Khan,	8

The Commissioner's camp, consisting of Sir West Ridgeway, Major Durand, Dr Owen, Nawab Mirza Hasan Ali Khan, Kazi Muhammad Aslam Khan, and myself, with an escort of 25 sowars of the 11th Bengal Lancers under Ressaldar Jeswunt Singh, left Zulfikar on the 26th, and camped that night at the top of the Zulfikar pass, where we were joined by Major Holdich, who, leaving Captain Gore at Chaman-i-Bed, returned with the survey of the country completed so far, on purpose to point out to the Commissioners the more prominent topographical features. There is no water at the top of the pass, but sufficient for the men was carried up in camel *pakhals,* and the majority of the horses were left at Zulfikar to march straight through the 26 miles to Ak Robat the next morning. The mules did not seem to suffer in the least from the want of water for one night.

The Zulfikar pass, as I have said before, is simply a defile leading up through the precipitous scarps of rock that run along the eastern bank of the Hari Rud. At the mouth of the Zulfikar pass the scarp rises straight up from the valley of the river to a height of about 800 feet. The land at the top slopes gradually down to the east for four or five miles beyond, and then rises abruptly again in a second scarp, just like the first, through which a second defile cuts its way, finally landing one in the ordinary undulating country of Badghis, some eight miles from the river-valley. The scenery in the pass is very wild, and at one place the rocky cliffs on either side are barely 30 yards apart. I noticed that at the narrowest corner in the western defile a stone wall had been built across from side to side, showing, I presume, that the passage had been disputed by some one in days gone by. The rocks are full of the nests of hawks and vultures, and the cliffs around abound with ibex and oorial. Unfortunately, we were all too busy to find time to go after them.

The 26th was spent by the Commissioners in inspecting and deciding on the sites for the boundary pillars from the valley of the river up to the top of the pass. Starting about 10 A.M., we rode first to the Russian camp, where Colonel Kuhlberg and his staff joined us, and all then rode up the pass together. The Russian *kibitkas* had all been taken down and sent off, and the reed-huts forming the Russian cantonment all through this past summer, were left standing, ready for their new occupants, the Afghans. As we all rode out together, we found the squadron of Cossacks drawn up in line on the roadside opposite their late quarters. After the salute Colonel Kuhlberg rode up to them, and giving some salutation, was at once replied to by the whole squadron in a curious and pleasant sort of chant, immediately after which they fell in behind us, and sang in chorus almost all the way up the pass. The governor of Herat and Kazi Saad-ud-Din, the Amir's agent, remained behind to take possession of the Russian lines, and make the necessary arrangements for the Afghan garrison to be located there. The protection of this portion of the frontier has been intrusted to Muhammad Amir Khan, the Khan of Ghorian, with 100 of his horsemen and a company of Afghan Khasadars. The Khan himself accompanied us all round the boundary-line within the limits of his charge, finally leaving us at Ak Robat, to return and superintend the erection of the pillars.

The 27th was spent almost entirely in the saddle. Starting at 8 A.M., we rode out some four miles, and climbed to the site for a pillar on the top of the Dengli Dagh hills, a commanding position, whence the line of frontier could be traced all across the lower hills and undulations for miles. Here a good deal of work was got through; and by the time all was settled, we were quite ready to sit down to the breakfast prepared for us by Sir West Ridgeway's *abdars*. I must say a word in praise of the Persian *abdar*. He is not a cook, but something akin to it. The cook prepares and gives him the breakfast, and he is ready to stop anywhere on the road and serve you up that breakfast fresh and hot in less than no time. Mounted on a sturdy pony with two large regularly fitted-up leather bags, one on each side, and another behind the saddle, he has all his utensils and everything with him wherever he goes, and a handier man I have rarely seen. Colonel Kuhlberg, Captain Gideonoff, and M. Lessar breakfasted with us on the hillside, and then we all rode on to Ak Robat together, getting in just at sunset,—after just one little halt on the way to partake of a glass of Colonel Kuhlberg's excellent Caucasian wine.

Ak Robat is a wide hollow in the downs, containing some fifteen or twenty wells with a plentiful supply of water, only some 12 or 15 feet from the surface. The *robat* or resthouse which gives its name to the place, consists only of a heap of bricks, hardly one now being left standing on another. The Russians had a strong post here all the summer; but this has lately been withdrawn, and, so far as I know, has not been replaced. Our two camps were close together. We thought we had a small camp, but the Russians had one much smaller. We had one row of officers' tents, all of small Kashmir or Kabul pattern, with the servants' tents and horses, each in a row behind, and the escort of twenty-five sowars in a line in front, all compact, and easily guarded by a couple of sentries. The Russian camp, so far as the officers were concerned, consisted of four *kibitkas*, while the Cossacks and infantry had apparently neither tents nor baggage. The Cossack ponies are never picketed in the way that our cavalry horses are, but are simply tied up in a double row with their heads together, and have neither *jools* nor felts nor anything to cover them at night. The men, too, apparently have nothing but the clothes they wear, and whatever they can carry on their pony to sleep in, and yet they do not seem to feel the hardship in the least. The Russian officers tell us that during the Turkish war, when the Russian soldiers lost their feet by scores from frostbite at night, the Cossacks escaped almost without loss in this respect.

One great difference in the size and life of the Russian camp is the almost entire absence of followers. Our camp, with our Indian and Persian servants, even at our present reduced scale, still presents a scene full of life and animation in comparison to the Russian camp, where twenty-five Russian infantrymen seem to do the servants' work for the whole party. They pitch and unpitch the *kibitkas*, and load them on the camels far better than the Turkomans themselves; indeed, as a matter of fact, the latter are quite useless at such work, as with them the women do all the pitching of their *kibitkas*, and the men are accustomed to look on with lofty contempt.

Ak Robat having been surrendered to the Russians under the terms of Lord Granville's agreement, we had simply to define the boundary half-way between it and Sumba Karez, the frontier Afghan station nine miles to the south. A pillar, No. 13 of the series, was accordingly located by the side of the road on the morning of the 28th, and another on the top of the hill to the east, and we eventually found our way into camp at Au Rahak, 16 miles from Ak Robat, at sunset.

The day's ride afforded us two instances of the *shikar* of the country. The first, as we were all standing around the pillar No. 13, when an antelope—or rather, I should say, a gazelle—suddenly appeared, trotting quietly past at a distance of some 200 yards. Major Durand had just time to get his rifle from his orderly and roll it over by a good shot before it got out of reach. The Russian officers, who had never seen an Express rifle before, seemed much struck at the shot, and examined the rifle with great interest. The deer of this country is something like, though larger than, the ordinary *chikara* or ravine-deer of India, with the same sort and size of horns, only with the difference that the tips of the horns bend inwards instead of backwards. These deer are very wild, and especially difficult to approach on these bare downs, and very few have been shot by us as yet. Several wild asses were also seen by Major Holdich, but all his efforts failed to bring one down. The flesh of these asses is regularly eaten by all the Heratis and Turkomans, though the Kabulis profess to turn up their noses at it on the ground that it is unlawful food. The flesh, though, is not much of a dainty. When I was first at Ak Robat in February last, the Khan of Ghorian's men, who were then garrisoning the place, brought in a wild ass and invited me to partake of it; but I have no desire to repeat the experiment.

The second bit of sport that day was the running to ground of a fox by my greyhounds. The foxes here are large, bushy-tailed animals, nearly as big as an English fox, and the two little fox-terriers who followed this one down into the hole, could not bring him out again, and refusing to leave him, spent the night there. I had to return the next morning with spades and picks, and dig them out, and I eventually found the two little dogs and the fox all together at the end of the hole several feet under ground, and all considerably the worse for the night's fray. Coursing in this country is almost an impossibility, owing to the mass of rat-holes everywhere. The ground is undermined in every direction, and a horse is bound to come to grief. I remember a sowar's horse of the 11th Bengal Lancers on the march up putting his foot through a rat-hole and breaking his own and very nearly his rider's neck on the spot. The rats are of all sizes, from a sort of marmot—which look in the distance like so many small rabbits scuttling about—to jerboas and field-rats with bushy tails, and even to mice. Apparently they never drink, and what they eat is a mystery. However, they and the land-tortoises seem to divide the country between them: the latter are everywhere, and their eggs and shells are strewn all over the downs. Some epidemic or storm seems to overtake them at times, as I have found tracts of country here and there thickly strewn with countless empty tortoise-shells. According to the Turkomans, the foxes live on the rats, and as long as the weather is mild and the supply is plentiful, they never leave the hills or come near the settlements. Hence the difficulty they have in catching them. The eagles and hawks that one sees about must prey a good deal, I think, on the tortoises, as I have often noticed half-eaten carcasses of the latter lying about, though I confess I have never yet verified the story of the tortoise being carried up and dropped from a height by the eagle.

Au Rahak, where we camped on the night of the 28th, was simply a bit of flat ground by the side of a stream of salt water. All our drinking-water had to be brought with us in *pakhals* from Ak Robat; but the horses managed to get a drink some two miles up the stream that runs in from the south, though I believe the drinkable water is difficult to find without a guide who knows the place, as it is only at one particular spot, where apparently some fresh-water spring rises in the middle of the stream, that the animals will drink. Sumba Karez, some 10 miles to the west of Au Rahak, has a plentiful supply of water. The old *karez* has been opened out by the Afghans, and there is now an ample supply of sweet water, sufficient, they say, for a party of 300 sowars. This place will doubtless be the Afghan frontier post in this direction, as now that Islim has been surrendered to Russia, it is the only place possessed of good water near the frontier in all the line between Zulfikar and Kara Tepe, a distance, as the crow flies, of some 60 miles, from each of which places it is almost exactly equidistant. The frontier on the Afghan side at Sumba Karez and Au Rahak has been put in the charge of a Herati Khan, and I was rather amused at a conversation I overheard between him and a Turkoman shepherd at the latter place just as we were leaving. The Turkoman hailed from Panjdeh, and the

Khan was impressing upon him that now that the frontier had been defined, he must keep his sheep to his own side for the future. The shepherd vigorously remonstrated, but the Khan was firm. "You have gone over to the Russians," said he, "and now you must stay with them." "Not a bit," said the Turkoman; "we have not gone over to the Russians, it is the Russians who have come over us." The argument waxed hot and strong, but I fancy the Turkoman was worsted in the end.

On the 29th we had an easy day, simply marching down the valley of the Shorab (salt water), or, as the Russians call it, the Egrigeuk stream, to Islim, a distance of some 12 miles. The boundary line crosses the road about three miles west of Islim, and then runs up to the hill marking the watershed between the Shorab and the Kushk, near Kara Tepe. Islim consists of nothing but a spring of fresh water on the right bank of the stream; and it was the knowledge of the position of this spring, I presume, that prompted the Russian Government to claim a boundary-line crossing the valley and running along the crest of the hillocks bordering its southern bank, instead of following the natural line along the bed of the stream. Unfortunately the point was so conceded without proper inquiry from those on the spot, and the consequence is that the Afghans are cut off from the water-supply at this particular portion of their frontier, and have 30 miles of waterless downs to cross to Kara Tepe instead of a connected line of frontier posts.

On the 30th we marched 16 miles to Chaman-i-Bed, a ruined old mud-fort on the right bank of the river Kushk. The Shorab was dry all the way down, the water we found running higher up having all disappeared below ground; but the bed of the stream was as white as snow from some saline incrustation, and with water so salt the valley can never be of much use for cultivation. Chaman-i-Bed is very different. Here the Kushk river provides a plentiful supply of sweet clear water — though it also sometimes runs dry, I have heard. Hitherto no one but a Turkoman has dared to show his nose in the place, and even the few adventurous spirits among the latter who did venture up so far, took good care to build their tower of refuge first, and to cultivate their fields afterwards. I noticed one or two of these buildings close to Chaman-i-Bed, and they generally took the form of a deep circular ditch with a walled enclosure inside large enough to hold the Turkoman and his cattle and all. Inside the man was quite safe, as the raiding-parties never ventured an assault on any walled enclosure, however weakly manned.

Some two miles up the valley, to the south of Chaman-i-Bed, there is one of the curious artificial mounds so common in these parts, marking the site of some ancient fort; a small higher mound, in the north-west angle, clearly marking the position of the former citadel. This place is known as Kara Tepe Khurd—literally, the small black mound—to distinguish it from the real Kara Tepe, the Afghan post, some 15 miles higher up the valley. We halted at Chaman-i-Bed on the 1st December, as the question of the settlement of the boundary where cultivable land was concerned was naturally a more difficult matter than that of the uncultivable downs through which we had hitherto been demarcating it. However, all differences were soon disposed of, and on the 2d we moved eight miles farther down to Hauz-i-Khan, where we are halting for the present. From this point the boundary has to be demarcated, in nearly a straight line, across to some point north of Maruchak, and that point will be the most difficult of all to fix. However, Major Holdich, Captain Gore, and Captain Komaroff have started to survey the country up to Maruchak, and as soon as that is done the Commissioners will be able to set to work again.

At Colonel Kuhlberg's request, the Afghans have undertaken the building of all the boundary pillars, and these have already been built all along the line from Zulfikar to Chaman-i-Bed, and the remainder up to Hauz-i-Khan will be ready in a day or two. The Russian topographer, Swetowidoff, who is finishing his survey near Zulfikar, is to inspect and report the completion of the pillars from Zulfikar to Islim, and I start shortly to inspect those on from the latter place to Hauz-i-Khan.

The main portion of the camp marches for Maruchak on the 6th, under the command of Major Bax; the Commissioners' small party, as before, waiting at Hauz-i-Khan, ready to move directly the necessary survey is completed. The Russian camp is exactly opposite to ours on the other bank of the river, while the governor of Herat and Kazi Saad-ud-Din are encamped close alongside of us. Now that we are halted, we are able to see a little more of our Russian friends, and M. Lessar, Captain Komaroff, and the Cossack officers have all been dining with us the last night or two; while to-night, Sir West Ridgeway, Major Durand, Dr Owen, Nawab Mirza Hasan Ali Khan, and myself, are all dining with Colonel Kuhlberg. It is unfortunate that the number of our guests must be so limited, but it is hardly a compliment to ask a man to dinner who cannot talk anything else but Russian— a language that all of us are absolutely ignorant of. Our social intercourse is thus most unfortunately restricted on that account. We hear that the Cossacks were hoping we should all be here together on the 9th, their annual *fête*-day, when they have a series of sports and festivities to commemorate the presentation to them by the Emperor of a special standard, in recognition of the gallantry displayed by the regiment at the storming of Geok Tepe. Unfortunately, we shall probably at that date be toiling across the waterless tract between here and Maruchak. However, we hope to be able to give them a day's sport on our side before we part. The Murghab river, we hear, is considerably deeper now than it was this time last year, and the ford we crossed by, just below the old ruined bridge at Maruchak, is now impassable. Captain Cotton got his party and stores safely across at Bala Murghab; but all his mule-loads had to be transferred to camels, and even then the empty mules were many of them swept off their legs by the strength of the current. It is to be hoped that the Helmand is not similarly affected, as there seems to be some difficulty regarding the return march of Major Meiklejohn's party through Nasirabad, in Persian Seistan, and they may still have to cross the river instead of marching round the lake at the end of it. Very probably the river may be in its normal state, and quite fordable; but even supposing it is not, the governor of Farah, Muhammad Yusuf Khan, will probably be able to get the big boat we had last year down from Girishk again, and under these circumstances I am not sure that it would not be easier to cross the river than to pass through all the network of canals on the Persian side, including the great Kohak canal, which Bellew describes as 60 feet wide and 8 feet deep, with nothing but rafts of reeds, called *tutis*, to cross it upon. Major Meiklejohn and his party started from the Herat valley on the 1st, and are now well on their way to India.

The Commissioners hope to complete the demarcation of the frontier up to Kilah Wali before the winter sets in, and in that case probably both Commissions will winter either there or at Chahar Shamba, ready to go on again the moment the weather permits. Sirdar Muhammad Ishak Khan, the governor of Turkistan, seems to be doing his best to arrange for the advent of the Mission, and to make things comfortable for them during their stay in his province. Sirdar Sher Ahmed Khan, who has just returned from a trip in advance to Maimanah and Andkhui, reports that he has been received everywhere with the greatest cordiality and distinction.

We are all looking forward to some pheasant-shooting in our old haunts at Maruchak when we get there. Here there is little to shoot. Sirdar Muhammad Aslam Khan and myself have bagged a few pheasants, but that is all, with the exception of some specimens for the natural history collection. We have not yet seen the Russian officers out shooting, but they have some guns with them, and we hope they will be able to join us. The climate, however, is so variable just at present, that it is impossible to reckon on the weather holding up for very long. One day is sunny and still, and so hot that one thinks of getting out one's summer clothing again; the next cloudy and raw, with a Scotch mist that chills one to the bone. To-day in my tent the thermometer is only 52°; and one envies the Russian officers in their working-dress, consisting of a short black-leather coat lined with red flannel, a pair of leather cherry-coloured pantaloons, and long boots. Certainly they are well equipped for cold and wet; but how they would fare in a hot-weather campaign, either in Afghanistan or India, is a very different matter. They have no helmets—nothing but their black, flat-topped cloth caps, which would be no protection whatever against an Indian sun, while the fur caps of the Cossacks would be absolutely unbearable.

CAMP, HAUZ-I-KHAN, 14th *December* 1885.

Our weather for some days here at Hauz-i-Khan was wet and raw, and though it has now cleared again, still we have had nothing much to do while waiting for the completion of the survey on ahead. Life in a tent on a raw, cloudy day, with the thermometer at 40° or 45°, is never pleasant, but nevertheless the days have seemed to fly. We are not early risers as a rule; on these cold mornings no one seems to stir much before 8 A.M., and personally I honestly confess I am rarely up before 9; breakfast follows immediately afterwards, and before we have got through the work of the day the afternoon is closing in, and by 5 P.M. it is dark.

Hauz-i-Khan is not an interesting place, as there is nothing much to tempt one out. In olden days it must have either had a considerable population or else have been one of the stages on some highroad for traffic. The place takes its name of the "Reservoir of the Khan" from the *hauz* or reservoir, now in ruins, said to have been built by the great Abdullah Khan of Bokhara, to whom the erection of most of the buildings in this part of the country is assigned by local tradition. The valley of the Kushk here narrows slightly just at the bend of the river between the Kilah Maur and Chaman-i-Bed plains, on the north and south respectively. The old reservoir looks like an ordinary mound, and might be passed without notice. On near approach one sees that it is a great heap of bricks, and that the western side, where the arched roof has fallen in, is open. Climbing down, one finds one's self in the centre of three vaults, radiating north, east, and south; each vault is some 30 to 40 feet in length, and 20 or more in height. The central dome and western vault have fallen in, but otherwise the building might easily be cleared out and restored. The bricks are all laid in mortar—where the lime came from I do not know; and in the lower five or six feet the lime has been mixed with charcoal or ashes, or something black, apparently to make it better resist the action of water. The reservoir must have been filled by rain-water collected in a ravine through the hills to the east; and the river, I presume, must have run dry occasionally in this part of its course then, as now, to necessitate the building of a reservoir at all. The ground around is full of bricks, and probably a *robat* or rest-house for travellers stood alongside.

About 50 yards or more to the north-west there is a small mound marking the site of some old fort, but this mound has long since been turned into use as a graveyard. One long tomb, some six or eight yards in length, is evidently supposed to contain the remains of some holy man, as all over this country the size of the grave seems to increase in proportion to the sanctity of the man buried in it. Unfortunately the name of the saint buried here is lost. Close by, though, there are a couple of old white-marble tombstones. One has been rendered illegible by the action of the weather, but the other bears the name of Awes, son of Amir Osman, and the date in Arabic of A.H. 848 or A.D. 1445, with some verses descriptive of the grief of the father for the loss of his son.

Hauz-i-Khan has no inhabitants at present, though the Panjdeh Sarik Turkomans have been in the habit of cultivating here of late years, living for the time being in a small hamlet at Kilah Maur, some 10 or 12 miles farther north. Kilah Maur is said to be the site of the ancient town of Bakshur. No doubt there was once a considerable population there, as the large artificial mound in the centre, now crowned by the ruins of an old brick fort, evidently of a much more recent date, is surrounded by mounds and ruins of houses for a considerable distance. Whether this was a big city, as is said, deserted on account of the river suddenly running dry, or whether the large extent of the remains was simply caused by the constant desertion and rebuilding of houses so common amongst the people of these countries, it is impossible now to tell. Cultivation nowadays, of course, is limited to the irrigable land in the river-valleys; but there is little doubt that, were the population to increase, rain crops might be raised on the downs above. Many places in Badghis bear evident signs of having once been cultivated, and I can distinctly remember my Turkoman guide once calling my attention to the marks of cultivation on the ground as far north as the old wells at Elibir, north of the Salt Lakes of Yaroilan; but as a rule, the farther north one goes, the sandier the soil becomes, as instanced by the fact that though rain crops are now largely cultivated by the Jamshidis at Kushk, yet the Sariks of Panjdeh say that they cannot do the same, as their soil on the neighbouring downs is so much lighter that the crops sown by them, though producing plenty of stalk, never come into ear.

On the morning of the 9th the main portion of the camp marched for Kilah Maur under the command of Major Bax, *en route* for Maruchak.

The evening of the 8th was signalised by a dinner-party given by Colonel Kuhlberg to Major Bax and Lieutenant Drummond and his own Cossack officers. Every individual officer's health was proposed in turn by their genial host, and the evening was wound up by Cossack songs and dances round a big bonfire; the entire squadron of Cossacks eventually insisting on escorting the British guests down to the river-bank, singing in chorus the whole way and giving them a hearty good cheer on departure. Two days afterwards, Colonel Kuhlberg and his Assistant Commissioners were similarly the guests of Sir West Ridgeway.

On the 9th I started to inspect the boundary pillars built between Hauz-i-Khan and Islim. I halted that night at Kara Tepe Khurd, and walking down in the evening to the reed-marsh close by to try for some pheasants, I gained some practical experience of the fearless character of the Badghis wild pigs. My dogs, catching sight of a sounder, went off in full chase; but the pig soon turned the tables by promptly charging down on the dogs, and not only drove them back, but followed them right up to within 30 or 40 yards of where I was standing, and this out in the open plain. An enormous old boar, almost as big as a donkey, who headed the party, grunted away, gnashed his teeth, and twice returned to the charge, following us for a considerable distance, but eventually drew off, much to the relief of the unfortunate Persian *farash* who was acting as my beater. At Kara Tepe, 16 miles farther up the valley of the Kushk, I found some good pheasant-shooting in a reedy swamp by the river-bank. It is a curious fact that in this country pheasants as a rule are only to be found in the swamps;

wood jungle and dry grass, and other places that one would think would be excellent cover for them, are invariably driven blank, and yet no sooner does one get into a *jheel* after the snipe than the pheasants begin to appear.

Kara Tepe itself is a huge artificial mound, some 50 feet high and about 100 yards square at the top, surmounted with the ruins of an old brick and mud wall with a gateway to the south. The mound is surrounded by a moat still in a very good state of repair, and rising up as it does in the middle of a wide flat valley, must have been a strong place in its day. When its day was, who can tell?. but still, even a century and a half ago, what a different place it must have been from what it is now! It is recorded in the 'Tarikh-i-Nadiri,' the Persian history of Nadir Shah, that the latter marched up here on his return from India, and that he was met by his son from Khorasan at this very place, Kara Tepe, which was then the scene of a three days' entertainment on a scale of almost unparalleled magnificence. All the plunder of India was exhibited, and amongst other things the banquet was held in an enormous tent, manufactured in India on purpose, of which the poles were of gold and the fringes strings of pearls. I have not the book to refer to here, but I believe Nadir Shah marched on by way of Maruchak and Maimanah to Balkh, exactly the road that we shall soon be following ourselves; but there, unfortunately, the similitude ends, as we are neither laden with loot nor are we contracting matrimony at the various places on the road. Whether Kara Tepe was inhabited at the time of Nadir's visit, or by whom, is not stated, but the plain now is knee-deep in thick grass, and covered with a perfect network of old irrigation-channels, showing what could be done if the land was only properly taken up. At present the pig and the pheasants are the sole occupants, with the exception of a tiger or two, whose footprints we noted in the swamp five or six miles farther down the stream. Curiously enough, although so deserted, yet the lands of all these different places are thoroughly well known. Take this part of the Kushk valley, for example. The Jamshidis and others can all tell at once how far the boundary of each place extends. Kara Tepe, for instance, is said to extend to the bend of the river some eight miles down the valley. Then comes another old mound, known by the name of Kilah-i-Shaikh Janai—the grave of the latter forming a well-known shrine close by. The lands belonging to this old ruin extend for another five or six miles down the valley till a fresh system of irrigation commences from a canal taken off from the river some three miles above Kara Tepe Khurd, to which place the land watered by it again belongs,—and so on down to Chaman-i-Bed and Kilah Maur. The fact that this is all so well known seems to show that the country cannot have been depopulated so very long, and that the former Jamshidi occupation that one hears about must have been in comparatively recent times. The Afghan outpost at Kara Tepe is to be moved forward to Kara Tepe Khurd, now that the frontier has been defined; and doubtless before long all this land will be repeopled by Afghan immigrants.

Major Holdich and Captain Gore are still hard at work on the survey of the country between here and Maruchak, and are endeavouring to make the most of our present spell of fine weather, which unfortunately cannot be expected to last for long. Although cold at night, the thermometer generally going down to 15° or thereabouts, still the days are delicious, and riding out on the downs, the view from the higher points is magnificent. There is not a cloud in the sky, yet the sun is only just hot enough to make a light helmet pleasant; the air is clear and bracing, and the whole range of the Paropamisus lies stretched before one just capped with snow at its highest points. Dawandah, to the north-east of Herat, is always the first to show signs of snow, and even the Band-i-Turkistan has a sprinkling on its top, although last year none fell on it till close on the New Year.

We hope to have Captains Maitland and the Hon. M. G. Talbot back again with us for Christmas, or at any rate before the severe weather sets in. When last heard of, the former was at Mazar-i-Sharif on his way back, and the latter was making his way from Haibak to Ghori, both having been received everywhere with the greatest honour and courtesy by the Afghan authorities. Captain Griesbach is also on his way to rejoin us from Zulfikar, and we hope to be all collected together again for Christmas, with the exception of Captain Peacocke, who, being engaged with the Russian topographers on the survey of the country between Maruchak and Andkhui, cannot be back in time. Captain Cotton is waiting for us at Chahar Shamba with his party of the 20th Panjab Infantry, but whether we shall be able to join him there by Christmas or not depends entirely on the progress of the demarcation. So far things have worked well and smoothly, but it is whispered in camp that we have difficulties in store for us at Maruchak, and even more beyond. Hitherto the line of the boundary has been pretty rigidly defined in the Protocol, and unreasonable claims have been out of the question: the farther we go through, the less precisely is the Protocol worded, and should the Russian Commissioner insist on putting forward claims depriving Maruchak, Kilah Wali, Maimanah, and Andkhui, not only of their pasturages but also of their wells, it will be very evident that it is not his intention to help on the negotiations. To the north of Kilah Wali and Maimanah there is a great stretch of desert, preventing all communication and population in that part of the country; and the best of it is, that there is not a single Russian subject whose interests touch on that part of the frontier. The Turkomans of Panjdeh, Yulatan, and Merv all have their recognised pastures to the west of the desert, while those living on the banks of the

Oxus have theirs on the east, and there are no others between. The Usbegs of Maimanah will naturally resent being deprived of the wells they have dug to the south of the desert and the pasturages pertaining thereto, especially when there is no one close who can use them; and we can only presume that it is the Russian intention to try by all means to get a foothold south of the desert, sufficient to be able to keep a raw open on that part of the frontier for use as occasion may arise.

Our news from Major Meiklejohn's party reports them progressing well on their way to Quetta. In all probability they will not after all enter Persian territory, but cross the Helmand at Chahar Burjak, as we did last year on the march up. Captain M'Ivor, of the Baluchistan Agency, started at the end of last month to meet the party on the Helmand, and arrange for their march across the Beluch desert to Quetta.

CHAPTER IX.

CHRISTMAS AT MARUCHAK.

Camp Maruchak, 27th December 1885.

HERE we are in the midst of winter once again, sooner than we expected it. Last year we had no snow or cold to speak of till after the New Year. This year not only have we had the cold for some time—the thermometer down to 11° or thereabouts for many nights past is certainly cold—but we woke on the morning of the 22d to find ourselves fairly snowed in, the snow lying some 6 inches deep on the ground, and no signs of it stopping. However, as the day wore on it began to freeze, and at night the snow stopped, and the clouds began to show signs of clearing again. As good luck would have it, our convoy of tents from India arrived in camp two days previously, and we were therefore able to replace all the men's old and worn-out tents by new ones, and also to provide shelter for the muleteers and camel-men. Our men's tents were in a terrible state after all the wind and storms of the past year, and the new ones arrived just in the very nick of time.

The officers' tents have lasted wonderfully considering, and the small Kashmir and Kabul tents in which most of us are housed have stood their trial well. For hard marching and for warmth at night nothing can well beat the Kabul 80-pounder; but for living for days and weeks together in standing camps, as we have been doing for so many months past, the Kashmir tent is by far the best. It is only one

Persian mule-load, say three maunds in weight, and is much cooler in summer; while in winter, by sewing up the ends and covering the sides with thin felt, it can be made very warm indeed. Of course, tents made for use in India are not suited to the changes of an Afghan climate: for instance, the bath-room of an ordinary Swiss cottage-shaped tent is utterly useless in this country as a rule. The wind in summer and the cold in winter entirely prevent its use for the purpose for which it was intended. The only plan is to have the bath-room made in one piece with the inner body of the tent, and not merely enclosed by *kanats* attached to the outer fly, as is usual. For this climate the inner tent, top, sides, and bath-room should all be of one piece, with extra *kanats* to attach to the outer fly at either end to keep out the wind, snow, or rain, as the case may be.

We arrived here at Maruchak on the 18th, and joined Majors Bax and Holdich, Captains Gore, Griesbach, and De Laessoe, Lieutenant Drummond, and Sirdars Muhammad Aslam Khan and Sher Ahmed Khan, who had all arrived here from various directions before us. The Commissioners' party, consisting of Sir West Ridgeway, Major Durand, Dr Owen, Nawab Mirza Hasan Ali Khan, Kazi Muhammad Aslam Khan, and myself, marched on the 15th from Hauz-i-Khan to Kilah Maur, 15 miles, camping some 3 miles below the old fort, just where the Maruchak road branches off to the east. The road runs down the right bank of the river to Kilah Maur, the valley gradually widening all the way. There is a plentiful supply of tamarisk wood in the river-bed, and a splendid plain of good culturable land on either side, a rich heritage for the Panjdeh Turkomans, who, by the present settlement, have become the actual possessors of all this land to the south of Panjdeh, which they formerly only enjoyed on sufferance. The old fort stands in the middle of the plain on the left bank and some little distance from the river, and consists of a flat-topped mound, some 30 to 40 feet in height and about 200 yards long and 150 yards broad, with the ruins of an old brick fort, some 70 yards square, at its north-west angle. The Turkoman hamlets seemed to have increased considerably in size since last year, and doubtless there will be plenty of applicants for a share in all the new land hereabouts.

On the 16th the camp marched 26 miles across the *chul* to Ab-i-Kashan, where there is now a fair stream of running water. The *chul* here consists of sandy hillocks and downs in endless ridges and confusion, inhabited by nothing but rats, and perfectly waterless. It has no drainage so far as we could see, and the water simply runs into hollows and is absorbed by the soil as it falls. The road is a good deal up and down over the various ridges, but our camels did the march without any difficulty. The 17th was spent by Sir West Ridgeway in a ride up the Kashan valley, nearly to Robat-i-Kashan, to examine the canal irrigation in the valley, and also to inspect the site for the boundary pillar proposed by Major Holdich and Captains Gore and Komaroff on the top of a hill, as near as they could fix it in the straight line from Hauz-i-Khan to Maruchak. Colonel Kuhlberg and the Russian Commission came down the valley for the same purpose from Robat-i-Kashan, and camped close to us the same day. They, having a smaller camp and not requiring much water, had marched the 35 miles across the *chul* from Hauz-i-Khan to Robat-i-Kashan in two marches, carrying water with them for the first day. For us it was easier to go *viâ* Kilah Maur, and make the one long march, instead of two short ones which Colonel Kuhlberg preferred, as, having only camel-carriage, it was impossible for him to get his tents and baggage up before dark with so long a march in these short days, whereas to us with mule-carriage 26 miles was nothing out of the way. The Kashan valley runs into Bazaar Takta, the headquarters of the Harzagi section of the Sariks at Panjdeh, and the land in it is mostly cultivated by them. The Maruchak road crosses the valley about a mile to the south of a curious whitish artificial mound, called Yahud Tepe, or the Jew's mound. Some four miles to the south of this again are a couple more of small mounds, just opposite the proposed site for the boundary pillar on the top of a high hillock to the west. The stream here runs close under the hillocks on the western side of the valley, and the land on the eastern bank is irrigated from a canal taken off from the stream another three or four miles higher up. The whole of this canal, of course, is claimed by Russia. Another canal taken off from the stream near Robat-i-Kashan, higher up again, irrigates all the land on the western bank close up to the site for the boundary pillar; and this also is said to be claimed by Russia. The question of the conflicting Afghan and Russian claims is still under settlement.

The march on the 18th into Maruchak was very short, only eight miles, through the sandhills lying between the valleys of the Kashan and the Murghab. The road debouches into the Maruchak valley through a narrow cleft in the hillocks, through which the old ruined Maruchak fort stood out particularly clear and plain—a sight not easily to be forgotten. Our camp is pitched in the narrowest part of the valley, some three miles north of the fort, which stands on the opposite or eastern side of the valley. We are separated from the Russian camp by a curious little mound, some 70 or 80 yards in length, used as a graveyard; and as a good view of the valley is obtained from the top, many of the officers from both camps were found congregated there in the evening. The river is so high this year that it is unfordable near the ruins of the old bridge, about half a mile below the fort, where we crossed last year, and we have had to come to another ford a couple of miles or more lower down. This accounts for our being encamped so far to the north. Immediately to the west of us is a dense mass of reeds and swamp, formed by an old bed of the river, through which runs the great Band-i-Nadir canal, which not only irrigates Panjdeh, but was formerly carried across the Kushk by the brick aqueduct at Pul-i-Khishti, and ran all down the left bank of the river right away to Yulatan. At present the old canal, though washed away by the encroachments of the river in places, as at Urush Doshan for instance, can still be traced all the way to Sari Yazi, the old traditional frontier of Panjdeh towards Merv. Sir West Ridgeway, with Captain de Laessoe and Kazi Muhammad Aslam, are the only members of our party who succeeded in getting so far north as Sari Yazi, and in actually inspecting the frontier decided on by Sir Peter Lumsden. I shall not easily forget meeting Sir West and his party starting out on their trip to Sari Yazi last February in the teeth of a bitter north wind and snow-storm, and I can only say that, had it not been for Sir West's determination to overcome all difficulties, it is fairly certain that not one of the Commission would ever have got so far north. I remember that I myself at the time was returning from Urush Doshan to Panjdeh, and I felt only too thankful to have the storm at my back and the prospect of shelter when I got in. Well, this Band-i-Nadir canal which I was describing is now the great bone of contention between the Russians and the Afghans. The Protocol has laid it down that the boundary is to be drawn in nearly a straight line from Hauz-i-Khan to a point on the Murghab north of Maruchak. Now the natural point for the boundary is of course where the hills on either bank approach each other at the northern end of the Maruchak valley, some three miles below the fort, and there divide Maruchak from Panjdeh. Unfortunately, though, owing to the Band-i-Nadir canal running through this old bed of the river, the head of the canal, where it takes off from the river, instead of being to the north, is due west of the Maruchak fort,

and some three miles within the Maruchak valley. The
Russians claim, and with reason, the head of the canal,
upon which the cultivation of Panjdeh is entirely dependent; while of course the Afghans wish the strict letter
of the Protocol to be adhered to, and claim the point at
the northern end of the Maruchak valley. Were the
Russians content even with the possession of the head of
their canal, things might be arranged; but taking advantage of having got the canal as the thin end of the
wedge in the valley, they seem to wish to drive it in still
farther, and there is no saying where their claims will end.

On the 19th, Sir West Ridgeway, with Majors Bax and
Durand, Captain de Laessoe, Sirdar Muhammad Aslam Khan,
and myself, rode up to the top of one of the highest hills
overlooking the valley, whence a capital bird's-eye view of
the whole tract in dispute could be obtained. One has
little idea what a very winding river the Murghab is, till
seen from above for a good length of its course; and to see
it as it is, there is nothing like riding to the top of the
nearest hill. By hill, though, I do not mean a hill in our
ordinary sense of the word, but a sandy mound of greater
or less elevation. There is no hill in this country which
one cannot ride to the top of. In the afternoon, on the
way home, Major Durand and I stopped to beat a patch of
reeds we came to, and brought in a bag of nearly 50
pheasants before sunset. It is extraordinary what a number of pheasants there are in the reed-swamps in this
valley; and this year they seem even more numerous than
last, despite the thinning they got at the hands of the
various members of the Commission last winter. I know of
no country in the world where one can get such good, real,
wild pheasant-shooting as this, and certainly none where
one can do as one pleases with the coverts, and if they are
too thick to beat, burn them with impunity. On the 21st
we also brought in a bag of 72 pheasants, but as on the first

day, lost a great many wounded birds. The reeds are so thick, and the birds, especially the old cocks, are so strong, that it is very hard to bag one's bird even after it is shot; even if killed dead it is very hard to find, and if a spark of life remains it will invariably manage to creep off and hide somewhere. A good retriever would be worth anything here, but, unfortunately, amongst all our dogs we have not one of that breed in camp. Were I coming out to this country again, I should make a point of bringing a good retriever or a couple of retrieving spaniels with me; they would stand the climate well, and make a day's shooting here really enjoyable. As it is, much as we enjoy the shooting, still our pleasure is constantly marred by the continued loss of wounded birds—a loss that tries the heart of every true sportsman. Fox-terriers and greyhounds are our only substitutes for retrievers, and we do our best with them; but though they find some birds, they lose many more.

The night of the 23d will, I think, live long in our memories—unless, indeed, we are doomed to a continued repetition of such weather. During the afternoon the snow-clouds cleared away, and night fell with a perfectly clear sky and a glorious frost. By dinner-time, though, it got colder and colder; and though we had pans of burning wood-ashes under the table, it was all we could do to keep our liquor from freezing as we drank it. By the time dinner was over, the thermometer was standing at $6°$, and during the night it went down to $2°$ below zero. One's breath froze into ice on one's pillow, and many of us found it difficult to sleep despite all the clothes we could pile on. I myself was awoke towards morning by a loud report, which I found was caused by the bursting of a bottle of what had been drinking-water, but which had turned into a block of ice, and burst under my bed; and once awake, the cold was too intense to get to sleep again. At nine in the morning the thermometer was still only at $6°$, and it continued to freeze all the day through despite the sun. In the afternoon I was out shooting, with the sun full on my face; yet my breath froze on my moustache the whole time. The poor cook, I think, has the hardest time of it. His eggs, he says, are all frozen hard, and he can make nothing of them. Writing with ink, of course, is an utter impossibility: every ink-pot in camp contains simply a solid block of ice; and it is no use in thawing it, as it freezes on the paper before it has time to dry. I am writing this, therefore, in pencil. It is wonderful how well the men and followers are standing the cold; but a liberal issue of meat and tea and sugar seems to make them all proof against anything. I must say, though, that they are precious quiet in the mornings, and loath indeed to get up. Their ablutions too, I daresay, are few and far between; but really I cannot blame them. When it comes to us having to thaw our toothbrush every time we have to use it, and when everything around is frozen hard, little wonder that the poor Hindoo is chary of touching water. The *bheesties*, I think, I pity most. They can fill their *mussucks* certainly at the running canal, although even that is mostly frozen over; but a little time after they get back into camp the water they have been carrying gets frozen, and absolutely refuses to run out of the *mussuck* again. The 24th was not quite such a cold day as the 23d: the thermometer only went down to 2° at night, but it was still below freezing-point all day.

M. Lessar arrived shortly after breakfast, and had a long conversation with Sir West Ridgeway and Major Durand over the boundary; but what transpired, I do not know. It is generally supposed that his demands have not diminished. In the afternoon Major Holdich started for Chahar Shamba, whence he goes on to Daulatabad to collect his staff there, preparatory to surveying the country beyond that place up to the Oxus. Captain the Hon. M. G. Talbot writes that he had a most flattering and cordial reception at Mazar-i-

Sharif, and he is now bringing his survey down from Balkh to Maimanah. The two sub-surveyors—Heera Singh and Imam Sharif—who have been away so long, have both returned. The former has completed a capital survey of the Band-i-Turkistan and the upper waters of the Murghab, in the Firozkohi country; and the latter worked down south through the Taimani country into Zemindawar, to join on to the old Kandahar surveys. Both men went through considerable danger—the former owing to the feuds raging amongst the various sects of the Firozkohis, and the latter in Zemindawar, where, though the people were quiet enough, the *talibs*, or religious students, were numerous and fanatical, and longed for the blood of an unbeliever. Imam Sharif tells us numerous tales of how they shot at him when working on the tops of the hills; and how one *talib*, more bloodthirsty than the rest, thinking that his survey *khalassis*, from the colour of their turbans, were Sikhs (it is curious what an innate hate the Afghan has for a Sikh, although he may never have seen one), came up to his tent flourishing a naked sword, which, he informed Imam Sharif, was known far and wide as the *kafirchap*, or the unbeliever-slasher, and that it was now his intention to use it on those Sikhs of his. On being persuaded that they were not Sikhs, he went away quietly enough.

Our Christmas-day was bright and cold—so cold, in fact, that we feared at first we should not be able to warm the mess-tent sufficiently to make it comfortable for ourselves and our Russian guests. Dining in uniform in a tent with the thermometer at zero is by no means a pleasure; but with the help of several layers of felt on the floor and a stove in each doorway, we succeeded in making the tent almost as warm and comfortable as a room. Colonel Kuhlberg and all his officers were the guests that night of Sir West Ridgeway, and a right merry evening we had. Twenty-three of us sat down to dinner all told, ten of us and thirteen of the Russians—viz., Sir West Ridgeway, Majors Bax and Durand, Captains Griesbach and De Laessoe, Dr Owen, Lieutenant Drummond, Nawab Mirza Hasan Ali Khan, Kazi Muhammad Aslam Khan, and myself; while the Russian party consisted of Colonel Kuhlberg, M. Lessar, Captain Gideonoff, Lieutenant - Colonel Prince Orbeliani, Captain Komaroff, Dr Semmer, Captain Kondratenko, Captain Varenik, Lieutenant Kiachko, Lieutenant Gorokh, Cornet Winnikoff, Councillor Neprintzeff, and M. Mirzaeff. After dinner Sir West proposed the health of the Emperor, and Colonel Kuhlberg that of the Queen. Colonel Kuhlberg's health was then proposed by Sir West, and drunk with musical honours, followed at once by Sir West's health being proposed and drunk by the Russian officers to the tune of a Georgian chant. The toasts of all the other officers were then proposed and drunk in turn; and after that we had various Russian songs and choruses, winding up finally with "Auld Lang Syne," and then, at Colonel Kuhlberg's request, with "God save the Queen." Altogether we had a most pleasant evening, despite the cold and other drawbacks.

The morning of the 26th was spent by the Commissioners at a meeting in Colonel Kuhlberg's *kibitka*, and all the rest of us were invited by the latter to breakfast after it. Midday was the hour named, but the meeting of the Commissioners did not break up till 2 P.M., and then we all sat down to a regular Continental breakfast—a dinner, in fact, in all but the name and the absence of soup—to which we all did hearty justice. One *kibitka* not being able to hold us all, we divided into two parties, and the Cossacks sang in chorus to us outside. After breakfast we had some Cossack dances, and then Colonel Kuhlberg and the officers and Cossacks all escorted us back to our camp, the latter marching along behind singing in chorus, while one or two of the more active amongst them amused themselves by galloping backwards and forwards and firing off their rifles on horseback. Major Bax, Captain Griesbach, and Lieutenant Drummond marched across the river the same evening to a fresh camp near the fort, and we all follow after them as soon as possible. The intense cold of the last few days has put a stop to the melting of snow in the hills, and the river is now much lower than it was, and we have little difficulty in crossing it; the only thing is that it is still too deep for mules, and all our kit has to be moved on camels instead. We expect to move to our winter-quarters at Chahar Shamba very shortly, as soon as the negotiations here are brought to a close. The Russian camp will probably remain where it is; and with a plentiful supply of wood, they will be very comfortable here for the winter. The Panjdeh coloured felts make a capital warm lining for *kibitkas*, and both the Russians and ourselves have been laying in a stock. The supply, though, is not nearly so great as it was last year, and prices have risen in consequence. As to Turkoman carpets, the supply seems to be quite exhausted. The Russian officers say they can get none, and we certainly can get hold of none at all. Whether it is that the Turkomans are afraid to come to our camp, or what, I do not know; but certain it is that they do not come, and we have scarcely seen a man of position since we arrived.

Almost all the leading and wealthy men of the tribe belong to the Sokti section, which inhabits the northern portion of Panjdeh up to Pul-i-Khishti, some 25 miles to the north of our present camp—those living near here being Harzagis, and apparently the poorest of the poor. In all the *kibitkas* forming the hamlets about here I have not seen a single carpet door *purdah*—the surest sign of poverty; as to floor carpets, I do not suppose they have one amongst them. The carpets, although very pretty, are of no practical use, so far as the cold is concerned. Nothing but felt can keep the floor of one's tent warm, and without felts the cold seems to strike up from the ground through and through one.

Yet these felts are of no use again, they say, in any other climate. In India they are far too warm, in England they absorb too much damp, and consequently, once the winter is over, their day is past and gone.

The Russian officers are all two and two in a *kibitka*, with the exception of Colonel Kuhlberg and his two Assistant Commissioners, M. Lessar and Captain Gideonoff, who have each a *kibitka* to themselves. Our Government, by the way, has limited Sir West Ridgeway to one Assistant Commissioner instead of two. Lieutenant-Colonel Prince Orbeliani is a Georgian officer, who has just arrived, and having spent seven or eight years as a boy in England, speaks English capitally in addition to his other linguistic attainments, and is a great acquisition in consequence.

We have had no Indian post for some days now, as the Band-i-Baba pass is quite blocked up by snow, and all communication with Herat is cut off. Our Mashhad postal line, though, is in capital working order, and we get our telegrams across Badghis in between three and four days. From Mashhad to Zulfikar the mails are carried by Persian sowars, and then from Zulfikar to Kushk Sir West Ridgeway has organised a line of Turkoman sowars, who are doing their work well.

The public telegrams have already published the fact that differences have arisen regarding the demarcation of the frontier, and how these differences will be decided remains to be seen. In settling a boundary like this it is only to be expected that differences should arise. To define a boundary between Panjdeh on the one side, and Sarakhs and Merv on the other, would have been an easy matter; but to define a boundary between Panjdeh and the rest of the Herat district is a very different thing. Rights enjoyed by the Sariks as Afghan subjects have now to be taken away from them, and the Russians are naturally sore at their loss. The Afghans equally insist on the maintenance of the integrity of Maruchak and other places guaranteed to them by the Protocol.

The Amir in ceding Panjdeh claimed that Zulfikar, Gulran, and Maruchak should be secured to him, doubtless supposing that all lands and rights belonging to those places should be his also. We know how long it took and what difficulty there was before a settlement could be arrived at regarding the limits of Zulfikar. Now the same thing promises to repeat itself with reference to Maruchak, with this exception, that M. Lessar, who had in the former case to deal with the Ministry at home, is now confronted with the British Commission and Afghan representatives on the spot. The case of Zulfikar was comparatively simple, as there were no inhabitants there on either side of the border, and the Afghans knew and cared comparatively little about the country beyond. At Maruchak all this is altered. On the Russian side are the Sariks of Panjdeh, for whom the Russian Commissioners appear to wish not only to obtain as a right the full possession of all former encroachments, but also scope for further encroachment in the future. The Afghans, on their side, are equally determined to resist, and claim to oust all Sariks within Maruchak limits, and the right to prevent all future extension of the Sariks to the south. Both sides have a certain amount of right on their side, and an equitable decision can only be arrived at by moderation on both sides. Unfortunately, that is the one thing wanting. Afghans are noted for their arrogance; but if rumour is true, the Russian claims, on the other side, are sadly wanting in moderation, and a boundary settlement conducted in such a spirit must naturally be full of difficulties. A meeting of the Commission, at which Kazi Saad-ud-Din, the Amir's representative, and the governor of Herat, will both be present, takes place to-morrow; but whether a settlement will be arrived at here, or whether the matter will have to be referred to the two Governments at home, remains to be seen. Sir West Ridgeway has in any case a most difficult task before him.

CHAPTER X.

WINTER-QUARTERS AT CHAHAR SHAMBA.

CAMP CHAHAR SHAMBA, *9th Jan.* 1886.

ON the 28th December the final meeting of the Commission at Maruchak took place, so far as the present is concerned, and Sir West Ridgeway and Major Durand bade adieu to their Russian *confrères* and crossed the river to the camp by the fort.

Sir West Ridgeway halted at Maruchak Fort for the 29th, while Captain Durand accompanied the governor of Herat and Kazi Saad-ud-Din on a farewell visit to Colonel Kuhlberg, rejoining the camp at Karawal Khana, 12 miles up the valley, the next day. Maruchak Fort, which the majority of us have probably now seen for the last time, has evidently been a fine place in its day. The outer walls are some 600 yards square, slightly rounded at the corners, and are still some 15 feet or more in height, and surrounded by a moat. The main entrance is on the west, facing the river, which here extends, in the form of a large swamp, right up to within 200 or 300 yards of the gate. There are also other and smaller gates at the north-east and south-east angles; but the whole enclosure is now the picture of desolation and decay. The centre is occupied by a circular mound some 30 or 40 feet in height, and about 250 yards in diameter, the remains, I presume, of an inner fortress. The walls on the top of this have been partially repaired, and a row of barracks were built last year all round the eastern side for the Afghan garrison. These were all occupied when I saw them in February last, but that was before the attack on Panjdeh. They were deserted directly after. The heavy spring rains played sad havoc with the unburnt bricks of which they were constructed, and they will require a good deal of repair before they are fit for habitation again. The citadel is comprised in a higher mound again, some 60 yards square, occupying the south-west corner of the fortress mound, and some 20 or 30 feet above it. The walls and bastions of this were built up to a height of some 10 feet by the Afghan masons before the winter set in last year, but nothing more, of course, was done this year. Next year, no doubt, as soon as the boundary is settled, the walls will be completed by the Amir's orders, and the place put in a state of defence. But however suitable for the accommodation of the Afghan frontier garrison, I doubt if the fort could offer any prolonged resistance to a Russian attack.

The road from Maruchak to Karawal Khana runs along the eastern side of the valley, close under the hills, twice crossing projecting spurs of the latter, and thus cutting off bends of the river. Woe to the unfortunate sportsman who crosses the canals by the bridge near the Maruchak Fort and shoots his way up the valley, fondly imagining that he can cross the canals and get back into the road again higher up. I myself can speak from personal experience on the subject, and I am not likely to forget how, after working my way through swamps and reed-beds right up to the southern end of the first spur, I found myself brought up at the head of the canal by precipitous banks some 15 or 20 feet in depth, and utterly impassable for man or beast; and how I wearily worked my way back for some five or six miles along the banks of this canal; and even then, after the canal had split up into several branches, I only got across with the greatest difficulty, at the cost of a thorough ducking to myself, men, and horses—a by no means agreeable termination to a day's shooting on a cold winter's evening, with one's camp almost as far off as when one started in the morning.

Karawal Khana is a small Turkoman hamlet just at the junction of the Kilah Wali stream with the Murghab. We were encamped round the Ziarat-i-Pistah, a tomb enclosed by a low wall, and so known from the one solitary pistachio-nut bush overhanging it. The place is the site of some ancient building, as the mounds about, of which there are several, are full of burnt bricks and other remains. The Turkomans located at Karawal Khana are separated from the Jamshidis of Bala Murghab by a low projecting spur of the hills, though their respective hamlets are within a very short distance of each other, the Turkoman hamlets going right up to the point, and a big Jamshidi hamlet being just beyond. As a matter of fact, it is impossible to the uneducated eye to tell the hamlets of the one tribe from those of the other. The people of the one dress just the same as the other, and there is little to choose between them in the way of poverty; the *kibitkas* of all are the same.

The Turkomans are not at all a forgetful race, and I was struck by the warm welcome I received from a little old man who was out with me as a guide last year, and who recognised and rushed up to me the moment he saw me again. His real name I forget, but we nicknamed him Jowan Bátúr, from the untiring way he rode any distance, and the pride with which he told us that he had just married a third wife, a little girl in her teens. Bátúr is a Turkoman title answering somewhat to the Indian Bahadur, and the little man has stuck to it ever since. I think the best Turkoman bread I ever tasted I ate in his *kibitka;* and I well remember, when riding last year on a cold snowy day the 22 miles from Maruchak to Bala Murghab, thoroughly appreciating the hot bread he gave us to eat as we sat warming our frozen toes over the fire in his *kibitka*. The

Turkomans at Karawal Khana, though they hold all the land at the mouth of the Kilah Wali stream, still seem not to extend far up its course. Within a very few miles we found that the Turkomans were superseded by Jamshidi flocks from Bala Murghab; and, in fact, the Jamshidis seem to hold almost all the land between the two Turkoman settlements at Karawal Khana and Kilah Wali.

From Karawal Khana we all marched up to Chahar Shamba in detachments. Captain de Laessoe and I started first on the 30th December to assist Captain Cotton in the collection of supplies for the winter. The cavalry followed on the 2d January, their party comprising Major Bax, Captains Gore and Griesbach, Lieutenant Drummond, and Sirdar Sher Ahmed Khan—Sir West Ridgeway, with Major Durand, Dr Owen, and Kazi Muhammad Aslam Khan, bringing up the rear on the 6th. The road is a good sample of the curious natural highways that exist in this country. The Kilah Wali stream is very small, not more than four or five yards in width at its mouth; yet imagine a perfectly flat level valley, some half-mile in breadth, running more or less all the way down from Kaisar to Karawal Khana, a distance of nearly 60 miles, bounded on either side by low hills, those on the north gradually merging into the undulating sandy *chul*, and those on the south into the lofty and now snow-clad range of the Band-i-Turkistan; yet all the way up this valley you might drive a coach-and-four with the greatest ease. How such little bits of streams work out for themselves such wonderfully level valleys it is hard to say; but judging from the curiously even way in which the hills on either side here and there have been cut through, it would seem to have been due to the action of ice. At the present time the stream runs almost all the way between high banks some 10 or 12 feet below the level of the ground on either side, and this is the general feature of all the streams in this country. How easily these valleys are traversed by wheeled carriage is proved by the fact that the Russian Commission have a couple of carts which they brought with them from Ashkabad, and which have been driven through all our marches along the frontier without the slightest mishap. I can only trust that the practicability of this country for light-wheeled transport may be borne in mind by the military authorities when the next force is being equipped for service up here. So far as I am aware, there was nothing to prevent us using Heyland carts or other light vehicles all the march up from Quetta to Herat; and the passes of the Paropamisus north of Herat that are passable for artillery, of course offer no impediment to their further advance.

The march up the 42 miles from Karawal Khana to Chahar Shamba is not of any particular interest. Some six miles up, the road through the hills from Bala Murghab debouches into the valley, and some five miles farther on the road crosses the stream at a place called Shukr[1] Guzar, though I cannot say that I saw any reason for *thanks* regarding that particular ford, as we found one of our mules, load and all, stuck in a mud-hole in the middle of it, quite unable to move, and which it took us some time to get out. I remember finding a lot of pheasants in the reeds there when out with Sir Peter Lumsden one day last year, and their numbers seemed to increase higher up. The only signs of ancient habitations that I noticed in that part of the valley were some mounds full of bricks two or three miles above the ford. On one side of the road there were the evident remains of an old *robat*, and on the other of a reservoir—both buildings, of course, being assigned by local tradition to Abdullah Khan of Bokhara. As a rule, the water in the Kilah Wali stream is brackish; but this year, owing to the late freshets, it is everywhere drinkable. There is a spring of sweet water, though, on the eastern side of the valley, a mile or two above these ruins, known as Yan Chashmah, or

---

[1] *Shukr*=thanks.

the wayside spring. Seventeen miles from Karawal Khana there is a small Jamshidi hamlet called Bokun, where some twenty or twenty-five families, who fled from Bala Murghab on the retreat of the Afghans from Panjdeh, after wandering about in the hills all the summer, eventually settled down with the intention of cultivating the land next season. It was here and at Kilah Wali that I first heard of an instance of pheasant-hunting on horseback. I did not witness the sport myself, I regret to say, but I was told by Sirdar Muhammad Aslam Khan that, when travelling through during the heavy fall of snow a day or two before Christmas, he found that the villagers had captured no less than thirty-five, simply by riding them down. The sport, it seems, can best be pursued just after a fall of snow. In this case the whole village turned out to beat the reeds; the birds soon got distracted, and after the first flight or two, sought safety by hiding under the snow and bushes. The horsemen, galloping up, marked where a pheasant settled, followed up its tracks, only too plainly visible in soft snow, and pulled it out of its hiding-place by the hand. No wonder the pheasants up this valley are comparatively scarce. At Maruchak the reed-beds are too vast and too dense to allow of such sport; but along the banks of the Kilah Wali stream the beds are narrow and thin, and the birds can more easily be driven out into the open.

The present village of Kilah Wali is some seven miles above Bokun, and three miles below the old fort of that name. It is inhabited entirely by Sarik Turkomans, emigrants from Panjdeh. Of the total of 420 houses or *kibitkas* which it is said to contain, 300 or more belong to the Harzagi section, and the majority of the remainder are Khorasanlis, with just a few Alishahs and Bairach amongst them. They are presided over by an Afghan governor, known as the Akhund Zadah. The fort is simply one of the usual rectangular ruins so common in these parts. The outer walls are some

100 by 80 yards in length and breadth respectively, with an inner fort some 35 yards square in the centre. In the middle of this again there is a curious double-storeyed circular tower of burnt brick, the first of its kind that I have seen, and built to answer the purpose of a citadel, I presume. The place is now entirely deserted. The valley here bends more to the east, and for some miles up is nothing but a mass of reeds. On the southern side of the valley the ruins of another old fort, called Guchmach, are distinctly visible just at the junction of a small stream running down from the mountains behind. A couple of miles beyond, the road forks, the northern branch running up to Chahar Shamba, and the southern up to Hirak, a parallel valley some three miles to the south, more immediately under the Tirband-i-Turkistan.

At Chahar Shamba we enter the Maimanah district, Kilah Wali being the confines of the Herat province in this direction. So we have left the Heratis for good, and now we enter into a fresh course under the jurisdiction of Sirdar Ishak Khan. Muhammad Sarwar Khan, the governor of Herat, accompanied us to Karawal Khana, and from thence was to return to Herat. I regret that I had not an opportunity of wishing him good-bye, as I have always found him most pleasant and cordial. In Sirdar Muhammad Ishak Khan we shall probably have a very different man to deal with. The treatment experienced at his hands by Captains Maitland and the Hon. M. G. Talbot in their travels, seems to have been very different from that we have hitherto been subjected to by Kazi Saad-ud-Din in the Herat districts. In Turkistan the cry is that India and Afghanistan are now all one—*ek doulat*, as the expression is—and the utmost trust and confidence were reposed in our officers. They were shown everywhere, paid the greatest attention, and treated as friends. Kazi Saad-ud-Din, on the contrary, sits at our doors, bent on preventing the slightest intercourse between ourselves and the people of the country, and doing his utmost to thwart our best endeavours for the good of the Amir and his dominions. Instead of friends and protectors, he would wish to make us out treacherous deceivers, and he has doubtless done his best to malign us and minimise the effect of all that the British Government has done for Afghanistan. Our attempts to keep the people loyal and true to the Amir in times of great difficulty, have invariably been met, not with thanks, but with virulent misrepresentation to the Amir, and any unfortunate man caught doing any of us the slightest service has always been flogged or otherwise severely punished. I have even heard it said that one poor man was badly beaten simply for hiring out his *kibitka* last winter to one of our officers. With such a man to deal with, it may be imagined how difficult it is for Sir West Ridgeway to keep things straight.

CAMP CHAHAR SHAMBA, 23d *January* 1886.

We are now fairly settled down into winter-quarters here, and very comfortable we are under the circumstances. The weather had been so warm of late that we had almost forgotten what real cold was, and many, getting tired of the monotony of camp life, were longing to be on the move again, quite forgetting what hardship is entailed by marching in bad weather at this season of the year. The only certain thing about this climate is its uncertainty. One never knows what the morrow may bring forth. For the greater part of this month we had a succession of fogs, mist, and rain, which kept us and all belonging to us in a continual state of dampness. Then suddenly we had a couple of warm sunny days, followed just as suddenly by a couple of days of snow and sleet. Then sun again, and then rain, suddenly turning into snow, all without any warning whatever. One thing certainly we escape here, and that is the wind. Had we remained in the Herat valley we should have suffered from it greatly, whereas here we have escaped it entirely so far. The soil of this valley is terribly muddy and slimy—a little mist and rain turns the whole place into one vast quagmire; even horses can hardly keep their feet in it, and travelling is almost an impossibility. Our camp roads have been improved as much as possible by layers of gravel and stone, but still in a thaw the mud is something indescribable. On a dry day our camp is almost perfect. We have lots of room, and, thanks to the exertions of Captain Cotton and Lieutenant Drummond, the greatest regularity. The cavalry and officers' horses occupy all the northern face. The main street, comprising the tents of all the various officers and members of the Mission, occupies the centre, running east and west, with the infantry, hospital, and commissariat on the south. All the troops and most of the followers have been provided with *kibitkas;* and as we have a plentiful supply of wood, they are all as happy as possible, and in the best of health. Owing to the reduction in our number, sufficient *kibitkas* have been procurable locally to house almost all the men. The officers, as a rule, prefer their tents. We have all got a good Swiss-cottage tent apiece, and we have each of us run up either a fireplace or a stove, so that we can defy the cold. Great experience have we gained in the building of mud-chimneys. The number of times that some of these have been pulled down and built again, and the way in which the most inveterate tendency of some of these chimneys to smoke has been triumphantly overcome, ought to make us authorities in the art of chimney-building for the rest of our days. Fireplaces are, no doubt, preferable to stoves, the sight of a fire making the tent look so much cheerier; and we have them of every pattern. We have the humble hearth, easily made by sinking the floor of the tent a couple of feet and tunnelling out the fireplace and chimney through the earth on one side; and we have the regular fireplace and chimneypiece, filling up the whole of one of the doors of the tent. I myself have a small iron stove, brought from Mashhad, with a pipe sufficiently long to carry the smoke through the side of the tent, and then outside a mud chimney which carries it on well beyond all chance of danger from sparks. Not that we are dependent on Mashhad, though, for our stoves, for one of the most effective I have seen was manufactured by Major Bax out of an old kerosene-oil tin, and would do credit to an inventories exhibition. We have almost all of us adopted the big Turkoman top-boots, lined with long felt socks, and there is nothing like them to keep one's feet warm; when riding in the cold they are simply invaluable. Their only drawback is the long pointed heels shod with iron, which Turkoman fashion prescribes, and which make the boots most difficult to walk in.

Chahar Shamba is not an interesting place to live in. Imagine a valley about a mile in width, with a small stream, some eight feet wide, running down the centre of it. On the north are the low hills, or rather hillocks, bordering the *chul;* to the south the same for a mile or two, and then another parallel valley known as Hirak, and then behind that again the range of the Tirband-i-Turkistan—a grand sight certainly in its snowy grandeur when visible, but that has been so seldom, owing to the fogs, rain, and snow, that we hardly yet know what it is like. There is nothing in the immediate vicinity of the camp to tempt one out. Last year at Bala Murghab we had a fine river running past the camp, and sportsmen were always sure of a shot at a duck or a pheasant within a mile or two. Here there are no duck; and though there are some pheasants five or six miles up the valley, the reeds they live in are so dense that it is next to impossible to get at them. We hope for a dry day and a good wind to give us a chance of burning those reeds, but till then we are helpless. Pigs, too, swarm in them; and when we do succeed in burning the thick cover, we hope to have some fine fun with them. Snipe certainly seem plentiful, but few of us have cartridges sufficient to waste on anything so small; and in addition to that, the necessity of wading about in black mud, almost up to one's knees, in this cold weather, makes one think twice about going after them, with the prospect of a cold ride home again afterwards.

The Usbegs certainly are neither a handsome nor an interesting race, so far as one can judge of those we see here. The village of Chahar Shamba is close to our camp, but only contains some 50 low, flat-roofed mud-houses, mostly small and dirty. Here, where wood, mostly juniper, is procurable in any quantity from the mountains behind, we no longer see the domed roofs which looked so picturesque in the less wooded districts we have been hitherto traversing. The rough sheepskin hats of the Herat district, and the black lambskin hats of the Aimak and Turkoman tribes, which we have got so used to during the past year, have here quite disappeared. The Usbegs wear nothing but small blue *lungis* or turbans, and are much the most abject-looking race we have been amongst yet. Generations of oppression have, no doubt, told on them, and they are all apparently miserably poor. I have not yet seen a man amongst them wearing arms, and they look to be anything but a fighting race. Still we know that they held out at Maimanah for long against the Afghans, and there are many tales of individual courage against the Turkomans.

Riding up the valley the other day, I came to an old deserted fort at Chachaktu, some seven miles from here, and asking the history of the place, I was told that it was sacked by the Turkomans ten years or so ago, and every man, woman, and child in it was carried off, with the exception of the head-man, by name Isfandiar, who still survives in the new village down below. The Turkomans, it seems, first sent on a few of their number with a long string of camels, who got admission into the fort under the pretence of purchasing grain. These men opened the gates to their friends hiding in the hills close by, and Isfandiar and his wife had just time to get into the round brick tower at the end of the fort before they were surrounded. Here these two bravely held out against all the attacks of the Turkomans, and the latter, in the end, were obliged to withdraw, with the loss of fourteen of their number, leaving Isfandiar and his wife in solitary possession of the village. It is only just lately, I was told, that Isfandiar has been able to ransom his other wife and children, who were then carried off.

All this country seems to have been terribly harassed by Turkomans, even up to a very recent date. On arrival at Narin, a village some 25 miles to the east, the other day, the Shahgassi, or village official, pointed out a well-known Panjdeh Sarik leader, who was with me as a guide, as the man who had carried off 637 of their sheep only two years ago. "At any rate, he looks quiet enough now," said I. "Ah yes," replied the Shahgassi. "He was a wolf, but now with you he has become a lamb." The Turkoman raids, though, have not been put a stop to even yet. The Kara Turkomans, or the Lab-i-Abi, as they are more generally called, from living on the banks of the Oxus in Bokhara territory, still go on the foray, and several raids have occurred even since our arrival. A flock of sheep was driven off not long ago, and I hear that a Cossack, on duty with one of the Russian topographers, was also rifled of all he possessed. No wonder that the Usbegs here are comparatively poor in flocks, and that the Turkomans are rich. Poor Usbegs! they have hardly dared to let their sheep out of their sight for many years past, and have been obliged to abstain from the use of their wells and pasturage in the *chul*, from fear of being carried off into slavery, and now have the mortification of seeing those very wells, dug by their ancestors, claimed by Russia on the ground that they were not using them at the time of the Russian occupation of Merv.

One thing the Usbegs exceed the Turkomans in the possession of, and that is cattle. These being always kept at home, I presume have suffered less in the raids in proportion to sheep, and consequently milk and *ghee* are procurable here in plenty. The breed is small and black, about the same size, but not so shaggy, as Highland cattle, and are always used for ploughing. Amongst the Turkomans, on the contrary, few oxen were seen in the plough. Horses were generally used, much to the astonishment of our Panjabi sowars, who had never seen a horse put to such a use before; and as often as not, camels and donkeys were yoked with the horse. I have even seen a camel and a donkey yoked together in a plough. Such, though, is not the custom here. The people of this valley are all now as busy as they can be, ploughing their fields for next year's crop—indeed most of the wheat is already sown—but I have never once seen a horse in a plough. The Usbegs are not great horse-owners. Only the head-men of the villages about here seem to possess a horse at all, and that generally is a very sorry beast. Sheep we have no difficulty in purchasing from the Turkomans—and such sheep, too, as they are! Our ration meat equals the best English mutton, without any *gram*-feeding or special preparation, as in India. The last batch of sheep purchased from the Turkomans averaged each, when dressed, 75 lb. in weight, and cost only sixteen *krans* apiece (Rs. 6-6-4); and yet I can remember a time when, as an ensign, I was weighing out the rations for my company, the commissariat sheep weighed on an average 13 lb. apiece, or about as much as a good big hare: that, however, was in the Rajputana famine year, I confess. Talking of rations, we have now got an ample stock in hand. Thanks to Captain Cotton's exertions, two months' supplies of all kinds have been laid in here; while Captain de Laessoe and myself purchased and stored about another month's grain and *bhoosa* at Narin, ready for our move onward in the spring. Our demands, too, have been considerably reduced by the dismissal of 250 hired Persian mules; so that we are now practically independent for the next three months, and by that time I hope the demarcation of the frontier will be in a fair way towards completion. It is hoped that all the necessary surveys will be finished by the end of March, if not before, and the demarcation then ought to progress apace, if the Russian claims have been reduced by that time within reasonable limits.

Our men here are all anxious to test their strength and agility with the Cossacks, but hitherto the constant rain and snow have quite put a stop to the practice of all outdoor sports. Last New Year's Day at Bala Murghab we had a capital day's races and sports, and the Russians have often spoken of giving us an exhibition of their men's prowess; but I fear there is little chance, so far as we know at present, of anything of the sort coming off. Had the two camps been wintering together, I have little doubt some friendly contests might have been arranged; but as it is, I doubt if we shall ever have the wished-for opportunity. We had hoped to have had some of the Russian officers up here on a visit, but almost all our invitations were declined. M. Lessar and Captain Komaroff, however, talk of taking a trip from Panjdeh into the *chul* to the east, and paying us a visit on their way back, but it is doubtful when their trip will come off. Lieutenant Kiachko and another Cossack officer are, though, it is hoped, really on their way up; but I pity them if they are marching to-day, as it has been snowing steadily now for the past twenty-four hours, and their trip would be hardly a pleasant one.

Sir West Ridgeway has just received a letter from Mr Ney Elias announcing his safe arrival at Khanabad. The messenger, a Yarkundi, who brought his note, had been with him throughout his journey for the past five months, and hurried away to rejoin and accompany him back to Yarkund.

CAMP CHAHAR SHAMBA, 2d *February* 1886.

The weather was wretched for the week before the 30th, and we were able to do nothing. Wet and raw, there was no comfort indoors, or rather in our tents, for we have no doors, and still less comfort outside. On the 30th the wet changed again into snow, and real cold set in. How long this will last remains to be seen. Mr Merk arrived just in time for dinner on the evening of the 29th, having ridden through the last 45 miles from Bala Murghab that day, and was lucky to get in when he did, just before the snow commenced to fall. His Christmas dinner was eaten with the return party at Chahar Burjak, on the banks of the Helmand, and starting back the next day, he and Ressaldar-Major Baha-u'-din Khan have been travelling hard to rejoin us ever since; and glad we are to see them both safe back again. We only trust that all our comrades with the return party are equally safe back in India. When our turn will come to follow them no one can say. True, the first half of the boundary from Zulfikar to Maruchak has been settled, but who can tell when the second half from Maruchak to the Oxus will be finished? The country through which the boundary will run is absolutely unknown, and till the survey is completed nothing can be done. Our first idea of it was that all the country between Maruchak, Maimanah, and Andkhui was one vast desert, but every day's experience shows us more and more how wrong our ideas were. Captain Peacocke, who has just returned from his survey trip in the country to the north and west of Maimanah, tells us that all the heads of the valleys draining down into the Ab-i-Kaisar, at an average distance of some 20 to 25 miles to the north of that stream, were formerly—that is to say, up to within about the last twenty years or so—well inhabited, and that the country is covered with old wells and former sites of *kishlaks* or winter habitations. These gradually succumbed to the attacks of the Turkomans one after another, in many cases being absolutely destroyed, the people—men, women, and children—all being carried off into slavery, and the result is that no one has dared to go out to those places ever since. Not only has the population of these outer districts been carried off bodily, but even that in the more settled districts along the highroad has suffered in proportion. Almar, a level fertile plain, some six miles in diameter, 16 miles or so on this side of Maimanah, supported twenty years ago—so Captain de Laessoe reports—a population of 2000 families, whereas now there are hardly 700. So with all the villages about here. Chahar Shamba, where we now are, instead of a village of fifty houses, was formerly the centre of a well-populated district, extending down the valley almost all the way to Kilah Wali, 16 miles to the east. Curiously enough, the villagers claim to be not Usbegs, but the descendants of a lot of mixed races, and call themselves the Doazdah Aimak, or the twelve nomad tribes, and have no idea where they originally came from or what their tribes were. They are now, to all intents and purposes, Usbegs in fact, if not in name. Nadir Shah, the tradition is, settled 12,000 families of different tribes down here, but that subsequently some returned whence they came, others moved elsewhere or were carried off by Turkomans, and now, of the original 12,000, only forty families remain, the remaining ten houses in the village being comprised of six Jamshidi and four Khojah and Syed families.

Chahar Shamba seems to have suffered heavily at the hands of the Turkomans. In 1846, they say, 500 Sarik horsemen attacked the village, killed 60 men, and carried off all the remainder—men, women, and children—with all their sheep, cattle, and everything. Hukumat Khan, the then Wali of Maimanah, succeeded in ransoming the majority of the villagers through some Syeds of the Eshan or Priest of Khwajah Kandu, a shrine 12 miles to the south of Chahar Shamba, who proceeded as his representative to Merv for the purpose, but the village never recovered its prosperity. So late as 1881 the last of their cattle and sheep were driven off by the Sariks to Panjdeh, and now they have only just sufficient to supply themselves with milk and *ghee*, and these animals they never allow to wander out of sight of the village.

Hirak, the valley under the hills to the south of Chahar Shamba, though boasting a population of 250 houses, almost all Usbegs of the Mekrit branch, still possesses only one owner of a flock of sheep. Being more sheltered, they suffered comparatively less from the Turkomans, till, in 1877, the Firozkohis came down on them on the other side, from over the Band-i-Turkistan mountains, and carried off 3500 sheep and 300 head of cattle—all they had, in fact. This was the last straw, and since then they have given up all attempts at keeping sheep.

Hazarah Kilah, the village on the other side of our camp, a mile or two to the east of us, has a curious history apparently. As its name implies, it was originally peopled entirely by Hazarahs, descendants of a party who remained here out of the ancestors of the present Kilah Nao Hazarahs, and who were originally brought down, it is said, by Shah Rukh, the son of Amir Taimur, from Kunduz to Kilah Nao, by this very road. What their numbers were originally it is impossible to say, but they have dwindled down, till at present they number only seven families, and these have entirely lost all their Hazarah characteristics, and are Usbegs in all but name—in no way differing from the other forty or fifty families of Usbegs who now share the village with them.

As an instance of the curious mixture of races up here, we find a colony of some 600 or 700 families of Kipchaks settled in the Kaisar plain and the hills behind it, some 12 miles farther east. Where they came from they cannot say, and they are the only representatives of that race in this country. They have two chiefs or Mirs, two brothers named Hakim Khan and Karim Khan, who claim descent from the great Changiz Khan. The latter died in 1227, and it is just possible that these are a remnant of some of his mighty hordes who overran the country. Up in the hills, above the Kipchaks, at a place called Chahar Tagou, live another tribe, numbering some 300 families, called the Karaie. Who or what they are no one can say, and it is impossible to get to their snow-bound valleys at this time of the year. All I can hear about them is, that they have three Mirs, named Peerhat Beg, Turah Beg, and Morad Beg, who have been fighting among themselves for years, but that lately they have settled all feuds by mutually giving daughters in marriage all round, and are now at last at peace. They are said to resemble the Kipchaks in appearance; and as the Kipchaks are very like the Usbegs, I do not suppose there is anything particularly noticeable about them. The common language amongst all these tribes is Turki in various dialects, but almost all understand and speak Persian as well.

Our party in camp has been enlivened for the past week by the presence of a couple of Cossack officers—Captain Volkovnikoff, of the 1st Caucasian Regiment, and Lieutenant Kiachko, of the 1st Toman Regiment. The latter belongs to the escort with the Russian Commissioner at Panjdeh, but the former comes from Pul-i-Khishti, where his squadron is now quartered, and has come up with his friend to have a look at our Indian troops. He is said to be a keen soldier, and it would have been a pleasure to show him what we could, so far as our small number of men would allow it; but, alas! the weather has been so bad that any parades or sports have been quite out of the question, and all that he has hitherto been able to do has been to take a sketch of the different types of our native troops here in camp. Captain Volkovnikoff wears the Order of St Jeanne, given him for some act of valour during the Turkish war. The decoration consists of a sort of red Maltese Cross, with crossed swords between the points of the cross, worn, as usual, on the left breast; but in addition to this, the decoration is also engraved on the hilt of the sword, and the idea of putting a decoration for valour on the sword seems a peculiarly appropriate and soldierly one. Pul-i-Khishti, or Tash Kepri, as the Russians call it, seems to keep up its reputation for unhealthiness even in this cold weather. Captain Volkovnikoff's sotnia, consisting of 125 men, has only been there two months, and yet 100 of these are down with Panjdeh sores, neither the cause nor cure for which have the Russian surgeons yet been able to find out. It is very curious that when we were at Panjdeh this time last year we never even heard of this disease.

Our *kafila* of treasure and stores from Peshawar arrived safe in camp on the 31st. It ought to have been here long ago, but was delayed some time at Balkh and by the bad weather since. We are delighted to get a fresh supply of stores; but if this intense cold lasts much longer, we shall have little left to drink. All the wines are frozen hard, and bottles are continually bursting. Captain Griesbach last night, thinking to save something from the wreck, put his half-dozen bottles of beer up in the corner of his tent, close beside his stove, but all in vain—they froze hard during the night, despite the heat of the stove, and all burst but one. Nothing, in fact, can withstand this temperature. For two nights running now the thermometer has been down to 11° and 12° below zero, and yesterday it never rose higher than 15° in the shade all day. With 17° of frost at the warmest in the day, and 44° at night, small wonder that bottles burst. The only wonder is that the health of all is so good. As it is, we have hardly a man sick in hospital. The glare of the sun on the snow tries the eyes of most of us; but Sir West Ridgeway, when at Mashhad, took the precaution to lay in a small store of goggles, and these are now served out by Dr Owen to such as require them, and are, no doubt, saving us many a case of snow-blindness. It is amusing at dinner to see the way in which our liquor and water has all to be thawed. No matter what it is, it all comes in a solid block of ice. The cruet-stand on the table, too, is a joke, as the vinegar and sauces and everything are simply hard blocks of ice. The difficulty is to keep warm at night. Sheets, of course, have been long since discarded, and most of us have our blankets sewn up into bags, with just an opening at the top to creep into; but a *postin*, I believe, rolled round one, is the warmest and most comfortable of all. At the best, though, it is anything but comfortable. One wakes aching all over from the crumpled position the cold forces one into during sleep, only to find the pillows and blankets all wet from one's frozen breath.

In this weather we cannot grumble at not receiving our Indian posts very regularly. Where the fault is we cannot say, but presumably with the postal authorities at Peshawar; for though we do receive a post about once a-week with the English mail-letters, we have never yet, since the line was changed, received a single newspaper. Where they have gone to we cannot think; and were it not for the Mashhad telegraph, we should be utterly without news of what was going on in the world. Thanks to Sir West Ridgeway's arrangements for a *dâk* of Turkoman sowars right across Badghis from Zulfikar to Kushk, we get public-news telegrams now even here, at a distance of 320 odd miles from Mashhad, in between four and five days, and this despite all inclemency of the weather.

CAMP CHAHAR SHAMBA, 12*th February* 1886.

Our two Cossack guests — Captain Volkovnikoff and Lieutenant Kiachko—left us on the 6th after a ten days' visit, taking Lieutenant Drummond back to stay with them at Panjdeh. The sky cleared on the 3d and gave us a fine day, bright enough for Major Bax to be able to have the escort out on parade and show the Russian officers what Indian troops were like before they left. The cavalry fell in about noon, and were put through a few manœuvres by Lieutenant Drummond, winding up with a short charge and the lance exercise; but the snow balled so in the horses' hoofs that they could hardly keep their feet, and it was difficult to do anything much out of a walk. The infantry paraded, under Captain Cotton, in the afternoon, and the Cossack officers, I believe, afterwards expressed themselves much pleased and greatly surprised at the regular and quick way in which our men drilled. They seemed to have an idea that because Indian troops, as they had heard, were irregulars, they were loose and slovenly in their drill, and in fact not at all like regular troops. Lucky it was that the opportunity of a few hours' sunshine on the 3d was taken advantage of for the parades, as on the 4th the snow came down again and fell continuously all day. The 5th was little better; but the men of the 20th Panjab Infantry, determined not to be beaten by the weather, and despite the falling snow, turned out with their spades, cleared a bit of ground, lighted a bonfire in the middle, and after dinner in the evening gave the Cossacks a Katak sword-dance, the like of which they had never seen before. The dancers all turned out in their loose flying white clothes, and the scene round that bonfire is one to be remembered. Never, I fancy, has a Katak dance been danced before in a snowstorm, but our men had their hearts in it, and nothing would daunt them. Those are the men for service in this country.

On the 5th our hearts were gladdened by the arrival of some of our long-looked-for newspapers. We got a bag of some 400 papers, sent up from Quetta, containing a varied assortment of odd dates, ranging from the beginning of December to the middle of January. I am referring to the 'Pioneer' of those dates. The English papers, of course, were much older. The Peshawar bi-weekly letter *dâk* comes in now very regularly despite the weather, and we have nothing to complain of in that line.

Captain Peacocke started on the 9th for Maruchak *en route* to the Kashan and Kushk valleys, which he is to survey on a large scale in conjunction with Captain Kondratenko, the Russian topographer. It has been agreed, in the settlement of the boundary-line across those two valleys, that the existing canals drawn off higher up from those streams on the Afghan side are not be increased, and a survey is therefore to be made conjointly by an English and Russian officer of all canals and cultivated lands for a certain distance up each valley. The object of the Russian Commissioner in making this stipulation is, I presume, to secure for the Sarakhs in the future the same amount of water for irrigation that they have been hitherto receiving. In a country like this, where water is so precious, there is always the danger of constant quarrels about the supply of it; and we can only trust that the present precaution will tend to lessen the chance of their occurrence here in the future as much as possible, and so prevent a state of things being brought about on this border similar to that which now exists along the Persian and Russian frontier on the Khorasan border.

The Russian topographers, Ilyin and Tolmatchoff, are still at work on their respective sections of the *chul*, some 20 or 25 miles to the north-east and north-west of us respectively, and do not apparently expect to finish their surveys for some weeks to come. Captain Peacocke's survey, however, of the country to the north of us, extending from the Kara Bel plateau to the north of the well at Kara Baba, nearly 30 miles north of Chahar Shamba on the west, almost up to Daulatabad, 38 miles north of Maimanah on the east, has given Sir West Ridgeway all the needful information to work upon at present, and so there will be no necessity to wait for the result of the Russian surveys. It is clear that the wells on the edge of the desert were all dug by Maimanah subjects there, and the habitations and rights of pasturage all belong to them. In fact, there never was anybody else to whom they could belong, as to the north of the Kara Bel plateau stretches a waterless desert right away to the Oxus, completely cutting off all communication with Merv, and the only way of approaching this tract on the south is either through Panjdeh on the west or Andkhui on the east. One by one these *kishlaks*, or winter habitations of the numerous nomad tribes of Maimanah, were destroyed by Turkoman raids, and the limit of the inhabited area was gradually lessened, till in 1877 an attack in force completed the depopulation of the border tracts, and even of the lower end of the Ab-i-Kaisar valley in addition, and for some time afterwards no one dared to go there. Now the land is cultivated, though no habitations have been erected on it yet. This last is owing to the Ersari raids. Though the Sarik raids have been put a stop to, the Ersaris still continue to harass the country, and no less than four different raids have occurred within the last five months, on each occasion two flocks of sheep, averaging probably 1000 to 1200 head each, having been carried off.

Even now, as I write, news has just come in that some 300 Kara Turkomans are reported to have started on a raiding expedition from the banks of the Oxus, and that the Wali of Maimanah has himself gone out at the head of all the sowars he can muster to try and intercept them. Winter is the time always chosen by the Turkomans for these raids, as not only does the snow on the ground enable the raiders to traverse country impassable in the summer owing to the want of water, but in the summer there are few or no sheep to drive off. During the summer months all the flocks in these parts are taken up to Kara Jangal and other highlands of the Band-i-Turkistan, and it is when driven down from the hills by the snow that the sheep are all taken out into the *chul* to graze. It must, indeed, seem to the Wali of Maimanah to be the real irony of fate when not only his people are debarred from the use of their own grazing-grounds from fear of Russian or Bokhara Turkomans, but the Russian Government in addition claim those very lands as their own, on the grounds that because the Maimanah people are not using them they do not therefore belong to them. The Andkhui pasturages are much the same as those of Maimanah, with this exception, that being so close to the Oxus they are more than ever exposed to the raids of the Turkomans living on the banks of that river.

The last few days have been beautifully bright and clear; and though too cold for much (as I heard it expressed) fiddling about with a pencil, still, so far as the atmosphere was concerned, clear enough at times for surveying. The snow, though, on the hills, makes it most difficult to distinguish the points, and adds greatly to the surveyor's troubles. Dr Owen sent out snow-goggles the other day sufficient to equip all the different survey-parties, and they received them, I believe, just in the nick of time. I know that, judging by myself, I could not work an hour without them. The snow in our camp is gradually melting, and soon, I suppose, we may expect to see the ground once again, and with it all the crocuses and spring flowers that so abound in this country. I give below the daily maximum and minimum temperature as registered by Dr Owen in camp since the beginning of the month. The average maximum temperature in the shade for the last twelve days has been only $29°7'$. This does not look much on paper; but think what this means living in a tent with the door wide open—and one must have the door open to let in light. If we had glass doors, the case would be very different; but as it is, it means that it has been freezing in our tents during all these days, and we have hardly been able to hold a pen in our hands from the cold. Ink, of course, can be kept thawed over the fire or stove, but not so one's hands. A yard away from the stove everything is freezing hard; and one's hands get so numbed that one has to jump up every minute to warm them, and in the end to give up work in despair and to take refuge either in exercise or the fire. Riding has been quite out of the question, and I do not think one of us in camp has been on a horse for a month. Many of us limit our daily exercise to an hour or two's walk up and down the main street of the camp; but this, though good enough for a constitutional, is not much fun; and every afternoon I generally trudge off with my gun through the snow and take my exercise in a walk up the banks of the stream, on the look-out for wild-fowl, and specimens for our natural-history collection.

The following is the register of the thermometer:—

1886.	Maximum.	Minimum.
1st February	15°0′	12°0′ (below zero)
2d ″	15 0	11 0 ″
3d ″	33 2	6 0 ″
4th ″	32 2	18 0
5th ″	33 2	17 8
6th ″	39 0	14 8
7th ″	33 2	16 0
8th ″	29 5	16 0
9th ″	21 0	6 0
10th ″	27 0	7 0 (below zero)
11th ″	37 0	7 0
12th ″	42 0	17 0

We have been highly pleased to hear by telegraph of the safe arrival of the return party, and we hope that we also may be returning before the year is out—though in this country it is never safe to make plans beforehand, as one never knows what may happen. I think I mentioned in my last that Mr Merk and Ressaldar-Major Baha-u'-din Khan had rejoined us, having left the return party on the banks of the Helmand. The following extract from a letter by Mr Merk gives a capital idea of the country they travelled through on their way back. Their route lay through Persian Seistan round to the west of the Seistan lakes, and thence up to the Herat valley and through the Ardewan pass to Kushk and Bala Murghab. Mr Merk describes the part of Seistan that he passed through as most uninviting to the ordinary traveller, though interesting to geographers. He writes: "From Chahar Burjak on the Helmand, where I said good-bye to the return party, I went down the river to Band-i-Kamal Khan, and then to the west across the strip of 50 miles of now waterless desert country which lies between the Helmand and the stream that, under the name of Sarshela, flows, in years when the Seistan Hamun is flooded, from the Western Hamun to the God-i-Zireh depression or swamp in the northern Beluch desert. My route took me along a wide trough or depression winding from Band-i-Kamal Khan through desert bluffs in a general westerly direction towards the Sarshela. The banks of this trough are dotted with numerous ruins of ancient forts, tombs, villages, and pleasure-houses, and in its bed are traces of the great canal called the Jui Karshasp, which, taking off from the Helmand at Band-i-Kamal Khan, formerly irrigated what is at present a howling wilderness in Southern Seistan. Last spring the Helmand rose to an unusual height, and much of the flood-water escaped through this trough to the Western Hamun. This fact, together with the position of the ruins and the general appearance of the country, are good reasons for believing that at no very distant period a main branch of the Helmand took this course, if indeed the whole river, instead of turning north at Band-i-Kamal Khan, did not flow by this bed into the Western Hamun within historical times. Anyhow, the discovery is interesting, if only as a possible opening for the diversion of part of the Helmand water into a region which sadly wants irrigation. At Trakun, in the centre of the desert strip, I found a large fort in perfect preservation. It must have contained from 400 to 500 families. The Hammam in the citadel looked as if it had been abandoned only yesterday; the large audience-halls were beautifully ornamented, and evidently Trakun was a position of much importance and strength. It is built on an isolated mound with scarped sides, situated in the centre of the depression I have mentioned. Local Beluch tradition says the last inhabitants left the place only three generations ago. Its neighbourhood swarms with ruins of old forts, villages, and tombs. At Sarshela I was met by Persians, deputed by the Amir of Ghain, who is also governor of Persian Seistan. They received me very courteously. Up to this point I had been escorted by Beluchis of the Helmand,—very good fellows, but men who, considered in their character of notorious robbers, were objectionable on account of their sensitive consciences, which did not permit them to plunder living men, and compelled them to slay diligently all their victims before they stripped them. They were long the horror of Eastern Persia and Southern Afghanistan. Now, however, the strong hand of the Amir, Abdur Rahman Khan, has changed all this; and as one of my friends remarked with a sigh, a child may drive a ewe-lamb along the frontier, and we must all look on. They told me that eight years ago a big *Feringhi* had visited Shah Godar, a point some 50 miles south of Sarshela, and had built a pillar there. Possibly they meant Sir Charles MacGregor, who visited these parts about that time. At a ford called Gardan Reg I crossed the Sarshela, which is here about 100 yards wide, on an average about two feet deep, and running with a good current southwards to the God-i-Zireh. It was too hazy for me to see the Koh-i-Taftan, or smoking mountain, the much-sought-after volcano which is believed to exist in the Persian district of Sarhad; but the Beluchis gave me circumstantial accounts of what, according to them, is the undoubted entrance to the bottomless pit. From Gardan Reg the road lay for the next four days along the shore of the Western Hamun in striking scenery. To the left lay a barren stony plain gently sloping towards sterile ranges, while to the right the horizon was bounded by a deep-blue sea, unbroken by a single reed. The opposite shore of the Hamun was not visible, only the flat-topped Koh-i-Khwajah could be seen as an island in the lake. Last year's heavy floods have completely filled the area shown on our maps as "liable to inundation," and Persian Seistan is now a peninsula which can be approached dry-shod only along the left bank of the Helmand. Traffic with Lash Jowain or Persia is carried on by means of rafts, which are made of bundles of reeds tied together: they are necessarily limited in size, and carry at the most four passengers, and are punted by a single boatman over the shallow water of the Hamun, which is rarely more than six feet deep. It is probable that the flood-water will not disappear for several years to come. Naturally, Seistan is frightfully unhealthy with such vast marshes and lagoons in its immediate proximity. The Seistanis appear to have a wretched physique, and the Afghan garrison, whom we met on the march to the Helmand in the Afghan portion of Seistan, had last summer suffered greatly from fever and the terrible plague of flies which follows the drying up of the land flooded every spring. The captain of a troop of Afghan cavalry near Nadali told me he had lost fifty horses last summer, owing partly to the flies and partly to a disease —apparently blood-poisoning—which is peculiar to Seistan. In winter, however, Seistan must be a paradise for sportsmen, as the Hamun and the pools and swamps along its border are simply crammed with wild-fowl of every description. At the point where the highroad from Birjand to Nasirabad strikes the Hamun, a spot which is marked by a high brick pillar said to have been erected by Nadir Shah, I turned westward to Bandan, and reached it after crossing a piece of desert without water, 30 miles in width. In fact, from the Helmand to Bandan the country through which I came is pure desert. Along the Hamun a few Beluch encampments with their flocks are to be found, and for the rest—nothing. Bandan is a small village remarkable only for a fine grove of date-palms. From Bandan I went straight to Dorah by three marches through uninhabited country. Dorah is the frontier village of Persia towards the Afghan province of Farah, and rejoices in a picturesque little border fort, perched on an inaccessible rock, and in a population of, for Persians, singularly uncouth manners. From Dorah I marched to Awaz, the last village of the Birjand district in the direction of Herat. It was not practicable to go to Birjand itself owing to the heavy snow in the passes. From Awaz I went to Yezdan, along the skirt of the aptly termed Dasht-i-Na Umed or "Desert of Despair," which is a series of arid plains broken by ranges of rocky hills without tree, or bird, or bush. From Yezdan to the Herat valley, the road was explored by our officers when we were at Kiliki last summer. Near Yezdan, at Burj-i-Gulwarda, I again heard of Sir Charles MacGregor. This time he was described as a Russian who endeavoured to reach Herat, and got as far as Pahrah, where he was arrested and taken to Mashhad, and thence into captivity in Russia!

CAMP CHAHAR SHAMBA, 21st *February*.

Life in camp here passes very regularly and quietly, and we have little to disturb the even tenor of our ways at present. We are now in the midst of mud and slush, consequent on a thaw at last after a good month of continuous snow. Up till within the last few days we have had six inches of snow all round us, which means that, letting alone the snowstorms, we have not had a day for the past month in which it has not been freezing hard in the shade all day. Now I trust that before long the ground will be clear of snow; and as soon as the mud is dried up, we may look forward to some fine spring weather again. Already we are all talking of moving; and Sir West Ridgeway, if the weather keeps fine, proposes to start for Maruchak early in March, taking the infantry detachment of the 20th Panjab Infantry under Captain Cotton with him as escort, and sending on the cavalry and heavy camp ahead to Akchah or Tashkurghan in the Balkh direction. However, nothing is definitely settled as yet; but without doubt, as soon as ever the weather permits, we shall be on the move to rejoin the Russian Commission at Panjdeh, and commence work anew on the frontier.

Captain Drummond, of the 11th Bengal Lancers, has just returned from a week's visit to the Russian camp, where he was entertained with great hospitality. Colonel Alikhanoff arrived from Merv while he was there, and General Komaroff was expected also at Panjdeh a few days afterwards. Captain Volkovnikoff, our late guest up here, has been appointed to the civil charge of Panjdeh, and he and his squadron have consequently moved up from Pul-i-Khishti, where they were quartered, to Bazaar Takhta, the headquarters of the Harzagi section of the Sariks, situated about the centre of the Panjdeh valley. There, I presume, they will be quartered permanently. The following extract from a letter from Captain Drummond, gives such interesting details of his visit, that I take the liberty of quoting it *in extenso* :—

"At Maruchak," Captain Drummond writes, "I was met with great cordiality by Colonel Kuhlberg and the officers of the Russian Mission, of whom the following were present—viz., M. Lessar, Lieutenant-Colonel Prince George Orbeliani, Captain Gideonoff, Captain Komaroff (Staff), Dr Semmer, Lieutenant Gorokh (Sappers), Captains Kondratenko, Neprintseff, Denisoff, and Petroff (Survey), Captain Varenik, Lieutenant Kiachko, and Cornet Winnikoff (1st Regiment Tomanski Cossacks), Captain Volkovnikoff (1st Regiment Kavkaski Cossacks), Lieutenant Mehemetoff (Lesghin Militia), and M. Mirzaeff (interpreter).

"I was put up in a fine large new Panjdeh *kibitka*, heated by *mungals* (pans of hot ashes), with wooden doors, and felt covering sufficient to keep out the smallest breath of cold air. At dinner, on the evening of my arrival, a number of Cossacks sang their charming national songs, commencing with the 'Maritza,' the march which we had all so greatly admired on our first meeting at Zulfikar. After dinner my health was proposed and drunk with great cordiality, accompanied by 'Three times three,' first in English fashion, and then in Russian, after which all the officers present sang the refrain which invariably follows their toast—viz., the 'Mramel Djamiya.' Next day I was entertained at breakfast by the officers of the Cossack squadron. We sat down at 11 A.M., and did not rise till 4 P.M. Song after song by the Cossack chorus, and toast after toast by my hospitable entertainers, passed the time most cheerily, until at the close of the entertainment, on taking leave of my hosts, I found a section of Cossacks in full uniform awaiting my exit from the *kibitka*. These men fired two volleys in my honour, and then proceeded to toss me in the air, cheering heartily during the performance. After this the section escorted me back to my own *kibitka*, singing lustily *en route*. The next day I spent in visiting the Russian officers whom I had not previously formally called on. In the afternoon I had a long conversation with M. Lessar, whom, I regret to say, I found looking extremely unwell. He suffers from a fever caught on the shores of the Caspian, and since his arrival on this frontier has scarcely been well for a single day. On the 11th, Colonel Alikhanoff arrived from Merv, having driven all the way in a *troika* drawn by four horses. He was escorted by a troop of Merv militia, headed by a white standard bearing the Imperial monogram and a Turki inscription. Colonel Alikhanoff is a tall fine-looking man, and was dressed in the uniform of the Russian cavalry, wearing two Crosses of the Military Order of St George, one of which he had gained for bravery whilst serving as a private soldier. Next day a photo was taken of all the officers of the Commission, including their two guests, Colonel Alikhanoff and myself; after which Colonel Alikhanoff drove off on his way back to Merv, to make preparations *en route* for General Komaroff, who is expected shortly at Panjdeh.

"On the 15th, Prince Orbeliani organised a *partie de plaisir* including Captain Varenik, Lieutenant Gorokh, Lieutenant Kiachko, M. Mirzaeff, and myself, and we started off for Bazaar Takhta in order to pass an evening with Captain Volkovnikoff. At a distance of three miles out we were met by a section of Cossacks commanded by a young cadet, who, after saluting, escorted us to camp, his men dashing forward at full gallop, firing off their carbines in every direction. At the *kibitka* destined for my abode I found two sections of Cossacks drawn up on foot, under command of another cadet, as a guard of honour. We spent a most cheery evening, in toasts and songs, after dining in true Cossack fashion on the ground. I was amused to find the Cossacks of the Kavkaski Regiment had also learned to cheer in British fashion. Next morning Captain Volkovnikoff kindly had a full-dress parade of his squadron, and showed me a few movements and the walk, trot, &c. Unfortunately the ground was in a wretched state, and consequently I was unable to form a really correct idea of Cossack drill. I was, however, greatly struck by the excellent condition of the horses, the steadiness of their parade movements, and the fine sturdy appearance of the men. After the parade we started back for Maruchak, escorted part of the way by Captain Volkovnikoff and his squadron. On the 17th I took leave of my hosts, and was again escorted by a full squadron of the Toman Regiment, under the command of Captain Varenik, who *en route* kindly showed me a little dismounted skirmishing. My escort was not content with seeing me to the banks of the Murghab, but insisted on crossing it with me, marching through the deep and rapid stream six abreast. On the farther bank I found that wine had been brought with a view to finally drinking my health in a stirrup-cup, after which a volley from a dismounted section, 'Three times three' from the whole squadron, a song from the chorus, and I bade farewell to as hospitable and courteous hosts as we could meet in the two hemispheres."

Here at Chahar Shamba we are hoping to be joined soon by Mr Ney Elias, who, I am sorry to hear, was taken so ill at Faizabad that he was unable to start on his return journey to Yarkand, and has had to turn back to join us for the sake of rest and medical treatment.

During the bad weather of late we have none of us been able to get out much about the country, and I can therefore describe little but one of the principal sights and places of resort near us—viz., the reputed Cave of the Seven Sleepers, the Ashab-i-Kahf, a place of pilgrimage which our Mahomadans are continually asking leave to visit. It lies in the Hirak valley, some four miles to the south-west of our camp. I rode out to it with Subadar Muhammad Husain Khan, of the 2d Sikhs, the other day, and we were both much amused at the immunity with which these worthy Sayeds or Eshans, as the descendants of the Prophet are called here, practise on the credulity of their neighbours. The story of the Seven Sleepers of Ephesus is pretty well known, and the tradition is confirmed in the eyes of all Mussulmans by the mention of it in the Surah-ul-Kahf, or Chapter of the Cave, in the fifteenth *Juz* or section of the Koran. It is there related how these seven men, firm in their faith in their own God, separated from the rest of their tribe who had taken to other gods, and taking refuge in a cave, were caused to sleep there, with their dog, for 309 years. The Eshans of Khwajah Altai Azizan change the scene from Ephesus to Turkistan, and tell a very different story. The King Dakianus, they say, was originally a shepherd of Shibarghan, and tended his flock in the hills for twelve years, till one day he found a slab of stone with an inscription on it. Not being able to decipher the latter, he showed it to a *moollah*, who told him that it was a record of hidden treasure. Having possessed himself of the treasure and killed the *moollah*, Dakianus took service with the king, and after some time rose to the command of the army. He soon got the army on his side, seized the kingdom, and eventually conquered the world. When thus in supreme power, the devil appeared before Dakianus in the form of the angel Gabriel, and tempted him by telling him that God had sent him to say that he was God of the heavens, but that Dakianus was God of the earth. Dakianus, who was a worshipper of the one God, refused to believe the devil, and told the latter that he was not the true angel Gabriel. The devil then offered to prove that he was, by proposing, as a test, that if a certain fish on the top of the water went down on his approach, he was the true Gabriel, but that if it remained up he was an impostor. Accordingly, Dakianus and the devil went together to the bank of the river, and no sooner did the fish see the devil than it at once dived down.

Dakianus believed the test, acknowledged the devil as the angel Gabriel, left off the worship of the true God, and at the devil's tempting, set himself up as a god on his own account. One day, however, when eating his food, Dakianus was bothered by flies, which, do what he would, he could not get rid of. His servants said to themselves, "He calls himself God, and yet cannot even get rid of the flies that bother him. He is no God." And they determined to leave him. Six men went off, and on the second day fell in with a shepherd, from whom they begged bread and water. The shepherd gave them all he had, and asked them where they came from, and where they were going to. They told him their story, and how they were fleeing from Dakianus, and wished to hide, and the shepherd agreed to accompany them in their flight. The shepherd's dog also followed his master, and the men told him to drive the dog back, lest he should betray their whereabouts. The shepherd objected, saying the dog had been his faithful companion for years; but the others insisted, and the shepherd at last struck the dog with his stick, breaking one of its legs. The dog still followed, and the shepherd struck it again, breaking another leg; but the dog continued to crawl after them, and the men, struck with pity, eventually took it in turns to carry it on with them. The shepherd guided them all to this very cave that he knew of, and once there they all went to sleep, and never awoke for 309 years. The fate of the dog, however, is left in uncertainty by the Sayeds. They cannot tell exactly how it came to die, but they point triumphantly to its grave — a heap of bricks, surmounted by a pole and a flag, by the side of the entrance to the cave. In the Koran it is distinctly stated that the sleepers were seven in number, and the eighth was their dog. But either the Arabic of the Koran is beyond the Sayeds, or they prefer a story of their own. Whichever it is, there is no doubt of the realism of the latter portion of their tale, as any one who knows the affection the shepherds here have for their great savage shaggy-coated dogs, and the huge sticks that the shepherds always carry, will testify. Further on in the story, however, the worthy Sayeds get more confused still, and they have it that the sleepers woke twice—once in the time of Hazrat Esah, or Christ, and again in the time of the Prophet. According to the Sayeds, the men in the cave have been asleep for 2312 years—viz., 309 years before the birth of Christ, 700 years from that to the time of Mahomad, and 1303 years up to the present time. As a matter of fact, the Mahomadan era commenced on the 16th July 622 of the Christian era; and therefore, reckoning their lunar by our own solar years, the time would be 2195 years. The story is, they say, that when these men and the shepherd awoke they felt hungry, and sent one of their number to go to the city near by, called Shahr-i-Afsoz, to buy bread. On arrival he found the place much altered, and the first baker he went to refused to accept his money. Another to whom he applied asked him where he got his money from. The man said that it was his own, and from his own house. He was then told to point out his house, but could not at first, and eventually recognised it by a mulberry-tree, and going in, he told them to dig in a certain place, and there they found, sure enough, his store, a jar full of Dakianus's coins. The then owner of the house protested, and claimed the house and coins as his, and eventually both the men and the coins were taken before the king. When the king, who was a Christian, heard the man's story, and found he had been asleep for 309 years, he looked on the man as supernatural, and offered to resign the throne in his favour. The man declined, and stated that all he wished was to be allowed to return to his companions in the cave. The king thereupon accompanied him. With the king were a hawk and a dog; and a deer being started on the road, it was caught by these two and brought in, thus making a third animal in the party. On arrival at the cave, not only the original six friends, the Altai Azizan, and the shepherd, but the king, and the dog and the hawk and the deer, all went off to sleep, and never woke again for some 700 years, when they were awoke by the arrival of the *chahar yar*, or the four friends of the Prophet—*i.e.*, Omar, Osman, Abubakr, and Ali, who, repeating the Mahomadan creed, at once awoke the sleepers. The latter got up, repeated the creed, and then fell asleep again, and there they still remain.

All this was told me by the Sayeds in the cave, and they pointed triumphantly to the relics in proof of their story. Holding our lighted candles between the palings of the wooden screen which debars nearer approach to the sleepers, we were shown some cloths on the floor, apparently a rough common sheet with a dark-coloured fringed cloth above it, which was said to cover the sleepers. We asked if it was allowed to look under the cloth; but that, they said, was impossible. Even they themselves, they said, knew not what was there. One man had once tried to look, and was immediately struck blind; but that if we doubted, " there [pointing in the direction] were the dog and the deer and the hawk." Holding the candles to the right, we could then see indistinctly something looking like dried bodies of some animals propped against the wall. They were very small. The first, said to be the dog, was about a foot in height, and the deer a few inches higher, but it was impossible to say in such light what animals they were. The bones of the legs were visible—in fact, the dog's legs had fallen off, which rather told against its being asleep, but the body seemed to be covered with dry skin; and yet, on the strength of these relics, some twenty families of Sayeds are kept in comfort, and live here on the contributions of pilgrims, with, in addition, as much land as they require free of any rent and taxes. In ordinary years, with such a scant population, the contributions of pilgrims cannot amount to anything very great; but still numbers are brought here for burial, and the little ravine in which the cave is situated is full of graves. The village of the Sayeds stands at the mouth of the little side ravine in which the cave is situated, a mile or two below the last of the eight hamlets in which the 250 families inhabiting the head of the Hirak valley reside. The valley is narrow, and simply a level stretch of culturable ground, some 400 yards in width, marked by old watercuts and Turkoman watch-towers between the usual low hillocks on either side. A long, low mud-built building, used as the village *musjid*, is at the mouth of the ravine; and here sit all the Sayeds in a row, with nothing else to do, apparently, than wait for the advent of visitors. The entrance to the cave is marked by a brick portico some 20 feet in height, surmounted, like all places of pilgrimage in this country, by the skulls and horns of wild sheep, the offerings apparently of the *shikaris* of the neighbourhood. Walking down the passage some 10 or 12 yards to a vaulted chamber, and then turning down another passage to the right, one comes to a small low passage at the end filled up with loose earth. This, the Sayeds declared, was a direct passage to Mecca, but that God would not allow it to be opened, as so fast as they dug out the earth from the entrance, it was filled up again by supernatural means. Turning, then, again to the right, we had to ascend a ladder into a dark chamber above, floored with boards, and in this is the wooden screen before mentioned as enclosing the sleepers.

Noticing what a number of the tombs in the valley around were built up with bricks, I asked where the bricks were procured from, and was told that all the little mounds in the valley were full of them. Curiously enough, it is just the same with us here at Chahar Shamba. Looking casually about, one would never suppose that there was a brick within miles. The villages are all built of mud, and there are no ruins or anything to catch the eye; but the moment we required bricks to build chimneys to our tents, it was found that every little heap and mound in the place was full of old burnt bricks, most of them of an unusually large size, showing that there was a settled population living in regular brick houses here once, but so long ago that the remains of their houses even are distinguishable only on close search. So it is all over the country; and we even hear rumours of the remains of a large city out in the desert, to the east or north-east of Panjdeh, called Shahr-i-Kishlak, said to have contained once 80,000 inhabitants. *Kishlak* is the word in common use all over these nomad countries to signify the winter-quarters, usually in the plains, in contradistinction to the *ailagh* or summer-quarters, usually in the hills.

Where Shahr-i-Afsoz may be, the Sayeds of Khwajah Altai Azizan, although they have maintained the tradition, could not tell me. They themselves are divided in their opinions. Some of them say it was at Ala Taimur, a place to the south in the hills, which they describe as an ancient fortress built of stone on the top of some precipitous rock. Others say it was at Chachaktu, the village to the east of Chahar Shamba, some seven miles up the valley; but none connect it with Ephesus. That Chachaktu was once a large place is very evident. It is the one place between Maruchak and Andkhui, mentioned in the history of Nadir Shah, in the description of that conqueror's march up from Herat to Balkh in the year A.H. 1152 or A.D. 1739, and presumably at so late a date as that it was a flourishing city. Now there is nothing to strike the eye but the ruins of an old mud-fort on a mound. I have mentioned in a former letter how it was devastated of late years by the Turkomans. Before that, some twenty odd years ago, I believe the Salor Turkomans settled at it (or rather at Sir-i-Chashma, the spring two miles above it which forms the source of the Kilah Wali stream) for a time after they were driven out of Maruchak by the Sariks; but they did not stop there long, and after plundering the Usbegs, they beat a retreat to Kara Tepe in the Kushk valley, whence they were driven to Zorabad in Persia, and they only finally settled at Sarakhs within the last few years.

CHAPTER XI.

MARUCHAK AGAIN.

CAMP MARUCHAK, 14*th March* 1886.

TEN days ago we were fairly launched into spring, and with the exception of the snow-clad Band-i-Turkistan to the south of us, all signs of winter had passed away. *Postins* and Turkoman felt-lined boots had all been discarded, and sunhelmets had taken their place. Instead of grumbling at breakfast at the cold saddle of mutton being frozen so hard that one might as well try to chop a bit off a stone with a hatchet as to cut a slice off it, we were grumbling at the heat. Certainly the change was very sudden and very great. The country entirely changed. The whole of the Chahar Shamba valley suddenly appeared covered with countless little yellow crocuses, looking for all the world like a mass of buttercups in the distance; while the lower ground, nearer the water, came out full of a white, or rather very pale lilac, variety of the same flower. Here at Maruchak the flowers are not so numerous, the ground is much wetter, and the reeds in the swamps bordering the river being mostly on fire, the valley looks black and dirty. Despite the fact that the winter seems over, however, we are still luxuriating in last autumn's fruits. We have both pears and apples from Mashhad; while the Amir, a short time ago, sent us some pony-loads of apples all the way from Kabul; and now, as I write, a pony-load of pomegranates has just arrived as a present from Sirdar Ishak Khan at Mazar-i-Sharif.

Our winter-quarters at Chahar Shamba have been broken up, and we all are, or soon will be, on the move again. Sir West Ridgeway and a small party are the only ones out as yet, but a few days more will probably see nearly all on the march—a march, too, which we hope will not cease till we are all back in India again. Once the demarcation of the frontier is recommenced, we hope it may be successfully carried through; and glad, indeed, our men and followers will be when once their faces are fairly turned towards home.

Our plans at present, of course, are quite uncertain; but, so far as we know, the probability is that if the boundary is demarcated up to the Oxus, we shall all march on to Tashkurghan or thereabouts, and then divide, the cavalry and main camp returning direct to Peshawar, and the remainder through Badakshan to Gilgit and Kashmir. Mr Ney Elias, whose arrival from Yarkand I mentioned in my last letter, tells us that a small party will be able to procure sufficient supplies by the Badakshan route, supposing that time is given for them to be laid out beforehand—and I, for one, am fully hoping to return that way. However, before building castles in the air regarding the future, we must wait and see what is in store for us here. If the Russian Commissioners have not considerably modified the claims put forward by them before we broke up for the winter, there is little chance of a speedy settlement being arrived at. Not only do they claim the wells and pastures in the *chul*, but also a considerable portion of the regularly inhabited and revenue-paying portion of Khamiab in the Khwajah Salar district on the banks of the Oxus. Neither of these claims has any connection with the cession of Panjdeh, and neither of them can be acceded to. Consequently, when these points are settled, it will be time enough for us to think of our return march.

As soon as the weather cleared, orders were issued by Sir West Ridgeway detailing the movements of the various parties, and the 4th March saw us on the move. Sir West himself, accompanied by Captain Maitland and myself, started for Maruchak through the *chul*, with a light camp; while the remainder of the Commissioner's party, consisting of Major Durand, Captain de Laessoe, Nawab Mirza Hasan Ali Khan, and Kazi Muhammad Aslam Khan, with an escort of twenty-five men of the 20th Panjab Infantry, under Subadar Arsallah Khan, and a few sowars of the 11th Bengal Lancers, marched down the highroad *viâ* Kilah Wali and Karawal Khana, for the same place. The cavalry and main camp, consisting of Major Bax and Captain Drummond, Mr Merk, Sirdar Muhammad Aslam Khan, and Ressaldar-Major Baha-u'-din Khan, march shortly for Tashkurghan, halting *en route* at Andkhui, pending further orders; while the remainder, consisting of Captain Cotton, Dr Owen, and Khan Bahadur Ibrahim Khan, with the remainder of the infantry escort, await the Commissioner's return at Chahar Shamba. The march of the cavalry on ahead is necessitated by the clause in the Protocol limiting the escorts of the Commissioners to 100 men a side; and Sir West is therefore obliged to divide the Commission so as to avoid the possibility of having too many men with him on the frontier.

As I have already described the march up from Maruchak to Chahar Shamba, I will not follow the march of Major Durand's party down the same road. Sir West Ridgeway's march, however, was through comparatively new ground. The route was as follows:—

		Miles.
4th. Alai Chalai,	. . . . .	13
5th. Kara Baba,	. . . . .	20
7th. Kara Bel plateau,	. . . . .	20
8th. Galla Chashmah,	. . . . .	25
9th. Maruchak,	. . . . .	18

These places in the *chul* are as yet unknown, but will come into prominence in connection with the boundary settlement. Starting on the morning of the 4th, Sir West Ridgeway first inspected Captain Cotton's detachment of mounted infantry, composed of sepoys of the 20th Panjab Infantry, mounted on ponies, with Turkoman saddles; and uncommonly well the little party drilled, considering the very short time they have been in training. The experiment shows what useful men we have in our frontier Pathans.

From Chahar Shamba the road to Kara Baba runs almost due north, and thence west to Maruchak. The level of the country slopes up gradually from the Chahar Shamba valley to the elevated plateau known as Kara Bel, which divides the watershed of the Murghab from that of the Oxus. Alai Chalai, for instance, is some 600 feet higher than Chahar Shamba, and Kara' Baba 300 feet above that again; while the Kara Bel plateau, consisting of an endless stretch of undulating downs, ranges from 350 to 600 feet higher still, or say, on an average, some 3600 feet above sea-level. The first day's march lay through a belt of tumbled hillocks too steep to be of much use for pasturage or anything else. Alai Chalai, as the halting-place was called, simply consists of a couple of wells near a small spring in a little ravine, but with a plentiful supply of water; north of this the hillocks get gradually lower and more rounded, and become more and more valuable for pasturage till the plateau itself is reached, which at this season of the year is one mass of grass and verdure as far as the eye can reach—very different from the desert we all supposed it to be.

Curiously enough, these hillocks swarm with pig, despite the absence of water and the fact that the hillsides do not afford cover for a rat, except underground. Twice near Kara Baba whole sounders were passed, but being collectively too formidable for the dogs to make any impression on, got off scot-free. Not so, however, an isolated couple. The first, an old sow, being descried by the dogs in the distance, was chased up a hill, but turning at the top, charged down on the dogs again, and sent them all flying back as fast as they came. Unfortunately, as if prompted by some evil genius, the beast finally came charging all the way down the hillside again herself, and stood at bay in the *nullah* at the bottom, and eventually had to be shot to save the dogs, who could not be otherwise got off. Very different was a fight with a solitary old boar the next day. The Turkoman guide—a well-known man of the name of Gok Sirdar, the leader of many a raid—hearing a row, galloped over a rise, and the first thing seen of him was his appearance galloping as hard as he could go up the next rise, with a boar in full pursuit. More than this, the old boar caught him and ripped up his horse's hock before he knew where he was. After that a regular fight commenced. The boar charged everybody and everything. The dogs, emboldened by their easy victory of the previous day, seemed to think the killing of a pig an everyday matter, and went in at the beast in the most reckless manner. I need not say that before very long they were all pretty well cut up. Sir West Ridgeway's bull-dog was slashed up the flank, the muleteer's big pie-dog was ripped up the back, and my kangaroo hound gashed across the throat in a manner that made one marvel how the dog escaped with its life. A Winchester rifle was tried, but the bullets seemed to have no effect whatever on the pig; and eventually the brave old beast was shot with a cavalry carbine, fighting grandly to the last. Had he stood at bay a little longer, the dogs must have been killed. To shoot the boar was the only chance of saving them, and even that was no easy matter in the midst of the fray; but how we all longed for a good spear and a fair fight! When measured, the boar was not very tall, only about 37 inches, but with immense breadth and bulk, and about 52 inches in length. The body was covered all over with long, light, rather fawn-coloured hair, forming a regular fleece, and giving it quite a different appearance from the ordinary black-bristled Indian boar.

Sir West Ridgeway halted a day at Kara Baba to have a good look at the country around from the heights about; and as there is no water on the road for the next 63 miles to Maruchak, it had been arranged to fill the water-*mussucks* at Kara Baba and take on a sufficient supply for one day from there, while a similar supply was to be sent up by the main party from Maruchak to Galla Chashmah. Unfortunately, however, the Kara Baba well was not equal to the demand, and our party were reduced to great straits. The well, on arrival, was found to be about 36 feet in depth, and to contain about 18 feet of water. The water, though sweet, had an unpleasant smell, and the muleteers were allowed to empty the well for their mules, in the belief that it would refill during the night, and the water next day be better. The story goes that Captain Peacocke, when out surveying during the winter, found this well nearly dry, and went down it to see what it was like, but that on arrival at the bottom he went plump into the carcass of a dead sheep, which had been thrown down some time before by a party of marauding Kara Turkomans, with whom it is a common custom thus to poison the water behind them to cover their retreat. No wonder, therefore, that the water did not smell very sweet. Next day, when the well came to be examined, it was found that it had not half refilled in the night, and that there was not even enough to fill a third of the *mussucks* for the next day's march. The horses and mules got nothing to drink that day, and the men very little, and the only chance was to send off the *mussucks* on camels to a small spring called Chashmah Pinhan, about four miles to the west, to get there whatever they could. The 7th turned out a very hot day, and the horses and mules, after a 20-mile march and no water the previous day, were frantically thirsty; but the *pakhals* had leaked on the march, and there was little more than enough for the men. However, despite the heat and the thirst, all did the 25-mile march the next day without loss; and glad indeed were we, on arrival at Galla Chashmah, to see the twenty camel-loads of good Murghab water sent up from Maruchak lying ready for us. Each muleteer, as he came in gasping with his tongue out to show how dry it was, soon revived under the influence of a good drink, and only one mule out of nearly fifty gave in, and could not be got up again till revived with water. With the exception of this want of water, these two marches across the plateau from Kara Baba to Galla Chashmah were most enjoyable. From Alai Chalai to Kara Baba the road led up the bottom of a narrow ravine, known locally as the Kara Baba Shor; the whole way the view was limited to the hills on either side. Two or three miles to the north of Kara Baba the crest of the plateau is reached; and once out on the plateau, the country changed all at once to rolling undulating ground covered with young grass and little yellow flowers. Not a sound was to be heard but the singing of the larks. The change that had taken place was marvellous. Ten days before, the country was a snow-covered waste; now it was found green and fresh, full of birds, beetles, and insects of every description, which had all suddenly appeared from goodness knows where. The road along the plateau crosses a succession of undulating ridges, known as Yedaram, a Turki word signifying seven ridges, and always used, so far as I can make out, to denote a country where the road crosses a succession of ridges at right angles instead of running parallel to them.

From the road at intervals the country could be seen sloping gradually and smoothly away for some miles to the south, till the smooth ground suddenly changed into the tumbled mass of hillocks lying immediately to the north of the Kilah Wali stream. The camp on the Kara Bel plateau, chosen by the Turkoman guides, was a little hollow immediately to the south of a low slope covered with Kandam wood—the curious, dry, low bush growing about the *chul*. It seems all rotten to the touch, and burns beautifully even when fresh cut, or rather broken. The hawks in the *chul* all seem to select this bush for their nests, and of these there were no fewer than eight in the small area close above the camp. Two of them were fresh nests, but with no eggs in them—though eggs were taken from similar nests in the Andkhui *chul* by Captain de Laessoe nearly three weeks before. The Turkomans have an idea that if these eggs are not laid before the close of winter and thoroughly frozen, they will not hatch; and I remember last year being gravely informed by my Turkoman guide that these hawks—I could not ascertain then exactly what species they were—always left their eggs for a certain time to be frozen, and then returned at the opening of spring to sit on them. None of their nests are more than eight feet from the ground, and the huge bundle of sticks of which they are built is generally visible for miles around—showing the most charming confidence and an entire absence of all fear of intrusion or molestation on the part of the parent birds. Near the road I picked up a small Bokhara knife, supposed to have belonged to some Ersari Turkoman from its make,—possibly to one of the two men who were found dead near the same place by Captain Peacocke and Mr Merk in their trip across the *chul* last year, when the knife, being hidden under the snow, may have escaped observation. These two men, it was supposed, were raiders, who had succumbed during the retreat.

The road from Kara Bel to Galla Chashmah was a gradual descent the whole way. From the last Kara Bel ridge on the western side of the plateau, some 7 or 8 miles from the camp above, the road led gradually down, finally opening into a valley some 11 or 12 miles below the crest of the plateau, about 300 yards in width, and full of soft wet soil, with a shallow stream of bitter salt water in the centre. The road then winds down by the side of this stream for the next six miles or so to Galla Chashmah—an open space covered with a succession of shallow pits, say 20 feet in diameter at the top and some 8 feet in depth, each containing a few inches of salt water, quite undrinkable by any animal except sheep, which, I have heard, will drink water that no other animal will touch. From Galla Chashmah to Maruchak the road makes a sudden descent from a small *kotal*, about 10 miles out, down a narrow winding valley full of mud and salt water in places, which makes it most difficult for baggage-animals, and with a descent of some 700 feet within the first three miles. This road does not seem as if it could ever have been a great highway in olden times, and there are no remains of any *robats*, or rest-houses, that I know of, to show that it was ever much used. The road following the Galla Chashmah salt stream is better, I believe; but that debouches into the Murghab valley at a place called Pusht-i-Hamwar, about half-way between Maruchak and Karawal Khana, and is not, therefore, much used, if at all.

Our camp at Maruchak is pitched a little below the fort. The Russian camp is still on its old ground on the opposite side of the river, about three miles to the north. So far the Russians seem to have made no preparations for crossing, beyond the fact that the Panjdeh boat has been brought up and established as a ferry near the ford, about half-way between the two camps. The Panjdeh boat, I must say, is a marvel of marine architecture. Imagine a flat-bottomed punt some 20 feet in length and 12 in breadth, constructed of nothing but logs of wood by no means straight or uniform in size, but averaging between 3 and 4 feet in length, and say 6 to 8 inches in diameter. The solid way in which these logs are all held together and the boat is made water-tight, certainly reflects considerable credit on the Panjdeh builder. The Murghab has not yet come down in flood, though it is certainly rising; and if the present hot weather lasts much longer, we may certainly expect the snow to begin melting in the mountains. We are generally supposed to have heavy rain in this country about the *Nouroz*—the 21st of March—and after that the snows begin to melt. The river is still fordable, though it is now impossible to ride across without getting one's feet and legs wet; and we are therefore only too glad to avail ourselves of the use of the boat, while our horses are led across the ford.

On the morning of the 10th, Lieutenant-Colonel Prince Orbeliani and Lieutenant Gorokh arrived with an invitation from Colonel Kuhlberg to Sir West Ridgeway and all of us to breakfast at noon the next day. The morning of the 11th, therefore, saw us all riding over. To our astonishment we found not only a large Cossack guard of honour drawn up to salute Sir West Ridgeway on arrival, but a band of one of the Trans-Caspian Rifle battalions in addition, just brought down from Aimakjar, who played a selection mostly of English airs throughout breakfast, in turn with songs from the Cossack chorus,—a wonderful treat to all of us, who have heard no music now for so long. We sat down a party of twenty: the English guests, with Colonel Kuhlberg, Captain Gideonoff, M. Lessar, and Prince Orbeliani at one table, and the remainder of the Russian officers at the other—all of us being easily accommodated in their fine large mess *kibitka*, which must be some 20 to 22 feet in diameter, and about the largest I have ever seen. The *kibitka* was made in Panjdeh, they told us, though the woodwork of it, it is thought, was brought from Khiva, where most of the best *kibitkas* are made, I believe. When Colonel Kuhlberg proposed Sir West Ridgeway's health, we were amused to hear the Cossack chorus outside break out into an English cheer, with a "Hip, hip, hurrah!" and a "One cheer more," in the most approved style; and we were even told that they all but knew "For he's a jolly good fellow," though, of course, without any very exact idea of the meaning of the words. A Turkoman race-meeting was to be held by Captain Volkovnikoff in Panjdeh, we were told, on the 14th; and there were also rumours that a Russian lady—the wife of the Colonel commanding the Russian troops at Aimakjar—was coming down to Panjdeh on a visit.

A meeting of the Commission was held on the 12th; and all preliminaries having been arranged, we shall probably soon be on the march again back to Chahar Shamba, this time in company with the Russian Commission. Kazi Saad-ud-Din, the Amir's representative, is in camp with us here, the governor of Herat being still at Karawal Khana. The latter has spent the winter at Bala Murghab, and probably will not be sorry to see the boundary demarcated up to the confines of his district at Kilah Wali, and be free to return. The Kilah Wali settlement, however, will probably require some looking to after our departure, as the Turkomans there have been rather uneasy of late. Having got hold of the idea that the Afghan Government intend to remove them from the frontier to the Herat valley, most of them are returning to Panjdeh in all haste; and here at Maruchak, my tent being close by the roadside, I am continually seeing Turkoman family-parties passing by on their way back. Imagine a string of camels, probably eight or ten in number. First of all comes, I presume, the father of the family on horseback; then a boy leading the camels, on the first of which will be a pair of those huge carpet-bags so much prized by us for their fine workmanship, containing all the household goods and chattels, and on the top the mother of the family with a child or two in her lap. One of the ladies I saw passing to-day was resplendent in a bright green silk mantle, and evidently considered herself rather young and pretty, though to our ideas their round flat faces and small eyes are not particularly interesting. On the next camel in all probability is loaded the *kibitka* and felts thereof; then follow half-a-dozen camels loaded with bags of grain, an old woman generally bringing up the rear on the last. Who are to take the place of these Turkomans at Kilah Wali I have not heard.

There is little news from Panjdeh. General Komaroff's expected visit has not yet come off, and apparently is indefinitely postponed. Colonel Alikhanoff at Merv holds the chief civil charge of all this frontier, but without any military command. He has under him, I believe, four assistants, in charge of Merv, Sarakhs, Yulatan, and Panjdeh respectively. Captain Volkovnikoff's appointment to the civil charge of Panjdeh is only temporary, pending the arrival of the permanent civil official. The Panjdeh Sariks seem to have tacitly accepted the position of Russian subjects, and the joke in the Russian camp now is (so all the Russian officers tell us) that the Maruchak pheasants have had such a rough time of it at the hands of the British officers, that even they are now petitioning to be taken under Russian protection. The pheasants certainly are the principal, in fact almost the only, inhabitants of the Maruchak valley at the present moment; but I do not suppose the Amir intends they should long remain so; and if ever we visit the valley again, it is highly probable that we may find our shooting-grounds much curtailed by the spread of cultivation.

The railway to Merv is progressing apace, and is now running, we hear, as far as Doshakh. Colonel Kuhlberg and all the Russian officers fully hope to return by rail from Merv, where it is expected to be open in time for them to avail themselves of it on their return from the Oxus. Work has also been commenced, it is said, on the section from Merv to Chahar Jui; but the general progress of the line, we are told, has been much retarded owing to the freezing of the Caspian during the severe weather in the winter, which prevented the bringing up of the requisite amount of material.

Major Holdich, Mr Merk, and Jemadar Azizulah Khan, who left us on the 27th February, have been engaged for the last ten days with Captain Komaroff in fixing the sites for the pillars along the boundary from Hauz-i-Khan to Maruchak. It will be remembered that the frontier was demarcated from Zulfikar up to Hauz-i-Khan, but that from the latter point onwards, though a settlement was arrived at, no demarcation was possible before the winter. This has now been done, and Major Holdich and Mr Merk have just returned. The following extract of a note from Mr Merk tells us of some of their doings. He says:—

"We reached the Russian camp on the 3d, and were hospitably received, and left for Robat-i-Kashan on the 5th. During the two days we were with the Russians they had sports, which were very enjoyable, as the weather was beautiful and warm, and the events were numerous and amusing. The programme included horse-races in heats for Cossacks and Turkomans, at first separately, and afterwards a combined Cossack and Turkoman race for the winners in both sections; foot-races, sack-races, a donkey and a camel race, wrestling between Cossacks and Turkomans, and, what was the most interesting of all, a performance of the *Jigitoffka* by Cossacks of the escort with the Russian Commission. We all sat on a low grassy mound, round which the race-course had been laid out, and at the foot of which the wrestling, &c., took place. The ground was very heavy from the effects of the recent thaw, but the little Cossack horses ploughed their way sturdily through it—although, of course, in the international race they were outmatched by the much larger and more powerful Turkoman horses, a Cossack nag being rarely over 13.2, and being built more for endurance than for speed, much in the style of the hill-pony of India. The Turkomans, moreover, were no novices in the arts that go to win a race, and 'had been there before,' so to speak. The donkey-race brought out a procession of little Turkoman boys, who with great solemnity trotted in single file round the course, the last boy finishing at the end as conscientiously as the winner of the race. Certainly the best part of the entertainment was the *Jigitoffka*. It consists of mounted Cossacks at full speed picking up caps from the ground, jumping off and remounting, firing their rifles, and drawing swords, while covering a measured (and short) space of ground, galloping past, standing in the saddle, &c. It was carried out with spirit and zest, and is evidently a favourite amusement of the men. The pace, however, cannot help being slow, and we saw no barebacked exercises such as are common in our cavalry. During part of the time in the *chul* we were accompanied by Captain Petroff of the Russian Topographical Department. It was interesting to meet him, as he had been on the staff of M. Khanikoff when the latter travelled to Herat, and thence by Anar Darah to Lash Jowain, and on through Southern Persia to Teheran in 1858. Captain Petroff also served on the Anglo-Russian Delimitation Commission in Asia Minor after the Crimean war, where he was with General Gordon, of whom he says that he then already formed the opinion that he was a ' noble soul.' "

Captain Griesbach has started on a fresh trip in the search for coal and other mineral wealth, and we can only trust his Turkistan explorations may meet with the success they deserve. The Mashhad telegraph line was interrupted for some little time owing to the late heavy rains in Khorasan; but the energy of the English inspectors, under Major Wells, R.E., soon put it to rights again; and now that the line is under British supervision, I trust we shall have none of the long and wearisome interruptions like those which occurred last spring, just at the time too when the line was most required. Jemadar Halim Khan, of the 20th Panjab Infantry, has just started for Zorabad on the Persian frontier, and several of the political orderlies are also engaged in looking after the Turkoman sowars who carry our Mashhad mails across Badghis; so that I trust there is little fear of our part of the line not being maintained at its present efficiency, despite the heavy spring rains which are now upon us. The rain has been heavy and continuous for the last three days, and now, as I write, it has just changed into snow. The ground is all white again; everything looks as if we are in for another spell of winter weather, so I fear our march may be delayed. The newspaper and letter *dâks*, however, continue to come in with wonderful regularity.

CHAPTER XII.

THE HERAT FRONTIER.

CAMP KARAWAL KHANA, 12*th April* 1886.

THE demarcation of the frontier from Zulfikar to Maruchak —or rather to the confines of Herat to the north of Kilah Wali, some 45 miles to the east of Maruchak—having now been completed, it is time that I should send a short description of the boundary, and a sketch of the line laid down. My previous letters have already described most of the places visited by the Commissioners, and I shall therefore give simply a brief *résumé*, showing, as connectedly as I can, the results of the settlement just concluded, defining the northern limits of the Herat province.

Commencing from the Persian border on the west, the boundary starts from the right bank of the Hari Rud, at a point as near as possible $1\frac{1}{2}$ mile to the north of the small tower at the mouth of the Zulfikar pass. Down the valley, to the north of pillar No. 1, there is little more than room for the road between the river and the rough ground at the foot of the cliffs; and the line of boundary thus demarcated gives the possession of all culturable land at Zulfikar to Afghanistan. Pillar No. 2 stands on the top of the cliffs immediately above No. 1, and thence the line runs in an easterly direction to pillar No. 5, on a prominent and well-marked point on the edge of the second line of cliffs. From this point the boundary runs south-east, following the edge of the second line of cliffs, crossing the second defile at pillar No. 7, about half a mile up the pass, and thence south and south-east for some 4 miles, still following the second line of cliffs, and then bending eastwards up a rocky ridge to pillar No. 10, on the top of the Dengli Dagh hills. From pillar No. 11, on the eastern point of these hills, the line of boundary can be followed running straight across the undulating ground below to the centre of three low hills, and thence to pillar No. 13, on the roadside half-way between Ak Robat and Sumba Karez. Pillar No. 15 stands on the roadside about half-way between Ak Robat and Au Rahak, and thence the line runs round eastwards for some 10 or 12 miles, and turning south, crosses the Egrigeuk, Shorab, or Islim stream, as it is variously called, three miles to the west of Islim. From pillar No. 19 [1] the boundary runs south-east to the top of the highest hill, marking the watershed between the valleys of the Kushk and the Egrigeuk streams, and thence down along the watershed to pillar No. 21, some three miles to the south-west of Chaman-i-Bed. Pillar No. 22 is on the highest point, the north-west corner of the mound marked in the map as Kara Tepe Khurd. The boundary-line runs straight across the Kushk valley at this point, just to the south of the spring and marsh at the head of the Chaman-i-Bed canal; and thence, turning to the north-east, follows the line of the tops of the highest hills to pillar No. 25, some three miles almost due south of Hauz-i-Khan.

From this point the boundary turns eastward to the pillar No. 27, about half a mile to the south of Chah-i-Nakhash, a narrow well lined with tamarisk, and some 80 feet in depth —the only well, in fact, between the Kushk and the Kashan. Then, turning a little more to the north, the line runs on across the hills to pillar No. 30 on the left bank of the

---

[1] This portion of the frontier from pillar No. 19 to pillar No. 35 was subsequently rectified in the final negotiations at St Petersburg, described in chapter xxvii.

Kashan stream, below Robat-i-Kashan, and on in a north-easterly direction across the hills and the western half of the lower portion of the Maruchak valley, to pillar No. 35, on the left bank of the Murghab river, at a point 150 yards to the south of the head of the Band-i-Nadir canal, and almost due west of the Maruchak fort. From there the boundary runs northwards down the centre of the river-bed to pillar No. 36, on the top of the low hills on the right bank forming the natural northern frontier of the Maruchak valley, at the point where the river, sweeping round to the extreme eastern side of the valley, cuts off all further communication along that bank. From this point the line follows a general easterly and north-easterly direction across the hills to pillar No. 41, to the north of Kilah Wali, beyond which the Maimanah district commences.

I have given this short technical description of the boundary to enable the line to be followed on the map, and also to be compared with the terms laid down in the Protocol of the 10th September 1885, published in the last blue-book, on which the Commissioners had to work.

The ground traversed by this boundary during its entire length of some 180 miles is almost entirely pastoral, the only exception being the narrow strips of cultivation in the valleys of the Hari Rud, the Kushk, the Kashan, and the Murghab. The only culturable land at Zulfikar lies to the south of the mouth of the pass, in the river-valley, and the greater portion of that is on the left bank in Persian territory. Zulfikar has been hitherto entirely uninhabited; but an Afghan frontier-post has now been located in the lines vacated by the Russians, and cultivators may possibly soon be settled in the valley under their protection. The bed of the Hari Rud is here well wooded with tamarisk and other low jungle, and the traces of irrigation-channels through all the culturable ground show that the place was once well cultivated. The Zulfikar pass, or rather the defiles known by that name, leading up through the two successive lines of cliffs that here run parallel to the river, has already been described. The boundary-line, running along the crest of the second scarp up to the top of the Dengli Dagh hills, is so well marked by nature that it can never be mistaken. Ak Robat and Sumba Karez, the two places beyond, are both at present uninhabited; but both possess a good supply of water, and will probably become the Russian and Afghan frontier-posts respectively, in this direction, though no troops have been located at either place up to the present, so far as we know.

Up to Sumba Karez there was no discussion between the Commissioners regarding the demarcation, the line to be followed having been so clearly laid down in the Protocol of the 10th September that no discussion or divergence of opinion was possible. A glance at the map, though, will show how the Russian claims went on increasing beyond that point. From Sumba Karez to Chaman-i-Bed the boundary-line was so drawn by the Commissioners as to give both Au Rahak and Islim, belonging to Afghanistan and Russia respectively, each its due share of grazing-lands on both banks of the stream, so as to prevent the chance of quarrels, if possible, by the too close contact of the shepherds and flocks on either side. Both places are uninhabited; and as the water of the Shorab or Egrigeuk stream is too salt for irrigation even, there is not much likelihood of there ever being any large population along its banks.

At Chaman-i-Bed, some 80 miles from Zulfikar, the second strip of cultivated land is reached. The valley of the Kushk here is entirely uninhabited, and has only been cultivated of late years by Panjdeh Turkomans. As a matter of fact, there are no habitations down the Kushk valley on the Afghan side north of the Jamshidi headquarters at Kushk itself; and the whole of Badghis having been depopulated by Turkoman raids, the Panjdeh Sariks were pretty well free to come and go when they pleased, their only restriction being the fear of Teke raiders from Merv. In this way of late years the Sariks have been in the habit of cultivating land at various places along the banks of the Kushk, each little field being cultivated under the shelter of one of their round mud-towers of refuge, in which a man armed with a gun was pretty sure to be let alone by any passing *alaman*. A glance at the approximate line of Russian claims on the sketch-map will show how the Russian Commissioners attempted to make capital out of this occasional cultivation, and how seriously they endeavoured to work the clauses regarding cultivation and pasturage in the Protocol of the 10th September—so seriously, indeed, that they actually claimed all the land for some 35 miles to the south, and up to within 15 miles of Kushk itself. Sir West Ridgeway, however, stood up firmly against this, and the boundary-line, as will be seen by the map, was, after some discussion, eventually drawn across the Kushk valley at Kara Tepe Khurd, 30 miles to the north of Chahar Darah, the point the Russians wished to lay claim to. The portion of the Kushk valley embracing Kara Tepe and Kara Tepe Khurd has already been fully described. I need only add that the Chaman-i-Bed valley is irrigated by a canal drawn from the stream a little less than a mile and a half to the south of the ruins of the Chaman-i-Bed fort, an old mud-building, of which only a bit of the walls is now left standing. The Kushk sometimes runs dry at this part of its course, but the canal is still fed from a spring rising in the middle of a reedy swamp, by the side of which the canal takes off from the stream. In former days the valley of the Kushk must have been largely populated; but now it is quite deserted, and the old canals have mostly fallen out of use. The last of these on the Afghan side takes off from the stream some three miles to the south of the Kara Tepe Khurd mound, and flowing north past Kara Tepe Khurd, exhausts itself about

M

half a mile to the south of the Chaman-i-Bed fort, on the high ground to the east of the Chaman-i-Bed canal. The boundary-line having been drawn straight across the valley at Kara Tepe Khurd, leaves a portion of this high level land, irrigable from the Kara Tepe Khurd canal, on the Russian side of the border; but a proviso in the demarcation Protocol records the fact that the Russians have no claim to water from any canal the head of which is in Afghan territory, and thus any disputes about water on this score will, it is hoped, be avoided.

The land, though, in the Kushk valley, only gets properly watered if a good spring rainfall brings the stream well down in flood; and the crops in this valley are often dried up and lost, they say, for want of water. Consequently, there will always be the chance of complaints from Russian subjects in the lower parts of the Kushk valley against the excessive consumption of water by the Afghans higher up; but this is only one of the many difficulties consequent on the surrender of Panjdeh. The water-supply, cultivation, and pasturage belonging to Panjdeh, is so mixed up with that belonging to the remainder or upper portion of the Kushk, Kashan, and Murghab valleys, that to delimitate a frontier across these valleys was not only a work of great difficulty, but, when done, the boundary is only an arbitrary line based on the circumstances of the moment rather than on any permanent and natural basis. The northern frontier of Panjdeh beyond Sari Yazi, on the other hand, is the natural and traditional frontier of Herat; and to have demarcated a boundary between Panjdeh on the one side, and Merv and Sarakhs on the other, would have been a work of no difficulty whatever, while the ample stretch of waterless country on either side would have been a sure safeguard against all future quarrels. Russia, by the acquisition of Panjdeh, however, has got past the desert frontier, and well down within the radius of Afghan influence; and at first sight it would seem as if there can be but little doubt that the Russian foot now advanced will at some future time be either advanced still further or withdrawn altogether, and that a frontier thus arbitrarily defined, as this has been, cannot be expected to be permanent. But the boundary has this essential advantage, that having once been defined, it cannot be crossed with impunity, and any future violation of that frontier must necessarily be an act of war. It is this latter circumstance that lends the frontier its importance, and renders it so incumbent on Sir West Ridgeway to take every precaution in his power to obviate the chance of border squabbles, and to secure as far as possible the smooth working of the frontier arrangements for the future. So far as the Kushk valley is concerned, a small Afghan frontier-post has been located at Kara Tepe Khurd; and we hear that a battalion of Trans-Caspian Rifles is to be located on the Russian side at Chaman-i-Bed. East of Chaman-i-Bed, the hills through which the boundary runs, like those on the west, are simply used for pasturage, though marks here and there in the hollows show that the ground in places has been cultivated for rain crops at some previous time.

The third strip of cultivation is reached some 37 miles to the north-east of Chaman-i-Bed, in the valley of the Kashan stream. This valley is comprised of a narrow strip of level culturable soil, about half a mile in width, with a small stream winding through it. The water of this stream, as a rule, is entirely used up for irrigation, and the stream itself below Robat-i-Kashan is generally dry except during the spring floods, when it becomes an unfordable torrent. The canal on which the Panjdeh Sariks depend for their cultivation in the northern portion of this valley takes off from the right bank of the stream, some three or four miles below Robat-i-Kashan, and irrigates the land down the right bank on to Panjdeh. Although the head of this canal lies some four miles to the south of the straight line from Hauz-i-Khan to Maruchak—the Protocol of the 10th September laid down that the line should be nearly straight—still, it was so desirable that the Panjdeh Sariks should have the command of the head of the canal upon which they were dependent for their irrigation, that Sir West Ridgeway agreed to concede this point in their favour; but not content with this, the Russians, as will be seen by the map, claimed the valley all the way up to Babulai, nearly 25 miles farther south. This, however, Sir West Ridgeway entirely refused to concede, and gained his point, as will be seen by the line of settlement. Robat-i-Kashan is simply an old ruined rest-house, and is entirely deserted at present; in fact, the whole Kashan valley is uninhabited. The Panjdeh Sariks have hitherto been its only occupants, cultivating the land but not residing thereon.

The Maruchak valley, some 14 miles farther north-east, the fourth and last cultivated strip, is also entirely uninhabited on the Afghan side. The nearest habitation on the right bank of the Murghab is at Karawal Khana, 12 miles to the south of the Maruchak fort; while on the left bank there is no habitation at all right away up to Bala Murghab, 10 miles beyond that again. Any land that hitherto has been cultivated in the Maruchak valley has been cultivated by Panjdeh Sariks. The natural frontier between Maruchak and Panjdeh is at the northern end of the Maruchak valley, where the hills, closing in to the river on both sides, separate the Maruchak lands from Panjdeh. The river, which seems at some former time to have run down the western side at the northern end of the Maruchak valley, has apparently changed its course, and sweeping across the valley, now washes the hills on the eastern side. As it is now, the river, thus sweeping so straight across the lower end of the valley, forms a capital naturally marked frontier of itself; and so far as the right or fort bank of the river is concerned, the present settlement leaves little to be desired. The Amir, I believe, specially approves of having the river between himself and the Russians. The Band-i-Nadir canal on the left bank was the cause of the great difficulty in the settlement at Maruchak. Whether originally taken off from the river in its old bed at the point marked Band-i-Nadir in the map, it is now impossible to say; but there is no doubt that in olden days the canal was a work of much greater magnitude than it is at present. Its former course, it is said, can be traced almost all the way down the valley of the Murghab to Yulatan, a distance of some 90 miles to the north of Pul-i-Khishti; whereas now it is practically exhausted before it reaches Pul-i-Khishti itself, barely 20 miles below Band-i-Nadir, and the water for the cultivation beyond is drawn from the valley of the Kushk. When or how the present head of the canal came to be dug in the Maruchak valley, some nine miles to the south of Band-i-Nadir, cannot well be ascertained; but presumably, when the river deserted the old bed, the remedy was applied of digging a canal from the river higher up into the old bed, so as to preserve the ancient canal-system in force. The result of this is, that the actual head of the Band-i-Nadir canal is now exactly opposite the Maruchak fort. That Russia should hold the command of the canal-head on which the very existence of Panjdeh is dependent was only fair; and for this reason Sir West Ridgeway acceded so far to the Russian claims as to assent to the boundary-line being drawn in a straight line across from the head of the canal in the Kashan valley to the head of the Band-i-Nadir canal on the left bank of the Murghab, almost due west of Maruchak, instead of to the "point north of Maruchak" laid down in the Protocol of the 10th September. By this settlement some culturable land on the left bank of the Murghab between the head of the Band-i-Nadir canal and the hills bordering the Maruchak valley on the west falls to Russia, which is irrigable from two canals taken off from the river higher up in Afghan territory; but owing to the proviso in the demarcation Protocol, Russian subjects are to have no claim to water for this land from Afghan canals.

The Maruchak fort I have before described. It will, I presume, now be regarrisoned by Afghan troops; but it is never likely to be a strong place, capable of any resistance worth speaking of, under Afghan *régime*. The bulk of the garrison will probably be quartered at Bala Murghab, as before. Maruchak will simply be held as the frontier post. By the demarcation of the frontier, Russian subjects for the future, so far as the Maruchak valley is concerned, will be cut off entirely from the right or fort bank of the river, and will be restricted on the left bank to the land north of the boundary-line between the Band-i-Nadir canal-head and the hills to the west. The Afghans, in their turn, are the principal gainers, as they will now be able to occupy all the land in the Maruchak valley on the right bank, and two-thirds of that on the left bank, which they have never been able to occupy before, and which has hitherto been only lying waste or been cultivated by Panjdeh Sariks.

The Russian Commissioners made great difficulties about the settlement at Maruchak, and put forward so many claims, that, what with the Russians on one side, and the Afghans on the other, it seemed at one time as if no settlement could ever be come to at all. The Russians, for instance, I believe, at one time demanded the cession of a strip of land some two miles in length on the right bank of the Murghab, close to the Maruchak fort, on the plea of building a *bund* across the river at the head of the Band-i-Nadir canal. Kazi Saad-ud-Din, the Afghan representative, and the governor of Herat, on the other hand, not only refused to accede to this demand, but refused to agree to any part of the settlement from Hauz-i-Khan to Maruchak without a reference to the

Amir on the subject. All these conflicting interests had to be reconciled, the Russian claims moderated, and the Afghan representatives brought to reason; and it was with no small difficulty that Sir West Ridgeway was able to effect any agreement at all regarding the boundary, before the two Commissioners separated to go into winter-quarters at the end of last year. During the winter a reply was received from the Amir cordially accepting the frontier settlement, and severely censuring his representatives for their ill-advised obstruction, at the same time giving his consent to the construction of the proposed *bund*, or dam, by the Russians across the river at the canal-head, on the condition that the *bund* was not to be used as a bridge, or held by any military post. As soon as the snow was off the ground again, therefore, the demarcation of the frontier from Hauz-i-Khan eastwards was carried out in accordance with the terms of the agreement previously recorded, and the settlement, so far as the Herat district is concerned, completed. The question of this *bund*, though, is one of the things that may still give rise to future complications. The possibility of making a *bund* at all at the head of the canal has still to be proved, as the banks thereabout lie low, especially on the Afghan side. The Murghab, as a rule, is a deep, rather slow-running river, some 40 or 50 yards in breadth, with comparatively few fords, and most difficult to cross at times. There are a couple of fords at Bala Murghab, and a similar number at Karawal Khana, Maruchak, and Panjdeh; but these are impassable during the spring and summer floods, and below Panjdeh they say the river is unfordable almost right down to Merv. The ancient bridges have long since been destroyed; and though there are the remains of one standing at Maruchak, and of another some 18 or 20 miles higher up, near Bala Murghab, still nothing has ever been done to repair them, and communication across the river is often entirely cut off. The Murghab in this respect is very different from its affluent, the Kushk, which not only often runs dry in its course, but at its best is almost entirely used up for irrigation. Last year, shortly before the Russian attack on Panjdeh, the Kushk, at its junction with the Murghab just below Pul-i-Khishti, was simply a sandy bed with a few inches of water flowing over it. Yet, like all streams rising in the mountains, the Kushk is liable to sudden floods, as the unfortunate Afghans on its left bank found out to their cost, when, owing to the spring rains in the hills, it came down in full flood just the night before the Russian attack, and cut off their retreat the next morning.

Panjdeh, as the home of the Sarik Turkomans is called, is not a village or a town, but a long narrow valley, some 25 miles in length, and averaging about two miles in breadth, containing a series of hamlets of Turkoman *kibitkas*. There is not a house in the place. The only building of any sort in use that I know of is a small, low, flat-roofed *musjid*, built of mud, at the northern end of the valley in the Sokti settlements, the peculiar property of Juma Eshan, the head priest of the Sariks, one of the men who behaved so staunchly to the British officers, and who stuck by them so faithfully when matters looked so threatening after the Russian attack. Juma Eshan, by the way, is a son of the old Khalifah of Merv, who in his time behaved so well to Dr Wolff on his travels.

What the name of Panjdeh, literally the five villages, originally arose from, I cannot say. From the fact of the Sariks being divided into five clans or sections, each with its separate settlements, it would look at first sight as if they had given the name to the place; but this is not the case, as the name is of ancient date, being mentioned, so Rawlinson says, by Hafiz Abru in A.D. 1417. The Sariks only occupied Panjdeh some thirty years ago, when they were turned out of Merv by the Tekes. Before then it was held by a section of the Ersaris, whom the Sariks in their turn displaced.

The Sariks have no hereditary chiefs or rulers. They are commonwealths pure and simple. Every man seems to think himself as good as his neighbour, and wealth is the only criterion. A wealthy man becomes naturally an influential man, and the title *Bai*, given to the more wealthy, is the only mark of distinction that I remember amongst them. For instance, Said Bai, our camel-contractor, is a man, I believe, who has suffered various reverses of fortune. He has at last apparently fallen on his legs, in so far that, after a year or more's enjoyment of our contract, he has now become the owner of so many camels that he richly merits the title of *Bai*, which he formerly only enjoyed on sufferance, in remembrance of the wealth he had lost. I must say, better camels, and more willing hard-working camel-men, I have never seen.

The title of *Sirdar* amongst the Turkomans has nothing to do with rank or position; it is simply a title given to the best leaders of raids, and to the most knowing guides—and well indeed they seem to deserve it. Gok Sirdar, Beg Murad Sirdar, and others whom I could mention, seem to know every bit of country from the Oxus on the east to the Hari Rud on the west. Every well, every pathway, every hill and hollow, seems to be engraven on their memory; and no matter where they are, they are never at fault, and the way they will guide you across country from one place to another is simply marvellous. Now that raiding has been put down, the peculiar art or faculty necessary for the making of a good guide will, I fear, to a certain extent die out; and I very much doubt if the next generation will be half as good men in that respect as their fathers across the *chul*.

Each section of the Sariks has certain influential men, who generally lead and represent the others; but the obedience accorded to them is purely nominal, and till one sees a certain number of the people collected together and under the influence of some excitement, one has little idea of what an unruly and turbulent lot they are. As a rule, the hamlets are so quiet that one little suspects what a slight breeze will blow down the veil and show the Turkoman in his real colours; but just witness a race-meeting or any scene of popular resort, and see how little attention is paid to the leading men, and how the mob cheat and quarrel amongst themselves for the prizes, and what thoroughly unscrupulous rapacious beggars some of them are. The more one knows of them, the more one marvels that, amidst all the excitement and temptation consequent on the Russian attack last year, the British officers at Panjdeh were left unmolested.

The different sections of the Sariks are by no means particularly amicably inclined to each other, and there is a great deal of internal jealousy. The five main sections have each their separate location, and mix comparatively little amongst themselves. The Soktis, the richest as well as the most numerous and influential section, hold the land on the left or western bank of the river from Panjdeh Kuhnah, or old Panjdeh, right away down to Sari Yazi, a distance of some 35 miles, though their cultivation does not extend at present beyond Kurban Niaz, some 13 miles north of Ak Tepe. The Harzagis hold the land on the left bank from Bazaar Takhta southwards up to Maruchak, while the Khorasanlis, who are comparatively small in numbers, are located between the two. The right bank is divided between the two other sections, the Bairach and the Alishah. This division of the lands, though, was only effected some time after the Sariks came to Panjdeh. They only came there by parties and detachments, as one after another they were driven out of Merv. The fighting at Merv went on, I have been told by a man who took part in it, for two or three years; and it was only when the Akhal Tekes came to the

aid of their Sarakhs brethren that the Sariks were finally
defeated and hostilities came to an end, though the enmity
then engendered between the two tribes still exists. Long
before all the fighting was over, the wealthy Sariks who had
anything to lose had left, and only the poorer portion remained to fight it out. The Soktis, the richest both in
flocks and wealth, almost all left Merv, I have been told, at
the first attack, and went off in a body to Panjdeh, where
they settled. The remainder of the tribe went off by degrees, some to Chahar Jui on the Oxus, others to Panjdeh,
each making their escape as best they could. Those who
went to Chahar Jui did not stay there long. The place was
already so thickly populated, they said, that land could not
be got except by purchase, whereas at Panjdeh it was free;
so they, too, left Chahar Jui and made their way to Panjdeh,
travelling along the banks of the Oxus to Karki, and thence
to Andkhui. From Andkhui those who had baggage-animals
and water-*mussucks* crossed the *chul* by the direct road over
the Kara Bel plateau, while the remainder went round
through Maimanah and Kilah Wali. At first the Soktis
held the sole tenure of the Panjdeh land; but each section,
as it increased in numbers, got strong enough to enforce its
claim, and the land was finally divided off in the manner I
have named, the only difference now being that a good many
Khorasanlis, and some of the Soktis, have moved into the
Kushk valley and settled at Kilah Maur and other neighbouring places, and the Harzagis spread southwards to Karawal Khana and Kilah Wali. The occupants of these two
latter places remain Afghan subjects, and the question of
their future disposal has only just been settled. The Afghan
Government, fearing a further extension of the ethnological
arguments formerly so successfully advanced by Russia in
the case of Panjdeh, decline to keep any Sariks near their
borders, and have decided to remove all the Sariks remaining
at Kilah Wali and Karawal Khana to Chahar Shamba and

other places farther south in the hills where they are better under control, and to put Afghan settlers in their place. The rumour of this move operated forcibly on the Sariks—so much so, that as soon as they heard it, they commenced to vacate Kilah Wali and to troop back to Panjdeh in numbers; and it is said that of the 300 odd families lately located there, hardly 30 are now left on Afghan soil.

At the time of the Sarik occupation of Panjdeh, Maruchak, and afterwards Kilah Wali, were both occupied by the Jamshidis before they finally settled down at Kushk after their return from Urganj in Khiva. No doubt the Jamshidis have the prior right to this ground; and the old ruined fort of Kaurmach, or Guchmach, as it is variously called, some four miles above Kilah Wali, is still locally known as the Jamshidis' fort, and is said to have been occupied by them both before and after their move to Urganj. At present the place is an utter ruin. The walls, some 300 yards square, are built of mud, and are almost entirely gone—so much so, that a few years hence they will simply form a square mound like all the other old ruined forts in this country. When visiting the place the other day, I was much struck at its utter desolation. The two gates—east and west—were still partly standing, and also the little inner fort, some 40 yards square. In the centre of that, again, there were the remains of a circular double-storeyed brick tower, similar to that in the Kilah Wali fort; but beyond that there was not a brick in the place. The whole inside was bare and damp, and the footprints of a tiger in the mud were the only noticeable feature about it. Yet this fort stands at the mouth of a fine valley, coming down from the Band-i-Turkistan, and ought to be a most fertile and favourite spot instead of the utter waste it is. However, I notice that now the boundary has been settled, the Jamshidis are flocking in numbers up the Kilah Wali valley; and if, as I hear, the governor of Herat has collected 1000 odd families of Afghan and

Ghilzai nomads to colonise the frontier, no doubt both Kaurmach and Maruchak will soon resound again with the signs of life.

The great want of Panjdeh, of course, is culturable land. The long narrow valley known as Panjdeh cannot produce nearly sufficient grain for the population of nearly 8000 families which it now contains, and the consequence is that they have to import it from Maimanah. This was the main reason of the emigration of Sariks from Panjdeh to Yulatan. The latter place was originally held by the Salors; but they all fled before the Persian advance in 1860, and were allowed to settle for a time at Maruchak, on the land vacated by the Jamshidis, till the Sariks fell out with them owing to their thieving propensities, and drove them clean away. Similarly, the Sariks drove out the Ersaris, who held Panjdeh before their advent from Merv. In fact, the shiftings and changings that have been going on amongst these Turkoman tribes are endless; and, possessing no houses, they are always ready to load up and move on at a moment's notice. The Sariks who first went to Yulatan had a very rough time of it, I believe, at the hands of the Tekes, who are said to have at once carried off all their sheep; and the consequence is, that the Yulatan Sariks are now almost all agriculturists and tillers of the soil, in contradistinction to the pastoral members of the tribe at Panjdeh. The great advantage about Yulatan is the unfailing supply of water, the canal drawn off from the Murghab at Band-i-Kazakli being, they say, deep enough to carry a camel off its legs.

As an instance of the enmity between the Sariks and the Tekes, I remember a story told me regarding a fight which occurred some years ago at Chaman-i-Bed. A prisoner, escaping from Merv, gave notice to his brethren at Panjdeh that a large Teke raid, numbering some 2000 men all told, horse and foot, was on the way up. The Sariks collected very nearly an equal number of men, and moved across to Kilah Maur, sending out scouts (of whom my informant was one) in all directions, to watch the Tekes. The latter were traced by these scouts to the salt lakes at Nimaksar, and thence on to Ak Robat. The Sariks moved up to Chaman-i-Bed; but thinking that the Tekes, from the direction they were taking, were bent on a raid into the Herat valley, they were not particularly careful. My informant, who had brought the news of the Tekes' whereabouts, was sent out again with a few men to keep watch on them, while the rest went to sleep. Scouting up through the hills on the left bank of the Egrigeuk stream, he found that the Tekes had moved in the meantime from Ak Robat to Islim. At the same time, as it afterwards turned out, the Tekes sent a scouting-party down the right bank to Chaman-i-Bed, who, seeing the fires of a large camp there, and having no idea that the Sariks had news of their approach, went back as hard as they could, and gave notice to the main body that a large *kafila*, or merchants' caravan, was encamped at Chaman-i-Bed. The Tekes at once started off to attack it, and the horsemen, in their eagerness to be the first at the plunder, left the footmen behind, and pushed on by themselves. They charged down on the camp with a yell, just before dawn, thinking they had nothing but a party of traders to deal with. The Sariks were taken by surprise, but still kept together, covered by their footmen; and directly it was light, charged the Teke horsemen, and routed them in turn, and then falling on the footmen, who were coming straggling up behind, intent on nothing but the expected plunder, cut them all up in detail, and killed almost every man of them. This is the Sariks' side of the story. What the Tekes say on the subject I do not know; but the Sariks aver that they were freed from Teke raids for many a long day afterwards. No wonder, though, that the feeling between the two tribes is not particularly cordial.

The chief wealth of the Panjdeh Sariks is in their sheep. These are reckoned by flocks, each flock consisting of from 1200 to 1500 head, which are grazed about the *chul*, summer and winter, under the charge of a shepherd and his assistant. These men, equipped with a suit of clothes and a couple of donkeys, one for water and the other for food, wander about the country with their flocks from year's end to year's end, rarely or never apparently coming into the settlements except with the ewes at the lambing-season in March. No wonder that they are wild-looking men, almost as wild as their own strong shaggy sheep-dogs. Yet even they are susceptible of the charms of music. Last year I remember meeting a couple of Salor itinerant musicians on their way back to Sarakhs after a round of visits amongst the Sarik shepherds grazing their flocks near the salt lakes. These men played a sort of flute made out of reeds—not the ordinary reed of the river-beds, but a stronger and larger kind grown in the hills, they said, on the Khorasan border. They gave me a performance on the roadside; and wonderful music it was, and much appreciated apparently by the shepherds, as they were driving back with them several sheep, the gifts of their patrons. The shepherds certainly seem to have wonderful power as to the disposal of their masters' sheep. It is a point of honour with them always to kill a sheep for the entertainment of any passing guest, and they are also allowed to kill as much as they require for their own consumption; but as a matter of fact, the wolves generally kill as much and more for them than they can possibly eat. These brutes are always hanging round the flocks; and often in a single night they will kill and maim many sheep, always, I believe, seizing and lacerating their tails, and going on to attack another before the first is dead, thus wounding far more than they kill. Between 20,000 and 30,000 sheep used to be sent annually to Bokhara, it is said, and sold there at prices varying from Rs. 8 to Rs. 10

apiece. A good deal of trade seems to be carried on between Panjdeh and Sarakhs, rice being largely exported, and oil-seeds brought back in return. A good many skins are also exported to Bokhara, more especially fox-skins, which sell for about a rupee apiece. The Panjdeh horses, though doing capital work for their owners, are not much to look at according to our ideas; and so far as I can learn, they are not highly priced—50 *tillahs*, or Rs. 270, being apparently considered to be a long price, and above the usual average. It is generally allowed on all sides that the Akhal Tekes possess by far the best breed of horses.

The great feature of Panjdeh, though, and in fact the chief manufacture, is the carpets. These are made entirely by the women, and really the best are so fine that they are more fitted for tablecloths than for carpets. Every girl is supposed to make the carpets for her husband's *kibitkas* before she marries, though how she does it I don't know, as it is supposed to take five women about eight months to make one of their usual large-sized carpets. The richer families generally hire the services of the wives and daughters of their poorer neighbours to assist in the manufacture of their carpets; and probably it is only the rich members of the tribe who attempt the manufacture of the fine silk carpets and bags with which the best *kibitkas* are ornamented. The wool they use is first steeped and washed in alum-water, and then dyed with dyes imported from Bokhara; but the silk used is purchased all ready dyed from Bokhara.

I wish I could give a just description of a Turkoman marriage procession. It is a sight worth seeing. The bride, who is generally hung all over with the curious massive silver jewellery peculiar to the Turkomans, seems to be escorted about by her lady friends (who are all dressed in the height of Turkoman fashion), and followed by a crowd of women and gaily decked camels. The wonderful scarves and mantles, and the half-concealed but not uncomely faces of the younger women, all make up a scene not easily to be forgotten.

The place marked " Old Panjdeh " in the map is simply the ruins of an old brick fort, built by no one knows who. New Panjdeh is merely a square enclosed on three sides by mud walls, now also entirely deserted. Band-i-Nadir is a small *bund* or dam, made of tamarisk-bushes thrown across the old bed of the river at the place where, I presume, the canal originally took off before the river changed its course: whether or no, the *bund* only serves now to catch the water brought into the old bed by the canal which takes off opposite the Maruchak fort. There is hardly a single tree in the whole Panjdeh valley: the Turkomans seem to be too wild and unsettled to care for arboriculture in any form, and are only now apparently just beginning to realise what a fruit-garden is. Panjdeh ought to be rich in antiquities; and had we been there only long enough, I have little doubt many good coins and relics would have been obtained. Several curious jars and household vessels were found in the site of an old buried city on the right bank of the river; and a most perfect set of caves, cut in the sandstone, were discovered and opened out by Captain de Laessoe on a hill overlooking the valley on the eastern side. I forget the exact length of the central corridor of these caves, or how many sets of rooms opened off from it on either side; but the rooms were all perfect in their way, many of them with a staircase leading to an upper storey; and it is curious to note that each set of rooms had a sort of well or shaft some 2 feet in diameter, and 8 or 10 feet in depth, sunk down in the solid rock, presumably for the storage of water, though how that water was ever carried up the hillside from the river away below, I cannot tell. These caves, however, are fully described in Captain de Laessoe's paper published in the Proceedings of the Royal Geographical Society for September 1885. The question of the ancient geography of this country, and especially the identification of the site of the ancient city of Merv-ul-Rud, located by Sir Henry Rawlinson at Maruchak, according to his paper published in the above-mentioned number of the Royal Geographical Society's Proceedings, is naturally the cause of much interest amongst the various members of the Commission, and many are the theories broached on the subject. The general idea at present is against Maruchak, I think. In the first place, Maruchak is on the eastern bank of the river, on the same side as Kilah Wali, which Rawlinson identifies with the ancient Talikan; whereas Ebn Haukel states that the river runs between Merv-ul-Rud and Talikan, and is crossed over by a bridge. Again, Abu Zaid states that Merv-ul-Rud is six stages from Herat, on the road to Balkh; and as the highroad to Balkh, one would think, would in all probability have run up the Kilah Wali valley, the great natural highway in the country, or else through the hills to the south of it, it would seem to follow that Merv-ul-Rud must have been somewhere opposite the roads into that valley, leaving Maruchak considerably out of the way to the north. Now, of the two old bridges still partly standing between Bala Murghab and Panjdeh, the first, just below Maruchak, may possibly be the bridge of Dizeh, which, as Rawlinson mentions, was twice repaired by Timur in A.H. 782 and 785 (A.D. 1380-83). The second is situated some four or five miles below Bala Murghab, where the road from Mangan debouches into the Murghab valley. Following up this road from Herat, we find that it is divided into exactly six stages, the very number named by all the ancient geographers as the distance from Herat to Merv-ul-Rud; each stage except Mangan being marked by a *robat* or rest-house, the ruins of which are still extant—viz., Robat-i-Baba, Kushk, Robat-i-Kolari, Torshaikh, Mangan, and Robat-i-Ishmail. One might suppose, therefore, that Merv-ul-Rud was situated somewhere on the left bank of the river, opposite or near to this bridge, which again is almost exactly opposite a road leading from the Murghab valley through the hills into the Kilah Wali valley. But unfortunately, not the least sign of any ancient city has been found as yet in that neighbourhood; and so far, all our inquiries and all our theories on the subject have failed to lead to any definite result. Certainly there are said to be the foundations of other bridges still extant, though under water, and there are two other roads leading from the valley of the Murghab to Maimanah, either of which may have been the highroad from Herat to Balkh in olden days. The first runs from Bala Murghab straight eastwards through the low hills at the foot of the Band-i-Turkistan to the old ruined fort known as Takht-i-Khatun, and thence on past the well-known *ziarat* of Khwajah Kandu to Kaisar and Maimanah, and is said to be a good and well-marked road the whole way. The second is the route known as the Kara Jangal pass, which passes from Herat through Karukh, Tagao Robat, Naratu, Kilah Nao, Darah-i-Bam to Darband-i-Kilrekta on the Murghab, and thence over the Tirband-i-Turkistan, locally known as Kara Jangal, to Takht-i-Khatun. This latter route over the Kara Jangal pass we have not as yet been able to explore, but it is passable for camels I am told, and therefore must be a fairly good road; and moreover, the ruins of an old *robat*, about half-way up the pass to the north-east of Band-i-Kilrekta, prove that it was once a regular caravan-road. Both of these roads, it will be seen, converge at Takht-i-Khatun. Who the fair lady may have been who made this place her throne I cannot say, but doubtless the place was important in its day. At present it consists of nothing but the remains of a mud-fort, 600 yards in length and 200 in breadth, situated at the foot and to the west of two low hills, between and near the junction of two streams known as the Kara Jangal and Khwajah Langari, which unite and form the rivulet running into the Kilah Wali stream at Kaurmach. The site is an excellent one, just at the foot of the mountains, in the midst of a wide level plain or valley of fertile land; and the remains of old *karezes* or underground canals show that the place was formerly well cultivated. When visiting the place the other day, I could not help wondering if this might not have been the ancient Talikan. There was not a stone or a brick in the place, however—nothing whatever to afford any clue to its age—nothing but earthen walls, and those not of the thickest. But then, neither are there any bricks at Herat or at Old Kandahar, or at any of the ruins of the ancient towns in Seistan; and here was a place, of course much smaller, but still very much after the fashion of Old Kandahar, as the hills above it had evidently been levelled at the top and fortified, something like the rocky Chihal Zinah range above Old Kandahar. However, speculation was useless, and the Jamshidis in the little hamlet below could not help me to solve the mystery. They could only tell me that the more modern mud square fort, away in the valley below, was the work, it was said, of their ancestors, and that the land right up to Khwajah Kandu belonged by tradition to them. Certainly, from what I could see, the Jamshidis had made up their minds to put this tradition into force, as I found lots of new settlements all about the Kilah Wali valley and the hills to the south of it—far more than were to be found there last year.

The Herat district extends as far north as Kilah Wali and Kaurmach; and it was with the view of getting this last north-eastern portion settled, at any rate with as little delay as possible, that Sir West Ridgeway consented, before leaving Maruchak for winter-quarters at Chahar Shamba, to an agreement fixing the boundary eastwards from Maruchak to the meridian of Sofi, at a distance of between 15 and 20 miles to the north of the Kilah Wali stream. For the actual demarcation of this portion, it was necessary to wait for the completion of the maps of the Russian topographers intrusted with the survey of this section of the frontier; and these maps were not completed till after the middle of March, some days after Sir West Ridgeway's return to Maruchak. What the delay was I cannot tell, but I must say the country just to the east of the Maruchak is the most hopelessly intricate task possible for a surveyor, and all the Russian topographers here declare that they have never had such troublesome work in their lives before.

Imagine a huge tumbled mass of hillocks, most of them very steep, and rising straight up from a succession of ravines and valleys, locally known as *shors*, which here run down in long parallel lines from the edge of the Kara Bel plateau and fall into the Kilah Wali stream, with the exception of one—the Galla Chashmah Shor—which falls into the Maruchak valley at Pusht-i-Hamwar. These *shors* are, most of them, very narrow in places—just wide enough, in fact, for the tiny stream of salt water and mud, which, running down in wet weather, makes the roads up these valleys almost, if not quite, impassable. The hillocks are mostly too steep to make good pasture-ground, and the tract near the Kilah Wali stream is not, therefore, nearly so rich in pasturage as the more level ground on and bordering the Kara Bel plateau, which at this season of the year is simply one vast meadow, covered with all sorts of grasses; whereas the hillocks are only scantily covered on their northern slopes, and have little or nothing on the southern. Standing on any high point in the hills, it is curious, on looking north, to see everything tinged with brown, and on turning to the south to find all the brightest green. In addition to the grass on the hills, there are plants of many descriptions, and lots of flowers, amongst which bright red tulips, mauve-coloured cowslips, buttercups, dandelions, and other little yellow flowers, are in endless profusion, while wild rhubarb grows everywhere. The camels, I notice, eat the rhubarb-leaves greedily, and in the winter I have seen the Turkomans digging up the roots for their camels; but the plant has no other use that I know of. The only water in all the country between Maruchak and Kilah Wali is at a spring called Khwajah Gogirdak, some 10 miles north of the Jamshidi hamlet at Bokun, 12 miles below or west of Kilah Wali. This place possesses, not one, but apparently a succession of springs, most of them sulphur-springs, as the name implies. At the head of the valley the stream is salt; then comes a narrow reedy marsh, with a spring of sulphur-water running out of a black hole, smelling and tasting most horribly bad, but not salt; while below that again, just where some white-coloured limestone rock suddenly crops up, the water is sweet and clear. The place must have been inhabited at some time, as there is a graveyard farther down the valley, where the stream falls into the *shor*, but now it is simply the resort of *shikaris* from all the country round. The banks of the stream are strewn with the horns of *mall* or wild sheep, which, I presume, have been killed and eaten here. They abound, they say, in the hillocks around, as also do pig; and man is not the only animal that preys on them, as the footmarks of a tiger were seen there—though how a tiger found his way to such a place I cannot think. The prompt conclusion of the settlement of this, the last portion of the Herat frontier, sets free the governor of Herat, who has been waiting at Bala Murghab all the winter; and not only will he be able to conclude his arrangements for the population of the frontier and return to Herat without further delay, but he goes back knowing full well that both lines of Russian advance up the Hari Rud and Murghab valleys have been closed, by this demarcation of the border, against any encroachment short of an actual declaration of war. The main object of the Mission has thus been accomplished.

CHAPTER XIII.

A SNOWSTORM IN THE CHUL.

CAMP KARAWAL KHANA, 15*th April* 1886.

AT last we have heard that the Russian Commission is crossing the Murghab at Maruchak, and that they propose to join us here. Small news in itself, but still all-important to us, who have now been encamped here nearly a month, awaiting the receipt of orders from his own Government by the Russian Commissioner, and for which there seemed every possibility of our being kept waiting another month. Had the Russians met us last month with the intention of settling the boundary, we should probably have been half-way to the Oxus by this time. However, better late than never, says an excellent proverb; and the breaking up of their winter camp looks as if the Russians had at last made up their minds, and consequently a few days hence may see us all at work again. We hope so sincerely, as this enforced idleness is trying to everybody. The weather is now charming, the thermometer not having risen above an average maximum of 65° in the shade this month; and we may fairly hope to have about done with all the snow and rain with which we have been visited so heavily of late.

As soon as the negotiations were brought to a standstill by Colonel Kuhlberg, Sir West Ridgeway moved his camp from Maruchak to this place, and the difference in the air caused by the change up those 12 miles of the Murghab valley was very remarkable. Maruchak is a notoriously unhealthy place—so much so, that I hear there is an old Persian proverb to that effect; but I must say none of our party have ever suffered there, though the Russians, I believe, have no liking for it. We set out on the 22d March, leaving the Russians at their winter camp on the other, the left bank of the river, at the lower end of the valley, some three miles within the Panjdeh border; and there they have remained ever since. At the time we left Maruchak the Murghab was still passable; but since then it has come down in flood, and now it is so high that for some days past the Russians have not been able to work their ferry-boat.

The camp at Chahar Shamba has been temporarily broken up, and all our winter tents and *kibitkas* have been left standing under the charge of an Usbeg guard, pending our return there with the Russian Commission. When Sir West Ridgeway found out that his stay at Karawal Khana might be indefinitely prolonged, he brought down Dr Owen and Captain Cotton, and the remainder of the infantry escort, and also Mr Ney Elias, who had remained there under medical treatment. We shall probably find most of the *kibitkas* in a state of collapse on our return, as I don't think they were warranted to stand the effect of such storms of snow and rain as we had on the 28th March and 5th April respectively, without some one to look after them. The cavalry escort, under the command of Major Bax, started for Andkhui some days before the snowstorm, and though they were detained on the road by the snow, they got through all right, and are now halting at Andkhui, pending further orders. Captain Maitland and Mr Merk are also *en route* to Andkhui, the former going on to Balkh, the latter making certain inquiries regarding the grazing rights, while Captain Griesbach is at Shibarghan on a geological tour. Captain Peacocke returned to camp here on the 11th, having completed his survey of the cultivation in both the Kushk and Kashan valleys, in company with Captain Kondratenko. He proceeded down to Maruchak again to-day to make a further survey of the ground at the head of the Band-i-Nadir canal, in company with Captain Gideonoff, and to report on the feasibility of, and amount of ground necessary for, building the *bund* across the river there proposed by Colonel Kuhlberg. His rejoining us here in camp was a matter of no small difficulty, as it turned out. The first we knew of his arrival was seeing him on the opposite side of the river; and as there was no other way of crossing, he just left his men and horses on the far bank and swam across to us. We rigged up a ferry with our little Berthon canvas boat in the evening, which enabled him to cross back again dry, but he had to wait till the next morning to swim his horses and camels across. The Russians, I believe, are crossing all their horses and camels over in the ferry-boat, which accounts for the time they are taking.

Major Holdich and I were out for some ten days with Captain Ilyin, putting up the pillars on the last portion of the Herat frontier, stretching eastwards from Maruchak, north of Kilah Wali, to the confines of the Maimanah territory, and we were caught by a snowstorm in the midst of the *chul*, which nearly did for us. I must say that such a thing as a snowstorm on the lowlands is said to be unknown here after the *Nouroz*, on New Year's Day on the 21st of March; and this storm, which was the severest we had all the winter through, seems to have played terrible havoc. The fruit-buds are entirely destroyed in many places, and all the little birds, that flocked here in numbers from I don't know where at the opening of spring, were killed in hundreds. Their bodies are still to be seen lying all over the country.

Starting from Karawal Khana on the 24th, our first day's

march led us up the Shor Sanam, a long narrow valley, which gradually got narrower and narrower, till, some 13 or 14 miles up, we found no road left at all except up the bed of the little salt muddy stream that formed the bottom of the ravine, and which was just wide enough for one camel at a time. The mud was so deep that it was all our horses and mules could do to get through it, and the wretched camels before long stuck altogether. This very narrow bit turned out to be some six or eight miles in length; and had we known it, we should have halted at the mouth; but not knowing what was before us, we pushed on, and the consequence was, that before we were half-way through, our animals were done, and we were only too glad to find a narrow ledge on the hillside, some 30 feet above the mud, to camp on. As luck would have it, down came a tremendous thunderstorm and caught us fairly in a trap. It rained hard all night and half the next day, and our camels and baggage were strewn all down the *shor*. The stream came down in flood, and the mud was worse than before. However, by evening of the 25th we managed to get all into camp. The Turkoman camel-men, always ready and willing to work, then set to and made a road along the hillside up to a side ravine, and next day we managed to get the camels out of the *shor*, and taking them over the hills, got all right to the water at Khwajah Gogirdak. The worst of it was, that our sheep, which it was impossible to drive up the *shor*, had to be tied on the camels, and were in a dying state when they got in, and had to be killed at once. The thunderstorm turned all the meat the same night, and we found ourselves started off on our trip the next morning without any meat rations at all, and no chance of getting any. We had a day's halt at Khwajah Gogirdak, to build a boundary pillar, and started again on the 28th for the Taidashti Shor, and the valley farther east, whence we hoped to get to the site proposed for the next pillar. The country there is very wild, just a tumbled mass of steep hillocks, with no way through it whatever, and almost utterly unknown and unvisited. Gok Sirdar was our only guide who had ever been near it, and he had a very hazy notion of the way about, but said he would be able to find his way to the next water at Pekenna, some 25 miles to the north-east. As it was, we only got about half-way to the Taidashti Shor when another storm came on, and we just got our tents pitched and our baggage up in time. At nightfall the rain changed into snow, and it snowed continuously for twenty-four hours. The 29th was a pretty miserable day for all of us. Snow being unknown, as a rule, out here after the *Nouroz*, we had made no provision against it. We had *mussucks* and *mussucks* full of water, just the one thing with the snow all round us that we did not want. Fortunately we had brought one or two camel-loads of tamarisk-wood from Khwajah Gogirdak, but not so much as we would have done had not the guides told us that we should find lots of wood ahead in the Taidashti Shor.

Not knowing, therefore, when the snowstorm might stop, we had to be very sparing of what wood we had, and I sat shivering all day in one of those wretched thin little 80-lb. Kabul tents that were sent up to us by the last convoy from the Rawal Pindi or Allahabad arsenals. The old 80-pounder was as warm a little tent as one could wish to have; but this new ordnance pattern is so thin that the wind whistles through it in every direction, and it is impossible to keep it warm. I tried to write, but the minute particles of snow driven in by the wind lay so thick on the paper that the ink ran in all directions; so beware for the future of the ordnance 80-pounder in a snowstorm. However, the snow stopped on the night of the 29th, and the morning of the 30th found us with a clear sky, but 12 or 15 inches of snow all round us. We determined at once to push on for Taidashti, so as to get some wood at any rate, and well it was that we did so. That night was bitterly cold, and the thermometer must have been very close to zero. When we sat down to dinner it was 22°, and when we got up for breakfast next morning it was only 12°; but what it was in the meantime we could only guess. We found lots of tamarisk-bushes all down the banks of the Taidashti Shor, and as our men could burn just as much as they liked to take the trouble to cut, they did not suffer in the least. The horses and mules were the things that suffered. Poor beasts! they had had nothing to eat for two days but a little barley, and now we were running short of that. We had brought no *bhoosa*, or thrashed straw, with us, knowing that there was plenty grazing everywhere in the *chul*. As a matter of fact, the grass was some three inches high in all the ravines, and the animals ate this so greedily that they even refused their grain. The muleteers, knowing this, had only brought a little grain with them to save the loads, and, worse than all, the Russians ran completely out. The Afghans sent over word to say that they were running short too, and to know if I could give them anything; and when I came to inquire, I found that the Russians, instead of having brought seven days' supplies from Karawal Khana, as I thought, had only three days' food all told. Here we were, three days' march in good weather from the nearest habitation, and not knowing how long we might be storm-bound in these hills! At last an old Jamshidi *moollah* said he thought that he could find a way by which horsemen might be able to get through the hills to Kilah Wali; so we at once sent him off with all the spare Afghan *yabus*, and with instructions to try and make Kilah Wali, and bring up some grain and flour from there to meet us at Alai Chalai. We threw away the extra pony-loads of bricks, &c., for the pillars, taking on just sufficient for a couple more, and sent the ponies back empty, as that was their only chance of getting across. We ourselves put all our men on short rations and gave the

Cossacks what we could, and as good luck would have it, on the march next day we came across a sounder of pig. First of all a family of little squeakers were descried, to which the Cossacks at once gave chase and ran down three or four in the snow. Just then we came up. My dogs got on to some big ones, and singling one out, ran it right down the hill, straight through the midst of all the camels, where the chase was joined in by all the Cossacks and followers, while we came pounding along through the snow behind. Poor piggy was eventually run to bay, and after a good fight with the dogs, in which the latter got much the worst of it and the little fox-terriers were all but killed, was at last shot by Major Holdich with his orderly's carbine. We presented it at once to the Cossacks, and were not they delighted! I shall never forget the handy way in which one of them jumped off his pony, took off the headstall, gave one end of it a turn round the pig's snout and the other round his pony's tail, and remounting, trotted gaily off down the hill, his pony dragging the pig behind it, to the place where it could be loaded on the camels below.

This welcome supply of meat kept the Cossacks going for the next three days, much to the astonishment of the Afghans and Turkomans, who had never seen the "unclean animal" put to such use before. Unfortunately, roast-pork would not feed the Cossack ponies. These hardy little animals, used to cold as they are, still found the snow too deep for them, and got more exhausted each day for want of food. I used to see them scratching up the snow with their fore-feet and doing their best to get at the grass below; but all their efforts failed to get them sufficient to fill their stomachs, and the night before we got in to Alai Chalai, so Captain Ilyin told us, they got nothing to eat but the last crumbs of the Cossack's hard-baked service biscuits collected from the bottom of the bag and made into a paste with a little melted snow. When this was the state of the Cossack ponies, how much worse was it for our Indian horses and ponies, that got no grazing at all! Major Holdich's orderly's pony died straight off; and M. Ananiantz's and my orderly's horse got so weak that they could hardly walk—in fact, M. Ananiantz's gave in entirely and had to be left out the last night on the road. One of the Afghan *yabus* also died, and the others were so done up that had we wished to put up another pillar we could not have done so. In fact we were very lucky to get the pillars built that we did. On the 31st, Gok Sirdar, our guide, managed to take us to Pekenna, and from there we found a point and survey-mark on the top of a high hill, from which we could see the last pillar we had built near Khwajah Gogirdak, and Major Holdich was just able to take his observations and the Afghans to build the pillar before dark. Precious cold work it was, I assure you.

On the 1st April we got in to Alai Chalai, after a hard march through mud and melting snow of some 18 or 20 miles down the Kara Baba Shor. The Pekenna Shor was quite impassable, but Gok Sirdar took us out of it and across the hills into the Kara Baba Shor, and we got down that all right, with the exception of some of the camels, which did not get in till next morning. The snow was now melting rapidly, and as I had never marched in snow before under the heat of an April sun, I little knew what an effect the glare had. All of us were more or less blind. One of Major Holdich's eyes was completely closed. Gok Sirdar, our only guide, and also Jemadar Azizulah Khan were both quite blind, and had it not been that M. Ananiantz had some spare goggles, I do not know how we should have got along. Several of the Cossacks, too, were suffering, and my *khidmatgar* was so bad that he did not get the use of his eyes again for some days after our arrival at Chahar Shamba. I had both goggles and a veil; but even with these all the skin of my face peeled off, and I have hardly recovered it yet.

On arrival at Alai Chalai we saw a couple of men with a bullock and some donkeys, and said to ourselves, "Ah! these men have brought us out some supplies;" but great was our disappointment to find that they were men who had been up to Kara Baba with supplies for Captain Tolmachoff, who is still surveying up there, and that they had nothing whatever for us. The Russians and Afghans had absolutely nothing left, and we were sadly contemplating our resources for dinner, when suddenly the men and ponies we had sent in to Kilah Wali arrived all right, having got through without loss, though with considerable suffering. It was not long before some mutton and fowls were roasting before the fire.

On the 2d we marched into Chahar Shamba. The camel-men declared that their camels were so snow-blind that they could not possibly march, and Captain Ilyin also said that two of his camels were perfectly blind; but they all got in somehow, and a couple of days' rest put them all right again.

I must say it was a comical sight to see us all on the march. The Cossacks with their heads completely muffled up in their *bashaliks*, never daring to look out unless obliged; the officers with their faces all swollen and burnt, and wrapped up in veils and pocket-handkerchiefs; and the Indian servants with their turbans all tied across their eyes, each trying his best to escape the glare.

Here in camp we have little to excite us, and day succeeds day with wonderful monotony. The pheasants are all breeding; in fact, the hens began to lay a month ago, and must have been sadly put about by the unexpected snowstorm. The cocks are incessantly crowing all over the valley, and it is amusing to watch an old bird, strutting about in the field, suddenly stand up and crow and flap his wings just like the old barn-door chanticleer. The hamlets at Karawal Khana and the whole of the Bala Murghab valley are entirely deserted; all the Jamshidis have moved up with their flocks and herds into the hills behind, and hardly a soul is to be seen. Standing on the top of the old ruined fort some three miles up the Bala Murghab valley, there is not a *kibitka* to be seen all the way up to the Bala Murghab fort, which stands out a square mud-building in the distance. I wonder, by the way, what this old nameless fort has been. Imagine a huge artificial mound of earth, measuring about 130 yards in length and 100 in breadth at the top, and say 50 feet in height, standing out in the middle of the valley on the eastern bank of the river, but without any particular signs of any old ruins around it. The mound is encircled by a broad depression, and then a gradual rise to the top of the lower mound—forming the ruins of the outer walls, which stand some 20 feet high in places—and measures about 300 yards square. No doubt it was a strong place in its day; and if Ebn Haukel can be read to mean that the Murghab ran between Kushk and Talikan, instead of between Merv-ul-Rud and Talikan, it might possibly have been the great Merv-ul-Rud itself.

CHAPTER XIV.

DELAYS IN THE NEGOTIATIONS—RETURN TO CHAHAR SHAMBA.

CAMP CHAHAR SHAMBA, 28*th April* 1886.

THE Russian camp joined ours at Karawal Khana on the 16th, as we had expected, M. Lessar coming on ahead to stay with us, and taking up his quarters in Major Durand's tent. Sir West Ridgeway rode over in the afternoon to invite Colonel Kuhlberg to dinner, but the latter accepted instead an invitation for himself and all his officers to breakfast next day. Accordingly, at noon on the 17th our camp once more shone with Russian uniforms, though in smaller numbers than hitherto, as only eleven turned up altogether. There was a meeting of the Commission in our mess-tent at 10 A.M., when Colonel Kuhlberg and Captain Gideonoff arrived and joined M. Lessar. No settlement or arrangement was come to, and it was agreed that we should all march up to Chahar Shamba together, and have another meeting there, Captain de Laessoe with a couple of Russian topographers being deputed to proceed across the *chul* from Maruchak in the meantime to settle the question regarding some reported wells at Aghamet, about which there was some doubt. This latter trip, however, never came off, as they could not cross the stream for some days, and Colonel Kuhlberg finally waived the point. Breakfast was laid in the *shamianah*, and fortunately the rain, which threatened all the morning, held off long enough, as a *shamianah* is not of much use in heavy rain, and without it we should have had some difficulty in finding room for our guests, having gone down to Maruchak with a very light camp, leaving all the big tents at Chahar Shamba. We were to have marched the following morning, but continuous rain for the next two days kept us prisoners in camp, and we were not able to start till the 20th. The Murghab came down in greater flood than ever, and had not the Russians got across when they did, they might never have got across at all.

The little Kilah Wali stream, as it was, turned out an impassable obstacle; and the Russians, disregarding the advice of their Afghan guides, crossed over to the northern bank on the morning of the 18th, and could not get back again till the 22d, and then only by crossing themselves and everything they had over on a raft made out of barrels. We marched on the 20th after the rain was over, and going up the Bala Murghab valley, crossed over through the hills, and on arrival at Bokun found M. Lessar there all alone. He, it seems, taking the advice of his Turkoman guide, had ridden up the left bank of the Kilah Wali stream, and when night fell and there were no signs of his party coming up, he tried to get shelter in the various Jamshidi hamlets about, but all in vain. One and all shut their doors in his face, telling him that were they to harbour a Russian, they knew not what dreadful fate would not overtake them at the hands of Kazi Saad-ud-Din Khan and the Afghans; and so there was nothing for it but to make for the tent of our postal sowars at Bokun. A bed, with half-a-dozen Turkomans in a little bit of a tent, was not the height of luxury to look forward to; so I can quite fancy he was not a bit sorry to find a tent of ours pitched there which Major Durand had sent on ahead under the charge of a Persian *farash*. Here we found M. Lessar very happy after a two days' sojourn with the tent-pitcher, living on whatever the latter could cook for him. He spent that day and the next with us, and when we marched on to Kilah Wali he rejoined the Russian camp, which in the meantime had got across the stream. The Kilah Wali valley is now at its best, being covered with grass, and flowers of every description and colour; so much so, indeed, that when I tried to examine the mounds that stretch for some 400 or 500 yards along the southern side of the valley, about a mile below the fort, and mark apparently the site of some old town, I found that it was impossible to tell which were natural and which artificial, as the thick grass concealed almost all traces of brick and pottery. The mounds round the old *robat*, some 12 miles farther down the valley, have lately been dug up— I presume, to get bricks for the boundary pillars—and it is astonishing to see what a mass of brickwork has been exposed there, stretching for about 300 yards on either side of the road. If these mounds at Kilah Wali were also dug up, it is highly probable that they would be just the same.

The Russians and ourselves all marched into Chahar Shamba together on the morning of the 24th—we taking up our abode in our winter camp, the Russians on the southern side of the valley just opposite. The 25th, Easter Sunday, the great festival of the Greek Church, was commenced by the Russian party with a full-dress parade. In the afternoon Sir West Ridgeway and all of us paid Colonel Kuhlberg and his officers a formal visit, which was duly returned the next day. The majority of the Russian officers, though, I must say, were not visible that Sunday afternoon: whether this was the result of the festival being kept as a feast, or what, I cannot say. The morning of the 27th was spent by the Commissioners in a formal meeting in Colonel Kuhlberg's *kibitka*, and we were all invited over to a mid-day breakfast at the conclusion of the meeting. We sat down a party of twenty-four altogether; ten of us—viz., Sir West Ridgeway, Majors Holdich and Durand, Captains Peacocke, Cotton, and De Laessoe, Khan Bahadur Ibrahim Khan, Kazi Muhammad Aslam Khan, M. Ananiantz, and myself,—and fourteen of our hosts, consisting of Colonel Kuhlberg, M. Lessar, Captains

Gideonoff and Komaroff, Dr Semmer, Captains Petroff, Denisoff, Tolmachoff, and Ilyin, Lieutenants Kiachko, Gorokh, Winnikoff, Mehemetoff, and M. Mirzaeff.

The Russian officers, with the exception of the Commissioner and Assistant Commissioners, who are in *kibitkas*, are all in tents—and precious hot, I fancy, they will find it a few weeks later, when our present rainy and cloudy weather has come to an end. The tents are square and low, the centre pole being barely 8 feet, and the four corner poles about 5 feet in height; and so far as I could see, they consist of only single canvas, though I have been told that officers' tents, as a rule, are double. The tents are small, say some 8 feet square at the top, with spreading sides some 5 feet in height, which peg down on to the ground. They must be very easily pitched, as they have only four ropes, one at each corner, with the same number of pegs. However well suited for a European climate, I fear the Russian officers will find them regular ovens, when baking out here under the rays of a midsummer sun. They hope, I know, to be back home before then; but what chance there is of their hopes being fulfilled it is impossible to say. So far as I have heard, the Russian claims have not abated in the least, and the prospect of any definite settlement is as far off as ever it was.

The cavalry, under Major Bax and Captain Drummond, are still encamped at Andkhui, with Sirdar Muhammad Aslam Khan, Ressaldar-Major Baha-u'-din Khan, and Subadar Muhammad Husain Khan. Mr Ney Elias has just left us on his return journey through Badakshan. Sirdar Sher Ahmed Khan joins him *en route*, to arrange for the collection of supplies at Faizabad for our party returning to India that way. Captain Gore and Mr Merk have just rejoined us here in camp; but Captains Maitland, the Hon. M. G. Talbot, and Griesbach are still away on tour in various parts of Turkistan.

CHAPTER XV.

BALA MURGHAB.

CAMP KILAH WALI, 26th *May* 1886.

WHEN last I wrote, we were still all in camp together at Chahar Shamba, and everything was unsettled. Since then the two Commissions have moved on from Chahar Shamba to Andkhui, and the boundary has been settled as far as Dukchi, a point some 25 miles almost due north of Andkhui. Various parties, one of which I am with, are out putting up the pillars to mark the line agreed upon, and thus I date this letter from Kilah Wali instead of from headquarters at Andkhui. Both Sir West Ridgeway and Colonel Kuhlberg proceed at once to the Oxus, I believe, where the final difficulty has to be settled. How that will be done I do not know.

The 1st of May saw the final break-up of our winter camp at Chahar Shamba. All the big tents were struck, and we moved out into a light camp ready for the march onward. A meeting of the Commissioners was held in Sir West Ridgeway's tent at 10 A.M., and shortly after noon I received orders to proceed with Captains Komaroff and Kondratenko to survey and report upon certain canals in the Maruchak valley. We accordingly marched west the next morning, while the camps of both the Commissions moved eastwards up the valley of the Ab-i-Kaisar to Daulatabad, and thence subsequently to Andkhui.

We three had a rough march of it down to the Maruchak valley, as we were just caught in the heaviest of all the spring floods, and consequently found every little stream an unfordable torrent. The little Bokun stream came down in such flood that a whole Jamshidi hamlet was carried away the night we were there; and the last I heard of the poor people was that thirty-three dead bodies had been recovered, but a great many were still missing. We managed to get down all safe to the banks of the Murghab, and there, with the help of some Jamshidis, I rigged up a little raft of inflated goat-skins, and crossed everybody and everything over the river without the least mishap till, last of all, I started to cross myself. What happened I do not know. I presume some excitable Jamshidi would pull at the rope just at the wrong time, when the raft was caught by the full force of the current; but whatever was the cause, the result was that the little raft turned clean over, and I suddenly found the raft on the top of me instead of me on the top of the raft, and consequently I had to swim the Murghab, clothes and all. Such a ludicrous scene as it was! Half-a-dozen Jamshidis at once plunged in to my rescue and raced me across in hot pursuit. All my servants on the bank commenced to howl, thinking no doubt their days were indeed numbered if their Sahib was drowned in the Murghab; and only one man that I know of took it coolly, and he was the man who had the sense to swim after my helmet and rescue it before it was washed away clean out of sight. I owe that man a very good turn, as what I should do without my sun-helmet in this present heat I do not know.

Mules are stupid enough beasts when set to swim across a river, but a camel beats everything. I never tried to swim a camel before, and of those I had with me, so far as I could see, not one could swim. They floated just like so many logs; and when once they were carried out of their depth, they simply floated away placidly down the river, not making the slightest effort on their own behalf, till fate finally stranded them again on the same side from which they started.

While I was at Bala Murghab, an amusing letter was received by the governor of Herat in camp there from the Sipah Salar, or commander-in-chief, at Herat, describing the advent of a European on an iron horse from Farah. This, I believe, was the American bicyclist, bent on making the tour of the world; but he so frightened the governor of Farah by his sudden arrival, that he was at once sent on under escort to Herat, where the Sipah Salar seems to have been equally puzzled. He sent Mirza Ghulam Ahmad, our agent there, and various others, to interview the stranger and find out what he was, but all without avail. All they could learn was that he came from the New World; and as Yangi Duniya conveyed no very precise ideas of nationality to the Sipah Salar's mind, he was left in greater doubt than ever, and wrote to say that he had lodged him for the present at Ziarat Gah, to the south of the city, and that if he could only be assured that he was an Englishman, he would bring him at once into the city, but that fearing he might be a Russian, he had lodged him outside. I believe that subsequently the gentleman returned to Persia.

At Maruchak we had an interview with Lieutenant-Colonel Tarkhanoff, the new Russian governor of Panjdeh. We met at the boundary pillar on the left bank of the river, and Lieutenant-Colonel Tarkhanoff afterwards returned to Bazar Takhta, his headquarters, 12 miles farther down the valley.

On my return to Bala Murghab I was much surprised by the arrival of General Ghaus-ud-Din Khan, the late Afghan commander at Panjdeh, with his aide-de-camp, as he calls him, Captain Muhammad Amin Khan, the officer who had charge of the advanced pickets at Sari Yazi at the time of the first Russian advance. We had a great greeting, both being equally surprised at meeting the other so unexpectedly. General Ghaus-ud-Din Khan was resplendent in a round white felt hat, ornamented with a broad green ribbon and bow, cloth uniform and sword, and long rough Hazarah boots. He informed me with much pleasure that he had been re-appointed to his former command and charge of the frontier, with headquarters as before at Bala Murghab; but we had not much time for any talk, as, after resting for an hour or so in my tent, he went on to see the governor, and in the evening rode back again to Band-i-Kilrekta, 20 miles farther up the valley, to hurry on the rebuilding of the bridge there which had been carried away by the late floods. All the officers of the Afghan regulars are now, it seems, known by the English names of the various ranks. They are all right in their generals, colonels, and captains, but apparently are a little puzzled about our Indian rank of commandant; and with them the commandant, or *kumedang*, as they pronounce it, is the name they give the second in command of the regiment under the colonel. The Khasadars, or Afghan irregulars, still stick to their old titles and organisation. They are all composed of separate companies, each one hundred strong and quite independent of each other. For each ten men there is a *Dah Bashi*, or commander of ten, all under the *Sad Bashi*, or commander of a hundred. Five or six of these companies, I believe, form the command of a *Sartib*, and he again is under the orders of the *Sarhang;* but what limit of strength is laid down for each I do not know. I believe it is quite unsettled, as at Bala Murghab, with only three companies, there is both a *Sartib* and a *Sarhang*, whereas at other places there is neither.

The building of this bridge at Band-i-Kilrekta had now become a matter of the greatest importance. At Bala Murghab I found that the whole of the Jamshidis were returning *en masse* to Kushk, and that their places were going to be taken by Afghan nomads who were already collected to the number of some two thousand families on the western bank of the river, while the Jamshidis were all massing on the eastern. As I left Bala Murghab, I found the roads full of Jamshidis, all trooping up with their flocks and their herds, their goods and their chattels, their wives and their children, all laden on bullocks and donkeys, and forming one of the most curious migrations I have ever seen. On my return to Bala Murghab a week later, not a Jamshidi was to be seen. Nothing but their deserted hamlets were visible, with empty reed-huts, and old sticks and rags lying about in every direction — the sticks, by the way, being carefully collected by the Afghans for firewood, a windfall that they are not likely to get again.

I had occasion to go up to the bridge to see the governor of Herat and General Ghaus-ud-Din Khan, and the sight there was a curious one. On this side were all the Jamshidis streaming across the bridge in one continuous line, while the hills on the far side were black with the tents and the camps of the Afghans, waiting for the Jamshidis to pass. The Jamshidis one and all told me that they were delighted to return to Kushk; and although all this country here on the northern slopes of the Tirband-i-Turkistan, from Bala Murghab to Khwajah Kandu, is known as the *Yurt*, or ancestral land of the Jamshidis, still they seemed to be leaving it with the greatest gladness—a gladness, I fancy, fully shared by the Afghan governor, who on his part is equally pleased to see his frontiers tenanted by pure-bred Afghans. Most of the latter whom I saw were nomad Ghilzais, who at once, after crossing the river, scattered themselves and their flocks over the rich pasturages on the slopes of the mountains, where they will remain till the autumn. Towards winter they will come down to the valleys and set to work in all probability to cultivate some lands—though for this, I believe, a special colony of Afghan cultivators is to be brought up.

Riding up the pass, I stopped for breakfast under the shade

of a well-known mulberry-tree, the only one in the country, a little more than two-thirds of the way through; and here I found the first of the new Afghan settlers, who had just arrived with his flock and his family and seemed thoroughly happy. He told me that he was a Ghilzai, a Hotak from the Kalat-i-Ghilzai district, whose forefathers had migrated to the hills near Herat some four generations ago. His language was still Pushtu, though he could speak Persian also. He was brimful of hope, and assured me over and over again that twelve thousand families of them were coming altogether, and that they would never allow a single Russian to cross the frontier. All they wanted, he said, was some guns from the Sirkar, and they would fight to the death. Other families, he said, were coming down from Kabul through Turkistan, and more from Zemindawar, all determined to fight. I was just wishing to myself that the Amir would send up the whole of Zemindawar to the frontier, when who should turn up but a veritable Zemindawari. He sat down under the tree to have his chat too, and told me all his history—how he fought against us at Maiwand, not from any love of Ayub Khan, but simply because the word went round for a *ghaza* against the unbelievers. Twenty thousand Ghazis, he said, were assembled that day. He himself was on the upper side towards Maiwand, opposite the Europeans; but before he got within a thousand yards of the fighting he was knocked over by a bullet in the groin. Directly he fell another Ghazi went off with his gun, and consequently he not only gained nothing by his *ghaza*, but he lost the gun that he had, and moreover, lay for six months on his back before he recovered the use of his leg. During this time he said he was fed by the Alizais; but when he got better he went down to Quetta, and there his wound was treated by an English doctor, and he was fed by the English all the time he was there. He then returned home; but hearing last summer that the Russians were going to attack Herat, he and lots of others like him had come up of their own accord to join in the *ghaza* against the Russians. He had no family or ties of any sort to bind him to this world; his life was of no value to him, he said, and all he wished was to meet his death fighting against the Russians—a true type of the real Zemindawari fanatic.

The Darband pass is a difficult one to describe. The Murghab here forces its way through the mountains, and the gorge more resembles a great huge hollow tooth than anything else I can think of. On either side are lofty cliffs. Those on the west tower up in one long straight line the best part of a mile back from the river, with low hills at the bottom down to the river's bank. Those on the east stand several miles away, with a regular series of low hills in between them and the river. At either entrance to the gorge, some 14 miles apart from north to south, a stratum of solid rock, tilted up with the dip to the south, comes running down from the main cliffs on either side right to the water's edge, thus completing the circle. The rocks at both entrances are marked by some old stone towers guarding the pass. The northern entrance, known as the Band-i-Joukar, is said by the Firozkohis to be the limit of their country. All the land in the pass they claim as their *Yurt*, and they have names for all the different spots. The bridge at Band-i-Kilrekta, the southern entrance, is simply formed by two rough but massive stone buttresses thrown out from either bank, joined by the trunks of two trees laid across about a 30-feet span in the centre. The depth of the river must be considerable to allow so much water through so small a space; and I only hope the bridge may stand till the old brick bridge at Bala Murghab has been rebuilt. The governor, I believe, intends to set to work on the latter as soon as the water goes down, and the sooner it is built the better. Last month, when we were in camp at Karawal Khana, a foolhardy Afghan sowar attempted to cross the river at the Tanur Sangi ford; but the current was so strong that both he and his horse were carried away, and neither man nor horse was ever seen again. Just that very day, or the day before, if I remember right, I winged an old cock-pheasant just at that very ford: he fell on the bank, and at once ran down and plunged into the river, and set to to swim for the opposite side. I had a little fox-terrier with me, who at once started in hot pursuit, and the swimming-match between the two was very amusing. The pheasant swam almost as fast as the dog, and was well out in mid-stream before it was caught; and what with the bird's struggles and the force of the current, it was almost as much as the little dog could do to bring it ashore. Poor little dog! never again will he catch me more pheasants. The heat the other day, marching across from the Kashan to the Maruchak valley, was so great that he died; and the other two dogs I had were only pulled through with great difficulty.

The heat just now in the Maruchak valley is tremendous. Not that I believe it registers anything excessively high by the thermometer, as with a good roof over one's head one would hardly feel it, but in the sun it is overpowering. The whole valley is uninhabited, and the ground is one dense tangled mass of thistles, flowers, grasses, and weeds of every description, standing between two and three feet high, and full of horse-flies and mosquitoes. For the last ten days there has not been a breath of wind, and very often a heavy dew at night. This all dries in the sun, and the steam or heat rising from this and the damp ground and the dense vegetation, all now drying up, without a breath of air to carry it off, almost suffocates one. I was encamped below an old mound, the remains of some former fort known as Kilah Kambar, close to the Afghan frontier-picket, and marched through the hills from there to Robat-i-Kashan, a distance of about 14 miles. I was rather amused, I remember, on the way, by the domestic troubles of the poor old Turkoman who was with me, which he related at great length, bitterly lamenting his fate all the time at living in such an age when he could no longer take the law into his own hands. From his account it appears that the ways of the gentler sex are just as inscrutable in the East as they are in the West. Poor old man! Whilst he was absent from home for two or three days, his brother-in-law arrived, and when he returned, he found that his wife had fled. She had simply jumped up behind her brother on his horse, and off she went; and why? There was the mystery. She was a Salor Turkoman girl, and "sixteen years ago," wailed the poor man, "I bought her for 600 *krans* (Rs. 240), and she has lived with me happily ever since; and now she has gone, and so have my *krans*, and I dare not do anything. Oh, if these Russians were not here, I would kill her and her brother too! and now all I can do is to give my petition to Tarkhanoff. What is the good of that?"

"But why did she run away?" said I; "did you beat her?"

"No," said he.

"Did the other wives beat her?"

"No; I have two other wives, but they each have their separate abode, and always got on very well together."

"Did she take anything away with her?" said I.

"Yes; she took all her jewellery and the child's clothes. She has three children, the youngest four years old. Now, why," said he, "did she leave the child and take its clothes?"

"Heaven only knows," said I. "How old was she?"

There at last I tickled the old man's humour, as, breaking out into his first smile, he replied, "Ah, I never looked at her teeth!" After that he forgot his woes, and became as jovial as ever again.

Robat-i-Kashan must have been a fine place in its day,

and evidently a stage on a much-frequented highroad; though whether the highroad from Herat to Merv ran down the valley of the Kashan or the Kushk, it is impossible at present to say. Taking into consideration the old bridge at Chihal Dukhteran, and the many ruins of important places in the Kushk valley, I am inclined to think that it followed the latter. The Kashan *robat*, or rest-house, is all built of burnt brick, and is of the usual design—an outer wall, some 50 yards square, with a domed corridor all round the inside, and open in the centre. It stands on the right bank of the stream, in the centre of a fine stretch of cultivable land; and the want of water, owing to the stream running dry, was provided against by the erection of a fine reservoir, some 70 yards to the south. This is now gradually tumbling in; but the four arched vaults, some 20 feet square, each radiating from a dome-covered centre, rather larger in size, are still perfect, and I see no reason why it should not be cleaned out and refilled. The place also boasts of its sets of caves, hewn out of the hillside, a little to the south; but I had no time to explore them, though, I believe, others of our party have done so. On my way back to Bala Murghab I took the opportunity of exploring a cave in a cliff, on the left bank of the river, that I had often looked longingly at, but had never been able to get to before. After climbing along the steep hillside above the cliff, at some risk of tumbling into the river in full flood 100 or 200 feet down below, and stumbling suddenly on the way on to a flock of young ibex, which certainly never expected to see us in such a place, I at last got to a slope where I could get down to the water's edge, and then, with the help of a rope, held by my two Sikh orderlies up above, I managed to climb along the cliffs, and after considerable scraping of elbows and knees, I got up to the cave, to find nothing but a simple vault, eight or ten feet deep. Two similar vaults, one on either side of the entrance, were partially broken away; but when the place was new, I daresay it was cool and pleasant to sit and meditate in, with the river rolling away just below. I must say, however, that the majority of these rock-caves, which so abound in this country, are most uninteresting to explore, as nothing ever seems to be found in them to give the slightest clue to the makers.

On arrival at Bala Murghab, I was only too glad to accept General Ghaus-ud-Din Khan's invitation to spend the day with him in the fort, while the tents and kit, &c., were crossed over the river on the raft. We sat in the north-west bastion—and very pleasant it was to have a roof over one's head again, after the last few days in the sun. The present garrison of Bala Murghab consists of three *bairaks* or companies of Khasadars. General Ghaus-ud-Din Khan and his five-and-twenty or thirty orderlies—men belonging to regular regiments—occupy the fort, and the Khasadars are quartered around. The fort, which was entirely rebuilt when originally reoccupied in 1884, is some 100 yards square, built on an artificial mound, about 30 feet high, with the gate on the northern face, immediately above the river. It contains a good residence, with a *hammam*, and an underground passage down to the river, and quarters for two companies, as the garrison, with magazine and storehouses, &c. Whether this mound was the citadel of an old city or not, it is impossible to tell. The site is well chosen, protected as it is on three sides by the river, and walled across on the fourth. The outer gateway lies to the east of the present fort, in this line of wall, and close by are the Khasadars' barracks, in the lines occupied the year before last by the battery of artillery, subsequently captured by the Russians at Panjdeh. The western side of the fort, a large space, some 500 yards square, in the bend of the river, lies low; and if any city ever existed upon it, it was probably washed away in some flood.

There is a mound marking the ruins of another old fort, I find, on the left bank, just at the bend of the river above the Robat-i-Ishmail ford, and only a mile or so above the mouth of the Mangan pass. It consists of a mound some 200 yards square, and 20 feet in height, with another mound some 50 feet higher again, marking the site of the citadel in the north-west corner. I could get no name for it, though there is one, as a Jamshidi told me that an old man had once given him the name, but he had forgotten it. The ground around, he added, had evidently once been all under garden cultivation; and this one can easily see for one's self. Everybody who remembers the deep rows of trenches and mounds on which grapes are grown in this country, will readily understand how very long it must take to eradicate all traces of a vineyard; and the marks of these parallel trenches are still to be seen all over both the Bala Murghab and Maruchak valleys at the present day. Ebn Haukel, if I remember right, specially notices the gardens for which the city of Merv-ul-Rud was noted, and yet at the present day there is not a tree or a bush in either the Bala Murghab or Maruchak valleys. Nomads like the Jamshidis and the Turkomans never cultivate trees on principle; and till a few settled cultivators are introduced, it will be hopeless to expect to get them. Once, however, the place has been populated and cleared, I see no reason why it should not become another garden again. With good land and climate, lots of water, and the hills around to go to in summer, what more could settlers want? At present, certainly Maruchak is nothing but a mass of thistles. But one must not condemn the thistle, about the most useful plant in the country. We have them of every shape and size, from the broad spreading leaf on the ground, to the high stalk not much thicker than one's little finger, and yet standing five and six feet in height. All the fuel of the country is composed of these thistles. Wood can only be procured from the mountains, but the thistle grows everywhere, and is regularly used as fuel. In winter I used often to see the Usbegs bringing in donkey-loads of thistle-stalks, and I don't think they ever burnt anything else. At this season the camels graze on them regularly, while almost all the little birds build their nests in them.

The Khasadars at present in garrison at Bala Murghab and Maruchak are almost entirely Logaris, and fine sturdy fellows they are. I have seen a good deal of the Afghan soldier during the past year, and I must say that the more I see of him, the more I like him. He is very independent, and is often thought sullen and discourteous from his habit of never saluting a stranger; but once get to know him, and see how he opens out under the influence of a few kind words, and what a ready and willing fellow he is. I only wish we had a few more of them in our ranks. I have heard it said that the Afghan is not a good fighting man, and certainly the Afghan regulars never once stood up against us that I know of; but this I believe to have been due to their want of organisation and competent leaders, not to the want of individual courage on the part of the men. Look how bravely the irregulars fought us time after time! and why should not those same men fight just as bravely for us as against us? The Afghan orderlies, men from Kabul and Logar, who were selected from the 11th Bengal Lancers for service with the Mission, are as fine a set of men as one could wish to see, and have done splendid service with us; and the more we can get of their brethren, the better for us, I should say.

CHAPTER XVI.

THE MARCH TO THE OXUS.

CAMP KHAMIAB, 15*th June* 1886.

WE are now encamped on the banks of the Oxus, at the end of our boundary-line; but, so far as I know, we are not a bit nearer the conclusion of a settlement than we were when we arrived here more than a fortnight ago. An earthen bank running in a long line between the Russian camp and ours marks the boundary here between Bokhara and Afghanistan, and never till now has there been the slightest disagreement about it. The Russian Commissioners, however, as I have mentioned before, are bent on upsetting if they can this settlement, mutually effected between the local Afghan and Bokharan officials some twelve years ago, and are now busily employed trying to get up a case to prove that, in accordance with the agreement between the English and Russian Governments of 1873, the Khojah Salih therein mentioned is not the Khwajah Salar district belonging to Afghanistan, as hitherto understood by the people on either side, but a small *ziarat* or saint's grave of the same name, some 20 miles higher up the river—a contention which, if allowed, would involve the surrender of all this thickly inhabited and regular revenue-paying district, that has belonged to Akchah from time immemorial. Matters for the moment are at a standstill pending the completion of a large-scale survey of the district in question, which Colonel Kuhlberg has insisted upon as a preliminary, presumably, I suppose, to gain time; but the Russian topographers are all at work, and the survey is to be completed within the next ten days or a fortnight, till when, I fancy, we must just grill and wait with the best patience we can.

The boundary pillars have all been built from Maruchak right up to Dukchi, some 30 miles west from here, so that nothing now remains but the settlement of this question regarding the land on the river-bank. That in all probability will have to be settled at home, but whether we are to await the result or not is not known. Diplomatic negotiations with Russia are so very uncertain in their duration, that it is generally thought that the whole Mission will not be kept waiting on here indefinitely for the result.

The country here is infinitely hotter than the Herat valley, where we were this time last year. The thermometer in our tents has ranged for some days past from 106° to 108° Fahr.; but fortunately the nights are comparatively cool, and consequently the heat does not tell on us as it otherwise would. The Oxus here is rather a slow-running river, apparently about a mile in width, with low-lying banks, and bordered on either side by a strip of thickly populated land well cultivated and well wooded. Having only just rejoined headquarters, however, I must reserve all description for a future letter, when I have made myself better acquainted with the place, and at present I will confine myself to an account of the march up here. The following letter, kindly sent me by Mr Merk, gives a vivid description of the Queen's birthday sports and festivities at Andkhui, which were a novel and interesting sight for the Russian officers and men, and were thoroughly enjoyed by all:—

"Colonel Sir W. Ridgeway and the headquarter camp of the Commission reached Andkhui on the 18th of May, where Major

Bax and the cavalry had already been for some weeks. The march to Andkhui was uneventful: we had a couple of hot days *en route*, but generally the weather was very pleasant. The most noticeable feature in the country—the usual rolling downs—through which we passed was the wonderful growth of grass, which, waving knee-deep, clothed the hills and valleys as far as the eye could reach. At this season of the year a division of cavalry moving anywhere between the Oxus and the Hari Rud would be almost independent of other sustenance for their horses: numerous flocks of sheep and herds of cattle that were pastured along our line of march appeared to make little impression upon the supply of grass. These tracts must be a paradise for sheep-farmers. Towards the end of May, however, the country becomes burnt up, and the sheep have to remove to the higher spurs of the Tirband-i-Turkistan. We halted for some days at Andkhui. The day after our arrival, Colonel Kuhlberg and the Russian Commission joined us and pitched their camp near ours.

"On the 22d of May we celebrated the anniversary of her Majesty's birthday. The proceedings commenced in the morning with a parade of the escort before her Majesty's Commissioner. The men of both detachments looked very fit indeed, and turned out very smartly; the horses of the 11th Bengal Lancers were in magnificent condition. After the usual salute, the cavalry and infantry marched past, and then went through a few simple manœuvres for the benefit of the Russian officers present, who repeatedly expressed their admiration at the appearance and turn-out of the troops. At five o'clock in the afternoon our Russian friends came over to witness the sports got up by Captain Drummond, who had prepared a small steeplechase course and a tent-pegging run. The programme was: (1) A mule-race for Persian mules, owners up. This race afforded the usual amount of fun, the riders trying to cut every corner of the course, and the honorary secretary bumping them back again. (2) A mule-race for Indian mules and drivers. This lot was more orderly and the mules were not so eccentric in their pranks. (3) A steeplechase for sowars' ponies. A large number of entries, and a scuffle in heat and dust, the winner turning up in a smart little nag ridden by Sowar Sirdar Khan. (4) A V.C. race. The sowars picked up the corpses of their dead comrades (represented by dummies), and returned over the hurdles in good style, under volleys of blank cartridge fired at them from a ditch close by. (5) Tent-pegging by the men of the 11th. This was the feature of the evening; it was performed in fine form, and was a sight as novel as it was interesting to Russians, who, I ought to have mentioned, had brought all their Cossacks and infantry to see the sports. Many of the British officers took part in the tent-pegging, after which the sowars performed a few feats, such as standing on the saddle and going past at full gallop, picking up a handkerchief from the ground, &c. (6) Sword *v.* lance. The last contest, between Sowars Sher Mahomed and Mahomed Hassan, was particularly good. (7) Lime-cutting, ring-tilting, and cutting off a dummy's head,—poor dummy had a good number of spare necks. (8) Infantry race, in marching order: the pace was good. (9) Dooly race. Three British officers, and Lieutenant Kiachko of the Cossacks, were carried by panting *kahars*, who with true courtesy bore their Russian guest first past the post. (10) *Bheesti* race with filled *mussucks*. (11) Foot-race for men of the 20th, which produced a close contest. (12) Tug-of-war between the old and young soldiers of the 11th, which was won by the lads after a long and most determined pull. (13) Tug-of-war between Khuttucks and Afridis of the 20th Panjab Infantry—the cheery Khuttucks pulling over their adversaries amid wild yells of the hillmen.

"This ended the day's programme, which was favoured throughout by lovely Queen's weather; indeed too much of it, for it was uncommonly hot. In the evening Colonel Kuhlberg and all the Russian officers dined with us: Colonel Kuhlberg proposed the health of her Majesty the Queen, and Colonel Ridgeway that of his Majesty the Emperor. After dinner the Khuttucks of the 20th gave us one of their wild and picturesque sword-dances round a blazing bonfire. The Russians were much impressed by it, and greeted with great applause the splendid sword-play shown by two well-known swordsmen of the 20th.

"Next morning Major Bax, with Major Maitland, Captains Gore, Talbot, and Cotton, the bulk of the cavalry and infantry, marched for the Oxus. On the following day, Colonel Sir W. Ridgeway, accompanied by Majors Durand and Holdich, Dr Owen, Nawab Mirza Hasan Ali Khan, and myself, escorted by 50 lances of the 11th under the command of Captain Drummond, marched *viâ* Jar Kudak to Khamiab, and reached the classic Oxus on the 28th of May. The evening we arrived, some of us went down to the river, where I heard an old native officer of the 11th Bengal Lancers remark, 'Long is the arm of the Sirkar, for I have watered my horse in the Tientsin river in China, and to-day in the Amu Daria!'"

The marches of the Mission from Chahar Shamba to Khamiab were as follows:—

		Miles.
May 6.	Chahar Shamba to Khwajah Isik Bulan,	8
,, 7.	Khwajah Gaohar, ...	18

			Miles.
May	8.	Kasawah Kilah,	15
,,	11.	Ata Khan Khojah,	14
,,	12.	Daulatabad,	20
,,	17.	Harfah Guzar,	17
,,	18.	Andkhui,	18
,,	24.	Ziarat Shah Murdan,	6
,,	25.	Neza Beg,	14
,,	26.	Kak-i-Tali,	18
,,	27.	Jar Kudak,	10
,,	28.	Khamiab,	19
		Total,	177

From Khamiab the main camp, under the command of Major Bax, marched on to Karkin, 18 miles higher up the river, where they are still encamped.

The character of the country changed greatly during this march of 177 miles. At Chahar Shamba we had the Band-i-Turkistan mountains immediately to the south of us, and the hillocks of the Maimanah *chul* to the north. The farther east we got, the more the mountains vanished and the less the hillocks became. At Daulatabad the latter had dwindled down to sandy undulations. At Andkhui they ceased altogether, and beyond that we traversed a great sandy waste. Isik Bulan, the first march out from Chahar Shamba, is a holy spot, as its designation of Khwajah implies, marking the resting-place of some pious saint. It consists of a small domed *ziarat*, well ornamented with flags and horns, on a little mound just above a spring of hot water, which here is collected in a reservoir, and forms a favourite bathing-place. The next march to Khwajah Gaohar strikes the valley of the Ab-i-Kaisar, down which the road runs till close to Daulatabad, where the stream falls into the Shirin Tagao. Beyond that, down to Andkhui, the united streams are known as the Ab-i-Andkhui, and there they come to an end in the sands of the desert beyond.

At Kasawah Kilah the valley of the Ab-i-Kaisar is little

more than half a mile in width, though it widens out to a mile or a mile and a half farther north. The stream is only about 30 feet in breadth, and pretty deep at this time of the year; but it overflows its banks in flood-time, and renders a lot of the adjacent land useless. Kasawah Kilah itself is an old mud-fort on the top of a small mound on the northern side of the valley, with mud walls and houses around it, and some patches of mulberry, *pashakhana* and other trees down below. The valley is well cultivated down to Ming Darakht, eight miles farther down, but beyond that habitation ceases. Ming Darakht means the thousand trees, and though there are hardly that number now left, still there are a great many, and some very fine trees amongst them. These trees all get their nourishment from a spring on the southern side of the valley. In the midst of them stands an old domed *musjid*, and walking here in the evening I found an aged Syed, the only guardian of the place. He told me that they were formerly a thriving community, and had held the place for the last eleven or twelve generations, but that now only four families were left, and they lived in the ruins of the old mud-fort close by. The trees, he told me, were planted by an ancestor of theirs a hundred and twenty years ago, though one close by the *musjid* was known to be three hundred years old. Poor old man! I fancy I was the first European he had ever seen. After looking at me for some time, he asked me if I was a Farangi: I told him I was. He then asked me if I was a Christian: acknowledging this also, he then asked me if I believed that Hazrat Esah was to return to this world again; and when I assured him on that point as well, he seemed perfectly satisfied, accepted me as a believer of the Book, and talked away without the least reserve.

To the north of Ming Darakht the valley of the Ab-i-Kaisar is now a desert. Formerly it was well inhabited, and there were large settlements of both Arab and Ersari nomads, who grazed their flocks in the *chul* to the west: these, though, were gradually reduced by Turkoman raids, and in 1877 the two last Usbeg villages of Ata Khan Khojah and Jalaiar were attacked and plundered, and since then the land has lain waste.

The raiders were Sarik Turkomans from Yulatan, and one of their leaders gave me a long description of this very raid the other day. The story was briefly as follows:—

"We were a party of 500 horsemen, and 200 *mirgans* or matchlockmen on camels; and passing down through the *chul*, *viâ* Chah Ata Murad, we arrived at Chashmah Pinhan. Here one of our scouts brought us news that an *alaman* of 50 Kara Turkomans was encamped at Kara Baba. We at once swept down on them. We found them all dismounted and unprepared, and charging down, only ten of them succeeded in reaching their horses and escaping; three were shot, and the remainder were all taken prisoners. We kept their horses and arms, &c.; but the men were subsequently let go, and found their way home through Andkhui. It was early spring-time, and the snow was not yet all melted. After this we went on to Yarghan Chakli and Kiamat Shor, and on the third day we attacked Jalaiar. We first surrounded and then stormed the place: there were only some fifty families of Usbegs in it. One man was killed; but the resistance was trifling, and the place was soon cleared. The men, women, and children were bound on the camels, and we all went straight on to the attack of Ata Khan Khojah. Here we found some twenty-five families, and the place was soon razed and the people bound and sent off with the rest to Pekenna. There we halted for two days, watering and resting our horses. On the third day the prisoners and plunder were all sent off with half the footmen to Khwajah Gogirdak, while we all went to Alai Chalai, and thence swept down on the villages of Pain Guzar and Chachakli. There we captured some forty families more, and taking them down to Kilah Wali, we rejoined the others at Khwajah Gogirdak. The male prisoners were let go; but the women, children, and cattle, &c., were then divided by lot amongst all the different leaders. I myself had ten men under me, and to our lot fell three women, one child, four cows, two horses, and some personal property. The women were good-looking, and ought to have been sold for 35 or 40 *tillahs* apiece (say Rs. 200 on an average); but when we got back to Yulatan, the headmen of the tribe assembled and decided to release the women and children, and consequently our three women and the child were taken from us and sent back through Panjdeh. The only result of our foray, therefore, was 140 *krans*, the proceeds of the sale of the horses and cows, &c.—of which 40 *krans* fell to my share, and 10 *krans* (Rs. 4) to each of my men. This was all we got for sixteen days' hard work. Truly, raiding was most unprofitable work. I was at it for many years, and left off 150 *tillahs* in debt (a *tillah* equals $13\frac{1}{2}$ *krans*, or Rs. 5-6-5), whereas I have saved and paid off 100 *tillahs* during the time I have been a servant of the English; and before I took to raiding, when I was only a shepherd, I saved enough to buy me a wife—more than I ever did by raiding."

It must have been small consolation, however, to the poor people carried off, that their captors were none the richer.

Some six or seven miles below Jalaiar, the road turns off into the low hills and emerges into the valley of the Shirin Tagao—a fine broad valley at least two miles in width. The village of Khairabad stands out green and fresh amongst its trees—a great contrast in that respect to the Turkoman village of Daulatabad just beyond, which has not a tree in the place. Nothing marks the difference between the two races (the Usbegs and the Turkomans) more than the inability or aversion of the latter to cultivate trees or anything else likely to tie them down to any one particular spot. They are such thorough nomads, that tradition forbids of their doing anything calculated to give them a permanent interest in any particular land. Everything they have must be movable at a moment's notice; and though doubtless they are gradually now being settled down, still it will be many a day before they go in for their gardens. Khairabad is the most northern Usbeg village of Maimanah, and I was sorry, when passing so close, not to be able to visit it. There are the ruins of a famous old fort there, known as the Jumjuma Kilah, about which there are many local traditions. The Usbegs also call the place Kilah Kazal; and it is believed by some of them to be the fort of Kazal Arsalan, mentioned, I am told, by Shaikh Sadi in the 'Bostan'; and the traditions and stories they have about it are the most curious mixture of faiths and dates that one can well imagine. One story I remember is to the effect that Jumjuma was the descendant of Kazal Arsalan, and a king of great power. One day an old woman came begging to his durbar, but he refused to give her anything. She then went off to Khwajah Roshnai—the Mahomadan saint whose grave is now the great *ziarat*, or place of pilgrimage, in the neighbourhood—and obtained from him a potion which killed the king. Fifty years afterwards Christ and His disciples arrived, and saw the skull of the king lying in the ground where it had been buried outside the fort. The disciples remarked on its size, and said how much they would like to see the man owning such a skull in the flesh. Christ thereupon raised the king to life again, and he ascended the throne a second time and ruled for years. He left one daughter, who grew up a most beautiful girl, but never married. She succeeded her father on the throne, and ruled well; but she was devoted to the chase, and used to spend days and days out hunting. It is a curious thing, but I believe there are many stories current amongst the Usbegs regarding a visit of Christ and His disciples to these parts.

Daulatabad consists of simply a collection of some 300 *kibitkas* and reed-huts inhabited by Ersari Turkomans, with a mud-fort to the north of them on the banks of the stream, held by a *bairak* or company of Afghan Khasadars, under the command of the Sad Bashi. Daulatabad formerly belonged to Maimanah; but as the inhabitants are purely Turkomans, the direct administration has been taken over by the Afghan Government, and the present *hakim* is one of the men who lived in exile with the Amir and Sirdar Ishak Khan at Tashkend.

The road from Daulatabad to Andkhui is most dreary and uninteresting the whole way. The valley of the Ab-i-Andkhui is about two miles in width; but the hills on either side get flatter and lower and more sandy the farther north one goes, and the road on the eastern bank runs through desert the whole way. The river is invisible, running in a deep channel full of tamarisk and other low jungle. Harfah Guzar and Chap Guzar are simply bends of the river which here approach the road and give water for a camping-ground.

Andkhui is not seen till one gets close to it. About three miles out, the road crosses the first canal just at the spot where it divides into four. Here the first gardens or trees commence, and the road runs on to the city past a succession of these. The city itself is nothing but a collection of mud-ruins. Formerly, it is said, there were 13,000 families in the place; now there are said to be 3000—but probably half that number would be nearer the mark. The houses are all flat-roofed, low, mud-buildings; the old city walls are in ruins, and the bazaar and the fort are the only two points of interest in the place. The bazaar consists of four cross-roads meeting in the centre, and roofed over, but of very limited extent. The market-days are Sundays and Thursdays, if I remember right, and on other days there is little or nothing doing. Passing through the bazaar we arrived at the gate of the fort—a high, irregular-shaped enclosure, some 250 or 300 yards in diameter, and defended by a garrison consisting of one company from the regular regiments at Maimanah, three companies of Khasadars, two guns, and 100 sowars. All are quartered in the fort with the exception of the cavalry, which are outside on the northern face. The governor—Colonel Abdul Hamid Khan—occupies a good set of rooms in the highest part of the fort, whence a capital view is obtained of the city below and of the desert stretching away to the north. Cultivation extends for a radius of six or eight miles all round the city, and the whole of this ground is one network of canals and water-cuts, into which the river is split up. How far north the river flows in flood-time, I could not see; but I noticed that the walls of the gardens at Khan Chahar Bagh, at the north-eastern corner of the oasis, were all washed down during this last flood-season, and much damage was done. I presume the water must extend some way farther before it is finally absorbed. The snowstorm, too, that overtook us at the end of March, is said to have done the greatest damage in Andkhui. The fruit-trees were all nipped by the frost, and all hope of any fruit there for this year is gone. Riding through these Khan Chahar Bagh gardens with my guide—an Ersari Turkoman named Shayak Yeuzbashi—I was shown a lot of mud-houses, the winter residences of some 400 Turkoman families who emigrated here—so my guide said—from the banks of the Oxus about eight years ago. At present I found all living out in their *kibitkas*, pitched in the open plain to the north. *Kibitkas*, I suppose, are after all the coolest during hot weather. The side-felts are all removed, and the walls consist of nothing but a reed *chik* or mat, which keeps out the glare, but lets in the breeze from whatever quarter it may be blowing.

The desert stretching from Andkhui to the Oxus is about as hot and wretched a country as ever I saw. The general feature is an endless stretch of rough, broken ground, very sandy in parts, and covered with wormwood and low bush. Water is very scarce—so much so, that one or two of our postal stations have to get their water from Andkhui on camels. Kak-i-Tali possesses four wells of brackish water; but the rain-water collected in a shallow tank off a stretch of hard clay is now exhausted, and the few Turkomans camped close by were all on the move when I passed through the other day. Jar Kudak has a plentiful supply of water in a well, and close to the surface—the character of the country changing there a good deal. The wormwood gives place to low tamarisk, and the sandhills increase. A mud-enclosure, some 60 yards square, marks the site of an

Afghan frontier picket-station, though at the present time one old man is its only occupant. Wherever a little stretch of hard or clayey soil affords the slightest chance of water running off it, a tank has invariably been constructed to catch it; but almost all these tanks are now dry. Wherever a few inches of mud and water are left, I used to see the white-breasted pintail sandgrouse coming to drink in small numbers; but, with that exception, I saw no sign of game. Lizards seem the staple product, and they are to be seen of all sizes and colours. First and foremost comes a beast of a yellowish colour with red stripes, some two or three feet in length, which never tries to run away, but stands and hisses, distending its stomach to an abnormal size. The dogs hate them cordially, as, when approaching to the attack in front, the lizard suddenly brings his tail round and gives the unwary dog a most tremendous wipe across the side of the head. The first interview between a dog and one of these animals is very amusing—the dog is always so utterly astonished at this unexpected attack on the lizard's part, and also so hopelessly wroth. The natives have a holy horror of these lizards, and kill them whenever they see them. The touch of them, they say, is fatal to a man's powers, besides which, they suck the cows' and sheep's udders dry. A harrowing story was told me of a fine promising young shepherd, just married, who was foolishly playing with some companions one day, and had the misfortune to be struck by one of these animals. All the *moollahs* in the country were consulted by him in vain, but not one of them could give him the slightest hope; and the only consolation he got was that "it was all that lizard." Another variety of lizard—perhaps the most amusing of all—is a little blunt-nosed fellow that sits up and curls his tail over his back like a squirrel, and then suddenly darts off, or else, by some imperceptible motion, buries itself in the sand. The sandhills between Jar Kudak and Dev Kilah are full of these, as well as of several other varieties.

Dev Kilah—a flat-topped rocky hill, precipitous on the eastern side, and very steep on all the other sides—is the great landmark hereabouts. It is only some two miles from our camp, and is a great object of veneration in the neighbourhood. Who held it, or where it got its name from, is unknown; but local tradition refuses to believe that any agency but that of demons could have constructed it. There is no water near it, yet the crest of the hill is surrounded by the remains of a thick masonry wall; and there are two shafts sunk in the solid rock, which apparently must have gone right down through the hill to the level of the water in the plains below. These wells are now almost entirely filled up, so the depth cannot be ascertained; but how such clean-cut circular shafts were bored through solid rock to the depth we would suppose is certainly a marvel.

Our camp here is pitched on some nice grassy land between the belt of cultivation and the river; but the great heat of the last few days has brought the river down again in flood, and the level of the five or six canals on either side of us has risen tremendously, so that we shall have to move camp to escape being swamped out. The water-level is getting dangerously close to the surface; and though it is very pleasant to have one's own little well of cool water in one's tent, still, when that well begins to overflow, it is about time to move on.

Mr Merk and Captain Komaroff are just starting to make some inquiries regarding an alleged former ferry higher up the river, and Sir West Ridgeway and Major Durand pay a visit to the other camp. Captain Griesbach has just rejoined us after a long tour through the mountains. Starting from Chahar Shamba, he first went up to Farad Beg—a little to the west of the Tailan pass in the Band-i-Turkistan—and thence across the Kara Gali pass into the Surkh Ab valley, and down to Maimanah. From there to Belchiragh and Deh Miran, where he found hundreds of old rock-cut caves, but no inscriptions

—caves, in fact, he found everywhere from Farad Beg all the way through the northern Hazarahjat to Bamian. From Deh Miran he traversed the Yekh Darah pass to Foughan in the Ferozkohi country, just on the northern slope of the Band-i-Turkistan, and about 9000 feet above sea-level. The Yekh Darah is so narrow in places, he says, that an unladen mule can only just be squeezed through. The walls are precipitous for some thousand feet up on either side, and the sun's rays in some spots never reach the bottom. He had the bad luck to be caught in a snowstorm in this pass; and had the Foughan people not turned out with torches to help, the servants and baggage would never have got through. From Foughan the road ran along the Astarab valley to Siripul. Thence Captain Griesbach traversed the Sangjairak district, inhabited by a mixed population of some 4000 families of Hazarahs and Usbegs, to Darah Yusaf, crossing the Balkh Ab river by a bridge at Ak Koprak. Here the Hazarahjat was entered, and extended throughout to Bamian—the boundary between Kabul and Turkistan being at the southern Ak Robat Kotal. The Hazarahs and all the tribes were, Captain Griesbach says, most civil and hospitable throughout. Everywhere the orders issued by Sirdar Ishak Khan for his safe-conduct were thoroughly carried out, and no restrictions whatever were placed on his movements.

CHAPTER XVII.

MORE RUSSIAN DELAYS—THE KHOJAH SALIH QUESTION AND THE BANKS OF THE OXUS.

CAMP KARKIN, 30*th June* 1886.

TO-MORROW the main camp, under the command of Major Bax, marches for Shadian, a place in the hills some 15 miles to the south of Mazar-i-Sharif, where we hope to find cool quarters for a time while the present negotiations are being brought to a close. Sir West Ridgeway, with Majors Holdich and Durand, Captains Peacocke, Gore, and Drummond, Mr Merk, Dr Owen, Nawab Mirza Hasan Ali Khan, Sirdar Muhammad Aslam Khan, and Kazi Muhammad Aslam Khan, remain at Khamiab, and we can only trust that the present uncertainty may soon be ended. The only question now remaining for settlement is that regarding the point where the boundary is to strike the Oxus, and known briefly as the Khojah Salih question. The land between Dukchi and the river is almost entirely desert, with the exception of a strip of cultivation about a mile in width, running along the banks of the Oxus and inhabited by Ersari Turkomans, and it is just this strip of fertile land that the Russian Commissioner is now trying to lay claim to. The land on the Afghan side of the boundary belongs to the district of Akchah, and on the other side to Bokhara, but both sides are equally inhabited by Ersaris, who apparently occupy the whole of this portion of the left bank of the Oxus.

Akchah came into Afghan possession some thirty-seven years ago, and the Russians acknowledged it to be an integral portion of Afghanistan by the agreement of 1873. By that agreement the Afghan boundary was said to extend as far down the Oxus as Khojah Salih, but the agreement apparently was written without any knowledge of the country in question, and the consequence was, that when the Boundary Commission appeared on the scene, it was discovered that there was no such place on the Oxus as Khojah Salih, but that the district along the river-bank was known by the general name of Khwajah Salar, from some old saint of that name who lies buried at a place called Ziarat-i-Khwajah Salar. It was also discovered that some little time after the agreement of 1873 between England and Russia, the local Afghan and Bokharan authorities met together and formally recorded the limits of their respective districts. The boundary was well known, and there had never been any quarrel about it; and the local authorities therefore simply marked out the frontier between their respective frontier villages—viz., Khamiab on the Afghan and Bosagha on the Bokharan side—and there the matter rested till the present day. Instead, however, of gladly accepting this settlement by the Bokharan authorities, the Russian Commissioner claims the letter of the agreement of 1873, and has been delaying and putting off the completion of the settlement for the last month on the plea of making surveys and inquiries in furtherance of his claim. Ziarat-i-Khwajah Salar lies some 20 miles up the river from the boundary-line, between Khamiab and Bosagha; but there was never any ferry or post there, as was supposed in 1873, and all the Russian inquiries have failed, so far as we know, to make out any case for the boundary being fixed at the *ziarat*, or any other place than where it now is.

The land at Khamiab having been in Afghan possession for the last thirty-seven years, will, of course, never be surrendered by the Amir except under compulsion; and on the other side, as the Bokharans have no claim to it whatever, we can only presume that the Russians are trying to get possession of it for themselves. One can quite imagine the desire of Russia to obtain a permanent footing, however small, here on the bank of the Oxus. I presume the day is not far distant when all the left bank of the Oxus in the possession of Bokhara will be permanently annexed by Russia; but still I doubt if the time is ripe for it just yet, and the Russians would get all they want at present if they could manage to force us to surrender a strip of Afghan territory, just sufficient for them to form a frontier station where their troops would be a standing menace to Mazar-i-Sharif and to all Afghan Turkistan. There is not the least doubt that any concession in the present case would enable Russia to avoid the annexation of Bokharan territory, and yet at the same time to hold out a visible threat to the Afghans, which all Turkistan could not fail to understand. However, the matter will, I suppose, be brought to an issue now without further delay, and we shall then await the final orders of Government as to the conclusion arrived at.

Mr Merk and Captain Komaroff were deputed to take the evidence advanced on both sides, and left Khamiab on the 15th, and the 16th and 17th were spent at Karkin visiting the river and places of interest in the neighbourhood. On the 19th they crossed over to Kilif and stayed there the 20th, and on the 21st went on to Chahar Shanga on the right bank, whence they returned to camp. Mr Merk writes me—

"The country on the right bank is very like a bit on the Indus: wide, muddy river fringe of cultivation and canals, then level bare *put*, then barren stony hills, and a fiery hot blast blowing over all. The Bokhara cultivation did not look so flourishing as the Ersari Afghan fields on the left bank; the canals were slovenly, walls all tumbled down, and houses poor-looking. I guess the Usbegs are more oppressed. I was the first British officer to cross the lower Oxus for the past forty years."

THE BANKS OF THE OXUS. 243

Sir West Ridgeway and his party will not be kept long, we hope, down in the heat at Khamiab, which is at its height during July. We had it for some days 108° and 110° in our tents, which was trying while it lasted, but fortunately it was always cool at nights. With a cool night and good sleep one can stand almost any heat in the daytime, and it is only when the nights are hot too that heat really tells seriously upon one. Our life at Khamiab for the last fortnight was a very quiet one. I mentioned in my last letter how the sudden rise of the river was driving us out of our pleasant camp on the low grassy land near its banks, and within a day or two the whole of this tract was waterlogged. There was no sudden overflow, but the water slowly and surely rose up through the ground from below, and every little hollow and depression became a pool. The Russian camp moved off to a garden some two miles down the river, while we found shelter under some trees just on the outer edge of the cultivation.

So long as the two camps were close together we saw a good deal of the Russians, and Colonel Kuhlberg and some of his officers were either dining with us or some of us with them almost every evening. When the camps separated, however, we were not able to see so much of each other. The Russian party, too, is gradually decreasing in numbers. Captain Gideonoff, the Assistant Commissioner, has started for Bokhara and Samarcand, and several of the topographers have been set to work to survey the country down the left bank from here to Chahar Jui. What the Amir of Bokhara thinks of this long stay of the Russian Commission in his dominions, I do not know; but he has deputed some high official to attend upon them, who doubtless keeps him well informed of what is going on. Who the official may be I do not know, as we have seen nothing of him; but I heard that Colonel Kuhlberg had paid him a formal visit and held a parade of the escort in his honour, so I presume he is a man of rank.

A good many Bokharans are coming in for treatment in Dr Owen's dispensary, as well as Ersaris from the neighbouring villages. By villages I do not mean a collection of houses in the ordinary sense of the term—a village here is more properly a district. Take, for instance, the country between our two camps at Khamiab and Karkin, 18 miles apart. A strip of cultivation a mile or more in width extends the whole way, and each Turkoman in this strip lives on his own homestead. His house is a long, square, flat-roofed mud-building, the walls of which are all built sloping slightly inwards, with no windows, only a door. There is sometimes a second storey, approached by a ladder, in which, I fancy, the silkworms are generally kept. These houses, though, are all empty at the present time. The Turkomans during the summer season live out in their *kibitkas*, pitched under the mulberry and other trees that surround the house. The fields are mostly enclosed by low mud-walls, and divided from each other by rows of willows and the pollard mulberries on which the silkworms are fed. Two or three fields distant from one mud-hut will be seen another, and so on all the way up. The road runs the whole way just along the skirts of the sandhills, and between them and the cultivation. There is a great deal of flood-water out over the sand at present, and I noticed that the drainage seemed to run from the river inland. This flood-water comes from the canals, which are all now full to overflowing and very deep, as one poor camelman, whose corpse I saw fished out of one, found out to his cost. His camels were on the sandhills above, and saying to his comrades that he was going to try some of the mulberries on the trees in the gardens below, he went off, but never returned. The night passed, and the next morning his comrades, searching about, found his shoes on the far bank of the canal. Getting some Turkomans together, they searched the canal, and found his body in the mud at the bottom. From the marks on the bank it was pretty clear that the poor man, thinking the canal was shallow, threw his shoes across and then waded in. The water is densely muddy, so he could not judge of the depth, and instead of a shallow stream, he found himself in a canal with precipitous sides and some 10 feet in depth, and being unable to swim, like most Pathans, was drowned on the spot.

From the road the river is rarely visible, and then only in the distance. The cultivation and orchards are green and pleasant to look upon, and behind them, away in Bokhara on the opposite side of the river, rises the great mountain known as Koh-i-Tan, a huge rocky mass rising directly out of the plain, something like Mount Abu in Rajputana, only some 3000 or 4000 feet higher. Captain Griesbach, our geologist, asked permission to examine this range, but Colonel Kuhlberg declined to allow him to cross the border. On the other or southern side of the road, the look-out is dreary in the extreme, nothing but a sandy desert stretching away as far as the eye can see. The only birds are some species of tern, which hover about over the pools of water caused by the overflow from the canals. In the trees amongst the cultivation there are lots of cuckoos, jays, and magpies, but very few other birds so far as I have seen as yet.

The Ersaris here differ greatly in appearance from their brother Turkomans, the Sariks of Panjdeh, having a much more Tibetan style of countenance, and being apparently more exclusive and much more religiously inclined, doubtless due to their propinquity to Bokhara. Here the *azan*, or the call to prayer, is heard continuously, whereas such a thing was almost unknown in Panjdeh. Very few of the Ersaris can speak Persian, and thus our intercourse is comparatively restricted. None of us can speak Turki, and we feel it a great want. Great efforts are being made, I see, to encourage the study of Russian in the Indian army: but I trust the

Government will not forget that a knowledge of Turki is equally indispensable; and I hope before long to see the study of it encouraged amongst Indian officers by the grant of the same rewards that are now given for passing in Persian and Arabic and other Eastern languages.

The Usbegs of this country, I must say, do not strike me as a pleasant race. In Maimanah and Andkhui the majority of the villagers appear a dirty, sullen-looking, lazy sort of people, not half so jolly or so hearty as the Turkomans. The Bokharans, what we have seen of them, appear to be tall cadaverous-looking men, whom one can quite imagine are outwardly intensely religious, but mean-spirited and cowardly at heart.

All these Usbegs, Turkomans, and in fact all Turki-speaking races of Central Asia, are of one stock—so a very genealogically inclined old Jamshidi once informed me; and I remember being much amused at the pains he took to impress upon me the fact that the Russians were of Eastern, not Western, origin. "Mogul, Kipchak, and Kazak," said he, "were three brothers, all the sons of one father Mogul, and from them are descended the three races of Moguls, Kipchaks, and Kazaks. These very Cossacks that we have here now," added he, "are not Russians. The real Russians are of the same stock, but they separated from it much further back. The Hazarahs and the Russians are brothers. They are both offshoots of the same Mogul family, but they have no affinity whatever with the Usbegs and Turkomans, who are of an entirely different origin again." Whether the old Jamshidi's idea of the Mongolian descent of the Russians and Cossacks is generally accepted in Central Asia, I do not know; but he himself absolutely declined to admit the least doubt of his theory. It hardly agrees though, I fear, with that of the writer who claims for the Cossacks a Polish descent. However, whatever their origin, there are rumours that we shall see more of them here before long. The

Afghans have got the idea that Russian troops are being moved up in this direction, and we have heard for some time that a steamer was coming up the river. Neither troops nor steamer have appeared as yet, though what may arrive in the future none can tell.

The party going to Shadian consists of Major Bax, Captains Cotton, the Hon. M. G. Talbot, and Griesbach, Khan Bahadur Ibrahim Khan, Ressaldar-Major Baha-u'-din Khan, and Subadar Muhammad Husain Khan, with half the cavalry and the whole of the infantry escort. Colonel MacLean also accompanies the party. Major Maitland is away on a trip up the Oxus to complete the examination of the ferries commenced by Captain Peacocke. The latter has just returned from a visit to Mazar-i-Sharif, where he had an interview with Sirdar Ishak Khan, who received him most courteously, and made arrangements for him to return down the left bank of the Oxus. Captain Peacocke describes this journey as follows:—

"On leaving Mazar, the road to Patakesar, the ferry across the Oxus on the highroad to Bokhara, runs almost due north over an open plain for some 26 miles, and then for the last 10 miles through heavy drift-sand covered with *saxsal* bush. Half-way the road passes through the old ruins of Siahgird, which cover an area of some 10 square miles. The ruins were mostly of mud, but there are remains of brick buildings in the centre, and the place must have been a very big one in its day, though when that day was nobody knows. The place was, at any rate, of sufficient importance to have a large canal all to itself. Of the three canals that take off from the Daria Band-i-Amir at the Imam Bakri bridge at the mouth of the Paikam Darah valley, some 12 miles west of Mazar, one runs to Balkh, one to Siahgird, and the third, the Shahi Nahr, supplies Mazar. These Siahgird ruins extend for some 10 miles along the roadside right up to the edge of the sand at Padah Khana. Where the road hits the Oxus the river is divided by islands into several channels, but below these islands, at the ferry, the river is 1000 yards in width. The whole of the river-bank is covered with thick jungle called the Hazarah Toghai, and abounds with tigers and deer. The trees are of large size, mainly of the sort known as Padah, a species of

willow, with a fringe of reeds along the edge of the river. There
are no inhabitants here on the left bank, with the exception of
the twenty boatmen and their families. The opposite side is flat
and fairly open, and populated with mixed Ersari Turkomans and
Usbegs. Some eight miles down the river, on the right bank, lies
Tarmiz, where there are vast brick ruins. The place has been an
important one, as the river is here confined by high banks in a
permanent channel, which is said by the boatmen to have been
once spanned by a bridge, the piers of which, they say, are still
to be seen at low water, and form a source of danger to boats
going down the river. There is a large domed *ziarat* too, said
to contain an inscription on marble and another on a silver plate,
recording the fact that the place was sacked three times, once by
Alexander and twice subsequently. A Russian traveller, moreover, it is said, tried hard to obtain possession of this silver plate
a few years ago, but without avail. Beyond Tarmiz the river
makes an abrupt bend, and there is no road along its banks.
The ordinary track runs across the sand for some 18 miles, and
joins the river again at Chobash. Thence down to Kilif, a distance
of some 36 miles, there is a strip of cultivation between the
edge of the sand and the low-lying grass and jungle-covered
land along the bank of the river. This is occupied by some six
thousand families of Ersaris, inhabiting the successive districts
of Chobash, Ganesh, Karujah, Dalli, Aranji, and Islam, each of
which has its own canal from the river, bearing the name of the
district, and lined on both banks with the usual orchards, houses,
enclosures, and mulberry plantations. The Ersaris are multi-
plying and spreading up the river. Three years ago they
resettled at Islam, and this year they founded a new colony
some 30 miles above Patakesar: that at present appears to be
the highest point up the river to which they extend. The river
is now in flood, and in some places below Chushka Guzar it is a
magnificent open sheet of water a mile and a half in width. Its
course, though, is tortuous, and broken by islands. There is a
local tradition that the river once flowed to the south of the Kilif
rocks and away to Jarkudak, but its course beyond that is mere
speculation.

"Chushka Guzar ferry lies about five miles below where the
road from Patakesar debouches from the sands at Chobash. The
course of the ferry runs diagonally across the river, and is about
a mile in length. Eight boats are employed in the service—four
on either bank—and are propelled by long sweeps. Horses are
only used to tow them in bad weather, both there and at
Patakesar. At the latter place there are six boats, three on
either bank. There is a large traffic over the Chushka Guzar,

but principally of travellers, as merchandise generally goes by Kilif. Curiously enough, a large number of Kashgari Hadjis were crossing the river at Chushka Guzar on their way to Mecca, *viâ* Kabul, Peshawar, and Bombay: 800 were said to have crossed this month, and 900 more were said to be on their way. These unusual numbers rather startled Sirdar Ishak Khan; but the reason given by the Hadjis was that they had heard the Russians were coming, and so they thought they had better make the best use of their time, and get to Mecca while they could.

"There used to be two other ferries, one at Shorab above, and the other at Kara Kamar, below Chushka Guzar; but these did not pay, and were discontinued some twelve years ago. The main routes to Bokhara from the Patakesar and Chushka Guzar ferries join at Sherabad in Bokhara, and are both equally direct from Mazar. From Mazar to Chushka Guzar the road runs *viâ* Daulatabad and Alti Tepe, which latter place is 18 miles short of the ferry."

Sherabad in Bokhara is described in Dr Yavorski's 'History of the Russian Mission to Kabul in 1878,' of which he was a member, and the town has acquired additional importance of late from the fact that the Russian Government demanded permission from Bokhara to establish a cantonment there; but the late Amir refused his consent, and the demand was not enforced. The endeavour, however, to establish Russian troops at a place like Sherabad, immediately commanding the two main routes into Afghan Turkistan, shows how longingly the Russian eyes are turned in that direction, and how directly Kabul is menaced.

CHAPTER XVIII.

AFGHAN TURKISTAN—KILIF TO BALKH.

CAMP SHADIAN, 7th *July* 1886.

HERE we are in an Afghan Turkistan hill station, and how welcome the change is can be easily guessed when I mention that yesterday at Dehdadi, at the foot of the hills, the thermometer was 114° in our tents, and to-day it is only 85°: not that we have gone up to any great height, as we are only 5000 feet above sea-level, but the change in the air is delightful. Shadian is simply a small mud-village of some 200 houses of Tajiks, and there is nothing particularly striking or picturesque in the place. Immediately above and to the east of us, is a line of tall bare limestone cliffs; to the west and south, bare stony undulating country rolling away to the pass below, and up again on the opposite side; and to the north, the gorge in the low hills leading down to the dusty-looking plains below.

Here we remain for the present till it is known what is to be the result of the Khojah Salih dispute. Sir West Ridgeway and his camp are still at Khamiab, and the latest news we have is that Colonel Kuhlberg had at last agreed to produce his final statement of claims within the week. Nothing of course can be done till that statement is received, and nothing of course is known for certain yet as to what those claims will be or what line of argument will be followed; but one thing is clear and certain, and that is, that Colonel Kuhlberg has had every opportunity given him of testing the merits of the case, and that if he has not been able to find a good and sufficient cause for upsetting the mutual settlement arrived at by the Afghans and Bokharans some ten years ago, during the last month and half that the British Mission have so patiently waited for him, he is never likely to do so. When we left Karkin on the 1st, Captain Kondratenko was out examining and reporting on the Chushka Guzar ferry, and Captain Gideonoff was also away making inquiries on the Bokhara side of the river; and as soon as their reports are received, I presume there will be no further excuse for delay.

Our route from Karkin, on the banks of the Oxus, to Shadian, was as follows, viz. :—

		Miles.
July 1.	Kilif,	14
" 2.	Chilik,	20
" 3.	Chahar Bagh,	23
" 4.	Chahar Bulak,	13
" 5.	Balkh,	12
" 6.	Dehdadi,	10
" 7.	Shadian,	16
	Total,	108

Both Kilif and Balkh were interesting places to visit, and we could have stayed longer at both with pleasure. In fact, so cool and pleasant was the breeze under the trees by the river's bank at Kilif, that more than one of us would have spent the next day there, and have ridden on to overtake the camp the next evening, had not the thought of those 20 miles across the sandhills deterred us. As it turned out, though, the sand was not so heavy as we expected. The sandhills ceased after the first eight or nine miles, and the ground beyond was comparatively hard and good going. The sturdy sepoys of the 20th Panjab Infantry started at 1 A.M., and did the march at the rate of three miles an hour including halts, and thought nothing of it, despite the fact that they had been fasting for nearly a month previously during the Ramadzan.

The Oxus at Kilif passes through some rocky ridges running down from the Koh-i-Tan mountain in Bokhara, and its bed is consequently very much narrowed there: the average breadth is only about half a mile, while at the ferry, from point to point of the rocks, the distance is only 540 yards. Kilif itself stands on the Bokhara side, and consists of a small picturesque-looking fort on a rocky mound just at the water's edge, with a bazaar and village behind it. On the Afghan side there is no village or cultivation of any kind, nothing but the huts of the few boatmen built out on the projecting spit of rock behind which their three boats are sheltered. Two bluffs, some 400 yards apart, overhang the river, each of which apparently was fortified in olden days; but the western bluff has nothing on it now but a *ziarat*, while the fortifications on the eastern one are all in ruins: so apparently the little fort opposite was too much for them.

The ferry is the chief attraction of the place, and great was the interest taken in it both by us and all our men. We were all sitting at breakfast, I remember, under the little clump of trees on the water's edge, when the cry went round, "The boat is coming." The cook left his pots and pans and all the servants scuttled out, and even we, phlegmatic Britons as we are, left our breakfast to get cold and went out to look at the novel sight of a boat being drawn across a swift and deep river by a couple of horses, as if it was a waggon on wheels. Nowhere else have I ever heard of such a ferry, and yet the arrangement seems wonderfully simple and easy. This first boat that we saw contained a light load of passengers only, and was drawn by a couple of horses fastened to the bow. The next boat that came across was full of camels, and this had three horses harnessed to it—two at the bows and one at the side. Another boat, that was brought out for Captain Griesbach to photograph, had four horses attached to it, and I presume that is the maximum. The boats are very heavy, being made of logs rather than of planks, and about 35 feet in length by 12 or so in breadth. The arrangement for harnessing the horses seems very simple, nothing in fact but a band round the body, by which the animal is suspended to a peg on any part of the boat that may be necessary. His weight is supported by the boat, and all that he has to do is to strike out for the opposite shore; but for all that, the poor beasts puff and blow tremendously, and I should say the work must be very exhausting. The men in the boat use their sticks freely, and I fancy the poor ferry-boat horse has decidedly a rough time of it. The boat is naturally swept a good distance downstream in crossing, but when land is reached, it is towed up by the horses along the bank to the regular ferry station.

From Kilif our road led round the rocky bluffs and then southwards across the desert strip to join the main Balkh and Akchah road. Owing to the heat of the sun in the day we had to do all our marching at night, and jolly cool and pleasant I must say the nights were. Hot weather as we know it in India is unknown here. During June and July, apparently, the sun in the daytime is terribly hot; but then the breeze, when there is one, is generally cool, and in a good house I don't believe the heat would be anything so great. It is only in tents that one feels it so much.

Starting from Kilif, Colonel MacLean and myself determined to try the effect of dividing the distance, and so, starting about 6 P.M. in advance of the rest, we rode till dark, then halted and had dinner, after which we lay down and slept till dawn, and then rode on quietly into camp at Chilik, arriving just about the same time as the camp colour-party, which had started shortly after midnight. The belt of low sandhills which we passed through for the first 10 miles or so, is thickly covered with a stunted small-leaved bush standing some four or five feet in height, which burns beautifully even in its greenest state. The supply of firewood, therefore, in this strip of desert is practically unlimited. Beyond the sand we gradually got on harder ground, and then into a plain covered with camel-thorn and low scrub as far as the eye could reach, till eventually we struck the outskirts of cultivation at Sardabah, a small collection of Turkoman huts. Chilik is a bare uninviting place, with no trees or gardens and few inhabitants. We passed lots of spill-water running to waste over the plain, and population is the only thing required to bring huge tracts of this arable land under cultivation.

Our march to Chahar Bagh was mostly done in the dark; but, so far as I could see, for the first two-thirds of the way we passed through another level camel-thorn-covered plain, all similarly run to waste for want of population. Just as dawn broke, however, we were astonished to find ourselves in the midst of acres and acres of old mud-ruins, and not at all the ordinary class of mud-ruins, but the walls of large high houses, perforated with double rows of arched windows. Each of these houses apparently formerly stood in its own garden, as they were mostly surrounded by the long parallel mounds, marking the site of former vineyards. Now the place is entirely deserted, and nothing but the name—Unpaikal—remains. How or when it was destroyed I did not ascertain. Another curious feature in the landscape was the unusually large number of *tepes* or artificial mounds in sight. Ten or a dozen of these were continually in sight at the same time; and not small mounds either, but many of them of large size. Ages must have passed, I suppose, since each of these was a flourishing village or castle, or whatever it was, but their presence shows what a thick population the land must have supported in olden days. In fact, the more one sees of this Turkistan plain the more fertile does the land seem to be. The soil is good, and we passed through enormous crops of ripe wheat standing ready for the sickle. Wherever I asked I was always told that the supply of water was far in excess of present requirements, and that cultivators were the only things wanting. The Balkh river, or, as it is here more generally known, the Band-i-Amir river, which emerges out on to the plains through the gorge in the Alburz range, some 15 miles south of Balkh, flows northwest to Akchah, and there expends immense volumes of spill-water in the desert beyond, all of which might be utilised were there only people to utilise it. But the people have all apparently been killed off. Three or four miles beyond Chahar Bagh, on the highroad to Balkh, we passed the ruined walls of Nimlik, or Minglik, as it is variously pronounced, which twenty years ago was a flourishing Usbeg town under a Mir of its own. It was twice, I believe, sacked by the Afghans; once in the time of Akhbar Khan, and finally, after an obstinate defence, by the troops returning from the siege of Maimanah under the then Sirdar Abdul Rahman Khan, when, so I was told, something like 1500 Afghans fell in the attack, and double or treble that number of Usbegs in the defence. Many other similar ruins dot the country, and we can hardly wonder, therefore, at the smallness of the population. A certain portion of the waste land has been taken up by Afghan immigrants from Kabul, who seem to be rapidly extending their gardens and orchards and to be good cultivators; but all along the road from Chahar Bagh to Balkh the cultivation is limited to a line of villages near the foot of the hills on the south, and the plain to the north remains a camel-thorn-covered waste.

Balkh is nothing but a vast ruin. The present population does not exceed some 500 houses, mostly of Afghan settlers, who cultivate a succession of gardens and orchards along the southern portion of the old city. The bazaar is simply a covered street with a few shops in it, running through the village. There are very few Usbegs in the place, but a considerable colony of Jews, who have a separate quarter of the village to themselves, and appeared, so far as we could judge, to be fair-looking men with most unmistakably Jewish features. I also noticed a Hindu shopkeeper in the bazaar, who smiled and salaamed with great gusto as we passed.

To describe the old city of Balkh I cannot do better than give a rough sketch of the place, merely premising that instead of a populated city it is now one vast ruin. The walls, some six miles and a half in circumference, are all in ruins. Nothing is left of them but a long line of dried mud, worn by the weather into all manner of desolate and fantastic shapes.

The southern and south-eastern portions, from the Burj-i-Azaran to the Mazar gate, stand high on the top of a large earthen rampart, something like the walls of Herat; but all the remaining portion, with the exception of the old fort and citadel, are low, and not more than 10 feet thick. The fort is an entirely separate building, standing a considerable height above the level of the country around, and the citadel, in its south-west corner, stands some 50 feet or more higher still; the whole being surrounded by a separate moat, rather narrow towards the city, but with steeply scarped sides. Taking one's stand on the top of the citadel, a capital bird's-eye view of the whole city is obtained. To the north lies the fort—an empty bare place, surrounded by high walls and ruined bastions, with no signs of habitations in it except the ruins of a lot of low brick buildings at its southern end. I saw no water in it, nor could I see whence its supply had been obtained. The citadel is nothing but a mound, with half of a glazed pillar, and a few low, plastered walls, remaining standing on the top of it. The walls have all been levelled and destroyed.

The whole of the northern half of the old city is nothing but a mass of brick and *débris*, and utterly waste. Entering

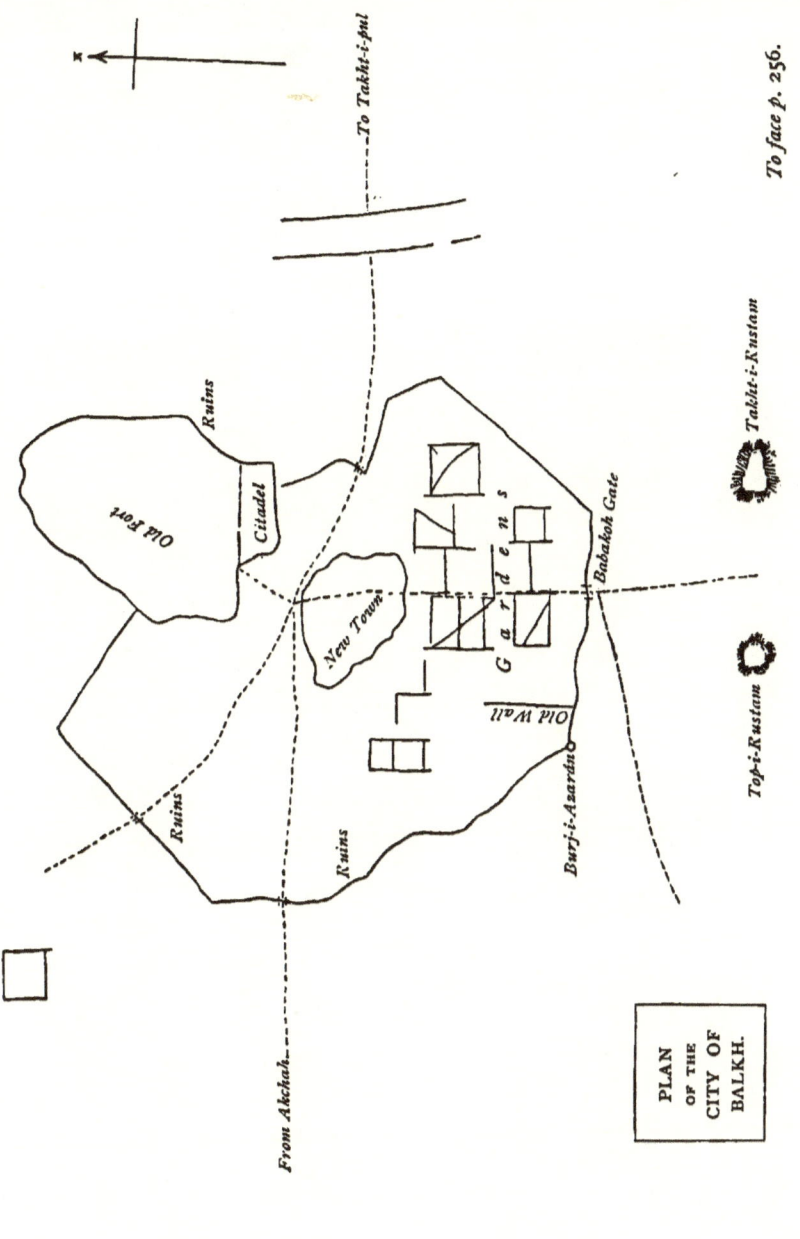

by the Akchah gate, one passes three lofty arches, said to mark the remains of the Jumma Masjid, and at the crossroads there are the foundations of what was once evidently a fine dome, said to have been the *chaharsu* of the city bazaar. A little to the east of it are the remains of two lofty gateways; and taking into consideration the remains of an old wall, that seems once to have run all the way from the Burj-i-Azaran to the south-west angle of the fort, it would look as if the city at first had only extended so far, and that these were the main city gates, the western portion of the city having been added subsequently. The most ancient Balkh of all is said to have stood to the east of the present city altogether. A mass of mounds and bricks on the road to Mazar mark the site of some old city, and in addition to these there is still standing a considerable portion of the old walls. An old Afghan with me described these ruins on the east as the Shahr-i-Hinduan, which he declared was destroyed by Changiz Khan, and the new city afterwards built. Whether these old walls, which now stand out in the plain a great thick mass of hardened earth, some 30 feet or more in height, and extending perhaps 200 yards on the eastern, and 600 yards on the northern face, were ever joined on to the present citadel, it was impossible to say.

The present town is nothing but a collection of the ordinary mud, flat-roofed huts, and the only garrison in the place consists of a few Khasadars. The regular troops are all stationed at Mazar-i-Sharif and at Takht-i-Pul, a sort of walled cantonment, about half-way between Balkh and Mazar.

The only two buildings of any note that I could find the remains of in Balkh, were the Masjid-i-Sabz and the Madrasah. The former consists of a handsome dome, ornamented with green tiles, and marks, I believe, the grave of the saint Khwajah Abul Narsi Parsar. I did not go into it, but I asked some bystanders if there was any inscription in it, and

I was amused to be told in reply that formerly there was one, but that the English had carried it away. When I asked if any Englishman had come to Balkh and carried it off, they said, "Oh no! but they got a Ressaldar at Peshawar to give a man a thousand rupees to go and fetch it"! The Madrasah or college is all in ruins, and nothing but the lofty arched entrance remains. I was told it was called Madrasah-i-Syad Subhan Kuli Khan, after a descendant of the Amir Taimur, who built it, in which case it was of no very great date. The walls were all knocked down, and the materials carried away by the late Amir Sher Ali's governor, Naib Alam Khan, to build a new college at Mazar, and nothing but the *débris* remains.

In a garden in the south-east portion of the city there is a house known as the Haramserai, built also by Naib Alam Khan, and used for the accommodation of travellers of rank. All of us who have visited Balkh have been put up there; and I myself spent a pleasant day there, very glad to have a roof over my head instead of a canvas tent. The house is of the usual structure, consisting of a lot of rooms in a long row, with wooden shutters instead of windows, and the walls and floors mostly unplastered; but it also boasts of a fine *hamam*, and the garden possesses some magnificent chenar-trees.

To the south of the city lie two most curious structures, known respectively as the Tope-i-Rustam and Takht-i-Rustam. My old Afghan gave it as his opinion that they were relics of ancient fire-worship, but it seems equally probable that they are of Buddhist origin. The Tope-i-Rustam is a circular building, some 50 yards in diameter at the base, and about 50 feet in height, much weather-worn and damaged by rain, and looking in the distance like a tall mud mound. On getting close, one finds that the base of it is built of large unburnt bricks, some two feet in length and four or five inches thick, and that the tope on the top of this was also apparently built of the same unburnt brick, but with a facing of burnt brick, now much defaced. There are no signs of mortar in the building, but the bricks are all of the same large size. Climbing up to the top, I found the summit flat, and nearly 30 yards in diameter, with four circular vaults inside, exposed to view owing to the domed roofs having fallen in. These four vaults or cells are not in the centre of the building, and consequently there may be others in it still intact. The base of the tope is pierced by four shafts, apparently meeting in the centre; but whether these passages were part of the original building, or whether they were run through afterwards, it is difficult to tell. If part of the original building, there may have been some internal communication with the cells above; but in such a case one would naturally suppose that the passages would have been properly arched and the sides made smooth, whereas, as it is, the side walls are rough and uneven, and the top of the passages is simply formed of the rough edges of the broken ends of the unburnt bricks, all laid horizontally without the slightest attempt at arching, and so rough that it looks most probable as if they had been subsequently cut through. The passages themselves are now so much filled up that one can only creep in for a few yards.

The Takht-i-Rustam is about the same height, but is wedge-shaped—not circular, like the tope. I saw no traces of bricks in it, and it seems to have been built of hardened mud, with straight perpendicular sides, say some 100 yards in length north and south, and 60 yards in breadth at the western and 20 yards at the eastern end. The top is perfectly flat, and full of rain-holes, but whether the rain runs down into cells inside or not I do not know. There were no inside chambers or entrances visible at any rate.

A road runs through various gardens from these old mounds to the Darwazah-i-Baba Koh, the southern gate of the city, so named from the Ziarat-i-Baba Koh, situated under some huge chenar-trees just outside. The ancient names of the city gates, given by Ebn Haukel and other old Arabian geographers, seem to have been entirely lost, and I could get no trace of where they were. However, further research might lead to their identification, though whether we shall have the opportunity for it or not remains to be seen. Apparently there are several Buddhist remains in the vicinity. Another tope, or something very like one, was clearly visible to the west of the city; and on our way out to Dehdadi, on the south-east, we passed between two other curious structures of a like nature, called respectively Chihal Dukhteran and Asiah Kuhnah. Both are built of the same large unburnt bricks; and while the former is lower and more irregular shaped, looking as if it had a vaulted chamber inside it, the latter is a simple solid cone, some 50 feet in height, and between 20 and 30 yards in diameter. The top seemed flat; but we could not stop to climb up to it, and there were no signs of any opening at the bottom, though, as there is a small village built close around it, it was not easy to examine it closely.

Our last march up to Shadian led, for the first 10 miles, across the bare open *dasht* or plain, at the foot of the hills, to a curious narrow rocky gorge, so narrow that it was spanned by an arch, and flanked on each side by tall precipitous cliffs: a more impossible place to force one can hardly conceive. Over the archway were rooms and loopholed walls, though now considerably out of repair. The road led through this gorge for some distance, till it opened out into the valley behind, and then gradually ascended for about six miles more to the village where we are.

CHAPTER XIX.

SUMMER-QUARTERS AT SHADIAN.

Camp Shadian, 11th August 1886.

Sir West Ridgeway, with Captain Drummond, Nawab Mirza Hasan Ali Khan, and Kazi Muhammad Aslam Khan, arrived here from Khamiab on the 6th, and the whole party are already the better for the rest up here in the cool. The heat and hard work down below had told heavily on them, and all were unwell and much in need of the change. The office work, too, had been unusually heavy of late, and Messrs Clarke and Chapman were equally in need of a rest. Writing all day with the thermometer 110° in the tent is apt to undermine the strongest constitution.

Much delay was caused owing to the dilatoriness and procrastination of the Russians in the preparation of the protocols recording the proceedings of the last few meetings of the Commission; but these were at last completed and signed, and now they have all been sent off with the final despatch detailing the history of the Khojah Salih case, and consequently there remains little else to be done except await the orders from home. Whether the new Ministry will order us to return to India at once, or to remain here and await the result of the negotiations between the two Governments, will probably be settled before this letter reaches you. In case of our return, there is nothing, I fancy, to prevent our starting next month and being back at Peshawar in October, as the distance from here *viâ* Ghorband and Charikar is not believed to be more than some 450 miles, which we shall do easily in 30 marches. If we are ordered to await the termination of the negotiations, there is no saying how long we may be kept, and in that case it is to be hoped that Government will arrange to relieve our present escort. Two years' service in this country away from their homes is a great strain on our men, who have little employment and less excitement, and no interest whatever in the boundary, and, considering that so many of them are not even our own subjects, it would be hardly fair to keep them here a third year. The conduct of all has been extraordinarily good throughout, despite all the restrictions they are necessarily subject to under the circumstances of our sojourn here, and they fully deserve every consideration and the most thorough and hearty recognition of their services.

The only work now remaining on hand is the completion of the compilation and copying of the maps, and these are expected to be ready for the Commissioners' signatures in another fortnight or so. Major Holdich and Captain Gore, with sub-surveyors Yusuf Sharif, Heera Singh, and Imam Sharif, are hard at work on them at Khamiab; but the great heat there in the tents makes the work much slower than it would have been could it have been done in a more temperate climate. Sir West Ridgeway will probably return to Khamiab in a fortnight or so — as soon as the maps are near completion—and in the meantime Major Durand, Assistant Commissioner, remains in charge of the camp there, with Captain Peacocke, Mr Merk, Sirdar Muhammad Aslam Khan, Sirdar Sher Ahmed Khan, and Munshi Allah Baksh, the Russian Commission being still encamped in the garden some two miles off on the Bokharan side of the border.

The Russian claims as presented by Colonel Kuhlberg

have been so far modified, that instead of extending the claim, as was first supposed, up to the old graveyard known as the Ziarat-i-Khwajah Salar, he only extends it to the site of a former ferry across the Oxus, between the villages of Islam on the Afghan and Chahar Shangah on the Bokharan bank, situated some 12 miles up the river from the recognised frontier at Khamiab. This ferry, it appears, was formerly known as the Khwajah Salar ferry, owing to the district on the Afghan side, both above and below it—so the Bokharan witnesses aver—being known as Khwajah Salar; but it did not pay, and was finally closed some eighteen years ago, when the boats were moved up to Kilif. Even at its best it was only used when robbers, or some such cause, made the Kilif ferry unsafe. For a few years after 1868 one boat used to be brought down for two or three months in the cold weather for local use; but there seems to be little doubt that the ferry, as a ferry, had been quite abolished before the agreement of 1873 was recorded. However, even supposing that this ferry was the one referred to, still there seems to be no reason why all local considerations are to be left out of consideration in the interpretation of that agreement, and that the lands belonging to and below the ferry must be surrendered to Russia any more than those above it. The Russian Commissioner claims up to the site of the actual ferry itself, according to the letter of the agreement as he reads it; but, according to the spirit of the agreement, no such reading need be taken, as it is clear from the context that it was never intended to deprive Afghanistan of any lands then in the Amir's full possession. There can be no doubt that the Bokharan authorities correctly interpreted the agreement when they demarcated the frontier between their village of Bosagha and Khamiab in 1874; and considering that possession is generally considered to be nine points of the law, and that Afghanistan is proved to have held continued possession of these 12 miles of now disputed territory for the last thirty-seven years, one would naturally conclude that the Russians had not a leg to stand upon. Curiously enough, too, the present boundary between Bosagha and Khamiab has been hitherto acknowledged by the Russians, and the frontier was correctly laid down some two miles to the north-east of Dev Kilah, as it at present stands, in their maps published so late as 1881. Consequently the idea of contesting it is apparently only of recent date.

The survey of the country under dispute between the Murghab and the Oxus was carried out conjointly between the members of the two Commissions. Colonel Kuhlberg, on his part, undertook the survey, with his staff of topographers, from Maruchak to Daulatabad; while Sir West Ridgeway agreed that our survey officers should carry it on from the latter place to the Oxus. The whole of the triangulation on which the survey of the boundary was based was carried out by the British officers from end to end, commencing from Mashhad, and terminating on the Hindu Kush, the Russian maps being adapted to the results of the English triangulation. It was in addition to this that Captains Gore and Talbot, with sub-surveyors Imam Sharif, Saiadulah, and Ata Muhammad carried out the topography of the desert from Daulatabad to the Oxus. The Russian plane-tables are quite different from those of the Indian Topographical Survey. Instead of the ordinary ruler and sights, they have a telescope mounted on a brass ruler. This telescopic power moving in a vertical plane gives considerable advantages in a country destitute of conspicuous natural objects, and is, consequently, much more perfect; yet it takes a much longer time to work, and appears needlessly minute.

The Russian Topographical Department is divided, I am told, into two branches—the Military and the Civil. The topographers attached to the Commission are all of the

Military branch; but so far as I have heard, they are not combatant officers or military men in reality, but have the rank of captains and lieutenants and a uniform of their own. They go on service with troops; and I believe a topographer is always attached to each general's staff, whose duty it is to explain to him the topography of the country they are operating on, though what their system of rapid sketches is I do not know. Their plane-tables, stands, and instruments are specially constructed to be slung over a man's back, and are always carried by Cossacks; but still, their plane-tables take much longer to set up than ours, and seem by no means adapted for quick work. Their maps, too, seem to be never inked in at the time. The topographer, on his return, hands over his board to a special draughtsman, who undertakes all this part of the work—a division of labour that one would hardly think to be conducive to a correct delineation of the various topographical features of the country.

The Russian topographers, I must say, had many difficulties to contend against in their survey of this frontier. One officer, I heard, lost several of his Cossacks' horses from thirst, and ran a good chance of losing himself and his Cossacks too, in addition, from want of water. Our officers were never sent out into the *chul* without a good supply of water in *mussucks* on camels, and plenty of spare carriage for wood and fodder in case of accidents; but the Russian topographers apparently were allowed nothing of the sort, and had to trust to luck and the Afghans. During the whole survey of the country from Maruchak to Daulatabad, the Russian topographers were entirely dependent throughout, for food, guides, and escort, on the Afghans. Everything they required was supplied to them, and every facility afforded them by the Afghans. Russia had no population, no wells, no anything along the Maimanah frontier, and any one working in the *chul* there was naturally dependent on Maimanah for supplies; yet no sooner was this *chul* surveyed than Russia, ignoring all Afghan assistance, laid claim to the whole of it. A good many mistakes were naturally made by the Russian topographers in the nomenclature of various places, owing to the want, I fancy, of good guides; but these, when found out, were corrected, and though the maps have taken a long time to compile, they are now, I believe, completed at last, and no time is being lost by our officers in copying them.

The floods in the Oxus are now beginning to subside, as the canals and inundations at Khamiab are rapidly getting dry, and it is only to be hoped that the ground there may not become malarious before we are able to leave it.

Here, at Shadian, we are in a glorious climate. The maximum temperature by day now rarely exceeds 77° or 78°, while it goes down to 49° and 50° at night, and the place certainly would make a capital sanatorium for troops. Standing here on the crest of the first line of hills, I can see the best part of Afghan Turkistan spread out before me. Balkh and Mazar are immediately below, the latter only some 14 miles distant, while the Oxus glitters on the horizon to the north. To the south stretches one continuous mass of hilly country for nearly 150 miles right away to the Hindu Kush.

The plain of Afghan Turkistan may be best described by dividing it into four belts. First on the north come the low banks of the river, covered in places with cultivation, and in others with jungle to a depth of three or four miles; next comes a strip of sand some 10 miles in width; then some 25 miles of fertile land watered by the Balkh river, as it is called in our maps, and other streams coming down from the hills; and finally, the usual belt of arid and gradually ascending plain immediately at the foot of the hills. The greater portion of this fertile belt, some 25 miles in width, and from Akchah on the west to Tashkurghan on the east, between 90 and 100 miles in length, consists of fine level culturable ground, while the ruins we have seen bear ample testimony to its former prosperity. All that is required is population, and that is increasing year by year owing to the number of Afghan immigrants that have now begun to find their way across the hills from Kohistan and other districts near Kabul. Amongst the Afghans, the western portion of this district is familiarly known as the Hizhdah Nahr, from the eighteen canals into which the Balkh river is divided for irrigation purposes. A great portion of this water runs to waste, as it is far in excess of present requirements; but the principal waste occurs at Akchah, where, according to all accounts, there is a huge swamp in addition to all the spill-water that is lost in the sands beyond. This swamp, I know, is full of pheasants; but I have not heard that there are any deer there. Major Maitland, who returned a little time ago from his trip up the Oxus, though he never actually saw any of the deer that are said to abound in the jungle along its banks, yet he managed to obtain a small broken specimen of their horns.[1]

We have no particular news of any sort from Bokhara. Captain Gideonoff has returned from his trip here, and now Captain Komoroff has gone off to Samarcand in his place. There are no further rumours of the advance of Russian troops, though 150 Cossacks are reported to have arrived at Chahar Jui. A Bokharan caravan on its way through Mazar is said to have given the news that all Afghans are being expelled by the Russian authorities from Samarcand and those parts of Russian territory, notwithstanding the many years they may have been settled there as traders, &c.; and also, that the Russians are commencing to build a canton-

---

[1] This horn was subsequently identified in the Indian Museum at Calcutta as belonging to the *Cervus Cashmerianus*, from the fact of the second brow-antler exceeding the brow-antler in length.

ment at Karki, between Chahar Jui and Khamiab. This report, however, has not as yet been confirmed.

It is amusing to us to see by the extracts translated from the Russian papers that they, too, have got the idea that we are bent on the annexation of Badakshan. This they must have got from Afghan sources. How the rumour arose, or what put the idea in the Afghan mind, we cannot think; but there is no doubt that it took firm hold of their imagination, and was even shared in by the Amir. First of all came the news of the arrival of Colonel Lockhart and his party on the Badakshan frontier from Chitral. Then it was heard that he had 300 armed men with him,—the truth being, I believe, that he had left his mule-carriage behind owing to the difficulty of the roads, and that this terrible army of his was comprised of nothing more formidable than Chitrali baggage-coolies. Just at that time, however, Sir West Ridgeway, in anticipation of an early settlement of this frontier, was making arrangements for a certain portion of the Mission to return to India *viâ* Badakshan and Gilgit, surveying the upper Oxus and the little-known regions of Roshan, Shignan, and Wakhan on the way. These arrangements, coupled with the arrival of Colonel Lockhart's party, by some curious misunderstanding, gave rise to the idea that the two parties were to act in co-operation, and to seize Badakshan.

All chance of any of us returning *viâ* Badakshan has, of course, long since been knocked on the head. The unforeseen delays and difficulties raised by the Russian Commissioner rendered any such trip out of the question, and the season is now too far advanced for a start. It is a great pity that the proposed survey-parties, who were all ready and equipped for the trip, were not able to carry it out, as the work must consequently remain over now for some future opportunity. However, Mr Ney Elias's explorations have given us a good insight into the country generally, and a professional survey is all that is now required to complete it. Had our survey officers been able to work through, and to join on to Colonel Woodthorpe's surveys on the other side of the passes, the thing would have been complete. I still trust, however, to have a chance of exploring that country in time to come, and of trying conclusions with the great *Ovis Poli* that are said to roam over its uplands.

I must say the freedom with which we have been able to wander about the country hitherto, has been wonderful considering. Whatever part of Afghanistan we have been in, we have always found ourselves as safe as, or even safer than, if we had been in India. In the main camp, of course, there are always the regular sentries; but the only cases of theft we have ever had have been those committed by our own men in the camp itself. Officers on detached duty have wandered about and camped night after night in out-of-the-way villages, inhabited by all kinds of people, and have slept safe and sound without the protection of a single sentry or watchman of any kind whatever. In Herat, certainly, Afghan sentries were always posted round us; but out in the districts this was never done, and our Afghan Mehmandar and his men always went to sleep with just the same confidence that we did ourselves, and not a thing has ever been touched.

We had a new arrival in camp yesterday in the shape of a merchant from Mazar with a consignment of all sorts of Russian goods. Wines, scents, sweetmeats, silks and furs, and even white kid gloves, were all turned out in turn, and last, but not least, the man himself turned out to be an old Jemadar and native Adjutant of the 2d Beluchis, who had served with them in both Persia and China, and who took his discharge some eighteen years ago, and has been trading ever since in various parts of Central Asia. He gave me correctly the names of almost all his own officers, and even of those in the 1st Beluchis as well; and the last time, it seems, that he visited his old regiment was at Kandahar in 1880, when his old comrade, Subadar Dost Mahomed Khan, was acting under me as Kotwal of the city. He has just returned from Tashkend, where he went with Rs. 20,000 some months ago to purchase goods, but apparently he purchased firearms, or in some way fell foul of the authorities, and was, further, arrested as a British spy, and only got away again after four months' imprisonment and the loss of half of his stock.

At Khamiab, too, lately, there has been quite an irruption of Indian *fakirs*. The way these men wander about these countries seems very extraordinary. We have had men in patchwork, men in sackcloth and ashes, men in chains, and men of all sorts at times. The last arrivals were, first, a couple of Sikh priests of sorts, who, curiously enough, came down from Bokhara, and after good entertainment and help from us, went on to Akchah; and secondly, a sort of mad Bengali Babu. Last year he was in England, and saw London, Liverpool, Glasgow, and Bristol, and, so far as could be ascertained, had worked on the Peninsular and Oriental Co.'s steamers as a sort of purser's clerk, and knew English well. Apparently he was dismissed for smoking *charas*, and is now off his head.

So long as Captain Drummond and his men were at Khamiab, they used to have small *gymkhanas* and sports every Thursday, which, I hear, were very amusing. The Turkomans used to turn up in great force, and appreciate the fun immensely. Up here, at Shadian, our men are amusing themselves by going out shooting after the oorial and ibex in the hills, and by trips to the hot springs at Chashmah Shaffah, some 16 miles off over the hills to the south-west. Now that the late Afghan restrictions on our movements have been somewhat relaxed, our Mussalmans all hope to get permission to make their pilgrimage to the famous shrine at Mazar, the tomb of Ali. It naturally is very disappointing to them to be so near, and yet not to be allowed to visit it owing to Afghan truculence; but this now, I trust, is at an end. A lot of our unruly Persian *farashes* and muleteers rushed off to Mazar in a body the day before yesterday, and have just been sent back under escort by Sirdar Ishak Khan, much to their disgust, and the amusement of the rest of the camp. They are a turbulent and easily excited set these Persians. A muleteer quarrelled with a commissariat weighman about his rations of *bhoosa*, knocked him down, and when dragged off, rushed at him again with a drawn knife, and was only just seized in time. Naturally he got a good flogging on the spot, but he turned out to be a Syed, and the opportunity was seized by a few men to excite some others, and induce them to rush off to Mazar. If they thought of taking shelter in the sanctuary in the shrine, and striking for higher terms or anything, they were sadly disappointed, as Sirdar Ishak Khan only let them in four at a time, and then at once sent them all back. So they have only got laughed at for their pains.

CHAPTER XX.

VISIT TO MAZAR-I-SHARIF.

CAMP SHADIAN, 10*th September* 1886.

SIR WEST RIDGEWAY is now back again at Khamiab, where the final meeting with the Russian Commission is being held, and we here are all busy packing up and preparing for an early move. The telegrams informed us some little time ago that it had been decided that we were not to remain here for another winter, and now we hear that a convention has been recorded with the Russian Government to the effect that demarcation having been completed as far as Dukchi, the joint Commissions are to be withdrawn, and the remaining 30 miles of frontier between Dukchi and the Oxus settled between the two Cabinets. Meanwhile the *status quo* is to be respected. This is most satisfactory, and another week will in all probability see us all on the return march to Peshawar.

The men are all in great delight at the thought of a speedy return to their homes, and the great topic of conversation amongst them is the amount of leave they will get. I only trust that the military authorities will treat them in this respect with the liberality that they deserve after two years of such good service under peculiarly trying conditions.

Major Maitland and Captain the Hon. M. G. Talbot have gone on ahead to Haibak, our starting-point on the main Kabul and Tashkurghan road, and we expect to follow them a few days hence, and to wait for Sir West Ridgeway and his party to rejoin us there on their return from Khamiab.

We are only a small party here at present—namely, Major Bax, Captains Cotton, Drummond, and Griesbach, Khan Bahadur Ibrahim Khan, and myself, with the greater portion of the cavalry and the infantry escort.

I hear that Mr Merk, Captain de Laessoe, and Munshi Allah Bakhsh will in all probability remain on the frontier for the present with Colonel MacLean, while Major Durand returns home *viâ* the Caspian, and Captain Gore returns to India *viâ* Persia, travelling through Kirman down to Bandar Abbas. Our return party, therefore, will be considerably diminished, and we shall arrive at Peshawar in very different numbers from what we started with at Quetta two years ago.

How long Sir West Ridgeway may be detained at Khamiab, or whether some fresh complication may not arise to still further delay his departure, yet remains to be seen. However, all our heavy tents and surplus stores have been packed up and sent off in readiness—some for the benefit of the Teheran Legation, and the remainder for the use of Colonel MacLean and his party remaining in the Persian frontier, as of course it would be useless to drag such things all the way back to India. We ourselves are to march very light with mule-carriage, leaving whatever extra baggage we have to follow us by camel *kafila* under Afghan escort.

Sir West Ridgeway started from here on the 28th August, going down first to Mazar-i-Sharif at the special invitation of Sirdar Ishak Khan. His party consisted of Colonel MacLean, Major Bax, Dr Owen, Nawab Mirza Hasan Ali Khan, Kazi Muhammad Aslam Khan, Ressaldar-Major Bahau'-din Khan, and myself, with an escort consisting of Ressaldars Jeswunt Singh and Tejah Singh, and 70 men of the 11th Bengal Lancers, under the command of Captain Drummond. We rode down in the evening and camped for the night at the foot of the hills, and made our entry into Mazar early the next morning. We had only some seven miles to ride in, and Mazar lay spread out before us as a great clump of green trees standing out in the plain, with the fortified cantonment of Takht-i-Pul four or five miles to the west of it, and Balkh in the distance beyond that again. The only distinguishing points about Mazar are the two blue-tiled domes of the shrine glistening in the sun from the midst of the surrounding trees. No houses or buildings of any sort stand up in sight, and even when one gets quite close, one sees nothing but a mass of gardens divided by narrow lanes between high mud-walls. The city is not enclosed in any way, and the only gates are the different entrances to the bazaar. We were located in a house called the Bagh-i-Sarhang, a little way outside the Tashkurghan gate, an unimposing-looking place consisting of two courtyards. The first contained a long row of stables round two sides, with just space sufficient for our servants and horses. The inner court or garden had a house with three sets of rooms on one side of it, and flower-beds round a square tank in the centre, with a clump of fine chenar-trees around it, under which a *shamianah* was pitched, which we used as our mess and reception room. The cavalry camped in an open space to the south. We all had a good deal of ceremonial to go through, though, before we got finally settled in those quarters. When we arrived about a mile and a half from the town we were met by Kazi Saad-ud-Din Khan, the Amir's representative, and Sirdar Sultan Muhammad Khan (Barukzai) on the part of Sirdar Ishak Khan, with an escort of one squadron of local irregular and a regiment of regular cavalry. The local irregulars were composed partly of Usbegs and partly of Turkomans, and were known as the Daulatabad levy. Each class had its own big red standard, but the men wore their own national dress and had their own horses and arms. The Usbegs were distinguishable by their turbans, and Turkomans by their black lambskin hats; otherwise the dress and accoutrements of each were much alike. The Haidari regiment of regulars turned out very weak, hardly 200 strong, and for an Afghan regiment were a poor-looking lot. Neither the horses nor the men came up to the standard of those that we saw in Herat; and in fact the same remark would apply to all the Turkistan troops that we saw, both officers and men, cavalry and infantry.

The regiment was drawn up in line and received Sir West Ridgeway with a general salute, after which the colonel—by name Afrasiah Khan—was called out and presented by Kazi Saad-ud-Din Khan. Both Sir West Ridgeway and Colonel MacLean rode down the ranks, and the regiment then filed off—one squadron in front and the remainder behind us. Thus escorted, with the kettle-drums and trumpeters immediately in front of us, we wound about through various lanes and passages amongst the gardens, till we finally emerged at an open space—a graveyard, of course—in front of the Tashkurghan gate. Here a regiment of infantry was drawn up in line and received us with another general salute, the band playing some Afghan air. The men were armed with Sniders, but were dressed in dirty *khaki* coats and white trousers, and were very badly set up, presenting a decidedly poor appearance. They, like the cavalry, were dressed in imitation Russian caps of dirty black cloth, with a red band and a huge peak, generally wrongly put on; and the cap, being worn well pulled down over the head, looked more like a shapeless nightcap than anything else. Why the Sirdar should go out of his way to dress his men up in such an unsuitable head-dress, I cannot think. The cavalry with any other head-dress—in their brown Russian cotton cloth coats and blue cotton trousers and long boots—would have looked comparatively well, but the badly fitting cap spoilt their appearance entirely. The latter were armed with smooth-bore carbines; but they had swords with small hilts to them—the first I have seen of the kind, as the Afghan regulation sword is a copy of the Cossack pattern, with a handle like that of a knife, fitting well down into the scabbard. I noticed that the officers of both cavalry and infantry were dressed according to their own individual fancy, without the slightest reference to the uniform of their men.

Passing through the bazaar—which consists of a series of cross streets roofed over with rafters and matting—we found small crowds at each of the corners waiting to see us; and beyond these, again, we came to the Sirdar's residence, with a small open space in front, where we all dismounted.

The Sirdar's residence is certainly a most unpretentious-looking place from the outside—a plain mud-building two storeys in height, with a particularly narrow and dirty entrance. Ascending a low, winding staircase, we were received at the top by the Sirdar himself. Sir West Ridgeway introduced us all in turn, and we soon found ourselves seated in a sort of open durbar-room, looking out on the open space in front, and on a garden courtyard behind, which apparently separated these public rooms from the private apartments.

As soon as we were seated, the Sirdar asked each of us individually after our health, and after that Russian cigarettes in boxes and silver cases were handed round, and subsequently tea was brought in. The table, which ran down the centre of the room, was covered with sweetmeats of all kinds, as well as with grapes and melons. Conversation went on for some time—the Sirdar repeatedly expressing his assurances that we should always meet with every comfort and consideration anywhere in the Amir's dominions. Finally, the Sirdar's presents for the acceptance of Sir West Ridgeway and Colonel MacLean were brought in, consisting first of trays of sweetmeats—perfect triumphs of the local confectioner's art, in the shape of sugar elephants, horses, goats,

&c.—followed by trays of Astrakhan lambskins, Bokhara silks, *barak*, *kurk*, and carpets, &c.; while three horses were led up in the open space below. The Sirdar was most affable throughout, and was handsomely dressed in a drab-coloured, gold-embroidered coat, with a large fur hat of sable or other skin, ornamented with a diamond decoration.

Saying good-bye to the Sirdar, we at once went on to call upon his son—Sirdar Ismail Khan—in the garden next door. We passed a new house for him in course of construction—the front of which, apparently, was being built mostly of wood, with partitions of unburnt brick; and then entering a big garden by a narrow doorway, we found the young Sirdar waiting to receive us in a tent under the shade of a fine plane-tree. He had little to say for himself, conversation being mostly kept up by Kazi Saad-ud-Din Khan; and despite his position as Commander-in-chief of the Turkistan troops, he was evidently little accustomed to the reception of strangers. Tea and cigarettes were again produced, followed by some more presents and a couple more horses; and then we all took leave and rode off, not at all sorry to find breakfast and a change of cool clothes awaiting us at the Bagh-i-Sarhang.

One feature worth noticing in Sirdar Ismail Khan's garden was his summer-house—simply a roof on poles, with the four sides filled up with green camel-thorn, which, when wetted on the windy side, acts as a *tatti*, and keeps the temperature within much lower than that outside. The light, too, coming in through the green thorns is soft and pleasant to the eyes; and inside one of these houses there is comparatively little to complain of, either regarding the heat or glare during summer in these parts.

We halted at Mazar on the 30th, and both days were thoroughly enjoyed by our men and followers in visiting the bazaar and the *ziarat*. After our long sojourn in the wilderness along the frontier, a real bazaar was a grand treat, and everywhere our men seem to have been well received. In such a sacred place as Mazar-i-Sharif one naturally expected to find the people extra bigoted; but so far was this from being the case, that the shrine itself was even thrown open to our Sikhs and Hindus, who were allowed to visit it in parties under Afghan guidance—a liberality that I have never heard of elsewhere. Major Bax and Captain Drummond also visited the local horse-fair, but did not succeed in finding anything worth purchasing at the prices asked.

The evening of the 30th was the time fixed for the return visit from Sirdar Ishak Khan to Sir West Ridgeway, but unfortunately the Sirdar was so unwell during the day that he had to send his apologies, and to request Sir West Ridgeway to receive his son in his place. With the son came, of course, Kazi Saad-ud-Din Khan and also General Nujbudin Khan, the Sirdar's latest father-in-law, a fine handsome old man, the Shahgassi, the Lalla, and various brigadiers, colonels, and adjutants, who were all duly presented; a very heterogeneous lot they were, too, with not a thoroughbred-looking Afghan amongst them. The Shahgassi is a Civil official, and the Lalla is the title given to the governor of all young nobles, an influential post in these countries. The young Sirdar was dressed in a large gold-embroidered grey Astrakhan hat, surmounted by a green plume, embroidered coat, gold-lace trousers, and patent-leather boots, and arrived under an enormous red-and-gold umbrella carried by an attendant, with a couple of gold-bridled and gaily caparisoned horses led in front, more after the manner of a Hindu Raja than anything I have yet seen in Afghanistan. On our side the cavalry escort were drawn up as a guard of honour on two sides of the courtyard, looking as clean and fresh as the day they left Umballa two years ago. Tea and ices were handed round, and then Sir West Ridgeway's presents to the Sirdar and his son were brought in on trays, after which the visit terminated.

VISIT TO MAZAR-I-SHARIF.

The morning of the 31st saw us all *en route* again, Sir West Ridgeway, Colonel MacLean, Dr Owen, Kazi Muhammad Aslam, and Ressaldar-Major Baha-u'-din Khan starting off for Khamiab, while Major Bax, Captain Drummond, and myself, with the cavalry escort, returned to Shadian. Ressaldars Jeswunt Singh and Tejah Singh, of the latter, both enjoyed their visit exceedingly; and I fancy there are few, if any, other Sikhs who, like them, have sat in an Afghan durbar, unless, indeed, we except the famous Diwan Nanak Singh, who was at one time *hakim* of Tashkurghan under Sirdar Abdur Rahman Khan, before the latter was finally driven out of the country by Amir Sher Ali Khan.

The celebrated shrine at Mazar is from all accounts a more imposing-looking place outside than in, and the building is not to be compared, I heard, to Ahmad Shah's tomb at Kandahar. Although claimed by some to be the burial-place of Hazrat Ali, still I think the superior claims of Najaf, near Baghdad, to this distinction, are generally admitted, and Mazar is simply reckoned as a *Kadamgah* —literally, " a place of the footsteps "—of Ali. Nawab Mirza Hasan Ali Khan, who duly went to pay his devotions, tells me that the shrine under the dome is surrounded by railings some six feet in height, lined throughout with cloth, so that it is impossible to see what is inside. The railings have a silver-mounted gate, but this is carefully locked. The outside and surroundings of the shrine are filthy in the extreme, and visitors are besieged by beggars at the gate. In spring, when the annual fair is held, the dirt and crowd must be tremendous. Inside, at the entrance to the shrine, there is a huge copper pot in which all donations are placed. Everything is acceptable, from a bit of bread upwards, and all is collected in this one huge pot.

The entrance is through a high archway on the east, ornamented with the " Al Rahman " chapter of the Koran inscribed on tiles, and a wooden gate worked in brass with a couple of minarets, one on either side. A similar archway on the west leads into a large garden, the property of the shrine. The original tiles with which these archways were covered are said to have been defaced, and the present ones to have been put on by Naib Muhammad Alum Khan, the governor of the province under Amir Sher Ali Khan. A small *musjid* has lately been built to the east of the shrine by Sirdar Ishak Khan, and immediately behind it lie the graves of Sirdars Muhammad Akram Khan, Muhammad Akhbar Khan, and Amir Sher Ali Khan. Near this, too, there are also a couple of mausoleums lined with old tile-work, now much defaced, but in which the remains of Cufic inscriptions can be traced. The eastern building apparently contains tombs only of ladies of royal descent; but unfortunately the stones mostly have either no name or no date, and the only real legible inscriptions are those to the memory of Kansh, daughter of Kilich Kara Sultan, dated A.D. 1543, and Sharifah Sultan, dated A.D. 1619. The tombstones in the western building are similarly mostly defaced: but amongst them the names of Khan Kara Sultan, A.D. 1543; Kara Sultan, son of Jani Beg, A.D. 1545; Kilich Kara Sultan, son of Kastin Kara Sultan, A.D. 1555; and Ibrahim Muhammad Bahadur, son of Siunj Bahadur, dated A.D. 1601,—were made out. Mirza Khalil, our Persian writer, tells me that the inside of the domes of the shrine are painted in imitation of the tile-work said to have been originally put up by Sultan Husain Baikrar, which painting is said to have been done by an artistic *moulvi* in the time of Sirdar Muhammad Afzal Khan, the father of the present Amir. The walls are covered with various Persian poems, giving the supposed history of the shrine, the general purport of which is to the following effect:—

During the reign of Sultan Sanjar, a man named Muhammad obtained possession of some historical book in

India, in which it was related that the grave of Hazrat Ali was in the Khairan fort near Balkh. Muhammad came to Balkh and spread the news. Some of the Syeds there acknowledged that they had had a dream to the same effect, and finally one Ahmad Kamaji went to the governor and laid the facts before him. A *moollah* who happened to be present in the durbar denied the facts, and maintained that Hazrat Ali was murdered at Kufah and buried at Najaf. That night, however, Ali himself appeared to the *moollah* and sharply reprimanded him for disbelieving these reports —a fact which was duly communicated by the *moollah* to the governor next morning. The governor, accompanied by a great crowd, at once went to the spot where the grave was believed to be, opened it, and found the body of Ali in perfect preservation. By the order of Sultan Sanjar, a building was at once erected over the grave. This was completed in A.H. 530, or A.D. 1136. On the advent of Changiz Khan this building was demolished and the grave alone remained, known as the Khwajah Khairan. Subsequently, however, a descendant of Bayazid Rustami made it again known that the grave was that of Hazrat Ali, and the coffin was reopened by the order of Sultan Husain Baikrar, when a red brick was found in the grave, on which it was recorded that this was the grave of Hazrat Ali. The present building was then erected in the year A.H. 886, or A.D. 1481.

So much for the historical claims of Mazar to distinction; and yet, on the faith of this, thousands of the halt and the maimed and the blind collect here every April in the hopes of a miraculous cure, and the failure to get it is simply put down to want of faith on their own part.

Dr Owen writes to me that, on their way from Mazar to Balkh on the 31st, Sir West Ridgeway and all of them rode through the fortified cantonment of Takht-i-Pul, which he describes as a huge cantonment, as near as possible a square, with double walls some 30 feet high pierced for musketry, and sundry bastions for guns, and a big moat. There are the ruins of what must have been once a fine fort to the south of it, but now the place is so surrounded by villages that it could never make a long defence.

Our life here at Shadian for the past month has been comparatively quiet and uneventful on the whole. All of us have thoroughly enjoyed the immunity from the heat which had to be borne in tents below by the remainder of our party detained by duty at Khamiab, and we have congratulated ourselves on our escape from it. Captain Drummond, who came up weak and ill from an attack of dysentery, pulled round in no time; and I myself, when laid up by the same complaint, had great reason to be thankful for the climate I was in. We have had an abundant supply of grapes and melons of late, and the men are all now in fairly good health, though there is a good deal of fever knocking about both here and at Khamiab. Every Thursday we have had our sports, which have been a great success, thanks to Captain Drummond's good management, and one day we were shown a new game by Kazi Saad-ud-Din Khan's local sowars called *Buzghalah Tazi*, or the race for the young goat. This game seems to be the common form of sport amongst the Ersari Turkomans, the Usbegs, and the local Afghan sowars of this part of Turkistan. One man starts off at a gallop with a goat across his saddle in front of him, and all the rest race after him and try to get the goat from him. The man who brings it in when time is called gets the prize.

The immediate neighbourhood of Shadian is stony and rough, and not very pleasant either for walking or riding; but once one gets to the top of the cliffs, which tower 2000 feet above us on the east, or over the Kotal at the head of the valley to the south, the country is much softer and more undulating. One favourite ride is to Malmul, another somewhat similar valley to this, about 8 miles to the east, but more cultivated and restricted, being only some 4 miles square, or about half the size of this, which is some 8 miles in length by 4 in breadth, and therefore not so good for a camp. Another ride is to Kafir Kilah, a great bluff some 10 miles to the south and about 8300 feet above sea-level, overlooking all the country right away to the Hindu Kush. Unfortunately the weather is so hazy and dusty at this time of year that it is impossible to see any distance.

One place I should much like to have visited is Band-i-Amir, the source of the Balkhab river, in the Northern Hazarahjat. Major Maitland, Captain Talbot, and Subadar Muhammad Husain Khan are the only members of our party who have seen it, and from their accounts it must be well worth a visit. The Subadar, who has just been describing it to me, tells me that the water collects there from all sides, and that, across the valley itself and also across the side ravines, there are a succession of natural *bunds* of rock which confine the water in a series of lakes, the overflow of one going in to the next, and so on, till, at the end, the Balkhab river is formed. There are some five or six different lakes in the valley, in the course of 10 or 12 miles, of unknown depth, but full of fish, many of them of great size, and all very tame and carefully preserved, the valley being renowned through the Hazarahjat as a place of pilgrimage. On the opposite side of the Kotal one of the sources of the Helmand is said to take its rise from a spring, the water of which is shot up out of the ground with great force, and is therefore supposed to come by some underground passage from the lakes on this side.

Fish seem to be common all over this country. At Mazar we got capital fish caught in canals drawn off from the Balkhab, and the Oxus is famous for them. At Khamiab we used to get a beautiful large white fish, with quite a different taste from the usual fresh-water fish. We all came to the conclusion that it must have been a fresh-run fish from the Sea of Aral.

Although here, at Shadian, we are not in the Hazarahjat, still we are close on the borders of it, as there are some four hundred families of Hazarahs camped about the hills quite close to us. I find, too, that these men are regularly employed by the Afghan Government as Khasadars or irregulars; and of the 400 families about here, 150 men are away at the present moment on duty at Daulatabad and Akchah and other places in the province. The Shadian villagers are all Tajiks, and it is amusing to see with what zest all the boys turn out for our races. Every boy from five years upwards turns out and runs his best, all expecting to win the prize. At first the Afghans would not let them appear, with their usual jealousy of our intercourse with their subject races; but fortunately this has somewhat decreased of late.

One curious feature of Shadian, which none of us have been satisfactorily able to solve as yet, is the number of large cylinders hewn out of solid rocks that are to be seen about the village. These cylinders are 6 and 8 feet in depth by some 3 feet in diameter, and the only explanation we can get about them is that they were water-mills; but how they were worked none can tell. One idea given to me was that, owing to the scant supply of water in the little rills about, the water was collected in these stone cylinders so as to bear with greater pressure on the mill below; but that is only a supposition. The immense labour of hollowing out these great cylinders would never have been undertaken, however, without good cause.

A good many of the villagers still come in for treatment at Dr Owen's dispensary, but many others are stopped by the Afghans. The Afghans themselves, when ill, invariably come freely to our hospital for treatment, but Kazi Saad-ud-Din Khan's constant opposition to the country people coming in has been most difficult to meet, and has prevented much good work that would otherwise have been done. As it is, there have been no fewer than 22,633 patients treated in the dispensary during the past year, including 80 major and 371 minor operations, and this although for more than half the time Dr Owen has had only one hospital assistant, Pati Ram, to assist him. I must say that Pati Ram deserves every credit for the way he has worked, and the interest and skill he has shown in his work. Last year the number of patients was only about 13,000; and it is wonderful that this year there has been so great an increase, considering how long we were encamped on the outskirts of all habitation along the frontier, and that Dr Owen and Pati Ram have had to do all the work themselves with a much reduced establishment, and without being able to leave camp and go into the villages at all. In June this year, when we reached the Oxus and found a decently populated district to work in, no fewer than 4521 patients were attended to during the month, which proves of itself what a still better return there would have been to show if Dr Owen had the same opportunities elsewhere. Patients have been coming in all the way from Khiva, Samarcand and Bokhara; and, curiously enough, even the Bokharan villagers of Bosagha and Karki send us their sick instead of going to the Russians, who are encamped in their midst. Dr Owen has certainly been unlucky in never having had the chance during the past year of camping in the neighbourhood of or in any large town for more than a day at a time; but, considering the wilderness that he has lived in, his show of work is decidedly encouraging, and it is to be hoped that the Amir will appreciate the work that has been done, and which has been the means of alleviating so much sickness and suffering among the people on his northern frontier.

CHAPTER XXI.

COSSACK AND SEPOY.

Camp Shadian, 12th September 1886.

Now that we expect to be shortly saying good-bye to the Russian Commission, it is time that I should send a few notes regarding the Russian troops, so far as we have been able to see and judge of them from the escort with the Russian Commissioner. Beyond that our experience is *nil;* but, taking the squadron of Cossacks and the small party of some five-and-twenty infantry as average specimens of their service, we have still been able to draw some few comparisons between them and our own troops—more especially our Indian native troops.

The dress of the Russian officers of all branches of the service that we have seen is of the same pattern — the flat-topped cap, a short frock-coat, double-breasted and buttoning up across the throat in front, with a double row of white silver buttons stamped with the Russian arms, and loose pantaloons and top-boots. The pattern is the same for all, the colour of the cloth alone marking the difference in the services; as, for instance, the cavalry is blue, the infantry is dark-green or black, &c. There is no such thing as an undress coat or patrol jacket with the Russians, as with us. The one frock-coat does duty for both, the only difference being that medals are worn in full dress and not in undress. In summer the officers wear a white cover to their cap and white or drab-coloured frock-coats, just of the same shape as their winter uniform. I have seen nothing with the Russians corresponding to our serge or *khaki* uniform, though I must confess I should be sorry to recommend our pattern. Why our military authorities should have selected such a short tight *khaki* serge coat as the one they have, with only two pockets, for our service coat, I cannot think, when they might have selected some nice easy jacket, such as the Beresford for instance, with four good pockets, and fitting loosely but equally well. It seems to have been forgotten that a man on service is not always buckled up in his belts. Again, look at the cut of our men's trousers. The Russian trousers, I notice, are always cut particularly wide and loose round both hips and thighs; yet how often do we see Thomas Atkins toiling along in a pair of trousers as tight as possible round the hips and thighs, and loose and flappy over the boots! When we go out shooting we take good care to have a pair of free and loosely made knickerbockers, or, at any rate, our trousers cut wide and easy, so as to give full play to the legs; and why should we not do the same for our men?

The rank of the Russian officer, as with us, is distinguished by the shoulder-straps, but instead of the simple badges that we wear, the Russian officers have a huge broad flat stiff lace-strap, some six inches in length by three in breadth, passing from the collar well over the shoulder, and removable at will. This strap has one narrow red stripe, perhaps a quarter of an inch in breadth, down the centre in the case of subalterns and captains, and two stripes for lieutenant-colonels and colonels. There is no rank of major in the Russian army. A subaltern has three little gold stars round the stripe, and the captain has none. Similarly the lieutenant-colonel has three little gold stars round his two stripes, and the colonel has none. The whole army has the red stripe except the staff, who wear a black stripe. Other departments have different colours. The topographers, for instance, have a blue stripe, the telegraphists a yellow stripe, and so on. The sword-belt, made of a narrow silver-lace-covered strap, is worn over the right shoulder, and the scabbard seems to hang easily and comfortably down the left side, and to be as much as possible out of the way. The sword is always worn back to the front, not like ours with the edge to the front.

The Cossack dress for officers is of the same cut as that of the men, though of finer material, and the pattern seems certainly to have the merit of simplicity; for, as one Russian officer laughingly told me, with shoulder-straps and with decorations it is full dress—with shoulder-straps but without decorations it is undress — and without either shoulder-straps or decorations it is night-dress. Think of that, ye native cavalry, with your dozen different combinations of dress!

If we are to judge of the number of decorations current amongst the Russian army by what we see here, they must indeed be a well-decorated body of men. Hardly one of the officers here has not three or four decorations of sorts. What they are for I don't know, but they mostly consist of light white and red enamelled sort of Maltese crosses, generally intermixed with crossed swords or gold filigree work. The Turkish war medal, which several wear, is handsome—a small thin gold medal, with a device on it of a cross above the crescent. The ribbons, too, instead of being worn straight as ours, are worn crossways through a ring, and we all certainly look very insignificant in the way of crosses and ribbons when confronted by our Russian *confrères* in all the glory of full dress. The Russians have no miniature medals, nor is it customary for them to wear the ribbon in undress as with us. The only decorations worn in undress are those for valour, and they are, I believe, always worn, and very rightly too. No Russian officer is allowed to wear *mufti*, and is always in uniform, unless, indeed, he may be travelling abroad on leave. Then, and then only, is he allowed to appear in plain clothes.

The Cossack dress, apparently the ordinary everyday national costume, consists of a loose short shirt with a waistcoat, or rather a sort of jacket with short skirts, fastening with hooks up to the throat, and loose baggy trousers tucked into a pair of top-boots. Over this is the coat, open at the neck, showing the jacket beneath, and hooked in front down to the waist, with long flowing skirts, reaching down below the calves of the legs. A narrow leather belt is worn round the waist, from which is suspended the knife in front and little ornaments at the side, with a revolver in addition in the case of the officers. The sword-belt, also a narrow leather strap, is worn over the right shoulder, the sword hanging by a couple of slings, back to the front, down the left side. Almost the whole of the hilt of the sword fits inside the scabbard, and nothing but the tip of the hilt is visible. The coats, of whatever material, or however many may be worn, are all of one shape and fit one over the other. In cold weather a *postin* or sheepskin coat of the same shape is worn on the top of all again.

The head-dress is a round lambskin fur cap without any peak or shape, and with a different-coloured cloth top, according to the regiment. This is the ordinary everyday dress of all Cossacks from the Caucasus.

The men have only one suit of uniform, consisting of a long black-cloth coat, with red facings and shoulder-straps in the case of the men of the 1st Regiment of Tomanski Cossacks here with us, and a thin red undercoat, fastening up to the throat; but this is never worn except on special occasions, and, so far as I have seen, every man wears, as a rule, his own private clothes, all cut in the same shape, but of whatever colour or material he likes best, the prevailing colour being dark brown, and the material the common Russian cotton

T

cloth to be found in all the bazaars in these parts. The non-commissioned officers have no distinguishing stripes on the arm like ours, simply a small band of gold lace across the shoulder-straps. All ranks, both officers and men, have a row of sham cartridge-cases across each breast. These are worn as ornaments in peace time, and are replaced by ball-cartridges in time of war.

Service of course is compulsory, and each man serves for his four years, practically speaking, without pay. His pony is his own property—in many cases, I fancy, bred by himself—and a hardier, stronger little animal it is impossible to conceive. Accustomed, I suppose, to roam about and pick up what it can all its life, it is the very beau-ideal of an animal for military service. In the coldest weather, with the thermometer at zero, it requires no clothing, but stands in the open, protected by nothing but its own shaggy coat. The ponies are all geldings, and are particularly quiet and tractable. At the end of a march they are all simply hobbled and turned loose, and allowed to graze where they like till dark, when they are brought in, and, instead of being tethered in lines like our cavalry horses, their heads are simply tied to a rope stretched between two pegs in the ground, as close together in double rows as the animals can well stand, and consequently the squadrons are accommodated in the smallest possible space. Each pony carries a head-stall and rope and a pair of hobbles, and is ridden with a snaffle-bridle of the simplest and roughest description. The saddle, like everything else, with the exception of his Berdan rifle, belongs to the Cossack, and is made apparently according to his own particular fancy. There is no such thing as any fixed regimental pattern in saddles, or in anything else. As a rule, the saddle is very narrow, hardly more than 12 or 14 inches from back to front, with two high flat wooden knobs forming the pommel and cantle, sitting very high, some three or four inches, off the pony's back, and with a seat composed apparently of a couple of stuffed leather cushions, one on either side, tied down by a leather surcingle. The saddle has two girths, narrow leather straps, one at the pommel and the other at the cantle, the surcingle being buckled round between the two. In one officer's saddle I noticed that the stirrup-leathers were tied down by the surcingle in such a manner that the stirrups had only three or four inches play, but I never noticed this in the case of the men.

Cossacks all ride well forward, with their heels as a rule tucked up under their ponies' ribs. They wear no spurs, and there is nothing for their knees to grip hold of. Their seat apparently seems to rest entirely on balance, and the power of managing their ponies on the use of their whips, combined with hard tugging at their bridles. Every man carries a whip, consisting of a short wooden handle about a foot long with a leather lash varying from one to two feet in length, with which, like the Turkoman, he belabours his pony on the slightest provocation.

Altogether, so far as I have seen, I should say the Cossacks' saddlery and accoutrements generally are of the roughest and most inferior description, and are by no means calculated to stand the wear and tear of a long campaign. The men, when left to themselves, seem by no means careful, and a large percentage of their ponies, despite the shape of the saddle-tree, are continually suffering from sore backs.

The Cossack drill I have never seen, so I can give no opinion on that point, but I should imagine it to be slow and simple. The rifle is carried slung over the right shoulder in a long-haired black-felt cover, except when, as often as not, on the march the men tie it to their saddle lengthways along the pony's off-side, just under the cushion forming the seat, where it lies flat and out of the way under their right knee. Similarly, their swords are often carried rolled up in their round felt cloaks, of the Caucasian pattern called *boorkas*, which each man carries strapped on to the saddle behind him. The rifle ammunition is carried in a soft long flat pouch slung over the left shoulder and resting under the right arm. Each pony also carries a small *kurzin* or double carpet-bag, strapped on like a valise behind the saddle; and this and the felt cloak is the only baggage they have.

Cossacks on service are allowed no tents or bedding, or anything beyond what each man can carry on his pony, and this felt cloak is his tent, greatcoat, bedding, and everything combined. The Cossack dress seems certainly admirably suited for the climate and work for which the men require it. The long skirts to their coats keep their thighs warm and protect their legs from cold and wet, and the small fur cap answers every requirement for a cold climate, while here, in the present hot weather, they seem to get along very well in their thin cotton underclothing, or else in a long print cotton coat of the same cut as their warmer ones. The light waterproof felt of which their cloaks are made is certainly a capital material, and I cannot help thinking that the Indian Government might take a profitable lesson from the Russians in the use of it. The Herat felts, for instance, are wonderfully close and good; and instead of going to the enormous expense that we do on campaigns, in the issue, to every follower even, of a waterproof sheet, each one of which has, I believe, to be procured from England at a ruinous rate of exchange, a piece of felt served out to each would answer the purpose of keeping his bedding dry almost just as well, and be infinitely warmer and more comfortable for him to sleep upon. We have all seen what little store the native follower sets on his waterproof sheet, and how little he appreciates its advantages; but give him a bit of felt to sleep upon, and see how tightly he will stick to it. Felts were served out to all our men and followers on this Mission during last winter with the happiest results, and I trust the experience thus gained here may not be thrown away. Another useful thing with which every Russian soldier is provided is the Caucasian *bashalik*, which has now been adopted throughout the entire Russian army. It consists of simply a peaked head-cover, fitting well over the cap and coming down on each side over the ears, with loose ends to wrap round the throat and chin. It is very light, weighing only a few ounces, and is a grand protection in cold or wet weather. The Russian sentries always wore it in bad weather, both day and night. Both felts and *bashaliks* could easily be manufactured in India at little cost, I should imagine, in comparison with waterproof sheets, and I feel pretty sure they would be much preferred for winter service in Afghanistan. The value of good Herat or Hazarah *barak* as warm clothing for troops in a climate like this I have already pointed out in a former letter, and I only hope that steps may be taken to increase the supply of it. Our men here are clothed in nothing else, and like it immensely.

The Cossack commences his service at eighteen, and the first two years are spent at the headquarters of his regiment learning his drill. At twenty he is sent to join the 1st Regiment of his corps wherever it may be, and serves with it till he is twenty-four. From the age of twenty-four to twenty-eight he serves with the 2d Regiment, and from twenty-eight to thirty-two with the 3d Regiment, after which he is free. The 1st Regiment is always permanently embodied, and apparently, in the case of the Cossacks, is generally on service away from its own district. The 2d Regiment of the corps is only embodied in the case of war or necessity, but the horses and men are all kept in readiness, and can be mobilised at any time within three days. The 3d Regiment, composed of men between the ages of twenty-eight and thirty-two, does not, I believe, keep up its horses. The discipline of the Cossacks, I fancy, is of the strictest, and the punishments severe. No body of men could be more respectful, as a rule, in their behaviour to their officers, not only to their own officers but to every Russian officer, whether combatant or non-combatant; and a non-commissioned officer or soldier, when addressed by any officer, invariably stands with his hand to his forehead at the salute as long as the officer is addressing him. Although, to our eyes, the absence of uniformity and the slovenly and untidy and often dirty appearance in their dress give the Cossacks outwardly a wild and irregular look, still, in the matter of interior economy and material discipline, they are, I fancy, equal to, if not stricter than, our own regiments. We pay great attention to uniformity, smartness, and the cleanliness of our saddlery and equipment; whereas the Russian officer, judging by the Cossacks, would seem to have no eyes scarcely for anything of the sort, but to be extra strict in the discipline and management of his men.

The Russian officers were much surprised, I believe, at the regularity of our native troops forming the escort of the Mission, and their steadiness on parade. They seemed to have an idea that all our Indian regiments were irregular, and their drill, therefore, as loose and slovenly as their own irregulars. The size of our men, too, greatly struck them. The Sikhs and Pathans of the 11th Bengal Lancers, mounted as they are on such fine strong horses, looked huge beside the small Cossacks on their ponies; while the Pathans and Afridis of the 20th Panjabis towered head and shoulders over the little Russian infantry. The only men of the latter that we have seen are the five-and-twenty men with the Russian Commission, belonging to a local Trans-Caspian rifle battalion. These men, though, I should say, are good specimens of their class, as these local battalions, raised for permanent service in Central Asia where there is no Russian population, have no particular districts to recruit from, and are composed of men from all parts of the Russian empire. I was surprised to find even Mussulmans in their ranks. Captain Komaroff's servant was a Tartar from Kazan on the Volga, rejoicing in the familiar name of Abdul; yet he lived with and was dressed just the same as the rest, his skin was as fair and his hair just as light coloured, and looking at him casually, I should never have noticed the least difference between him and the pure-bred Russian soldiers. Turki, though, was his native tongue, and he came under notice from the fact that he was always brought forward to interpret between his master and the Turkomans. I even heard an amusing account of his being the medium of communication at a visit his master paid to the governor of Herat. Captain Komaroff said what he wished to say to Abdul in Russian, Abdul translated it into Turki to a Turkoman, the Turkoman repeated it to a Jamshidi, and the latter finally conveyed it in Persian to the governor; and so on all the way back again. Yet it is only a few years, I believe, since these same Tartars rebelled when conscription was brought into force amongst them, and refused to perform the required military service. The Russian Government simply ordered a money payment to be levied instead, and after a few years the Tartars soon got tired of paying, and a few decorations judiciously distributed amongst the headmen finally removed all opposition, and now the Tartar puts in his service just the same as everybody else. Apparently they live, cook, and feed with the Russians, and to all practical intents and purposes are now Russians in all but name. The same thing is being repeated, I believe, with the Circassians and the Lesghins and other Muhammadans of the Caucasus at the present day. The conscription has only lately been put in force amongst them, and just now they are going through the money-payment stage; but before long that will probably be brought to an end, and they will be finally welded into Russian regulars just like the Tartars. The Caucasian Muhammadans, however, seem to be just as much Europeans as the Russians themselves, and consequently there is only the difference of religion to contend against, no diversity of race. The Caucasians are mostly fine-looking men, but the Russian soldiers, I must say, of whatever class that we have seen, are certainly very small men; and if those native editors who are so fond of dilating on the size and ferocity of the Russian soldier only interview the sowars and sepoys of our escort on their return, they will soon find out how little the latter think of them.

We have had no opportunity of testing it by practice, but I believe that our native troops are infinitely superior to the Russians in all feats of strength and agility, and without the least doubt all our men here consider themselves to be so, and look down on the Russian attempts at prowess with the greatest contempt. They all say that whenever they have tried the Russians at anything in their own camp they could always beat them, and though I have often seen the Russians standing round and watching our men practising, jumping, or putting the stone, or anything of that sort in our camp, I have never seen one of them attempt to join in. As to the Cossack *jigitoffka* (or mounted sports), our sowars have the meanest opinion of it.

The Russian infantryman is dressed in a dark-green jacket reaching down to the hips, and trousers of the same material tucked into a pair of top-boots, with the usual low, flat-topped, round-peaked cap to match. In the summer they wear a white cover to their cap, and a red cotton blouse, worn with a small black belt round the waist, making them look for all the world, as I heard it described, like the London Shoeblack Brigade.

The Russian boot I do not like. Our ammunition boots, with gaiters or *puttees*, seem infinitely preferable; and it stands to reason that a long top-boot, more especially with the tops loose and wrinkled, cannot be a good boot to march in. It is the national boot, however, and worn from infancy.

Never having seen the infantry on parade, I can say little or nothing about their drill or equipment. As far as I know, they have been employed on this Mission almost solely as officers' servants, and I always saw them putting up and taking down the *kibitkas*, loading the camels, and doing the general fatigue-duty of the camp. The only time I ever saw one on duty was as sentry over some commissariat stores, and the small size of the man in comparison with his rifle was then particularly striking. When standing with his rifle at the "order," the muzzle was well above his shoulder, and the bayonet above that again made him look smaller than ever. I never saw a Cossack sentry carrying a rifle—always a drawn sword, though once I saw one carrying two rifles slung down the left side, in addition to his drawn sword, possibly as a punishment.

The Cossack himself is a cheery, hardy little fellow, and I cannot imagine better material for an irregular soldier. They are all great singers, especially in chorus, and every squadron has its special chorus, whose duty it is to inspire the rest, and admittance to which is a post of honour. The men, as a body, I should say are religious, and they are always very particular about crossing themselves both before eating and at prayers. The Lord's Prayer and the evening hymn are regularly sung by the squadron chorus at retreat every day, and sound particularly well on a still evening.

The more one sees of the Cossacks, the more I think is one inclined to wonder what part they are destined to play in action. Mounted on ponies, sturdy though they are, still too small to meet regular cavalry in the open, and armed with light swords without any guard to the hilt whatever, they can hardly, one would think, be classed or utilised as regular cavalry, while their want of a bayonet and dress generally seems equally to unfit them for use as mounted infantry. There is nothing for it, therefore, but to class them as irregulars pure and simple. One great difference I noticed between them and our men is the freedom the Cossack enjoys in the use of his horse and his arms. The horse, or rather pony, is certainly the Cossack's own property, but so it is in the case of our own sowars, unless, indeed, the horses may be called regimental property; but whether or no, our men rarely or never take their horses out except for duty and parade, and to fire off their carbine is looked upon as a terrible thing—nothing less than trial by court-martial, in fact, for making away with Government ammunition. I remember when out in the *chul*, not long ago, my Sikh orderly came running up to tell me that he had just passed a whole sounder of wild pig. "Why did you not shoot one?" said I. "Oh, I did not dare to use my Government ammunition," said he. "I should be court-martialled if I did!" Here, no sooner do the Cossacks spy a sounder of wild pig, than off they go in full chase, firing freely at them both from horseback and on foot; and I know a Cossack who succeeded in killing three pigeons at one shot with his rifle. All this tends to make the men good shots and good riders, and to accustom them to the use of their arms; and why should our Sikhs, who love a wild pig just as dearly, be debarred from similar use and enjoyment of their horses and the arms in their hands? Of course, up here our supply of ammunition is limited; but still, when practicable, the example of the Cossacks, one would think, might be followed with advantage.

Russian officers, again, out shooting—not that many of them apparently do shoot, but still those that do—have no one but their own men with them; and why should we not follow the same plan? Why should an officer in India be dependent on coolies when he has his whole troop or company at his back? What better opportunity is there for the officer to get to know his men, or the men their officer, than away from barracks, and out in the freedom of the jungle; and why should not the men be encouraged to volunteer for such trips? There is no rule against it that I know of, but still it is rarely the custom.

To draw actual comparisons between our Indian cavalry and the Cossack is a difficult matter, they are so utterly dissimilar. The Cossack is an irregular, a scout, a forager, and an outpost man, rough and ready for any contingency, but he is a conscript who can be ordered about anywhere. The sowar, though theoretically an irregular, has been gradually worked up into the most regular of regulars, but, withal, is a volunteer, and to be treated accordingly. There, of course, lies the difference. The Cossacks are numerous, they can be ordered out in almost any number, and put to any sort of work, and freely expended in war. The sowar, on the contrary, enlists voluntarily, and belongs, as a rule, to a class unaccustomed to menial labour, and would not enlist if put to such labour. Moreover, their numbers are too small, and their losses too difficult to replace, to allow of their being expended like the Cossacks, or of their being frittered away on lines of communication and other such duties; and for the latter work, I must say, we sadly want the counterpart of the Cossack. The Cossacks do everything, from carrying *dâks* and parcels, to survey or any other work. We here hire Turkoman and Afghan sowars to carry our *dâks*, and send out coolies to put up survey-marks, never making use of our fighting men for any such purpose. No sooner, however, does a Russian topographer set to work than he sends out his Cossacks in different directions, and they go on in front of him putting up marks on different hills for days together; and when he has to send in a letter to headquarters, he sends it by the hand of one of his own men, and never dreams of hiring a Turkoman or any other man to take it.

One instance I may mention of how the Cossacks are worked occurred in the winter, when Colonel Kuhlberg sent us up a box of felt-lined Russian boots from Maruchak to Chahar Shamba, a distance of 55 miles. This box was big enough and heavy enough to require two men to carry it, yet a couple of Cossacks brought it all the way through, and thought nothing of it. They slung the box on a pole and carried it between them, each man resting one end of the pole on the saddle in front of him. What would have been the difference in numbers, supposing that an escort of two of our sowars had been required to take some similar box down from us to the Russian camp? First, the two sowars would have required a syce and a pony for horse-gear; next, a muleteer and a mule for their baggage, bedding, and tent, and another for the box. Total—two sowars, two followers, two horses, one pony, and two mules, all to do the work done by a couple of Cossacks and a couple of ponies as a matter of course.

Again, look at the Russian topographers. They are sent out with an escort of a dozen or fifteen Cossacks each, who do everything for them. One Cossack is the topographer's private servant. Four more carry his plane-table, stand, and instruments, and do all our Indian *khalassi's* work, such as the putting up of survey-marks, &c. The topographer has one canvas tent, and the Cossacks another, though that is a luxury not allowed them on service, whatever may be the weather. Total—one officer, fifteen men, sixteen ponies, two tents, and, say, one camel-man and four or five camels to carry the officers' baggage, supplies, &c., though the camel-man is not a necessity, as in one case I know the topographer had his private camels, and the Cossacks looked after them as part of their duty.

A Russian topographer must of course be compared as regards equipment with an English topographer, of whom we had none with us on the Mission. A survey officer doing triangulation in addition, necessarily requires more extensive equipment, and consequently comparisons between him and a Russian topographer hardly hold good. Still, supposing one of our survey officers to be sent out with a native cavalry escort of similar strength to the Russians, what a different party he would have! The escort alone would number fifteen sowars, eight *saises*, fifteen horses, eight ponies, four tents, and ten baggage-mules with three muleteers, or twenty-six men and thirty-four animals against the Russian fifteen men and sixteen animals, without counting the survey, followers, or private servants, &c.

The Cossack, so Russian officers tell me, prides himself upon his power of endurance. The Cossack pony, they say, has no speed, but is trained to endurance. Yet, if there is one thing more than another at which our Indian cavalry ought to and do excel in, it is in the power of endurance to do long marches, and I feel confident that when the time comes they will excel the Cossacks in this just as much as in everything else.

The men of our escort are now so accustomed to long marches, that 20 miles is thought nothing of by the sepoys even; and as to the sowars, they would think no more of double that distance now, than, I believe, a march of 20 miles would be thought of in India.

All the men on this frontier, I notice—men accustomed, as a rule, to ride from morning to night—always have a cord attached to their horse's headstall, sometimes aided by a small running chain noseband, sometimes without, but always with a small iron peg at the end of it. This cord on the march is looped up, and the iron peg is hung over the pommel of the saddle. Whenever they stop to rest, or drink tea, or chat, or anything else, they simply drive the iron peg into the ground with the heel of their boot or anything else that comes handy, and the horse is then left to graze quietly, while the man rests himself at his ease. Indian cavalry have the cord, but no iron peg at the end of it; and consequently, when they halt on the march in a treeless country like this, where there is seldom anything to tie the horses up to, they have to sit and hold their horses, and thus lose half the benefits of the rest they would otherwise enjoy—unless, indeed, they make use of the picketing pegs carried in marching order, but that is hardly worth while for a simple halt.

There are many good points to be found amongst these frontier men up here, and if ever we wish to raise the counterpart of the Cossacks, what a capital selection we might have amongst them!—good men, inured from their youth to ride long distances, and just as handy and as hardy as the Cossacks themselves. Our service is already most popular all along the frontier, as is evidenced by the ready manner in which even the Panjdeh Turkomans come forward for engagement in our postal line; and were the men to be allowed to bring their own horses and saddlery, and to wear their own style of dress, a regiment might be raised up here in no time, ready to take the field at a moment's notice, without a single follower or baggage-animal—and right good men they would be too.

We have already no less than 176 Turkoman sowars and 36 Persians in our service, employed in the carriage of the mails from here to Mashhad, a distance of 740 miles. The Turkomans are posted along the line from here to Zulfikar, 630 miles in length, and the Persians take the remaining 110 miles from Zulfikar to Mashhad.

These Turkomans, with their felt *numdahs* and their *kurzins* at the back of their saddles, are independent of all transport, and quite used to forage for themselves. What a capital squadron of irregulars they would make! but then they would have to be localised on the frontier. Transfer to India would ruin them. In fact, they would be almost as thoroughly spoilt there, as a corps of the sort raised in India would be out of place here. I have oftened wondered that the military authorities, when raising new cavalry regiments last year, did not try to include in their programme the raising of some local corps of this sort on the Baluchistan frontier. But it is not the raising of one, but of many such corps that we require.

The Afghans, I am sorry to say, are just as surprised as the Russians at the smallness of our army. An Afghan general only the other day asked me, "Why don't you keep a larger army? Look at the Russians," he said; "they have no money, but they have lots of men. You have lots of money, but no men. Why don't you get more? We are all ready to fight with you, side by side," he added, and I believe he was sincere in saying so; but still he shook his head over the small number of our men. The Russians cannot understand how we hold India at all with the force that we do, much less how we can spare a man to send out of it. It takes 90,000 of their men to hold the Caucasus, and yet they find us holding the whole of India with little more than double that number, and expecting to meet them in the field as well at no very distant date!

If, instead of wasting the money that we do in palatial barracks, high education, civil officers' tents, grand dispensaries, ornamental *kutcherries*, and suchlike luxuries, we were to content ourselves with a more moderate standard, and to spend the balance in extra battalions or a good reserve, how much better off we should be! However, to return to our Cossacks.

Not long ago, when out with a couple of Russian officers, we had occasion to cross the Murghab, then in high flood, and I was struck at the little the Cossacks seemed to think of swimming a river, though whether a larger proportion of them can swim well than of our men, I am doubtful. I arrived first at the banks, and getting some Jamshidis to help me, rigged up a raft of inflated goat-skins, and crossed my men and kit over. Next morning the Russians arrived. They declined all help from the Jamshidis, and said they had men enough themselves. The Cossacks, however, did not seem to get easily into the knack of managing the raft, and very soon broke all their ropes by trying to haul against the current, and did not get the last of their kit over till nightfall, and then only by the help of our postal *dâk* ropes, over which I and my sowars passed their light things, such as rifles, swords, and saddles, &c. The three sowars I had with me worked with a will, and helped the Cossacks right well throughout the day. When it came to swimming the horses over, though, the Cossacks had the best of it, as they got all theirs over without help, which was more than we did. Of my three sowars only one could swim, a young Sikh, and I will say he took his horse across in capital style. Our other horses, though, had all to be swum across by the Jamshidis, who took them over one by one. The Cossacks adopted a different plan, the result of the way their ponies are trained always to keep together. The banks were steep, and it was necessary to enter the river high up, and to swim down for some 200 yards before the horses could get out on the opposite bank. At first the leading Cossack tried it alone, swimming by the side of his horse, but the current overpowered him, and the horse broke loose about half-way across, and made back for the bank whence it came, and eventually got out some way down the river, and returned and rejoined its companions.

The Cossack, nothing daunted, swam back again, and after consultation with his men, I saw them all take off their cotton trousers and shirts, the only things they had left on, wind them round their heads, and prepare for a general start. Three men went ahead, each mounted on his pony barebacked, and without bridles—only a halter. Having gained wisdom from their leader's first attempt, they stuck to their ponies and rode them all the way across this time, instead of trying to swim alongside. The remaining five or six men brought in the other ponies behind these three, but as soon as they got well into the river they slipped off, and drove the ponies before them into the deep water; and once started, the ponies, all of their own accord, followed the leaders, and swam across all right. It was an amusing sight to see the three men, very much in a state of nature, cantering back across country to the camp nearly a mile away, followed by a dozen or more riderless ponies, the other men having gone back to cross by the raft.

Talking of swimming a river, I remember an anecdote told me by one of my Turkoman guides. He, with a party of his friends, had been out on a raid across the Oxus into Bokhara territory, and had captured a lot of camels, either double-humped or long-haired, I forget now which, but exceptionally valuable. They drove them all right down to the banks of the Oxus, and were just congratulating themselves on getting them away when the pursuers appeared. Behind them, as my guide said, were the gleaming swords and certain death; in front of them the vast river, with almost equally certain death. However, there was nothing for it but to chance it, and plunging in just as they were, they swam for their lives. All escaped, he said, but three, and those three sank with their horses and were never seen again. The cause was, he presumed, that the horses caught their feet in the stirrups—the only reason he could think of to account for their going down so suddenly. Whether this is possible or not, I do not know.

If ever our cavalry have to swim the Oxus, they will find a capital example ready to hand in the ferry-boats at Kilif and elsewhere. I have already described the manner in which these ferry-boats are towed across the river by one or two pairs of horses; and once our men have seen how easily it is done, I fancy they will jump at the idea, and, given the possession of one of these boats, they will soon learn to utilise their horses in towing it across, while they themselves, with their baggage and saddlery, are all accommodated inside.

U

With reference to the respective service equipment and establishments, one great advantage which the Russian has over the Indian army is the absence of followers. In the Russian camp here there is not a single follower that I know of, unless, indeed, it be the Mission cook. The waiters, the servants, and all are soldiers.

In the Cossack squadron there is no one but fighting-men. What a contrast to our squadron of Bengal cavalry, with its *saises*, and *bheesties*, and sweepers, and servants of all kinds and degrees! Why should our sowars' horses require a grass-cutter and a pony to feed them any more than the Cossacks'? Why should not our horses be rationed on service as well as the Cossacks'? As a matter of fact, the rations of the Cossack ponies here are better, both in quality and quantity, than those of native cavalry horses.

The Russians are intensely amazed at the idea of our sowars all having their servants, as they call it; and although there is only one *sais* between every two sowars, still I have heard that, when all the followers of a native cavalry regiment are totalled up, even on Kabul scale, they are not far short of one for every fighting-man; and the Russian idea, therefore, that each man has his own servant, is not so very far wrong. There are comparatively few places in Afghanistan where the grass-cutter can find any grass to cut; and of the two years that we have been in the country now, I don't suppose our grass-cutters have been of any use in the way of procuring fodder for their horses for half that time, and I have little doubt that it would have been much cheaper for Government to have rationed the horses throughout, and to have left the grass-cutters and ponies in India. Not that I would abolish the grass-cutter, or his pony either: I think that Government ought to be only too glad that such a nucleus of trained transport men and followers is kept up for them in peace-time, ready for immediate use in case of war. But, considering the barren nature of many parts of

Afghanistan, and with reference specially to service in that country, to the frequency with which native cavalry have to be dependent on the commissariat for their fodder when on service there, and to the length of time that both grass-cutter and pony have consequently often to be fed for doing little or nothing, I cannot help thinking that it would be easier in the long-run for the commissariat to undertake the feeding of the horses, and to relegate the grass-cutter and pony to transport duty. It is the case that in India the whole carriage of a native cavalry regiment is often furnished by these ponies and their grass-cutters; but that does not apply to Afghanistan, where the winter climate necessitates a much larger scale of bedding, clothing, and tentage. Moreover, this pony-carriage includes neither shops nor ammunition. To keep one man for every pony is excessive, too, for transport duties, even supposing the carriage to be sufficient. I see no reason, though, why some arrangement should not be come to, so that, on the outbreak of war, the grass-cutters and ponies of each cavalry regiment ordered on service to Afghanistan should be at once available for transport purposes, with their own regiment. Each grass-cutter would only have to be supplied with two extra ponies or mules, and the regiment would be completely equipped at once, shops and ammunition included, the grass-cutters being taken on for the campaign as public drivers instead of remaining as private servants.

As to other followers, *bheesties* are surely a luxury unnecessary on service; and if any men in the world ought to be able to cook their own food, Hindustanis ought, from whatever part of India they may have come from.

The Russian officer, even with us here on a commission of peace, has only his soldier-servant to look to, while most of us have four or five native servants of sorts. This number, of course, is cut down on service; but I well remember, during the Afghan campaign, that officers who lost their native servants were usually able to get a man from their regiments quite willing and able to wait upon them, and do for them generally, just as well as the regular servant whom they replaced; and I see no reason why the system should not be more frequently adopted when practicable, and an officer in a native regiment be allowed a servant from amongst his men when the man is willing to serve. Every step tending to reduce the fearful number of followers on service must be a step in the right direction. How can we hope to compete on even terms with the Russians, in a barren country like Afghanistan for instance, when every army-corps of 25,000 men we put in the field, means 25,000 followers in addition, who have all to be equally fed and clothed, and also protected? Our native troops, I feel sure, would willingly go on service without their usual number of followers were Government only to give them an inducement to do so, in the shape of increased field allowances. I see lots of recommendations in the papers for increasing the sepoy's pay, but surely the first thing we require to get sanctioned is not so much increase of pay in peace-time, but extra inducement to go on service in case of war. The present system of granting *batta* and donations, one cannot help thinking, is a bad one, being uncertain in its amount, and rewarding all alike, whether they have been simply a day across the frontier, or whether they have borne the heat and burden of the day throughout a long campaign. It tells equally unfairly on officers and men. The medal-hunter, up for ten days, and the man who serves throughout, get the same money reward. Then, again, the satisfaction caused by the grant of *batta* is in a great measure marred by the irritation caused by stoppages for rations and other suchlike inconsiderate retrenchments.

Take the native cavalry, for instance, and see how unfairly the stoppages for horse rations fall on the men, and what irritation these stoppages cause. Why cannot Government, instead of raising by some trifle the sowar's pay, say once and for all that free rations will be granted on service for both man and beast? I can think of nothing better calculated to sharpen the sowar's desire to go on service than such an order; and I know of nothing more calculated to deaden that desire than the present orders regarding stoppages, which leave the sowar, so far as I am aware, worse off on service than he is in cantonments.

The Russian army, I believe, has a regular scale of field allowances, and the officers and men here on duty with the Boundary Commission are now drawing, I am told, in some cases something like treble and quadruple the amount of their ordinary pay. This is possibly exceptional. Still the system of field allowances seems to be a good one, and one that we might adopt for our Indian army with advantage.

The ordinary pay of a captain of Cossacks is, I have heard, 85 roubles a-month in Russia, raised to 130 roubles when serving in Central Asia; a rouble being equal to 2s. at the present rate of exchange. The Cossack soldier's pay is 27 roubles a-year, or $2\frac{1}{4}$ roubles a-month. Out of this by no means large amount, hardly sufficient for much more than tobacco one would think, the Cossack has to pay for his horse and equipments: if he does not bring his own pony, he is provided with one; and the cost, which, I believe, varies from 25 to 50 roubles, takes up his first, and possibly his second year's pay, as the case may be. Then his sword costs 3 roubles more, and his saddlery something else, so that, altogether, I doubt if he even gets enough to buy his tobacco after all; but then the Russian theory is that every man is bound to give his service for his country free of pay. Rations, of course, are always provided by the Government. Then all Russian soldiers, when on service, have the privilege of being entitled to draw their pay in gold instead of in paper directly they cross the frontier. Not that they are actually paid in gold, but they are paid in paper roubles at the current rate of exchange with gold, and this nearly doubles their pay at a stroke. In addition to this, they have their field allowances. I don't quite know what these amount to, but the result is, I hear, that the Cossacks who are now with us on this Mission get 9 roubles a-month apiece instead of 2¼, or exactly quadruple their ordinary pay, and this in addition to free rations for man and horse. If all ranks on service get extra pay at the same liberal rate, we can hardly wonder at the invariable anxiety of the Russian army for war, and all the more reason that we should give our own men some similar inducement to be equally ready to meet them.

Another point, apparently, in which the Russian service differs much from ours, is in the strength of their hospital establishments. Here we have an establishment of forty-five men, with five *dandies*, thirteen mule *kajavahs*, and a Takht-i-Rawan with their muleteers; while, so far as I know, the only sick-carriage possessed by the Russian Commission is one stretcher carried on a camel, and a couple of pony-carts available for sick if required, with an establishment of perhaps three or four hospital apprentices.

The number of our hospital establishment, too, has only been reduced to its present limit after considerable time and trouble. Something like nearly half the number of *dooli-walas*, with which the medical authorities wished to burden us, were sent back from Quetta before we started, and the balance was subsequently reduced again when the return party went back, their places being taken by Persian mule *kajavahs*. When we on a Boundary Commission find the excessive number of *kahars* an unbearable nuisance, what must it be with an army in the field? Why the medical authorities should continue to insist on the sole use of *dandies* for the carriage of the sick and wounded in a country like Afghanistan I don't know, when I presume there can be no doubt that a large percentage of sick, at any rate almost all simple ordinary cases, can be carried just as well in light ambulance-carts or mule *kajavahs*. Surely the fifty mules or the twenty-five or thirty pony-carts necessary for the carriage of 100 ordinary sick, are more easily fed and protected, and take up less room on the line of march, than the 700 *kahars* and their 100 *dandies*, more especially when the *kahars* themselves are generally the first to fall sick, and to fill the *dandies* they come to carry. Every one who remembers what rear-guard work was like on Sir Frederick Roberts's march from Kabul to Kandahar, will, I am sure, have a lively recollection of the *dooliwala*, and will have no wish for a larger percentage of them with him on another long march than is absolutely necessary. So far as I have seen of Afghanistan, I know of no impediment to the use of mule-panniers, or even of light ambulance-carts; and certainly, so far as we on this Mission are concerned, we might have had the latter with us all the time, I believe.

The ordinary small Indian mule is not, I know, big enough to carry two men, but Persian mules can carry two men with ease. Many Persian mules are too big even for artillery purposes, and why should not a certain number of these latter be kept up for ordinary transport work in peace-time, ready for hospital service in case of war? The number required would be nothing so very great, and could easily be procured. A large number, I believe, could be purchased in Mashhad alone, and I know of nothing to prevent them being marched down direct from there to Quetta, instead of being sent all the way round by sea. Nothing showed us the utility of mule-pannier sick-carriage more than the snowstorm that overtook Sir Peter Lumsden's party when crossing the Paropamisus in April 1885. *Kahars* and *dandies* were useless then, and had we been dependent on them, not a man could have been moved; whereas, with the help of the Persian mule *kajavahs* and some Mosley crates over the ordinary pack-saddle, forty or fifty frost-bitten men were sent in from Chashma Sabz to the camp at Tirpul, a distance of 25 miles, two and two on a mule, in a single march, without the slightest trouble or mishap.

The Russian commissariat establishment, again, seems to be quite on a different footing from ours. Here, on this Mission, our commissariat numbers some thirty men—after all reductions with the return party; while that of the Russian Mission is practically nothing at all but the officer, as everything with them is done by contract. The Russians have neither butcheries nor bakeries. The troops apparently do the work of the former for themselves; and as for the latter, they are content with the bread of the country. I have before once or twice mentioned the excellence of the country *nan*, and I can only say that I have myself lived on it for weeks at a time, and that I never had any desire for change. In fact, to my mind, good fresh *nan* is infinitely preferable to bad commissariat bread; and bread baked hurriedly on the line of march is almost always bad.

Our Indian commissariat might well follow the Russian example in this case, I think; and if, instead of burdening themselves on service in Afghanistan with those huge unwieldy iron ovens, they were to leave them and their convoys of white Cawnpore Mills flour behind, and to content themselves with the ovens and the flour of the country, they would find their work much simplified; and the men, I believe, would get, on the whole, better bread than they do at present. A fresh *nan* nicely warmed is capital eating, very different from the so-called commissariat brown bread; and if the services of a few good Afghan and Persian bakers were only secured to teach the Indian bakers how to make and use the ordinary country ovens made here in the ground, the necessity for carrying iron ovens would be done away with. These country ovens are to be found everywhere; and were the commissariat to take up the baking of *nan* instead of bread, not only could all Mahomadans have their rations issued in baked *nan* instead of in *atta* should occasion arise, but I really believe the Europeans would prefer the *nan* to the bread.

CHAPTER XXII.

THE DEPARTURE OF THE JOINT COMMISSIONS—TASHKURGHAN AND HAIBAK.

CAMP HAIBAK, 26th September 1886.

I MENTIONED in my last letter that we at Shadian were expecting to march shortly for Haibak, but instead of marching straight across the hills as we had expected, we moved down to the plains on the 14th, and camped at a place called Ziarat-i-Ali Sher, just at the mouth of the Shadian gorge; and after a few days' halt, while Sir West Ridgeway's party were marching up from Khamiab to Balkh, we marched on by the following route to Haibak:—

		Miles.
19.	Gor-i-Mar,	12
20.	Naibabad,	11
21.	Tashkurghan,	13
22.	Gaznigak,	15
23.	Bad Asiah,	11
24.	Haibak,	14
	Total,	76

Sir West Ridgeway, coming up behind us, arrived here at Haibak to-day, and we shall now all march on together.

Gor-i-Mar is the most eastern village watered from the Balkhab river, and is divided by a low arid ridge from the Tashkurghan lands beyond. Our road from the mouth of the Shadian gorge cut across the plain three or four miles to the south of Mazar, and joined the highroad running parallel to the canal which waters Gor-i-Mar a little beyond it. The latter village, as its name—lit., the Grave of the Snake—implies, was the traditional scene of an encounter between Ali and some huge fabulous serpent, in which, of course, the latter was vanquished.

Naibabad is a little place, the houses of which are mostly quite new; some twenty families and a few Khasadars and *dâk* sowars having been settled there to keep open communication along the highroad. A small rill of water has been brought down with some trouble from the hills; and if the supply can only be maintained, it will be a great boon to travellers, who would otherwise have to do the 25 miles on to Tashkurghan at a stretch. The road here we found very uninteresting, the great rocky hills on our right rising straight up some 4000 or 5000 feet above the plain, and on our left an uninhabited and uncultivated waste stretching away towards the Oxus as far as the eye could reach. Even the *tepes*, or artificial mounds, marking the sites of former fortlets, which were so numerous between Mazar and Gor-i-Mar, here ceased, and there was nothing to break the monotony of this great level plain—not even a tree or a bush. The undulations of the ridge between Gor-i-Mar and Naibabad in former times used to conceal many a raiding party, I was told, who at times rendered the road almost impassable; but a couple of strong circular towers, with their garrison of Khasadars, have quite put a stop to all that, and highway robbery is now quite unknown.

Tashkurghan is the great trade-mart of Afghan Turkistan, and about its most important place. Here the caravans from India on the one hand, and Bokhara on the other, all break bulk, and from here the merchandise is distributed all over the country. Nothing is obtainable at Mazar even, except through Tashkurghan. Approached from the west, the latter town appears to be nothing but a huge mass of gardens, composed of apricot and other trees, surrounded by the usual mud-walls, and it looks double or treble the size of Mazar. As we passed along the southern side of the town, Sirdar Sher Ahmed Khan pointed out to me a new garden-house lately built as a guest and reception house, in which he was most comfortably lodged by the governor when on his way through to and from Badakshan. Our camping-ground just beyond was a confined stony waste, a mass of rocks and boulders. Last year, they told us, it was a fine level plain, but the town was overtaken in the spring by a great flood, which washed down from the hills right across this *maidan* and into and through the town, doing no end of damage—a thing which had never been known to happen before, showing that the storms and floods we had to go through in the spring were as unusual here as in the Murghab valley.

Just to the east of our camp lay the old fort of Tashkurghan, built on a rising ground, and with precipitous sides except to the west, where the buildings all down the slope of the hill are fully exposed to fire. The place is mostly in ruins, and I presume was originally built to guard against raiders issuing from the gorge in the hills just opposite; but now the times have changed, and instead of guarding against raiders from the hills, we have to prepare to defend the hills against invaders from the plains; and certainly a more wonderful gorge to defend I never saw. Looking south from our camp, there was nothing to be seen but high, rocky, and almost precipitous hills, rising some 5000 or 6000 feet above the plain on either side of the gorge, with a great wall of rock running down between them, through which it seemed hardly possible that we should ever find our way. However, before describing the gorge, I must tell you of our visit to Khulm, the ruins of which lie between two and three miles to the north of Tashkurghan. Riding out in the afternoon with Colonel Bax, Captains Cotton and Drummond, Sirdar Sher Ahmed Khan, and

Ressaldar-Major Baha-u'-din Khan, we first visited the Tashkurghan bazaar, a long street covered with matting and rafters, and culminating in a curious sort of *chaharsu*, forming the centre of the cloth-market called the *Tim*. The shops were mostly shut, as is usually the case in these parts except on market-days; but the building was worth seeing, being nicely domed and ornamented with lots of small china saucers let into the walls. The money-changers all sat on a raised platform in the centre, but did not seem to be doing much business.

Khulm we were rather disappointed in, as it took us some time to get there, and when we did arrive, we found nothing but a huge flat-topped mound, with some old mud walls and ruins behind it. These latter, I was told, were the remains of the later Khulm destroyed by Ahmad Shah Abdali, who founded Tashkurghan some century and a half ago, and took all the inhabitants away from Khulm to populate it. Only a hundred families or so of Usbegs now remain on the outskirts of the former city. The real old Khulm consists simply of the great mound, some 600 yards in length by 300 or 400 yards in breadth, and say 30 or 40 feet in height, and covered with broken pottery. On the western side there are the remains of a detached fort and a succession of smaller mounds, marking the site of the oldest city, I suppose; but beyond that there is nothing to see. Riding back, I found that it took me thirty-six minutes as fast as my horse could walk to get through the gardens and town of Tushkurghan, which will give some idea of its size—not that there is much of a town to look at. We rode through nothing but a succession of lanes, bounded by 8-feet-high mud-walls on either side, with just the tops of the apricot and fig trees beyond peeping over them. Few houses were to be seen and fewer people, and each lane had a canal running down the centre of it just the same as the last. I know of nothing more dreary and monotonous than an Eastern town. Except in the actual street devoted to the bazaar, there is no sign of life—everything is shut up and hidden behind those interminable mud-walls; and were it not for a few men sitting solemnly and silently here and there at the various corners, one might be in a city of the dead.

Tashkurghan is the most easterly portion of Sirdar Ishak Khan's province, and belongs to Afghan Turkistan, though it has a subordinate governor of its own, Mirza Purdil Khan. The district extends for some 15 or 20 miles to the east up to the confines of Khairabad, the first habitation on the Badakshan side, a place built lately by Sirdar Abdullah Jan, the governor, as a resting-stage for travellers on the highroad to Khanabad, his present capital.

All this country was formerly entirely independent, under various Usbeg Mirs, such as those of Badakshan, Kunduz, Ghori, Haibak, Saighan, Tashkurghan, Balkh, Nimlik, &c.; and Khan Bahadur Ibrahim Khan, who knows the country thoroughly, tells me that it is a well-known fact that Amir Dost Muhammad Khan and his son Muhammad Akhbar Khan, when flying through it on their way to Bokhara at the time of the first British occupation of Kabul, were the first to discover the weakness of the Mirs; and no sooner was Dost Muhammad seated on the throne again, than he at once despatched Akhbar Khan with a body of troops against them. Muhammad Akhbar Khan succeeded in bringing the whole country under subjection, with the exception of Badakshan and Maimanah. Muhammad Afzal Khan, afterwards Emir, was appointed the first Afghan governor, and he it was who finally demolished the Nimlik fort, making use of its wood-work and material for the construction of Takht-i-Pul, which was then his capital. After the death of Amir Dost Muhammad Khan in 1863, the province passed through various and many vicissitudes; but in 1866, when the Amir Sher Ali Khan had finally established himself on the throne, he sent Naib Muhammad Alum Khan to Balkh as governor of the province. The latter was a Shiah, a follower of Ali, and for that reason made Mazar his capital, and it has continued so to the present day. Naib Muhammad Alum Khan at once attacked Badakshan, and his troops, under General Hafizullah Khan, defeated and made a prisoner of Mahmud Shah, the Mir of Badakshan, and Badakshan was occupied as well as Shignan, Roshan, and Wakhan. Muhammad Alum Khan subsequently annexed Maimanah, as previously related, and just before Amir Sher Ali's death, the entire Turkistan province was for the first time brought completely under Afghan subjection. After Naib Muhammad Alum Khan's death, Shahghassi Sherdil Khan, and on his death his son Kushdil Khan, succeeded him; and on the death of Amir Sher Ali, General Ghulam Haidar Khan, Wardak, was appointed governor by Yakub Khan. Ghulam Haidar Khan fled to Bokhara on the arrival of Amir Abdur Rahman in March 1880, and the province was then divided in two by the latter. Sirdar Abdullah Jan Tokhi was appointed governor of Badakshan, including Shignan, Roshan, and Wakhan, as well as Kunduz, Ghori, Baglan, Khinjan, and Bamian; while Sirdar Ishak Khan became the governor of the western portion, with the exception of Maimanah, which was given semi-independence. Bamian and Haibak have since been taken by the Amir under his direct administration, and have their local governors appointed from Kabul.

The local Mirs have almost all been ousted, and Mir Sultan Murad Khan, the son of the late Mir Atalik of Kunduz, and the Mir of Roshan, are, I think, about the only ones left. The former lives at Talikan, instead of at Kunduz, which, I believe, is most unhealthy and unpleasant to live at. The country round it, however, so Sirdar Sher Ahmad Khan tells me, is covered with wood and jungle, and is full of tigers and game of all kinds. I trust I may be able to visit it myself some day. Badakshan is described as a very cold and poor country, and one that never can be rich owing to the want of culturable land,—very different from most of the western portion of Afghan Turkistan, which has plenty of arable land, and wants nothing but the population to cultivate it. Before closing my description of Afghan Turkistan, I must not forget to mention the tradition current amongst the Afghans here to the effect that the British and Russian troops are destined to fight some day at Dasht-i-Arzanak and Dasht-i-Bakwa, when much blood is to be shed. The Dasht-i-Arzanak is a plain some 15 miles west of Balkh, and Dasht-i-Bakwa lies between Farah and Kandahar, so that it is not so very improbable that the Afghans may see their tradition fulfilled after all, though what part they are to take in the fight is not stated.

Our march on the morning of the 22d through the Tashkurghan gorge was one of the most interesting that we have had for a long time. Our road first wound along for some $2\frac{1}{2}$ miles up the bank of a swift mountain-stream, past a succession of gardens, till we crossed a little brick bridge just at the entrance of the gorge. Here a wonderful sight met our eyes. Imagine a solid and precipitous mass of rock rising up on either side to a height of a thousand feet I should think, leaving just sufficient room for the stream and roadway by its side. At one place these precipitous walls are hardly 40 feet apart, and I do not suppose the width exceeds double that distance at any point for the first 300 yards or more. After that the rocks recede a bit, but the defile continues for some 10 miles, bounded on either side by almost impassable hills, with an average of hardly more than some 200 yards of level ground between them all the way. Then comes the little village of Sayat, and beyond that the road emerges into the comparatively wide and grassy plain of Gaznigak. Farther on the road is comparatively uninteresting, and Bad Asiah has nothing particular about it but an old mud-wall on the top of a hillock to represent the traditional windmill that gave its name to the place. Haibak is a beautiful fertile valley dotted all over with villages and gardens. The hills here are several miles apart, and every bit of available ground seems to be under cultivation. The governor lives in an old mud-fort on the top of a low hill, at the head of the valley immediately above the bazaar, which consists of a couple of short streets, roofed over with sticks and grass, and containing, strange to say, many Hindus' shops—though what Hindus are doing here I do not know. The old barrack square for troops, just below the bazaar, is now mostly in ruins, and the garrison only numbers some 200 Khasadars all told.

The highroad to Bamian leaves the valley at its southern end, and wanders through a beautiful gorge, bounded by high cliffs on either side, and all the space between one mass of gardens and orchards. The road we shall follow to Ghori branches off to the east. I do not think I have ever seen finer apricot-trees than those growing here, though the walnuts are not of any great size. The inhabitants of Haibak call themselves Chagatais, a Persian-speaking race, supposed to be of Turkish origin, though now generally mixed up with the Tajiks, and are most friendly and civil to meet. Altogether, I should say that Haibak ought to form a capital site for a cantonment. The valley, I believe, stands at an elevation of something like 3100 feet, and ought to be warm in winter, and not too hot in the summer. At some time or other it seems to have been a favourite resort of the Buddhists. Only a couple of miles from the fort there is a wonderful tope, called, as usual, Takht-i-Rustam. It is a great beehive-shaped *stupa*, some 70 feet in diameter and 30 feet in height, hewn out of the solid rock, with a platform, or, as it is locally called, a throne, on the top of it, also hewn out of the same solid rock, and some

20 feet square and 8 feet in height, with a small chamber exactly in the centre of it, entered by a passage from the south.

The entrance to the tope lies through a wide tunnel in the hillside, and the effect of suddenly finding one's self in the deep circular cutting around it is very strange. A rocky hill to the north is honeycombed with caves, from the large-domed vault to a long double corridor, while on the top of the hill there are the remains of some old building of unburnt brick. The view from the top of the tope, with the whole of the Haibak valley, say some ten miles in length and two in breadth, full of villages and orchards, spread out below one, backed by the hills beyond, is very fine, and worthy of Buddhist selection for such a site. There are many other Buddhist remains about, such as Hazar Sum, or the thousand caves, in the hills at the northern end of the valley, and the Sum-i-Sangi, or rocky caves, some way off to the south-west; but unfortunately we have no time to visit these. Captain Talbot, I hear, though, spent some days examining them.

Our party now is a very small one, as Majors Holdich and Maitland, Captains Peacocke, Talbot, and Griesbach, are all ahead examining and surveying the various passes over the Hindu Kush, and we do not meet them again till we get to Charikar. Colonel MacLean, with Mr Merk, Captain de Laessoe, and Munshi Allah Bakhsh, started for Mashhad on the 15th from Khamiab, Captain Gore having started for Bundar Abbas some days before. Major Durand, who, I am sorry to say, has been suffering for some time from a bad sprain, the effect of his horse falling with him, and is still unable to ride, has been kindly invited by the Russian Government, at the instance of M. Lessar, to accompany the Commission on its return march *viâ* Chahar Jui, on the Oxus, to Merv, and thence by rail to the Caspian—a much shorter journey than marching all the way *viâ* Mashhad to

Astrabad, the nearest port on the Caspian, and a much quicker and more interesting way of going home.

On what date the Russian Commission started we have not yet heard. All its members, I believe, were delighted at the thought of an early return to the civilisation of Ashkabad and Tiflis, and were very glad to get away so soon. The orders for their return were evidently quite unexpected, as I hear that a party of some fifty Cossacks arrived only a day or two before Sir West Ridgeway's departure to relieve their time-expired men, and these would hardly have been sent so far had the authorities had any idea of such an early break-up of the Mission. How it was, too, that the Russian Government recorded the agreement for the withdrawal of the joint Mission on the 26th August, and then never communicated it to their Commissioner till the 12th September, is one of those strange facts of Russian diplomacy that I suppose no fellow can be expected to understand. However, once the orders were received, no time was lost. The British Mission dined with their Russian *confrères* the same evening, and next day Colonel Kuhlberg and all his officers were the guests of Sir West Ridgeway, when the two Commissions finally said good-bye to each other.

Sir West Ridgeway has been suffering greatly from fever on the march from Khamiab, and is consequently much pulled down; but the change to the hill air here will, it is hoped, soon drive the fever away. The health of the camp generally has much improved, and with plenty of warm clothing, we hope to get over the passes in front of us without risk. Last year Major Maitland and Captain Talbot had heavy snow at an elevation of only some 8000 feet early in October, whereas we shall be crossing passes some 13,000 or 14,000 feet in height; but if the weather keeps up, we have every hope that we may get through in time. With Sir West Ridgeway we have Colonel Bax, Captains Cotton and

Drummond, Dr Owen, Nawab Mirza Hasan Ali Khan, Kazi Muhammad Aslam Khan, Khan Bahadur Ibrahim Khan, Sirdar Muhammad Aslam Khan, Sirdar Sher Ahmad Khan, Ressaldar-Major Baha-u'-din Khan, and Subadar Muhammad Husain Khan, and myself, with the whole of the cavalry and infantry escort. The whole camp seems to be afflicted with the desire to buy ponies, and we shall probably march into Peshawar with a goodly number of animals of sorts. Prices, though, have gone up here wonderfully of late.

We shall probably halt for a day or two at or near Kabul on our way back. The Amir has given Sir West Ridgeway a most cordial invitation to Kabul, and everything betokens a very friendly reception for us there.

CHAPTER XXIII.

OVER THE HINDU KUSH.

CAMP CHARIKAR, 12*th October* 1886.

I HAVE already telegraphed our arrival on the southern side of the Hindu Kush; but I must now try to take up the thread of the narrative from the date of my last letter from Haibak, where we had collected for our march across the mountains. The origin of the name Hindu Kush it is impossible to tell. There is a tradition here that these mountains were all formerly included in the general name of Himalaya, but that, at a time while Balkh was still held by Hindus, some ancient conqueror invaded the country from the north, and all the Hindus fled for refuge into the mountains, and were there overtaken by a sudden snowstorm and killed to a man: hence the name Hindu Kush, from the Persian word *kushtan*, to kill. However this may have been, no doubt these mountains are liable to sudden and severe storms at this time of the year, and had not the storm encountered by Sir West Ridgeway and his party on the top of the pass on the morning of the 6th luckily passed off, there is no saying what might have been the result. To have been snowed up in such a place, with nothing for our horses and mules to eat, would have been very hard on the latter, to say the least of it. Rations for men we could carry with us, but fodder for such a number of animals—nearly 1300 all told

—could not be carried with us; and as the Afghan stores very soon ran out, a forced halt on the top of the pass would have been anything but pleasant. In fact now, as I write, there is a storm raging over the hills, and whenever the clouds lift a bit we can see the freshly fallen snow even on the lower ranges, which shows what we have just escaped on the higher.

Our march over the Chahar Dar pass has been quite a novelty to us after all the time we have spent amongst the rolling downs of the *chul*, and I for one have enjoyed it immensely. At Chashmah-i-Sher we had our last day's pheasant-shooting. We found a lot of birds in the high reeds there, but they were difficult to get at. Colonel Bax, Captain Drummond, Sirdar Muhammad Aslam Khan, Subadar Muhammad Husain Khan, and I, with a dozen sowars of the 11th Bengal Lancers, formed a line across country and did our best to get the birds out, but our bag was only a small one after all. The marvel is that any pheasants, or even *chikor*—the local partridge—survive at all. In the winter, as one of my guides explained to me, when the snow is fresh and a foot or more in depth, the birds all come down into the open valley in search of food, and the people turn out *en masse* after them. As soon as the birds are flushed a horseman gallops after them, and if he can only mark where they settle he is certain to catch them, as they rarely fly a second time, but hide in the snow, where their tracks betray them, and they are pulled out by hand without difficulty. In Badakshan, I am told, they use dogs for the purpose; and an Afghan sowar, with whom I was out the other day, gave me a graphic account of the big hunts they have there after these birds in the winter.

The Ghori valley is a broad level plain full of villages running down both banks of the Surkh Ab or Kunduz river. We camped at the head of the valley, and here it was that, owing to the difficulties of the road ahead, Sir West Ridgeway determined to break up the camp into three. Sir West, with Dr Owen, Nawab Mirza Hasan Ali Khan, Kazi Muhammad Aslam Khan, Sirdar Sher Ahmed Khan, Subadar Muhammad Husain Khan, and an escort of 50 sowars of the 11th Bengal Lancers and a working party of the 20th Panjab Infantry, under Captain Drummond, went on ahead; the remainder of the camp, with Captain Cotton, Khan Bahadur Ibrahim Khan, Sirdar Muhammad Aslam Khan, and myself, under the command of Colonel Bax, followed the next day; and the camel *kafila* of heavy baggage, under Ressaldar-Major Baha-u'-din Khan, followed us again.

Our first march of 24 miles over two *kotals* and a very rough road to Dahan-i-Kaian was stiff work for the mules, but they did it all right. The hills we passed over were covered with pistachio-bushes, not so high as the Badghis bushes, these rarely exceeding 8 or 10 feet in height, while the nut, I was also told, is not so good. The Shaikh Ali Hazarahs, who live about Ghori, make their living a good deal, I fancy, by gathering these nuts for the Kabul market. They are a wild but cheerful and pleasant set of men. Up the Iskar valley we passed through a good many juniper-trees, and the place swarmed with *chikor*. I also shot a mountain-hare there—a beast more like a rabbit, but with black-tipped ears. Chahar Dar is a curious little valley, or rather a circular sort of hollow in the hills at an elevation of about 6570 feet; but to get to it we had to cross the Kotal-i-Fazak at an elevation of 10,000 feet. Such a climb as it was too! and an amusing sight it was to see all the cavalry *saises* going up in a long zigzag, each man holding on to his pony's tail. On the top we had a grand view, with a high, rugged, rocky range of hills in front of us, covered with patches and rifts of last year's snow. The Kotal-i-Bargah was not so high as the Fazak, but the descent was a real steep one, and we all felt very glad that we had not to go up it. Chahar Dar is so called from the four valleys or doors that here open into this little valley at right angles to each other. The main stream is full of trout, and Captain Griesbach tells me that they took a fly greedily: the water, however, was icy-cold and as clear as crystal.

Standing on the camping-ground I noticed curious little cylinders of mud full of some white stuff, about half an inch to an inch in length, which none of us could make out the origin of till we called our guide, a local Hazarah. He at once scratched up the ground and pulled out lots more and bigger, and showed us that each was full of locusts' eggs, and that what we first saw were the empty shells out of which the eggs had been eaten by birds, more especially the choughs which here abounded. The whole of this part of the country has been almost depopulated, it seems, by the locusts, which have been settled down now for the last three or four years; and so terrible is the plague of them that the unfortunate people have been unable to raise any crops, and have been driven away one after another to try and get their living at Balkh and other places. Strange to say, these locusts' eggs, laid in these little mud cases just below the surface of the ground, do not appear to be killed by the cold of winter, and the young come out as fresh as possible in the spring.

The morning we left Chahar Dar we started in rain and mist, which quite hid all the beauty of the scenery from us. We wound up along the banks of a nicely wooded mountain stream, and being unable to see the bare rocky mountains above, we might for all the world have been in a Highland glen in the north of Scotland in the midst of a good old Scotch mist. By the time, however, that we got up to Chap Darah, 4000 feet above Chahar Dar, we found that what had been rain and mist below was snow up there, and when we joined Sir West Ridgeway's camp we found out what a very unpleasant morning they had had of it. When *réveillé* went the snow was several inches thick and still falling, with a bitter cold wind, and the only thing to be heard was that old familiar sound we are so well acquainted with—namely, the beating of the tents with sticks to clear off the accumulated snow. Morning after morning in the winter did we go through that to get the weight of snow off before the ridge-pole of the tent gave way, but we never thought, after the heat of summer, that we were destined to hear it again. However, the snow ceased, and Sir West Ridgeway's party got off all right; but it still looked threatening, and when Colonel Bax arrived he determined to push straight on and get over the pass, if he could, that night, and not run the risk of being snowed up. So on we went, and that march of 28 miles over the Hindu Kush will long be remembered by most of us, I fancy. We halted at Chap Darah for breakfast, and what a glorious appetite for breakfast an elevation of 10,580 feet at this latitude does give one! Breakfast on the roadside is now a regular institution with us, and, following the example of the Persian *abdars*, our Indian *khidmatgars* always now have all their materials for breakfast in the *kurjins* or carpet saddle-bags on their ponies behind us, and wherever we stop they have our tea and breakfast ready in less than no time. While we sat and breakfasted—all wrapped up in our greatcoats, for it was precious cold—the clouds gradually rose and eventually the sun came out, and we had a fine day after all. The top of the pass we made out, by aneroid readings, to be 13,500 feet above sea-level, and the scenery all the way up was very wild but desolate. The road followed the banks of the stream, but all trees, bushes, and, indeed, vegetation of any kind, gradually ceased, and we passed through nothing but a bare, wild, rocky country without a sign of life. Just near the top of the pass we crossed the first real snow, a great furrowed frozen mass as hard as a rock: the result, I should fancy, of the freezings of many years. The freshly fallen snow all melted immediately the sun came out, but we apparently just touched the permanent snow-line, as there were patches of old frozen snow all about. The view from the top was very disappointing, as we could not see over the succeeding ranges, and on the southern side our road took us down a little narrow valley to the first village, called Deh Tang, and rightly too, for I do not think I ever saw a village in so tight a place before. Deh Tang stands at an elevation of some 8580 feet, so that our march of 28 miles at such an elevation, ascending about 4000 feet and descending another 5000 feet on our way, was no slight march in itself, and I doubt if it has ever been equalled by any body of regular troops before.

At Deh Tang we passed from the jurisdiction of Sardar Abdullah Jan of Badakshan into that of the governor of Ghorband, and we have been marching down the Ghorband valley ever since. One trophy of the Hindu Kush was secured by Sir West Ridgeway, in the shape of a specimen of the mountain-partridge, a beautiful bird some 2 feet in length and 5 lb. in weight. It was captured in a curious manner. It was being pursued by an eagle, and was seen by an Afghan sowar to take refuge under a rock, where he ran up and caught it. They are rare birds, living only up in the snows; and Captain Talbot is the only one of us who has seen them. Unfortunately this one did not survive its capture, but I have its skin preserved.

The country down the Ghorband valley is very pretty now with the fruit-trees all in their autumn tints. Pul-i-Rangar, where the Deh Tang stream falls into the Ghorband river, is especially so. Above are the ruins of a curious old fort called Kilah Morad Khan, with the rocky hills above that again, and below the stream rushing through a dense mass of fruit-trees of all descriptions. From there Captain Griesbach paid a visit to the lead-mines at Farinjal, which, he tells me, are well worth seeing. The old gallery worked by the ancients—or the "Kafirs," as the Afghans say, a word which to them covers all unknown races of former time—runs far into the hillside. The present workings are at the end of this gallery, some 1200 feet into the hill, of which about 200 feet constitute the present workings. The annual out-turn is some 6000 maunds.

Our camp to-day is stirred with unwonted activity. Lieutenant-Colonel Ata Ulah Khan, the British agent at Kabul, has just arrived on a visit, and the men of his escort belonging to the 10th Bengal Lancers are busy fraternising with their friends with us in the 11th Bengal Lancers. All our detached parties have come in. Majors Holdich and Maitland, Captains Peacocke and Talbot, and Sub-Surveyors Yusuf Sharif and Heera Singh have all rejoined from their various explorations and surveys of the different passes over the Hindu Kush, and Ata Muhammad is expected in shortly.

All survey operations have been brought to a close here now that we have joined on to the Kabul series carried out during the late war; and our survey officers may well be content with the work done during the past two years. The survey operations during the first year before the meeting of the joint Commissions embraced geographical work chiefly. The surveys of the Baluchistan desert, of the Helmand valley, the Persian border up to Mashhad, of Badghis and the valley of the Hari Rud, with part of the country between it and Kandahar, were all completed then. The longitude of Mashhad was fixed to give a starting-point to the demarcation survey, and triangulation which commenced from a base at Kuhsan was gradually extended over the whole country, including Eastern Khorasan, reaching as far south as Zamindawar and Seistan, and eastwards to the Koh-i-Baba mountains within sight of Kabul.

The necessity of placing Herat in a state of defence somewhat interfered with survey work about the end of the first year of the Commission's existence; but as soon as the demarcation of the boundary had been finally arranged, the survey party was again extended so as to complete one uninterrupted map of the whole region of Afghan Turkistan and of the province of Herat to a junction with previous surveys from Kabul on the east and from Kandahar on the south.

The demarcation survey forms a chapter of its own. This was carried out chiefly during the winter of 1885-86. A special boundary series was run from Zulfikar to the Oxus, the object of which was to fix accurately, and to obtain a computed record of, the position of every pillar or boundary-mark as far as possible. At the same time, a complete reconnaissance of the country adjoining the boundary was to be carried out, as well as large-scale surveys of all parts demanding special attention. To this was added a considerable portion of the topographical survey at first undertaken by the Russian staff, as it was necessary that the British survey party should take a share of the topographical work in addition to the triangulation. Our survey staff, however, even when strengthened from India, was not strong enough to complete the whole of the programme, owing to the want of topographers; but enough was accomplished to secure a final record of every position of importance. Afghan Turkistan up to the limits of Badakshan was speedily reduced to mapping, leaving nothing but a few small and comparatively unimportant blanks for future enterprise.

The last manœuvre of the survey party, with the help of the officers of the Intelligence Department and their well-trained *duffadars*, was to deploy along the northern face of the Hindu Kush between Bamian and the Khawak Pass, and to cross that range by every known available pass to Kabul.

Thus a fairly complete map of the whole system has been secured. In all, about 120,000 square miles of Persia, Afghanistan, and Afghan Turkistan have been added to our geographical mapping. Captain Gore and Sub-Surveyor Imam Sharif, moreover, are still in the field, mapping a most important line of route between Herat and Bandar Abbas.

CHAPTER XXIV.

THE MAIMANAH AND ANDKHUI FRONTIER.

KABUL, 17*th October* 1886.

My letter of 12th April 1886 gave a description of the first half of the boundary from Zulfikar to Maruchak, and it is now time for me to send a brief account of the second half from Maruchak to the Oxus so far as it has been settled. My description of the first half has so far to be altered that the position of pillars Nos. 30 and 31 was subsequently changed,[1] a concession having been given to the Russian Commissioner by fixing these pillars, one on either side of the valley at the head of the Band-i-Kashan canal, about half a mile below Robat-i-Kashan, instead of in their former positions some little way lower down, in exchange for an abatement on his part of the Russian claims to the Maimanah pastures in the *chul* farther east. The reason for this was that some Panjdeh Turkomans had sown crops during last winter on the left bank of the Kashan stream close to pillar No. 30, but, as the head of the canal irrigating this land remained in Afghan territory, they found themselves in the spring, under the terms of the boundary Protocol, debarred from the use of water for it. This caused considerable discontent in Panjdeh, which culminated as the hot weather came on and the crops began to dry up; and had

---

[1] These were again changed by the final negotiations at St Petersburg, described in chapter xxvii.

it not been that just at this time the concession in question was agreed to, the probability is that there would have been a collision between the excited Sariks and the Afghan frontier picket. By giving the Turkomans the head of this canal disagreement was happily avoided; and when last I saw the place, there were several scores of men and boys all hard at work cleaning out the canal and letting in the water as fast as they could. Not only on this canal were they engaged, but also on others lower down the valley; and I well remember how agreeably I was surprised at the way the men in these various parties came forward to claim acquaintance and shake hands as I passed through them, and the willing manner in which one and all turned to extricate one or two of my mules that got stuck in the mud. This was the last I saw of Panjdeh, and the recollection is certainly a pleasant one.

In the western half of the Maruchak valley down the left bank of the Murghab, just above where the boundary-line from pillars No. 34 to 35 cuts across the valley to the head of the Band-i-Nadir canal, there has also been a good deal of dispute regarding Turkoman cultivation. Some time after the boundary had been settled and demarcated, Colonel Kuhlberg discovered that the Sariks in the southernmost Panjdeh hamlet of Khojah Ali, just on the Russian side of the border, had sown a lot of wheat during last winter on ground subsequently awarded to Afghanistan, while at the same time, just as in the Kashan valley, the irrigation of the land cultivated by these Turkomans below the boundary-line was dependent on canals, the heads of which were some eight miles up the river in Afghan territory. I mention this to show how mixed up the Maruchak is with the Panjdeh cultivation, and how difficult it was to define a boundary between the two places under the circumstances. An examination of the irrigation system of the western half of the valley showed that there were six canals running down it, the heads of which were all in Afghan territory : of these, three canals watered land almost entirely on the Afghan side, two similarly almost entirely on the Russian side, and one half and half. The object of the original clause in the Protocol giving Russian subjects no right to water from any canal the head of which remained in Afghan possession, was to prevent Russia hereafter claiming powers of interference in the sources of the water-supply, such as, for instance, has lately happened on the Persian frontier. The Russian Government subsequently did advance a claim to the head of these Murghab canals, but the claim could not be acceded to without ample compensation to Afghanistan elsewhere, which the Russian Commissioner was not disposed to give. The Afghan authorities allowed the Turkomans for this one year to reap the crops they had already sown on the Afghan side of the border, and they also granted them the free use of water from the canals as a set-off against the abatement of Russian claims elsewhere; but this concession was not made until the Afghans had received from the Russian Commissioner a written agreement to the effect that this grant of water was a loan for this year only, and not a right to be enjoyed in perpetuity; and there the matter rests. Probably the claim to these canals will be again brought forward by the Russian Government in connection with the settlement of the Khwajah Salar question, and may form the basis for some compromise should the Home Government be willing to discuss such terms. It was distinctly specified, however, in the London Protocol, that the boundary was to be laid down at a point to the north of Maruchak, and Sir West Ridgeway has already stretched a point in the Russian favour by agreeing to fix the boundary at the head of the Band-i-Nadir canal to the west of it. This further claim, therefore, for land on the left bank to the south of Maruchak is quite against rule, and can only be entertained as a special case; in consideration, for instance, of some liberal offer by the Russian Government for an exchange of territory elsewhere.

The Sariks, I can quite imagine, are very sore at losing land which they have once cultivated, and the incident shows of itself what a loss Panjdeh is to Afghanistan, and how injuriously the forced separation acts on both sides. The Sariks have little culturable land, and are much in want of more. This they can most easily get by spreading southwards into Afghan territory, but from this they are now debarred. Afghanistan, on the other hand, is debarred from making use of its former Panjdeh subjects for the cultivation of its waste land in their neighbourhood. The Russian Government, however, by a little expenditure of money on irrigation works, will have no difficulty in reopening the ancient canals and giving the Sariks plenty of culturable land in the valley of the Murghab, north of Panjdeh, and this is what they ought to do.

The possession of the heads of these Maruchak canals would, without doubt, be of the greatest advantage to Russia, but she is bound by the terms of the Protocol just as much as we are; and, considering what little consideration has been shown by the Russian Commissioner for the wants and necessities of the Maimanah population, despite the agreement in the Protocol on that point, and how the Russian claims have been advanced over every little bit of ground where the terms of the Protocol could in any way be worked to the disadvantage of Afghanistan, it is only just that the same strictness should be shown on our side in maintaining the conditions laid down in the Protocol, even though they fall somewhat heavily on Russian subjects. But it is to be hoped that the Russian Ministers will now approach the subject of the final settlement in a more liberal spirit.

The second half of the frontier touches Herat territory from Maruchak up to Kilah Wali, and beyond that Maimanah, Andkhui, and Akchah respectively. Maimanah is now the last of the petty Khanates of Western Afghan Turkistan

under a ruler of its own—all the others having been one
after another annexed to Afghanistan. Not that it is independent by any means; far from it. The Wali only rules
under the constant supervision of the Afghan Resident,
backed up by a couple of Afghan regiments quartered in the
town. Mr Merk, who has been studying the Maimanah
history of late, tells me that the State apparently attained
its highest prosperity during the reign of Mizrab Khan from
1830 to 1845. Mizrab Khan died in 1845, and in 1846
Wazir Yar Muhammad Khan, of Herat, marched up with
a large force and took the town. In 1855, Wali Hukmat
Khan submitted to the Amir Dost Muhammad; and then in
1858, and again in 1859, Shah Nawaz Khan, of Herat,
invaded Maimanah with a considerable force, and plundered
the country generally. In 1860, Hukmat Khan was killed
by his brother Mir Hussain Khan, the present Wali, who
seized the chiefship. In 1868, Sirdar (now Amir) Abdur
Rahman besieged Maimanah with 16,000 men for thirty-six
days and then retired. In 1869-71 came the great famine,
when the sheep were almost all swept away; and sheep, it
must be remembered, form the staple wealth of the country.
Finally, in October 1875, Naib Muhammad Alum Khan laid
siege to the city again with 24,000 men, and in March
1876 the place was stormed, and a general slaughter took
place. Mir Hussain Khan was taken off captive to Kabul,
and from 1876 to 1879 Maimanah was administered by
Afghan governors, and held an Afghan garrison. The
troops were withdrawn during the war, and Dilawar Khan,
the son of Hukmat Khan, was sent to govern the chiefship.
In 1882, however, after the accession of the present Amir
Abdur Rahman, 5000 troops from Afghan Turkistan and
1200 from Herat were moved on Maimanah. After some
delay the city surrendered, and Mir Hussain Khan replaced
Dilawar Khan as Wali, and a considerable tribute was imposed. Altogether, therefore, the State has passed through

terrible vicissitudes during the last forty years, and the only wonder is that it has held together so long.

The city of Maimanah I have not seen, so I can only describe it from hearsay. I believe it is about two-thirds the size of Herat, strongly walled and surrounded by a moat, but completely commanded by some high ground on the east, and quite indefensible. The inside of the city is mostly in ruins and buildings are few, many of the people living in *kibitkas*. The shops in the bazaar are poor, and the regular residents all the year round do not exceed some 2500 families. In addition to these there are as many more half-nomad families, who live up at their *ailaghs* in the hills during the summer, simply coming down to Maimanah for the winter months. Most of these live entirely in *kibitkas;* and now that the Afghan garrison are quartered inside the city, many of them prefer to remain outside and pitch their *kibitkas* in the environs, instead of inside the walls as formerly. Another 10,000 families probably cover the whole remaining population of the Maimanah districts.

Nothing shows the richness and fertility of Maimanah more than the manner in which it has survived its successive famines and sieges. The cheapness and abundance of supplies of all kinds is even now remarkable, and after a few good years of settled government the out-turn would be enormously increased. The country may be divided roughly into three belts. First, the rich culturable land lying at the foot of the hills stretching from Chahar Shamba to Maimanah, and then down the Shirin Tagao to Khairabad; secondly, the hill-tracts and summer-quarters in the Band-i-Turkistan to the south; and thirdly, the grazing-lands in the *chul* to the north. It is with these latter that we have had most to do.

The waterless country stretching between the lower Murghab and the Oxus terminates to the south in an elevated plateau, known generally as Kara Bel, some 3500 or

4000 feet above sea-level, and running parallel to, and on an average about 40 miles to the north of, Chahar Shamba and Maimanah. From the southern edge of this plateau the ground gradually descends in a succession of *shors* or valleys for some 1500 feet to the level of the Kilah Wali and Ab-i-Kaisar streams, into which these *shors* empty themselves. The first half of this descent is through undulating ground affording capital pasturage, but the latter half is comprised in a rugged belt of steep hillocks of comparatively much less grazing value. The water in the *shors* is generally salt; but in the centre of the undulating strip there are a series of wells of drinkable water such as those at Aghaz Paz and its neighbourhood, marking the site of former nomad habitations. Water apparently is plentiful in the valleys just below the crest of the plateau, though its depth varies greatly in different places, some of the wells being only 30 and others 130 feet in depth. These habitations, though, were all deserted one after another owing to Turkoman raids, and the probability is that they have not been used for the last twenty years or more. Almost all the wells were subsequently filled up to prevent the Turkomans from making use of them in their raids, and the water in those now open is mostly bad-smelling from long stagnation, and often unfit for use.

The right of Maimanah to all these wells, of course, was undisputable. The Panjdeh grazing-lands were admitted, even by the Sariks themselves, to extend only as far east as the western edge of the Kara Bel plateau, and, with the exception of the Maimanah people, there never was any one else to use them. The Panjdeh Sariks held the grazing as far east of the Murghab as the water-supply allowed them to penetrate, and the Bokharan Ersaris on the left bank of the Oxus as far west as they could go; but the central space between the two rivers being a waterless wilderness, without any inhabitants whatsoever, Maimanah enjoyed sole rights on its southern border, and consequently possessed all the land as far north as its people could go.

The natural frontier, and the one claimed by the Afghans, ran along the Kara Bel plateau, and the wording of the London Protocol of 10th September 1885, No. 109 of the Blue-book—in which it was laid down that the boundary should "follow a line north of the valley of the Kaisar and west of the valley of the Sangalak (Ab-i-Andkhui)"—might be taken to imply the same place, as, when talking of the valley of the Kaisar, it was not supposed that the actual banks of the stream itself were intended, but the valley including both the stream and its affluents. This reading, however, was contested by the Russian Commissioner.

The names used in the Protocol are misleading, and I must here explain them. The stream called by the Russians the Kaisar is the one which rises a little to the east of Chahar Shamba, and flowing west through Kilah Wali, falls into the Murghab at Karawal Khana. This stream is called by us the Kilah Wali stream, as we were never able to find any local name for it, and it was necessary to distinguish it from its next-door neighbour, the Ab-i-Kaisar. This latter takes its rise in the hills south of the Kaisar plain, and running north-east, joins the Shirin Tagao near Daulatabad, and the two streams combined are, beyond that, known as the Ab-i-Andkhui. This Ab-i-Kaisar is the Sangalak of the Protocol, so named, I believe, from a ford across it called Sangalak on the road from Kaisar to Almar; but this did not deter the Russian Commissioner from taking advantage of the wording of the Protocol to try and advance a claim to the Shirin Tagao, farther east, as the stream referred to, despite the fact that the Ab-i-Kaisar valley was inhabited and cultivated by Maimanah subjects to the west of it—a claim, too, which was upheld by his own Government. The Russian Commissioner, moreover, quoting Lord Granville's memorandum of 22d May

1885—No. 32 of the Blue-book—claimed all land not actually in use at the time of the Russian occupation of Merv in March 1884. The wording of this memorandum is to the effect that her Majesty's Government " have not asked for any extension of the Afghan pastures, but only that the inhabitants of Maimanah and Andkhui, which, under the agreement of 1873, were recognised as belonging to Afghanistan, should not be deprived of their cultivated lands, or of those pastures the use of which they were actually enjoying before the Russian occupation of Merv established tranquillity in those regions."

As a matter of fact the Russian occupation of Merv had nothing whatever to do with the tranquillity of the Maimanah *chul*. The Teke Turkomans of Merv confined their attention mostly to the Persian and Herat frontiers, and, without doubt, thoroughly succeeded in depopulating those borders. The depopulation of the Maimanah border was due to the Sarik Turkomans of Panjdeh and Yulatan, and in a lesser degree to the Karas and Ersaris from the banks of the Oxus in Bokhara. The raids of the latter still continue, but the former were put a stop to by the Afghan occupation of Panjdeh in June 1884. The present improved state of affairs on the Maimanah border was thus due entirely to the action of the Afghans themselves, and in no way to that of the Russians. Of course, as to Andkhui, Merv had nothing whatever to do with it, as the distance across the desert was far too great to tempt raiders from Merv in that direction, and the Russian occupation of Merv had naturally no effect on the immunity of the Andkhui people from Bokharan raids. These facts, though, were unknown before the arrival of the Boundary Commission on the spot; but still the terms of Lord Granville's memorandum were held to be binding, and all that Sir West Ridgeway could do was to obtain the best terms he could.

The result was that, after much discussion, an agreement

was finally come to by which a belt of pasturage, averaging 15 miles in width, measured to the north of the Kilah Wali and Ab-i-Kaisar streams, was to be left to Maimanah in consideration of concessions to Russia at Band-i-Kashan and Khwajah Gogirdak and the temporary grant of water in the Maruchak valley, with a 12-mile belt of pasturage onwards towards Andkhui and 15 miles again beyond it. Khwajah Gogirdak is a spring about 10 miles to the north of the Kilah Wali stream at Bokun, and has been described before. It was conceded to Russia in exchange for more land farther on, as the river being comparatively close there, its water was not of such vital importance to Afghan subjects. The boundary consequently runs eastwards from pillar No. 36 on the right bank of the Murghab below Maruchak to pillar No. 39 on the top of a hill just to the south of Khwajah Gogirdak, and thence onward, passing some 9 miles to the north of Alai Chalai, to pillar No. 44 on the top of a high peak known to the survey as Askara Hill Station. Thence the line, turning northwards, follows the watershed of a range of hillocks known as the Bel-i-Paranda, and running down a spur to the north-east, it crosses the Kiamat Shor and again the Shor Aghaz Kin, the northernmost of all these Maimanah *shors*, and gradually inclining inwards, joins the 12-mile radius at pillar No. 54, almost due west of Daulatabad, and some 110 miles from Maruchak.

By this settlement Russia gains the wells at Kara Baba and Pekenna, and all those at Aghaz Paz and at the head of the Kiamat Shor, and along under the crest of the Kara Bel plateau up to the head of the Shor Aghaz Kin, west of Daulatabad; but, as a matter of fact, these wells and grazing-grounds having been unused by Maimanah now for the best part of a generation, their loss, consequently, is not felt at present, and both the Afghan and Maimanah authorities are only too pleased at the settlement as it stands. Of course the question of a few miles of *chul* here or there seems a little matter and not worth fighting or arguing about; but that, I take it, is not the way to look upon it. The future has also to be considered. At present the Maimanah sheep are not calculated to number more than some 350,000, but with good seasons and under a peaceful administration, each flock is calculated to double itself in five years; and supposing this much-troubled State of Maimanah to have a rest now from wars and famine for some years to come, so as to recover something of its former prosperity, the number of sheep will be enormously increased, and then the question of pasturage will again come to the front. Under present circumstances the pasturage on the low ground at the foot of the hills and the 15-mile radius beyond the Ab-i-Kaisar is more than ample for all their wants, and the Maimanah people are well pleased at having got so much.

The word *chul* is a difficult word to translate, and the Maimanah *chul* can by no means be represented by the word "desert" that has generally hitherto been used to describe it. It is not a desert in any sense of the word; perhaps wilderness would better describe it. It is waterless in so far that water is only to be found in certain localities and at a considerable depth below the surface, but still it is not a waste. On the contrary, it is covered in the spring with a fine crop of grass and plants of sorts, sufficient to feed enormous flocks of sheep. The custom is with all these nomads to take their sheep up into the mountains during the summer, and to bring them down to the plains in the autumn, and to spend the winter and spring out in the *chul*. So long as the snow remains on the ground, both sheep and shepherds are almost entirely independent of water. Unlike the Panjdeh Turkomans, who leave their flocks under the sole charge of a shepherd and his assistant all the year round, the Usbegs and Arabs and other nomads of the Maimanah districts always live with their sheep themselves; and wherever they go, their wives and families and all go with them. Consequently in former days there was a regular migration in spring and autumn to and from the Band-i-Turkistan and the *chul* below. Latterly this has all been altered owing to fear of raids, and the Usbegs in the winter have had to content themselves with the pasturage at the foot of the hills within the line of habitation; while the Arabs and others have gone off in a body to Siripul and its neighbourhood, well within the frontier, and out of reach of the raiders.

The Andkhui *chul* is very different from the Maimanah *chul*, being much more sandy and much less productive. The grassy hillocks and undulations that distinguish the Maimanah pasturages come to an end at Daulatabad, and the ground gradually merges into the sandhills and wastes to the north. In describing the Andkhui *chul*, I cannot do better than quote from Captain de Laessoe, who was deputed to put up the pillars from Daulatabad to Dukchi, and has kindly given me the following account of the country he passed through:—

"The main *chul*, consisting of high rolling downs, is, to the north-east, limited by a belt of low sandhills about 25 miles broad. These hills are covered with gandum-trees, and afford a fair amount of grazing for sheep and numerous herds of antelopes. The hills are, so to say, grouped round a large valley, which, starting from somewhere near Andkhui and running in a north-westerly direction, is joined by numerous lateral valleys with excellent grazing, and water 50 to 100 feet from the surface. Former inhabitants have taken advantage of this to dig wells, many of which could be cleaned out with very little trouble and expense. Continuing north-east, the hills finally give way to a plain with very long, low, and broad undulations, with an occasional isolated sandhill. For about 30 miles the soil is loose and sandy, and covered with grass and gandum. Afterwards the soil becomes harder, grass is very scarce, and the gandum is replaced by butah; but about 20 miles from the Oxus the sand again appears, the country becomes slightly hilly, and gandum is again predominant till we reach the belt of movable sands along the bank of the Oxus. All over the above-mentioned plain we found small round or oval valleys, where rain-water naturally collects. The bottom is frequently formed of a sort of *pat*, which retains the water for a long time, and in the centre of these valleys the sheep-owners have built tanks, locally known as *kaks*, where sweet water is found from March till the end of June. Many of the valleys have wells, dug hundreds of years ago and usually brick-built. They are 150 to 200 feet deep, and the water is, as a rule, salt, and sometimes quite undrinkable; but this is simply due to the fact that they have been abandoned for the last century or so. When a well is cleaned out, the water immediately becomes, if not perfectly sweet, at least quite drinkable.

"A remarkable feature in the Andkhui *chul* is a large *shor*, which seems to have been, if not an old bed of the Oxus, at least a branch of that river. Starting from a place east of Kilif, it passes by Dungez Syot and Zaid, and continues past the Hulu wells, west of Burdalik. At present no water from the Oxus reaches this *shor*, except by refiltration; but in very rainy seasons it affords an outlet for the surplus Akchah waters, which this year are said to have reached Hulu. This *shor* may possibly be the branch of the Oxus which in former times reached the Caspian. The isolated stony hills known as Kara Tapeh Kalan, Kara Tapeh Khurd, and Dungez Syot, are conspicuous objects in the plains, and form, with Chash Baba and Kilif, the solitary remnants of a prehistoric mountain-chain, destroyed by the ancestor of the present Oxus, as Captain Griesbach calls the river which, some dozen of million years ago, formed one of the main features of the country."

Andkhui itself I have before described. The three neighbouring towns of Akchah, Shibarghan, and Siripul I have not seen, but from all I have heard, I gather that they are very like Andkhui: the same amount of ruins and tumble-down walls, about the same population, and the same sort of citadel commanding the town, similarly occupied by the governor and a small Afghan garrison. All the old Usbeg rulers of these States have been displaced, and Afghan governors now rule in their stead. The last Mir of Andkhui, Gazanfar Khan, died in 1873, and his son and successor, Daulat Beg, is now an Afghan State pensioner at Mazar. The prosperity of Andkhui was at its height under the rule of Mir Shahwali Khan, from 1821 to 1843. The invasion of Wazir Yar Muhammad Khan in 1845, and the famine which followed, depopulated and ruined the oasis. It came under Afghan supremacy in 1864, and was finally taken under direct Afghan administration in 1881. The present governor, Colonel Abdul Hamid Khan, is the brother of Colonel Abdul Ghani Khan, the governor of Akchah, and both are young and pleasant men, the sons of one of Amir Sher Ali's generals, named Nujbudin Khan, who, fortunately for himself, possessed a handsome daughter whom he gave in marriage to Sirdar Ishak Khan, directly the latter arrived, and was thus enabled to make a home for himself at Mazar, and so far to escape the fate that has overtaken the other adherents of the late Amir.

Regarding the antiquities of Andkhui there is little to relate. In these old mud-built places there is little to find, and inscriptions on the mosques and tombstones are about the only record of former times. These latter Munshi Allah Bakhsh, our native *attaché* at Andkhui, has been doing his best to decipher; but the oil and dirt accumulated on the tombstones, owing to the practice pious ladies have of burning lamps on them at night, renders the deciphering a very difficult job. The oldest building in Andkhui apparently is a dome containing the grave of a saint, and known as the Ziarat-i-Baba Wali, which dates from the year A.D. 1386, there being an inscription on the walls to the effect that "the year of the death of Hazrat Eshan Baba Wali is 787 Hijrah." Another inscription on some iron-barred lattice-work is as follows: "On the 20th Zu'l Hijjah 1088 A.H. (A.D. 1677), during the reign of the Great Khan Rahmatulah Khan, a much-respected Sirdar of Turkistan, the Hakim of Andkhui—may God protect him from envious eyes!—the son of the gracious, the greater than the great, the late pardoned Niyaz Mahomed Khan Wali of Ummul Bulad (mother of cities—*i.c.*, Balkh), the lattice-work of the blessed and sacred shrine of the Chief of Saints and Priests Baba Sangu, the brave—may God make his grave happy and turn it into paradise!—was completed and safely finished." The grave is covered with a wooden frame, which was put up—so it is recorded on it—" By the order of Alijah Amin-ul-Doulah, Mir Daulat Khan, in A.H. 1289 (A.D. 1873).

Another domed building containing fourteen marble slabs, twelve white and two black, is known as the Ziarat-i-Chahardah Ma'sum, or the shrine of the fourteen innocents. Three of these slabs have no inscription; but the others, to the memory of four men, five women, and two children, are covered on the top with Cufic inscriptions, giving the names of the deceased and their ancestors and the date of death, mixed up with various Arab phrases, and on the sides with texts from the Koran and Persian verses imploring heavenly blessings on the dead and grieving at their untimely death. The inscriptions show that the deceased were Syeds, some of their pedigrees being traced back to Ali. The following translation from the Arabic is a good example: "This is the tomb of the Amir, the late pardoned Amir Syed Abdul Matlab, son of the great Amir Syed Kamil, son of the great Amir Syed Alaika, son of the great Amir Syed Ali, son of the late Amir Syed Yahiya, son of the pardoned Amir, the Amir Syed Ali, son of the great Amir Syed Malik, son of the pious Amir Syed Hasan, son of the late Amir Syed Husain, son of the pardoned Amir Syed Ahmad, son of the great Amir Syed Ismail, son of the great Amir Syed Ali, son of Syed Isah, son of Amir Syed Hamza, son of Syed Wahab, son of Amir Syed Hashim, son of Amir Syed Kashim, son of Syed Mahomed, son of Amir Syed Abdulah, son of Amir Syed Musa, son of Amir Syed Hasan, son of the Amir of Musalmans, the brave lion of God, Ali, the son of Abu Talib." Then follow six lines of Persian poetry, and finally, again in Arabic: "Died in the year of the Prophet

—may peace be on him!—[A.H.] 889 " [A.D. 1472]. The latest inscription is dated A.D. 1577, and marks the tomb of the gentle, graceful, and pious Hamidah Bano [lady], daughter of Syed Muhammad Kasim, [who] died during the month Shaban in the year of the Hijrah 984."

About the other buildings in Andkhui no reliable information could be obtained. It is said that there are inscriptions both in the Juma Musjid and in the Madrasah, but that they are now hidden by whitewash. Local tradition says that the Juma Musjid was built a hundred years ago by Abdul Momin Khan Padar Kush (patricide), son of the great Abdullah Khan of Bokhara; and that of the two Madrasahs or colleges, one was founded about a hundred years ago by Nasarulah Khan, a descendant of Shah Rukh Mirza, of Herat, and the other by Shahbaz Khan, Chulush Turkoman, from whose family the governorship of Andkhui was transferred to Niyaz Khan, the first Usbeg ruler, in A.D. 1470; though what reliance can be placed on these traditions I cannot say.

The settlement of the Andkhui frontier differed so far from that of Maimanah in that, instead of there being an unoccupied wilderness in front of it and no rival claimants, here in Andkhui the Bokhara territory was close, and the wells and pastures given up by Andkhui, owing to fear of Bokharan raiders, were soon occupied and made use of by Bokharan shepherds; and, as a matter of fact, the Andkhui people were only too pleased at the settlement effected, giving them a radius of some 23 miles to the west and north of the town—or nearly 15 miles beyond the limits of cultivation.

The boundary, commencing from pillar No. 54 near Katar Kudak to the west of Daulatabad, runs north for some 25 miles, nearly parallel to, and at a distance of 12 miles from, the Ab-i-Andkhui, up to a point almost due west of Ziarat-i-Baba Yataghan. Thence it circles round parallel to the outskirts of the Andkhui cultivation, leaving the wells at Yaman Kudak, Sarimat, Jelajin, Chichli, Oikal, and Chah-i-Imam Nazar, and several minor wells and tanks, to Afghanistan. Pillars Nos. 59, 60, and 63 were built close to Sarimat, Chichli, and Oikal respectively; and the last pillar,[1] No. 66, lies about 1½ mile north of Chah-i-Imam Nazar and 3 miles south of Dukchi, on the main road from Andkhui to Karki, a total distance of nearly 190 miles from Maruchak and some 80 miles from Daulatabad.

Russia by this settlement gets a connected line of wells all along her frontier from Panjdeh to the Oxus. This road is passable for camels all the way, and, in fact, better for camels than any other animal, as they require no grain and there is plenty of grazing for them everywhere. I believe camel caravans can do the distance from Panjdeh to Andkhui in five days. The Russian route along the frontier is as follows :—

From Panjdeh to—	Miles.
1. Galla Chashmah,	18
2. Kara Bel,	25
3. Kara Baba,	20
4. Yedikui,	19
5. Hazarah Kudak,	12
6. Chah-i-Pirjik,	18
7. Tezakli,	30
8. Sehchanche,	13
9. Gandeh Chah,	8
10. Dukchi,	22
Total,	185

This line runs all the way within the Russian border; but crossing the frontier, there is a direct road to Daulatabad, from Hazarah Kudak *via* Katar Kudak, with four wells on

---

[1] The position of this pillar was subsequently altered, and the wells of Imam Nazar made over to Russia by the final settlement at St Petersburg, described in chapter xxvii.

the way. Similarly, going from Panjdeh to Andkhui, there is a road from Chah-i-Pirjik to Chap Guzar, and thence down the river to Andkhui.

The only stages on the route without water are the first two; but supposing water for the first march to be sent out from Panjdeh, there will never be the slightest difficulty in making use of these routes.

Beyond Dukchi the boundary is not yet settled; but roads run from there both to Karki and to Bosagha, the present frontier Bokharan villages. Karki, we hear, is shortly to become a Russian cantonment; and should that be the case, of course with a direct road through Dukchi, Andkhui could be occupied by Russian troops from there at any time without difficulty—with this condition only, namely, that now that the frontier has been defined any such occupation would be an act of war—a most conclusive proof in itself of the utility and necessity for a defined frontier. As it is, the settlement and demarcation of about 325 miles out of a total of some 350 miles of frontier is no slight thing of itself, and the Mission has every reason to congratulate itself on having effected so much in the teeth of so many difficulties. In addition to this it must be remembered, too, that the Mission has collected a vast amount of information regarding these hitherto unknown regions, and future operations in Afghanistan will now be greatly simplified—as, instead of having to rely solely as hitherto on the chance reports of casual travellers, the Government will have at its disposal a trained body of thoroughly experienced officers possessing an intimate knowledge of the resources and features of all North-Western Afghanistan.

The only question now remaining to be settled is the point where the boundary is to strike the Oxus. It has already been decided by the two Commissioners that the line is to run eastwards from pillar No. 66, near Dukchi, to the north of Jar Kudak; and there will, therefore, be no difficulty in putting up the pillars across the remaining 25 or 30 miles of desert between Dukchi and the Oxus, as soon as it has been decided by the Government at home whether the present frontier between Khamiab, belonging to Akchah, and Bosagha in Bokhara, on the banks of that river, is to be maintained or not.

CHAPTER XXV.

THE COMMISSION AT KABUL.

CAMP JAMRUD, 31*st October* 1886.

WHEN I wrote from Charikar we were just starting for Kabul, and the Amir, we heard, was away at Bagran, where, by all accounts, he had been successful in bringing a considerable amount of land under cultivation which had formerly lain waste for want of water. At Tutam Darah we were shown the head of a large canal, taken off from the Ghorband river, which has been newly constructed under the Amir's own orders, all previous attempts at making a canal there having failed.

We heard that the Amir would not reach Kabul for a day or two after us, but that all arrangements were ready for our reception; and so, on we went. The Charikar valley was so well known in the last war that I need not try to describe it. We marched leisurely according to the stages fixed by the Afghans, viz.:—

		Miles.
13. Robat,	. . . . .	6
14. Siah Ab-i-Charmgah,	. . .	15
15. Kabul (Aliabad),	. . .	15
	Total, . .	36

The change to this densely populated and thickly cultivated valley after the wildernesses that we have wandered through was a pleasant surprise to those of us who, like myself, had not seen it before. We did not see many of the people on the whole; and, doubtless, all those who suffered so severely at our hands six years ago kept out of our way. Those that we did see were most civil, and I really think I received almost as many "Khush Amadeeds" and suchlike salutations of welcome during these three marches as I have during the whole of the past two years.

Our arrival at Kabul was signalised by an entertainment in real Afghan fashion. Aliabad consists of a large garden and house in the Chahar Deh valley, just at the back of the Asmai heights, and a little way to the north of the Deh Mazang gorge through which the Kabul river runs into the city. The Amir being away, almost everybody of position was away with him. The Sipah Salar Gulam Haidar Khan was absent suppressing some disturbance in Laghman, and Sir West Ridgeway was received by the Brigadier-General commanding, with a couple of squadrons of cavalry, some two miles out, and escorted by him to the residence set apart for us at Aliabad. The Brigadier appeared in a long gold-embroidered green coat, with a general's sword and belt, and a white-plumed gold-laced shako, escorted by some Turkistan Lancers, men in huge sheepskin hats, blue coats and trousers, and a long lance painted green, with a blue-and-white pennant; in fact, their lances were so long that they had no lance-buckets to their stirrups, but had to order their lances on the ground. The Brigadier advanced to meet us, and as soon as he had been introduced by Kazi Saad-ud-Din Khan, he cantered back to the troops drawn up in line and received Sir West Ridgeway with the usual salute. The Hizdah Nahri Regiment, which formed the escort, were all dressed in old British red tunics, and armed with muzzle-loading carbines and Cossack swords. None of the Afghan cavalry except the Amir's own body-guard are yet armed with breech-loading carbines; but this, no doubt, will come in time. The Afghan soldier's head-dress, I must say, is the most curious I have ever seen; and it was only on arrival in Kabul that we saw it for the first time in general use. Imagine a small beehive of brown felt without any shade or peak, or anything to relieve the rigidity of its appearance, except in some cases a small tassel at the top and a black band round the bottom, with now and then a rosette on one side. This cap is worn by all arms of the service, and looks better on a body of men than might have been expected.

On arrival at Aliabad we found a couple of guards drawn up who duly presented arms, and we then all dismounted and entered the house. A house in this country is hardly in conformity with our English ideas on the subject. A narrow entrance, turning three or four times at right angles, took us into a courtyard some 20 yards square, surrounded by open rooms on three sides, and by a *hamam* on the fourth. Who the rightful owner is I don't know, but it is State property at present, and has, I heard, been lately presented by the Amir to Sirdar Yusaf Khan, at present governor of Farah. In olden days, I believe, it belonged to the family of Ressaldar-Major Sirdar Muhammad Aslam Khan, and this was almost his first look at the home of his ancestors, as, having left Kabul thirty-seven years ago, when a boy of eleven, he had only vague recollections of what it was like. It was wonderful how his memory returned to him directly he saw the place, and how well he knew the names of everything he saw; though, as he told me, he was much surprised to find how small everything looked to him now after the vastness with which his boyish ideas had pictured each place.

Everything that could be done in the short time at their disposal had been done by the Afghans to fit up the house for our reception. All the doors, windows, and shutters had been freshly painted, the walls whitewashed, and the floors carpeted with felts and white cloth. The cornices of the rooms were even ornamented with rows of apples, pomegranates, and quinces, and very good those apples were, as I have good reason to remember. We were first of all ushered into the rooms on the south side, which had been fitted up as ante-room and dining-room respectively. The table in the latter room round which we sat was covered with sweetmeats of all shapes and sizes; and soon afterwards tea was brought in and handed round in little china cups, and after that again, cups of hot spiced milk and sugar. This refection having been done good justice to, Kazi Saad-ud-Din and the Brigadier took leave, and we were left to settle ourselves down.

Sir West Ridgeway occupied the couple of rooms above the dining-room, which had been expressly furnished and carpeted for him. I took possession of a room down-stairs, and the Commissioner's office and Nawab Mirza Hasan Ali Khan were located in others. The majority preferred to pitch their tents in the garden outside, which was in reality a wonderfully pretty place. These Eastern rooms, though so clean and nice to look at, have not the bath-rooms and conveniences which we are accustomed to, and, moreover, are very cold at night, as they are all open on the inner side, and though they can be closed by wooden shutters, still these, after all, are poor protection. Outside in the garden we found several Turkoman *kibitkas* had been pitched for our use, and two capital pavilions or summer-houses, which were all lined and carpeted throughout with red cloth. Certainly everything possible had been done for us in the way of preparation.

Hardly were we settled than breakfast was announced, and we all sat down again to another Afghan feast. First of all, a company of infantry arrived bearing huge wooden trays of sweetmeats, which were set down on the ground outside and covered the whole courtyard. These were divided amongst all our men, and a grand feast they must have had. Our breakfast arrived in a long procession of metal trays covered with *kincob* and gold-embroidered cloths. These latter, when removed, revealed huge *pilaos* of various kinds, a lamb roasted whole with pistachio-nuts, and finally, a sheep roasted whole—a huge dish with the sheep lying flat and four legs sticking straight out at each corner. All sorts of pickles and spiced meats in little china dishes and a few sweets completed the repast, and a right good repast it was too. I did my best to do justice to it; but I confess, despite all my efforts, I was beaten by Khan Bahadur Ibrahim Khan and Subadar Muhammad Husain Khan, who were sitting next to me.

The Amir did not arrive in Kabul till the 18th, and we did not pay our formal visit to him till the 20th, so we had nothing much to do but rest ourselves after our travels for the first four days. Captains Peacocke and Cotton, and also Messrs Clarke and Marshall, paid a visit to Sherpur early on the morning of the 16th; but after that we were asked not to visit either the city or Sherpur till the Amir arrived, and consequently we had to content ourselves with short rides in the neighbourhood. What surprised us most were the excellent roads laid out in all directions both in the Kabul and Chahar Deh valleys, planted with rows of poplars on either side; and the work is still progressing, as we found a battalion of sappers or pioneers encamped in the Deh Mazang gorge, busily engaged in blasting away the rock for a good 30-feet road in place of the track that formerly existed. The Amir's visit to Rawal Pindi was, I heard, the cause of all this activity in roadmaking, and very probably this is the case. But the Amir's attention has by no means been confined to roads. Riding out on the evening of the 17th with Sir West Ridgeway, Dr Owen, Sirdar Sher Ahmad Khan, and Ressaldar-Major Baha-u'-din Khan, we paid a visit to his Highness's new garden, called the Bagh-i-Baland, on the slopes of the Ao Shar Kotal. The whole hillside has been levelled and terraced and planted with vines, and we found fruit and sweetmeats all ready laid out for us in a pavilion, where we had a splendid view over all the valley—the lake, Sherpur, Siah Sang, and Kabul, all lying spread out before us.

Ten o'clock on the morning of the 20th was the time fixed for our visit to the Amir, and accordingly that hour saw us all in full dress on our way to the Bagh-i-Babar, a garden round the tomb of the Emperor Babar, at the back of the Sher Darwaza hill, where the Amir generally resides pending the completion of his new palace. At the gate we found a band and guard of honour drawn up, who received Sir West Ridgeway with the usual salute. Dismounting and walking up the garden, we were met by a procession of generals, brigadiers, and colonels, all in single file, headed by the Naib Salar, or acting commander-in-chief, Parwanah Khan, who were all introduced one by one to Sir West Ridgeway by Kazi Saad-ud-Din Khan. The latter having been away from Kabul with us for the last two years, got a little mixed over the various names and ranks, and the promptness with which each corrected any mistake in announcing his rank was rather amusing. This introduction over, the Naib Salar conducted Sir West to a large open pavilion all lined and carpeted with red and white cloth, where he was received by Sirdar Shums-ud-Din Khan and four or five other Sirdars, the Khan Mullah Khan or High Priest of Kabul (the father, by the way, of Kazi Saad-ud-Din Khan), the City Judge, and one or two others who alone were allowed seats at the durbar, all the military officers having to stand in a row outside behind them. We were all seated down one side of the room and the Sirdars down the other, and hardly had we got into our places when sounds of "Allah" and other cries of salutation announced that the Amir was arriving from his residence close by, and a minute later the Amir himself appeared riding on horseback, with a huge gold-embroidered umbrella held over his head, despite the fact that he had hardly twenty yards to come, and the sun was shaded by the trees. His Highness was preceded by some twenty or thirty men of his body-guard, fine-looking men, all Barukzais, I believe, armed with Martini-Henry carbines and bandolier belts, and clad in a dark uniform with round Russian-shaped fur caps. In addition to these there was also a guard of Turkistan Horse in their huge sheepskin hats, and another in the ordinary uniform felt hat. These all ranged themselves around while the Amir dismounted and entered the pavilion. His Highness first shook hands with Sir West Ridgeway, and then, after a few words of welcome, with each of us in turn as we were separately introduced by Sir West, after which he sat down on a small sofa placed at right angles to our line of chairs. His Highness was plainly dressed in a drab suit, with a plain leather sword-belt without any embroidery or ornamentation beyond mauve-coloured velvet facings and Russian shoulder-straps—his only decoration being the Afghan Order of Bahadari in diamonds, worn on the side of his grey Astrakhan hat.

The conversation lasted for about an hour, chiefly upon subjects connected with the boundary. His Highness welcomed us all to Kabul after all the wanderings we had gone through, expressed himself as very glad to see us, adding that he hoped we should not be the only British officers he should see at Kabul, as, till the boundary was finally settled, British officers would be continually coming and going. His Highness finally invited us all to breakfast at his new palace the next morning. Before we left, our presents to the Amir from the Government Toshakhana were brought in and presented. These included handsome rifles, a large telescope, a diamond-mounted watch and certain jewellery, and also full-dress general officers' swords and belts for each of his two elder sons, and a third in miniature for the younger one, as well as various other rifles, pistols, &c., and a couple of valuable Arab horses for the Amir and a Waler for each of the sons. Neither of the sons, however, was present at the durbar, and, as a matter of fact, we never saw them the whole time we were at Kabul. A younger brother of Sirdar Ishak Khan's, a tall man in a white Russian uniform, stood behind the Amir, and various other young Sirdars were also standing in the background, no near relations being allowed to sit. Sirdar Sher Ahmad Khan also stood throughout the interview—a mark of respect which, I believe, greatly pleased his Highness. The only peculiarity I noticed at the visit was that the Amir, after shaking hands with Sir West Ridgeway, sat down on his sofa and shook hands with all the rest of us sitting down.

In the afternoon I had my first ride through the city of Kabul. We were a large party, consisting of Sir West Ridgeway, Colonel Bax, Captains Peacocke, Cotton, and Griesbach, Dr Owen, Sirdar Muhammad Aslam Khan, Ressaldar-Major Baha-u'-din Khan, and myself, and we were everywhere received with perfect civility. The bazaars are so well known that I need not describe them. The only change, I fancy, since the time of our occupation, was the sight of the Naib Kotwal, well known by the name of Naib Sultan Khan, administering justice in the Kotwali. This man is, I believe, probably the most hated and most feared of all the officials in Afghanistan. He is at the head of all the secret police, and is popularly supposed to have a spy in every family; and so strict is his vigilance, that no two or three men dare to gather together anywhere, much less, they say, to talk to each other openly.

A fine new bridge is being made across the river, but the old buildings are mostly in ruins. The palace occupied by the Amir Sher Ali Khan and Yakub Khan is now half in ruins, part being occupied as a barrack and the remainder as a prison—a prison, too, they say, from which a prisoner never returns. The Upper Bala Hissar is still perfect, but the lower portion has been almost entirely demolished, and the old foundations are now being utilised for the excavation of saltpetre.

Our breakfast at the Amir's new palace on the morning of the 21st was a great surprise to us all, as we had no idea that such a magnificent building existed in Kabul. First of all, riding along the river-bank, we found a regular embankment under construction, which the Amir afterwards told us he was going to complete and adorn. And beyond that again, we came upon a new and spacious bazaar also in process of building. Just outside the city we came to the new palace, which, on the outside, is simply a large rectangular fortification with mud-walls and ditch all round it. Outside the entrance-gate is a row of new buildings designed for public offices. The Amir explained to us that he had found all the Mirzas working separately each in his own house, by which arrangement it took ten days to get one day's work properly done; so he had determined to locate them all together close to himself, and for the future, I suppose, office hours will be enforced with as much regularity in Kabul as they are in India.

Entering the palace-gate, we pass through a fine garden of big trees, down a road bordered with iron railings on each side, to a long white building with a corrugated iron roof. This constitutes the private or ladies' apartments, known as the Haram Sarai. The public or men's portion of the palace consists of an ornamental and lofty pavilion in the midst of an enclosed garden, with entrances on each side and a high domed octagonal room in the centre, in which we were all received. The garden around is beautifully kept, and inside everything was good. The doors, carvings, and fittings of all the little rooms and the central reception-hall were perfect, and I have never seen anything like them in

India. Above, in the balcony of the second storey, there were fine china vases full of flowers, and a large chandelier hung from the centre of the dome.

The Amir entered just after we arrived, shook hands with Sir West Ridgeway, bowed to each of us, and sat down on his favourite sofa, while we were seated around the hall on one side, and the Naib Salar and various generals and colonels occupied the other. Sirdar Ishak Khan's brother again stood behind the Amir's sofa, and also the long-haired youth in gold cap and belt and the crutch stick, who apparently is always in close attendance, as I even recognised his face in one of the Rawal Pindi photographs hung up on the wall. The Amir talked long, mostly on subjects connected with the army, and evidently for the benefit of the officers of his army who were present. Little tables covered with sweetmeats were brought in, and also tea and cigarettes; but eleven o'clock struck and then twelve, and it was not till about half-past that the Amir began to get angry and to ask why breakfast was not brought. Finally, he wrote a note, apparently to the cook, which must have frightened him, as at last tables were brought in, cloths spread, and breakfast produced. The Amir left us to breakfast at the tables alone and went outside, where carpets were spread all round for his own officers to sit and breakfast upon. All our native officers and men of the escort were also invited in, and regaled with a sumptuous repast, the Amir personally welcoming them as friends and brothers who were always to be allies for the future. As soon as breakfast was over and the cloth removed, the Amir joined us again, and further conversation commenced, during which he referred to the British Parliament, and pointing out to us the two paintings, one of the House of Lords and the other of the House of Commons, that hung on either side of him, suggested that we ought all to go to England and personally enlighten Parliament on the state and condition of Afghanistan—a proposal we assured him we should be delighted to carry out, were it possible.

We finally took leave, and started off under the guidance of his personal officials to see the interior of the palace, which, being not quite finished, has not yet been occupied by the ladies for whom it is intended. Entering by the big gateway, we found ourselves in a fine courtyard, some 80 yards long by 50 yards broad, surrounded by handsome corridors, all finished with carved gypsum plaster. Crossing the corridor and ascending wide flights of steps, we found ourselves in a series of lofty rooms, all beautifully carpeted and lighted, with all the shelves and recesses filled with vases and china, the last room of all containing a capital collection of Kashgar china bowls. Each room was double— that is to say, one to the front, with another at the back opening off from it, and the whole were warmed by hot-air pipes built into the walls. The only articles of furniture that we saw were huge iron and brass bedsteads, brought back, I believe, by the Amir when he returned from Rawal Pindi. Chairs and tables there were none. The other two sides of the court were filled up with servants' rooms, &c. When we had finished our inspection of this, we were taken to see the Durbar Hall, which is a separate building beyond. Here another surprise awaited us, as we found ourselves in a vast hall, 60 yards long by 20 broad, with a painted roof, supported by two rows of pillars. All this took some time to see, and it was not till late in the afternoon that we got back again.

The 22d was an equally busy day. We were all invited to breakfast by the Naib Salar, or acting Commander-in-Chief, and the Afghan generals and colonels conjointly, and a great breakfast we had of it too. I may here mention that evidently, in the Afghan army, anything under the rank of a colonel is a nobody. They have captains, but I have met only a few of them, and they are not held to be of much account, or apparently admitted into society. Certainly none were present at the breakfast. On arrival at Parwanah Khan's house, we found ourselves in a great big yard or enclosure where a half-battalion of the Kandahari Regiment was drawn up as a guard of honour, with band and colours, and also a party of pipers. We passed through into the private apartments which had been fitted up for our reception, and here we found a long table covered with sweetmeats, on one side of which were ranged the Afghan officers, and ourselves on the other. Sir West Ridgeway was given the seat of honour at the head of the room, with the Naib Salar on his right and Kazi Saad-ud-Din Khan on his left. Afghan ideas of hospitality appear to be diametrically opposed to ours. When they ask a man to dinner, instead of giving him his dinner at once, they amuse him first with tea and sweetmeats, conversation, and the circulation of a friendly pipe or two for some hours, so as to give him a chance of getting up an appetite, and then they produce the dinner. So it was with us. We sat from ten o'clock till noon amusing ourselves with sweets and cigarettes as best we could, and it was not till afternoon that the breakfast appeared. The sweetmeats were cleared away and the table laid for us in their place, while the Afghans and our native officers and *attachés*, who had not yet mastered the mysteries of the knife and fork, sat down in a solemn row in the adjoining room, and then round went the dishes. Tray after tray was brought and distributed between the two rooms, all the servants, in regular Afghan fashion, being armed to the teeth. Wherever we went it was just the same, everybody was armed, and I don't think I know of any other place where I have been waited on by so many servants in such gorgeous-coloured cloth coats and such ornamental sword-belts as I saw in Kabul. Every man wore a sword and pistol, and all wore good English boots; in fact, English boots, and trousers with straps to them, seemed to be the Kabul regulation from highest to lowest. A few only wore long Russian boots.

Shortly before we sat down to breakfast, just as the last cup of tea came round, Sir West Ridgeway proposed the health of his Highness the Amir, to which the Naib Salar at once responded by getting up and proposing the health of her Majesty the Queen, a toast that was fully honoured, and I do not suppose her Majesty's health has ever been more heartily drunk in any liquor than it was by us on this occasion in green tea. No sooner was the cloth removed and all the Afghans back in their chairs again, than the Dabir-ul-Mulk, a functionary corresponding somewhat to our Foreign Secretary, appeared with a written speech, which he read out in the name of the Naib Salar, welcoming the Mission to Kabul, and offering congratulations on the friendship now established between the two nations, evidenced to all by the officers of both thus meeting together in mutual friendship. Sir West at once replied, thanking the Amir and his officers for all their hospitality, and expressing his conviction that the friendship now so happily established would be lasting, and that, for the future, the two nations would always be found side by side.

During the entertainment a regimental band and the party of pipers played alternately in the court below, and uncommonly well they played too. The bandmaster and the pipe-major were both apparently Hindustanis trained in India, and they deserve every credit for the way they have taught the raw Afghans they have had to work upon. The bagpipes looked much as if they had been locally manufactured, and I fancy, as in the case of the heliographs, the Amir got possession of one and had the others made up like it. The Amir told us himself that he had now a body of some two hundred trained signallers, and communication was regularly kept up by them between the city and his camp all the time he was away,—all of which speaks much for his Highness's application and ingenuity.

The 23d was again another busy day. First of all the Dabir-ul-Mulk arrived at 10 A.M., with presents from the Amir. He was received with all ceremony, and first of all presented an autograph letter from the Amir to Lord Salisbury, which Sir West promised to safely deliver. After that the presents were brought in, the principal point about which was a little tray containing a decoration for each officer, as an acknowledgment of the Amir's gratitude for all their labours on his behalf. Sir West Ridgeway was first decorated with a diamond star, the first class of the Afghan Order of Chivalry, and Colonel Bax with a smaller star of somewhat similar pattern, being the second class of the same Order. All the other officers were presented with the gold decoration of the Afghan Order of Honour, and each also received a dress of honour. On the conclusion of the presentation we all put on our decorations and rode off to the Bagh-i-Babar to pay our final visit to his Highness. Sir West Ridgeway, first of all, had a private interview, at which, it is said, his Highness expressed his entire satisfaction at the boundary settlement so far as it has gone. After this we were all introduced, and took our final leave of his Highness. The Amir received us this time in another pavilion erected at the top of the garden close to the Emperor Babar's tomb, which stands in a marble mosque, with an inscription on the arches recording the fact that Shah Jehan, after conquering Balkh, Shibarghan, and Tashkurghan, came to Kabul and built the mosque, and erected the tombstone over his ancestor's grave in the year A.H. 1056, or A.D. 1643; the date of Babar's death being recorded by the Abjad reckoning in certain Persian verses on the tombstone itself.

From the garden we rode straight off to the other side of the city to witness a review of the Afghan troops. The

Naib Salar and Afghan generals met Sir West Ridgeway at the new palace, and escorted him to the parade-ground on the large Chaman near Siah Sang, immediately below Fort Roberts, where we found all the troops drawn up in readiness. After the salute the march past commenced, and was gone through with wonderful regularity, taking everything into consideration. The force was a small one, as some of the troops in Sherpur were not present; and then no less than two batteries of artillery and seven regiments of infantry were away with the Sipah Salar in Laghman, and three more had been lately despatched to Ghazni. Altogether 32 guns, about 2800 infantry, and 800 cavalry were present. The artillery came first, a couple of mountain batteries of six screw-guns each heading the column. These were not mounted on mules as with us, but on *yabus*, and capital strong ponies they were too. Next came a couple of light batteries of four guns each, and then a couple of heavier batteries of six guns each; none of these batteries had any waggons, and whether to call them field or horse artillery I do not quite know. Every man was mounted, but on the gun teams; they had no mounted detachments. The two light batteries had only five horses, and the heavier batteries six and eight horses, respectively, to each gun, and each horse carried his man. The men, however, though badly dressed, seemed to manage their guns well, and all looked serviceable.

After the artillery came the infantry by companies. It was difficult to distinguish the regiments, as only a proportion of the men were clad in uniform—that is to say, in red British tunics, and distance was not very regularly kept. Almost all the men, however, had the regulation felt hat, and were undoubtedly fine material for soldiers had they only good officers. The company commanders looked hardly up to their work, and the want of good officers is probably the weak point of the Afghan army. Such men under

British officers, ought to make capital soldiers. As it was, they kept good step and good line, and were wonderfully steady considering.

The cavalry turned out about the best of all. The two troops of the Shahi or Royal Regiment of the Amir's own body-guard looked uncommonly well. They are all Barakzais, mounted on Government horses, with Government arms and equipment, and both horses and saddlery were in good condition and well kept. They carried their Martini carbines in buckets. These were the only men armed with breech-loaders, all the rest having muzzle-loading carbines carried slung over the back or else hooked on to the waist-belt. The infantry were armed, some with Martinis, a larger proportion with Sniders, and some with muzzle-loaders. The last were principally confined to the young lads in the training battalion.

It was too late in the day by the time all had gone past for any manœuvres, so, after wishing the Naib Salar and his generals good-bye, we all rode home; but not to rest, for Kazi Saad-ud-Din Khan had to be received in durbar in the evening, to receive his presents and to say good-bye. The Kazi on his part came down with an autograph letter from the Amir to Dr Owen, specially thanking him for all his hard work and attention to the sick during the last two years — a graceful parting acknowledgment. The Kazi, when the time came, seemed sorry to say good-bye; and I daresay he was, as life with the Amir, I fancy, is not at all bliss for his officials. However, all things must have an end, and so had our visit to Kabul.

The morning of the 24th saw us all on our way again. Riding out to Butkak in the early morning, we paid a visit to Sherpur, where some of us, like Sir West Ridgeway and Dr Owen, who had lived there before, were anxious to have a look at their old quarters. The place, I believe, is in very much the same state as when we left it, except that part has been demolished by the Amir for the sake of the woodwork, which he utilised in the new palace. He told us himself that he did not like the place, and very possibly he may dismantle it all in time. Colonel Bax and Dr Owen paid a visit to the cemetery, which, they said, was very little disturbed; some of the graves had sunk and fallen in, and most of the tombstones were down on the ground, and the names carved on them had been chipped and defaced, apparently by mischievous boys, but a little repair would put all to rights again. This the Amir himself promised Sir West Ridgeway should be done, and, in fact, before we left Kabul orders were issued by his Highness for the wall to be built up afresh, and the whole cemetery to be repaired and preserved. We had a last leave-taking of Kazi Saad-ud-Din Khan and the Farash Bashi, a capital fellow, who had looked after us so carefully during our stay, and one or two others, on the road; and then we bade final good-bye to Kabul and fairly started for India.

The country from Kabul to Peshawar was so well known during the last war that I need say nothing more than that we marched by the following stages, viz.:—

		Miles.
24. Kabul to Butkak,	. . . .	15
25. Barik Ao,	. . . .	25
26. Safed Sang,	. . . .	32
27. Rozabad,	. . . .	18
28. Ali Boghan,	. . . .	19
29. Busawal,	. . . .	23
30. Landi Kotal,	. . . .	25
31. Jamrud, .	. . . .	16
	Total, . .	173

Here we are fairly, at last, in British territory, and we march in to Peshawar to-morrow. Captain Leigh, the political officer in charge of the Khaibar, met us at Landi Kotal, and there we finally said good-bye to our Afghan friends, and came under the welcome protection of the Khaibar Rifles

—the first sign to us that we were really back in our own territories. I must say, however, that we owe a great deal to the Afghans. For two years not a shot has been fired at us, and not a thing even has been stolen from us, and I know of no country where we could have experienced such entire immunity from theft. We had a troop of Afghan cavalry on duty with us from Kabul to the frontier, and the way they watched over us was something wonderful. Not only was there a circle of vedettes round our camp both day and night, but even when Sir West Ridgeway halted on the roadside for breakfast, there was a circle formed all round in no time. I was particularly struck in the Jagdalak pass how quickly each hill-top in the neighbourhood was crowned by one of these men, and how well they seemed to understand their duty; without doubt, the Afghan sowar has the makings of a fine soldier in him.

At Landi Khana we found the Maliks of the neighbourhood assembled, with an address of welcome all ready written for presentation to Sir West Ridgeway; and the men of the Khaibar Rifles, with their brothers and their cousins, were all waiting to welcome their commandant, Ressaldar-Major Sirdar Muhammad Aslam Khan, back again.

Here, at Jamrud, we have been met by Colonel Waterfield, C.S.I., the Commissioner of Peshawar; Mr Anderson, the Deputy Commissioner; Mr Hastings, the District Superintendent of Police,—and we are all thoroughly happy in the enjoyment of Colonel Waterfield's genial hospitality, enhanced by the knowledge that all care and anxiety is at an end, now that we are once more back amongst our own people. To-morrow, we hear, we have a grand reception in store for us, on arrival at Peshawar, by all the troops in garrison under the command of General Sir Hugh Gough, in addition to special entertainments for both officers and men. I need not say how proud and gratified all of us are, from the highest to the lowest, at such a cordial welcome.

CHAPTER XXVI.

RECEPTION AT LAHORE.

LAHORE, *6th November* 1886.

SIR WEST RIDGEWAY started for England last night, and the Boundary Commission is now being broken up. Never shall I forget the reception that has been accorded to us since our return. When last I wrote we were just starting from Jamrud, the whole of the little garrison of the fort there being drawn up on the roadside waiting for us to pass.

On arrival at Peshawar we were met by Brigadier-General Sir Hugh Gough, V.C., K.C.B., at the head of all the troops in the station, consisting of M Battery 3d Brigade Royal Artillery, 1st Bengal Cavalry, the Wiltshire Regiment, the 4th Battalion King's Royal Rifles, the 21st, 29th, and 31st Panjab Infantry, all drawn up in line in review order on either side of the road to salute us as we passed. We were played in all the way to our camping-ground by the bands of the different regiments, and escorted by the General and his staff. Many were the kind greetings we received, and many were the encomiums we heard passed on the fine appearance of our men. We then began to realise what a difference the invigorating winter air of the northern regions we had been living in had made in the *physique* of both our men and followers—how it had filled out their chests, and made them much more robust than their brethren who had never been out of India.

Our day in Peshawar was a busy one. Our orders were to proceed at once to Lahore, where his Excellency the Viceroy had graciously signified his intention of receiving us; and as his Excellency was to leave Lahore on the 4th, it was as much as we could do to get our equipment and stores and everything settled up and handed over in time to allow of our departure in the morning. The night of the 1st was a gay one for all. The officers of the station gave a ball in our honour, while all the native officers, *attachés*, and men were each entertained at various feasts and entertainments, followed by fireworks, illuminations, and dances that lasted till a very late hour in the morning. However, midday of the 2d saw us all on our way, the General and many of the officers kindly coming down to see us off.

On arrival at Rawal Pindi in the evening we had another and most unexpected welcome. Brigadier-General Sir John Hudson, K.C.B., with all his staff, a regimental band, and many of the officers of the station, were waiting to meet us on arrival and bid us welcome by the special request of H.R.H. the Duke of Connaught, commanding the Division, —and proud we were at the honour.

On arrival at Lahore on the morning of the 3d we were met at the railway station by Major-General Murray, C.B., commanding the Division; Mr H. M. Durand, C.S.I., Foreign Secretary to the Government of India; and the Deputy and Assistant Commissioners of Lahore; and we found a camp pitched for us all ready for immediate occupation.

The first thing to greet us on arrival was the receipt of the following notification:—

"*NOTIFICATION.*

"No. 1885 F.

"SIMLA, *the 1st November* 1886.

"On the return to India of the Afghan Boundary Commission, the Governor-General in Council desires to place on record his high appreciation of the valuable services rendered by officers and men during their two years' absence from British territory.

"Colonel Sir West Ridgeway and the political officers under his orders have shown skill, judgment, and tenacity in their endeavours to secure the primary objects of the Commission, and the results obtained in other departments have been highly satisfactory; while the military escort, composed of detachments of the 11th Bengal Lancers and 20th Panjab Infantry, have upheld throughout, by discipline, endurance, and good conduct, the credit of her Majesty's army.

"The Governor-General in Council heartily congratulates the members of the Commission upon the completion of their trying duties, and welcomes them back to the British frontier.

"By Order of the Governor-General in Council,
"H. M. Durand,
"*Secretary to the Government of India.*"

This was followed on the afternoon of the 4th by the investiture of Colonel Sir West Ridgeway with the insignia of a Knight Commander of the Star of India, and the public reception of the officers and men of the Commission, by his Excellency the Viceroy at Government House. In describing this, I cannot do better than quote the following extract from the 'Civil and Military Gazette,' the local journal, of this morning's date:—

"INVESTITURE OF SIR WEST RIDGEWAY.

"The most significant, and albeit its narrower dimensions as a spectacle, the most imposing, functions of the Lahore festivities came off on Thursday afternoon at 4.30 P.M., when a Chapter of the most Exalted Order of the Star of India was held to invest Sir West Ridgeway with the insignia of the second class of the Order. At the same time the opportunity was taken of welcoming the members of the Afghan Boundary Commission. Notwithstanding that the Chapter had been ordered at very short notice, it was a scene solemn and impressive. One of the upper rooms in Government House had been cleared and arranged in a manner suitable to the occasion. At the head of the room was the throne for his Excellency the Grand Master, and on either side of the centre passage were seated the Knights Grand Cross and Knight Commanders, and below them the Companions. Below the Companions, on either side, were seated the officers and native *attachés* of the Boundary Commission. All heads of departments were present, and many distinguished visitors attended the installation, who were provided with seats behind the members of the Order. His Honour the Lieutenant-Governor was present, welcoming the Maharajahs of Bahawulpur, Nabha, Jhind, and Nahun, and before the proceedings commenced he took his seat among the Knights of the second class. The entrance to the robing-room was guarded by non-commissioned officers of the 11th Bengal Lancers, and the archway leading into the drawing-room behind the throne was guarded by two non-commissioned officers of the 20th Panjab Infantry. At 4.25 P.M. his Royal Highness the Duke of Connaught arrived, all present rising and the band outside playing the National Anthem. After a few minutes' interval the curtains leading to the robing-room were drawn apart, and his Excellency the Grand Master appeared, preceded by the members of his staff, and followed the secretary of the Order, who wore his robes. All the assembly rose as his Excellency entered, and remained standing until the Grand Master had taken his seat. His Excellency wore the ribbon of the Order, and his breast was covered with the stars of the many orders of which he is a member. As soon as the Viceroy had taken his seat, the Secretary of the Order advanced and informed the Grand Master of the business before the Chapter—viz., that of the installation of Sir West Ridgeway as a Knight of the second class. The two junior Knight Commanders, Sir Dinkur Rao and the Raja of Natore, accompanied by the *attaché* in the Foreign Department, then proceeded to the robing-room and led up Sir West Ridgeway to his Excellency. The Grand Master then rose, and in a clear and distinct voice said, 'In the name of the Queen-Empress of India, and by her Majesty's command, I hereby invest you with the honourable insignia of the Star of India, of which most exalted Order her Majesty has been graciously pleased to make you a Knight Commander.' Sir West Ridgeway then knelt before the Grand Master, who, after touching him on the shoulder with the sword of the Military Secretary, said, 'Arise, Sir West Ridgeway.' The new Knight, after making a profound reverence, then retired on one side, and the Junior Knight Commander attached the Star of the Order to the left breast, the *attaché* in the Foreign Department at the same time presenting the collar and badge of the Order as custodian to the Grand Master, who invested the new Knight with the collar and badge. The newly invested Knight, having made his reverence to the Grand Master, was led by the Secretary to his seat. The Secretary of the Order then reported that there was no other business.

"Thus ended a most imposing scene, and all the more so from

the quiet way in which all the actors in the performance went through their duties. His Excellency after this expressed a wish that the officers of the Boundary Commission should be presented to him. Every member of the Mission in order then made his reverence to his Excellency, Colonel Sir West Ridgeway naming each officer as he approached the chair. This ceremony having been carried out, his Excellency the Viceroy next addressed the assembly in the following terms :—

" ' Knights, Princes, and Gentlemen,—Great as has been my pleasure in conferring upon Sir West Ridgeway, the distinguished Chief of the Boundary Commission, the honours which have been so justly awarded him by the gracious favour of the Queen, I feel that my satisfaction would not be complete unless I took this opportunity of welcoming back to India those other officers who have returned with him to Lahore, and who have so ably seconded his endeavours in carrying out the difficult and arduous duties imposed upon him. There are, indeed, few tasks more ungrateful or more exposed to mortification than that of delimiting a frontier in the interests of an ally. In matters of this kind there are always disputable points, almost impossible to settle without exciting a certain amount of discontent in the minds of those in whose behalf we are mediating; for it is difficult to make them understand that there must be a certain amount of give and take, and that right is not always on one side. I am happy to think, however, that, thanks to the good sense and intelligence of the ruler of Afghanistan, we have already been able on more than one occasion to settle controverted matters in a pacific manner; and I am certainly of opinion that the moderation and conciliatory spirit shown by his Highness in regard to the demarcation of the western portion of his frontier ought to facilitate the arrangement of the only remaining matter in dispute, in a manner consonant to his interests, and as I conscientiously believe, to his rights. Be that, however, as it may, I desire to assure Sir West Ridgeway and all his associates that their countrymen and the whole Indian community are heartily glad to see them back amongst us. From their first departure to the present moment we have watched their proceedings with the deepest interest and sympathy. We are fully aware of the arduous and trying circumstances which have attended the execution of their mission, and that they have been exposed to privations and hardships, sickness, and on more than one occasion to considerable peril; but from first to last their conduct has been deserving of the highest praise, and they have exhibited a degree of fortitude and patience which has been exemplary. Nor is it inappropriate to remember that, apart from the diplomatic object upon which they have been engaged, they also are able to show, thanks to the energy and industry of their scientific colleagues, geographical and scientific results of a most interesting and valuable character. Last, not least however, I would desire to congratulate them on the auspicious circumstances under which they passed through Kabul, and on the rapidity of their march from that capital to the British frontier. That an English Mission so constituted should be received as honoured guests by the Amir, and with the most hearty and friendly welcome at the hands of his subjects along their entire route, is in itself a remarkable and significant circumstance, which cannot fail to have a most beneficent effect upon the future relations between the Governments of India and Afghanistan. In conclusion, allow me to hope that, however disagreeable may have been a great portion of the period you spent in Afghanistan, at all events hereafter it will suggest none but pleasant reminiscences; for I am happy to think that the one thing necessary to all servants of the Queen, European or native, civil or military, to make a retrospect agreeable, is the consciousness that they have nobly and faithfully done their duty.'"

The assembly broke up as soon as his Excellency had finished speaking, and shortly afterwards his Excellency, accompanied by H.R.H. the Duke of Connaught and General Murray, inspected the escort, who were drawn up in the grounds of Government House. The escort received his Excellency with a royal salute, and, the inspection being finished, his Excellency addressed the men in the following words :—

"In the name of the Queen and the Government of India, I have come here to-day to bid you all a hearty welcome back to your country. I assure you that I am very proud to find myself surrounded by soldiers who have so admirably done their duty. I am well aware that during the period which has elapsed since you first crossed from Hindustan into Afghanistan you have been called upon to encounter great privations and other trials of a very serious kind, but all your officers assure me that they have never seen men under such trying circumstances exhibit more fortitude, more patience, more good-humour, or more untiring devotion to a sense of duty. You may take my word for it, that all your countrymen in India are very proud of you, and that the recollection of the way in which you have behaved during the time you have been absent will be a just source of pride to you all your lives."

The grounds of Government House at this time were full of guests who had come to attend Lady Aitchison's garden-party, and the inspection of the escort was a picturesque sight, such as is seldom seen in India. The local journal, commenting on the scene, says that those who missed the sight missed the finest of all our recent spectacles—and very truly too.

This and the dinner given to the officers of the Boundary Commission by the hospitable members of the Panjab Club, wound up our festivities at Lahore, and now we are all on the move again. The infantry escort left last night to rejoin the headquarters of their regiment, and the men of the cavalry are all being paid up and sent off to their homes, on the nine months' furlough which has been specially granted to them in consideration of their long and good service across the frontier. The various officers are all starting for their respective destinations, and I myself am off to Calcutta to wind up the various business and accounts, &c., connected with the Mission. What the result of the negotiations in Europe may be, the future alone can tell.

CHAPTER XXVII.

NEGOTIATIONS AT ST PETERSBURG—FINAL SETTLEMENT.

LONDON, *August* 1887.

THE Blue-book showing the result of the negotiations at St Petersburg and the final settlement of the Frontier question has now been published, and nothing remains but the demarcation of the boundary-line agreed upon.

After the adjournment of the joint Commissions on the Oxus in September 1886, it was doubtful whether Russia would consent to complete the work, as it seemed evidently to her advantage to leave the frontier unsettled. However, by March 1887 it was found that the time had come for a resumption of the negotiations, and it was agreed that these should take place at St Petersburg, partly as a matter of expediency and partly as a question of etiquette—the former arrangements having been concluded in London.

Colonel Sir West Ridgeway was accordingly directed to proceed to St Petersburg, and arrived there in the middle of April. The Russian Government deputed as their delegate M. Zinoview, the head of the Asiatic department, assisted by Colonel Kuhlberg and M. Lessar—Sir West Ridgeway on his side being assisted by Captains Barrow and De Laessoe.

The first important question to be decided was whether the district of Khwajah Salar, with its area of about a thousand square miles and a population of some 15,000 souls, belonged to Afghanistan or Bokhara. The British contention was, that by the agreement of 1872-73 it had been decided that in principle all territory which at that time was actually in the possession of the Amir of Afghanistan should belong to Afghanistan, and that a certain place on the banks of the Oxus, designated by the British Government as the "Post of Khojah Salih," and by the Russian Government as the "Point of Khojah Salih," should form the western limit of Afghan possession on the Oxus. The Commission had been unable to find any place corresponding to the "Post" of the arrangement of 1872-73, and it was evident that some geographical mistake had been made, and it would be necessary, therefore, to decide the question with sole reference to the spirit of the agreement; and as it was admitted that the whole of the Khojah Salih, or Khwajah Salar district, had been in Afghan possession at least since 1850, it was clear that the whole district must continue to form part of Afghanistan.

The Russian Government considered the case from a different point of view. Their delegates argued that in 1872 the British Government had claimed the whole of Badakshan and Wakhan for Afghanistan, and an extension westwards to a point on the Oxus situated between Khojah Salih and Karki. The Russian Government had, on the contrary, been of opinion that Wakhan and certain parts of Badakshan did not belong to Afghanistan, and that in the west Afghan possessions did not extend beyond Khojah Salih. Subsequently the Russian Government, maintaining their view as to actual possession, had, in deference to the wish of the British Government, consented to consider the whole of Badakshan and Wakhan as being within the limits of Afghanistan; while the British Government, in their reply, had stated that as long as the post of Khojah Salih remained in Afghan possession, they would not insist on defining the frontier as meeting the river below that place; that this was a distinct concession made to Russia in return for her concessions on the upper Oxus, and that there could consequently be no question of general principles so far as Khojah Salih was concerned; that, in addition to this, there were even stronger reasons preventing Russia from admitting that the case could be decided as a matter of principle. The agreement of 1872-73 declared the Turkoman tribes north of Andkhui, Akchah, and Maimanah to be generally independent of Afghanistan, and subject to Russian influence; and the London protocol of 1885 gave the control of the Panjdeh Turkomans to Russia, thus admitting that their country was independent of Afghanistan. Yet the Boundary Commission had by recent demarcation deprived these Panjdeh Turkomans of a large extent of pasture and lands, and consequently the principles of 1872-73 had been distinctly violated in this case, and it was not possible for Russia to admit that the principle should be applied where it was in favour of Afghan claims, and neglected when its application would favour Russian subjects.

Russia must consequently insist upon the literal application of the terms of the agreement. The words "Point" and "Post" could not possibly be made to mean a large district; they referred to some definite place of small extent, and the only definite places called Khojah Salih were a graveyard called Ziarat-i-Khojah Salih, and an adjacent ruin called Sarai Khojah Salih; that this ruin had once been a fortified building, and was the only place which in any way corresponded to the expression "Post." This ruin was therefore, in the opinion of the Russian Government, the Point referred to in the agreement of 1872-73, and the frontier line must be drawn to that place.

This Sarai Khojah Salih, I should add, is situated at the upper end of the district, and consequently concession of the line thus claimed by Russia would have deprived Afghanistan of more than some 600 square miles of land, with some 13,000 inhabitants, and a revenue of some £1300. How far the contentions of each party were justified is immaterial. It is sufficient to say that the British Government maintained their view of the case, though admitting that the letter of the agreement of 1872-73 was in favour of the Russian claims. Finally, in order to prove their respect for treaty engagements, they offered to compromise the matter.

The Russian delegates, on their part, admitted that lands which had been in Afghan possession for many years past ought to remain Afghan, but said they could not surrender their claims unconditionally, having to consider the interests of their Turkoman subjects, and that they were willing to agree to a compromise which would leave the Afghans in possession of the Khojah Salih district, if it restored to the Panjdeh Turkomans the lands of which they had been deprived by the recent demarcation.

Negotiations on this basis finally resulted in the settlement now published.

The main result has been to confirm the Afghans in the possession of Khojah Salih, and to give the Panjdeh Turkomans the greater part of the land they formerly occupied. This land is at present uninhabited and yields no revenue, and the Amir loses nothing by the exchange.

The frontier line, instead of running, as described in my former letters of 12th April and 17th October 1886, will now run from pillar 19 to the Kushk river, near the point where it is joined by its affluent the Moghor, and thence up the bed of the Kushk as far as Chihal Dukhtaran, and from there north-eastwards again to the highest point in the Baba Taghi hills, and along the crest of that range to the Kashan stream, which is crossed a little below Torshaikh, and thence along the crest of the hills again to the head of the Yekiyeuzi canal on the left bank of the Murghab river at the head of the Maruchak valley, and down the bed of that river to pillar No. 36 below the Maruchak Fort. This change gives the Turkomans some extra 800 square miles of pasture-land, of which perhaps 20 square miles may be culturable. The remainder is only fit for sheep-grazing. The Kara Tepe side of the Kushk valley, Chihal Dukhtaran, Torshaikh, and Maruchak Fort are all retained for the Amir, the only difference being that the Turkomans are given their formerly cultivated lands on the left bank of the Kushk up to Chihal Dukhtaran, at Robat-i-Kashan, and along the left bank of the Murghab in the Maruchak valley. The Turkoman cultivation on the western side of the Maruchak valley has already been noticed in my letter of 17th October last, and I had then occasion to mention how sore the Turkomans were at the loss of it. As there is no one else on the Afghan side to cultivate this land if the Turkomans do not, the restitution of it to the latter is no loss to the Amir. The doubtful question of the water-supply to the Panjdeh hamlets opposite the Maruchak Fort has thus been settled, and one essential result of the settlement is, that while treaties have been respected, tranquillity has also been better assured. The fact that by this last settlement the Russian frontier has been advanced 10 or 15 miles nearer Herat, as I have seen mentioned in the newspapers, does not appear to me worth discussion. Once the old frontier from Sher Tepe to Sari Yazi proposed by Sir Peter Lumsden was given up, and Pul-i-Khatun and Panjdeh, the only two points of any strategical importance, were surrendered to Russia, the question of 10 miles here or there on the sterile downs of Badghis became of little moment.

As a matter of fact, the removal of any likely cause of irritation is more likely to conduce to the duration of the settlement than the reverse; and while the Russian Government is to be congratulated on having obtained satisfaction for the Panjdeh Turkomans, the British Government is to be equally congratulated on having at last secured a recognised treaty frontier. Without this final settlement the work of the past three years would all have been lost, and Afghanistan would have been left without any recognised frontier from the Hari Rud to the Oxus — either party being at liberty to act according to circumstances. A large and influential party in Russia considered this an enormous advantage, and the influence exercised by that party made negotiations difficult and precarious. The success of the negotiations may be taken as a proof that the Emperor and his most trusted advisers wish to improve the relations between the two countries.

Captains Komaroff and Kondratenko have, it is said, been appointed the Russian representatives for the final demarcation of the frontier; and Major Peacocke and myself expect to be sent out shortly to join them, proceeding across the Caucasus to the Caspian, and through Persia from Astrabad to Mashhad, and thence along the frontier to the Oxus, putting up the pillars on the way.

CHAPTER XXVIII.

COMPLETION OF THE DEMARCATION, AND RETURN THROUGH TRANS-CASPIA.

CAMP KARAWAL KHANA, 28*th Dec.* 1887.

THE last pillar of the rectified line of frontier between the rivers Kushk and Murghab has now been erected, and we start to-morrow for the Oxus. The demarcation commenced at Kara Tepe, in the Kushk valley, on the 21st November, and was completed here on the banks of the Murghab on the 25th December: and a most unexpectedly festive Christmas Day it was for us too. When Captain Komaroff met us in the morning to build the last pillar, he told us that Colonel Alikhanoff, the Governor of Merv, with Colonel Tarkhanoff, the Governor of Panjdeh, a couple of travelling French officers, a German baron, and a Russian count, had arrived the evening before, and were coming to join us; and sure enough, soon after, they all turned up. Colonel Alikhanoff rode up, preceded by a troop of Turkoman irregulars, headed by a man with a large white standard, and followed by a crowd of others, all apparently got up in their very best and gaudiest coats. Our Turkoman postal sowars, seeing this, all rushed into their finest fancy coats, and came across the river to swell the throng. The building of the boundary pillar thus suddenly became the subject of most unwonted interest, and our French travellers lost no time in photographing the scene. I doubt if so many nationalities were ever collected together on the banks of the Murghab before, or so many different types of the Central Asian soldier. Cossacks and Turkomans, Bengal Lancers, and Afghan cavalry all looked on around, and I wonder if they speculated as to who was next to be arrayed against whom. However, there was little time for speculation, as no sooner was the pillar built than we all adjourned to our camp for lunch, and festivity was the order of the day. While healths were passing in I do not know how many languages in our mess-tent, the Cossacks and the Turkomans were all being variously regaled outside; and it was well on in the afternoon before we all mounted our horses again, and rode out to where Jemadar Khan Sahib Amir Muhammad Khan had his little escort of some five-and-twenty men of the 11th Bengal Lancers drawn up to show our guests what Indian cavalry were like. Colonel Alikhanoff, an old cavalry officer himself, expressed the keenest interest in everything, and I am bound to say he had nothing but praise to bestow. They were the finest irregular cavalry he had ever seen, was his final verdict, and doubtless well deserved. His astonishment was great at finding that the native officer in command was an Afghan, a native of Kabul; and I don't suppose he had realised that we had so many Afghans in our ranks, or what good soldiers they could be made. Jemadar Amir Muhammad Khan's show of medals, ranging from Lucknow to China, Umbeyla, Kabul, and Kandahar, attracted much attention, and was an honest and instructive record of the service done for us by our Indian army. Christmas night was a memorable one for us. We dined with the Russians, and had a capital dinner and a most festive evening, which we thoroughly enjoyed despite the fact that we had eight miles out and back again to ride on a cold winter night. We were a party of three Russians, three English, two Frenchmen, a German, and four Caucasians, all of different religions and nationalities, and all enjoying ourselves together, while the Cossacks sang in chorus round the bonfire outside.

Of the new frontier there is little to tell. The line we have demarcated is a little more than 100 miles in length, and the watershed of the Chingurak range running east and west between the Kushk and Kashan streams forms the principal feature in it. The main difference between the present and the former frontier is the surrender to Russia of the right bank of the Kushk below Chihal Dukhtaran, and the western half of the Maruchak valley along the left bank of the Murghab. The Maruchak valley is still uninhabited and uncultivated, and except that the reeds have been a good deal cleared, there is little difference from what it was three years ago. The Kushk valley at Kara Tepe, though, we found had greatly altered. This was formerly nothing but a waste of camel-thorn and reed-swamps inhabited by tigers and pheasants; but now we found it peopled by a colony of some 500 or 600 families of Zamindawari cultivators, who had been brought up and located here by the Amir's order, and whom we found settled in regular mud-villages all about the valley. Nearly half of these people were settled on the Russian bank and had to be moved; and this, with winter so close at hand, was an equal hardship both for the poor people themselves and for the Afghan authorities, who had to provide for them.

However, all was arranged and the ground was vacated even before Alikhanoff's visit to the place. I was in their villages almost every day, and no sooner did I appear than men and boys used to flock out for a chat, with offers of snuff or any other little thing they had—all so different from the surly and fanatical spirit Zamindawaris are generally supposed to possess.

That Alikhanoff should seize the earliest possible moment

to start upon a tour along his new frontier would seem to show that the Russians set greater store upon their new acquisition than we thought. The Panjdeh Sariks, we know, are terribly hard up for cultivable land, and I have not the slightest doubt that the new field now thrown open to them will be taken advantage of at once. By the possession of the left half of the Maruchak valley they have got some of the most fertile land along the banks of the Murghab. The Afghan colonists brought up to Bala Murghab by the Amir's order are as yet almost all nomads, and prefer to camp up in the mountains above, where firewood is plentiful, to settling in the valley below, where not a stick is to be found. But this, I daresay, will soon be altered. General Ghaus-ud-Din Khan, who still reigns at Bala Murghab with charge of all the frontier districts, is bent upon bringing as much land as possible under cultivation; and with a man of his energy in command, a few years will probably effect a great change. The General was to have accompanied us as the Amir's agent, but he was occupied in the Firozkohi country when we arrived on the frontier, and it is only now at the very last that he has been able to join us. His brother, Mullah Abdul Aziz Khan, the governor of Kilah Nao, has been acting with us as his deputy during his absence, and we now leave them both in the Bala Murghab fort, where the General has taken unto himself a new bride from amongst his lately imported nomads, and has apparently settled down for good and all.

The reed-beds in the Maruchak valley, though thinner than formerly, we found were still thick enough to provide cover not only for pheasants, but also for tigers. Shooting down the valley one day towards the old fort, we came across half-a-dozen Turkomans, some on horseback and the others on foot, with a pack of about a dozen great shaggy dogs—on the hunt for pig, they said: not that they would eat pork themselves, but that they wanted some to feed the dogs upon. We left them beating a patch of reeds that we had vainly tried to get the pheasants out of; and though we heard the dogs barking behind us, we went on, thinking nothing more of the matter, till some time after, when one of the Turkomans came galloping up to tell us that the dogs had found a tiger. We at once went back, but instead of having a long and difficult business to beat the beast out of the reeds, we found the dogs had already done this; and before we were aware that we were within a mile of the fray, we suddenly saw a riderless horse galloping and men running about, one with a drawn sword, another with a very old gun, down which he was vainly endeavouring to ram a bullet, and all shouting and yelling and wildly gesticulating. To jump off one's horse and seize a rifle was the work of a moment, and stepping up on to the bank of a small dry canal to see what all the row was about, I found myself face to face with the tiger within five-and-twenty yards—and uncommonly angry he was too. The dogs were baying round him at a little distance, but there was no time to stop and watch the fun. The tiger was evidently coming straight for us, and to let drive at him was the work of a moment. Fortunately I rolled him over in his tracks, and a second shot settled the matter, and then all the dogs rushed in and worried the beast to their hearts' content, with a pluck that I have never seen equalled before. These large Turkoman dogs are certainly grand animals in many ways; and the way they stuck to and worked this tiger out of his retreat in the reed-beds—reeds, mind you, 8 and 10 feet in height and utterly impassable for men—out into the open, and there never left him for a second, but worried him to his death, is worthy of every praise. We found that one of the Turkomans was badly mauled, the tiger having seized him and dragged him off the horse we saw galloping about just before we came up; so we bound him up as well as we could and sent him off to our camp at once, where his wounds were properly dressed, and two days afterwards he left hospital and rode off home again, apparently not in the least put out by his wounds, nor having the least idea of what shock to the system or suchlike civilised ailments meant. The tiger was a large full-grown male, quite as big as an Indian tiger, but much dingier in colour. The skin was more of a dirty brown, with very little black about it at all. Just a few of the stripes on the back were black, but the majority were simply of a darker shade of brown than the rest of the skin.

While we were at Maruchak the garrison of the fort there, consisting of 100 Khasadars under a Sad Bashi, and some sowars, did everything they could for us; and I must say that wherever we have thus come across Afghan troops we have found them willing and obliging. Nothing can better exemplify the change of feeling that is apparently coming over the Afghans towards us than the cordial reception which our escort met with on the march up. The men of the escort were full of it when they joined us, and they told us how everywhere on the march they had been cordially received and well treated, and how at Farah even the Afghan sepoys in garrison there had come out to them with presents of pomegranates, &c.—all so different from what the feeling of the country was even three years ago, and evidencing a most welcome change.

The escort, consisting of 30 men of the 11th Bengal Lancers, under the command of Jemadar Khan Sahib Amir Muhammad Khan, and accompanied by Assistant Surveyor Khan Bahadur Yusuf Sharif, Hospital-Assistant Amir-ud-Din, and various other details, numbering altogether 103 men, 38 horses, and 109 mules, all under the charge of Subadar Khan Bahadur Muhammad Husain Khan of the 2d Sikhs, left Quetta on the 12th October and joined us at Kara Tepe on the 22d November. I do not know accurately what the distance is, but the Subadar estimates it at a total of 609 miles, which was covered in forty-one marches, of which they made ten from Quetta to Kandahar, 137 miles; sixteen from Kandahar to Farah, 234 miles; and ten on to Pahrah, close to Herat, 153 miles, from which place it was five marches, or 85 miles, *viâ* the Ardewan Pass, to our camp at Kara Tepe.

Of our own journey to the frontier I have little to tell. Major Peacocke and I left London on the 22d September, and travelling *viâ* Constantinople (where we were joined by our Russian interpreter, Mr Woodhouse) to Batoum, we reached Tiflis on the 8th October. There we halted a day to pay our visits to Prince Dondukoff Korsakoff, the Governor-General and Commander-in-Chief of the Trans-Caucasus, General Zelenoy, Colonel Kuhlberg, and others whom we had known on the Boundary Commission. Prince Dondukoff received us most civilly, and gave us all the information he had about the arrangements for the demarcation of the frontier. He also gave us an account of his recent visit to Merv, and told us what a rich country it was going to become. He had been to Bandi-i-Sultan himself, and told us that the remains of the masonry of the old dam across the river Murghab there were still to be seen, and the old canals taking off from it could still be traced along either bank. The estimates for the rebuilding of this dam had now been completed and sanctioned, and when done, the large tract of country to be irrigated from it would enable all the cotton required for Russia to be grown at home instead of being imported from abroad. The Prince afterwards showed us his collection of curiosities, arms, brass and bronze ware and armour, &c., which he said it had taken him forty-five years of his life to collect, and was certainly well worth seeing. One room, I remember, was furnished throughout with Bombay black-wood furniture which I never expected to see in the Caucasus. Last of all the Prince showed us his two special objects of interest. The first was a quill-pen in a glass case—the pen, he said, with which Williams signed the capitulation of Kars; and the second was the coat of the Afghan colonel who was killed at the Russian attack on Panjdeh.

At Baku we had just time to drive out to Sorakhana and visit the old Hindu monastery there, but found it deserted. The last of the *fakirs* left about three years ago, and now the place is simply an empty enclosure surrounded by the works of a Russian oil-refining factory, and would be hardly recognisable were it not for the Hindi inscriptions on the walls. The enclosure is an irregular quadrangle surrounded by a high wall, with vaulted chambers and cells all around the inside, and a domed cupola in the middle ascended by steps, in the centre of which in former days the sacred fire fed by natural gas was kept alight.

Leaving Baku on the afternoon of the 10th October, we breakfasted the next day at Uzunada, the terminus of the Trans-Caspian Railway, where the lines of the ordinary gauge, about 5 feet, but lightly laid on the sand, run right up to the piers alongside of which the steamers lie. The railway station and houses were all log-huts, and very comfortable they looked too. Uzunada is only the temporary terminus, I believe, as we were told the line was eventually to be carried on to Krasnovodsk, which has the best harbour on that side of the Caspian, and will probably become the port of the future. Chikislar, which we passed early in the morning of the 12th, seemed to consist of nothing but some huts on an arid sandbank. Some 500 troops, we were told, were stationed there, and a hotter or more wretched-looking place to be quartered at one could hardly conceive. The island of Ashurada, the Russian naval station, which we reached about 1 P.M. the same day, was much pleasanter-looking. Here the scenery entirely changed. Before us we had the lofty mountains of Persia, wooded down to the water's edge; and the island itself, though only a few hundred yards across, seemed full of houses, and with its church and buildings looked comparatively civilised. We had no time to inspect the place, as the steamer only stopped long enough to land the mails and supplies, and then ran straight across to the Persian post of Bandar-i-Gaz just opposite, where we landed. There we found Gok Sirdar, our old Turkoman guide, and various Persian servants sent down with some tents by General MacLean from Mashhad to meet us, and we soon settled down into camp life again. At the entrance to the village we found the local garrison, consisting of some twenty Persian matchlockmen, drawn up as a guard in our honour, and passing through we had tea with the Sartip or General in local command.

Khorasan is comparativly well known, so I will simply give a list of our marches to Mashhad, in case it may be of use to some future traveller that way. Starting from Bandar-i-Gaz we proceeded as follows:—

		Miles.
1.	Langoran,	23
2.	Astrabad,	13
3.	Kujlak,	19
4.	Tash,	20
5.	Shahrud,	22
6.	Khairabad,	8
7.	Maiamai,	30
8.	Miandasht,	22
9.	Abasabad,	20
10.	Mazinan,	24
11.	Mehr,	18
12.	Sabzawar,	30
13.	Robat-i-Sir-Poshidah,	14
14.	Shorab,	23
15.	Nishapur,	22
16.	Bagh-i-Shan,	20
17.	Sharifabad,	23
18.	Mashhad,	22
	Total,	373

At Mashhad we were the guests of General MacLean for a week, while the arrangements for our transport, servants, and camp equipage were completed; and starting again on the 5th November, we reached the Afghan frontier at Zulfikar on the 10th, two years to the day from our first arrival there for the meeting of the Joint Commission. We found the Afghan Sad Bashi in command duly expecting us, and with orders to afford us every assistance; and once again in Afghanistan, we felt quite at home. We marched across Badghis by the old route *viâ* Gulran to Kara Tepe, where we arrived on the 15th, and were joined by the Russian Commission, consisting of Captain Komaroff, Topographer Ilyin, Interpreter Mirzaeff, and an escort of 25 Cossacks of the Caucasian Regiment, on the 19th. We set to work on the frontier without delay, but demarcation in such a country is by no means so easy. First of all we had to send out men and camels, and dig out and bring in bricks from various ancient mounds and ruins about. Then lime had to be burnt and brought in from a distance; and last of all, the site for the pillar was often 10 or 15 miles away from our camp or from the nearest water, and we had thus to take out everything with us all that distance; and sometimes it was not at all an easy matter to get the things out so far, to find and fix upon the site, and to build the pillar and get home again before dark. Fortunately for us, the weather kept up, and though the survey work was several times brought to a standstill by cloudy, foggy weather, still we have had only one day's snow as yet; and if we can only reach Andkhui before the winter breaks, we shall have nothing to fear, as in the low country there along the banks of the Oxus the snow never lies very thick.

ON BOARD THE S.S. GRAND DUKE MICHAIL,
BLACK SEA, 12*th February* 1888.

The demarcation of the Afghan frontier up to the Oxus has now been completed, and we are all on our way home again. When last I wrote, we had just finished the first portion up to the Murghab and were starting onwards. Our march up to Andkhui was of no special interest. We followed the same route down the valley of the Ab-i-Kaisar that we took in 1886, and the only thing worth noticing was the extraordinary difference in the climate. Instead of the intense cold of the winter of 1885-86, we experienced warm, fine, sunshiny weather, and with the exception of a day at Andkhui, we were never once stopped by the snow.

At Chahar Shamba our Afghan agent from Herat, Abdul Aziz Khan, was relieved by the Turkistan agent, Nazir Nurudin Khan, whom we found waiting for us some three miles out with an escort of a troop of Afghan cavalry, who drew swords and received us with a salute with all due formality, and we then rode in together. It was curious to see the old mud chimneys and fireplaces still standing in rows on either side of the gravel walk that had formed the centre street of our camp two years ago; and I daresay they will remain like those at Bala Murghab for many a day yet, to mark the site of the British encampment.

At Khwajah Isik Bulan, our next day's march, there is a curious hot spring, and I think almost every man, not only in ours, but in the Afghan camp as well, had a real good wash that day. All our men and the Afghans bathed away most amicably together all day; but in the afternoon, when the Cossacks joined in, Afghan fanaticism began to show itself, and Nazir Nurudin had eventually to post sentries over the water, and to put a stop to the bathing for fear of a row.

We found the wild boar just as numerous as ever down the Ab-i-Kaisar valley, and we had some capital runs, spearing several of them. The Cossacks killed several, shooting them with their rifles off horseback; but that is dangerous sport with unskilled men, as the Afghans found out to their cost by shooting one of their own men through the shoulder one day.

At Jalaiar we were joined by Muhammad Sharif Khan,

one of the Wali of Maimanah's sons; but being unable to talk anything but Turki, our conversation could only be carried on through interpreters. His men all prided themselves on their skill in shooting off horseback, but unfortunately we had then no opportunity of testing it.

At Andkhui we exchanged visits with our old friend the governor, Colonel Abdul Hamid Khan, an ardent sportsman, like his brother Colonel Abdul Ghani Khan, the governor of Akchah. The latter was to have met us at Jarkudak, but was prevented by illness, and thus we never saw him at all.

Owing to the dry season and want of water in all the wells, we found that it would be impossible to take any large party along the frontier that we had to demarcate; so at Andkhui we divided. Major Peacocke and Captain Ilyin struck off due north to Imam Nazar, and constructed the pillars across the *chul* from there to the confines of Khamiab; while Captain Komaroff and myself, with the main party, pushed through to Khamiab, and there built the pillars through the cultivated land between that place and Bosagha —a division of labour that enabled us to push the work through with much greater rapidity. The Afghans made all arrangements for bricks and masons, &c., for Major Peacocke's party, and the Bokharan officials did the same for Captain Komaroff and myself; and thus we were able to work both sides at one and the same time.

At Jarkudak I had my first day's deer-hawking. Nazir Nurudin's hawks and dogs arrived from Akchah, and we hunted along across country during our day's march. He had three hawks (*chirkh*)—all procured young, he told me, from the nest in the cliffs on the Koh-i-Tan mountain in Bokhara, and then subsequently trained to the sport. I found, however, that they would not touch bucks—being afraid of their horns,—and that they invariably singled out some poor little doe for their quarry. The general turn-out of Nazir Nurudin's men was certainly very handy. Three men, mounted on strong sturdy ponies, each carried a hawk on his wrist; and each had a dog, the native greyhound, fastened to his left leg by a long leather thong—the best way of slipping a dog when riding at full gallop that I think I have ever seen. One end of the thong was fastened to the man's waistband, the other end had a slit in it; and the man on mounting simply passed the thong through a ring in the dog's collar, and then put his foot through the slit just before putting it in the stirrup. The dog then ran easily along by the side of the horse, and could be slipped at any moment by the man simply drawing his foot out of the stirrup. We had some capital runs; and I was much struck at the way the hawks and dogs worked together, and how well the dogs always followed the hawks, although they themselves had no idea at the time where the game was—as in all the sandy bush-covered country where the deer were, the dogs could see nothing till close up. The brushwood was very thick in parts, and once or twice it took us some time to find out where the deer had been killed. In one run a hare was started half-way, and the hawks at once left the deer and went for the hare; and the moment the dogs caught the latter, it was curious to see with what confidence the hawk dived in between them and insisted upon having its share of the sport as well.

Captain Komaroff and I arrived at Khamiab on the 14th January. We were rejoined by Major Peacocke and Captain Ilyin soon after, and the demarcation of the frontier was completed by the 18th, though it took us some days longer to compile and copy the maps and to complete the records on the final close of the Mission. Both Afghans and Bokharans seemed pleased with the settlement, and assisted us in every way they could. By the 27th the final arrangements were completed—the last protocol had been signed; and the morning of the 28th saw us all on the move.

Major Peacocke, Mr Woodhouse, and myself, it had been arranged, were to return by the Trans-Caspian Railway from Chaharjui. The Indian escort party were to march back to Quetta by the route they came; the Persian party, under the charge of Mirza Abdulah, turning off at Kushk and marching *viâ* Zulfikar to rejoin General MacLean at Mashhad. Captain Komaroff had already sent on his Cossack escort by route-march to Chaharjui, and had secured the two boats belonging to the Ak Kum ferry just below Bosagha to convey us down the river. He, with Captain Ilyin and Mirzaeff and two or three Cossack servants, took one boat, and we three with our Persian servants the other, and by about 9 A.M. we were all under way. Nazir Nurudin, Subadar Muhammad Husain Khan, Jemadar Amir Muhammad Khan, and all the men of the escort off duty, came down with us to the river-bank to see us off, and our last link with British India was the hearty cheer given us by the latter as our boats pushed off into the stream.

Life in a boat on the Oxus is anything but lively work. The boats themselves are clumsy heavy things, some 40 feet in length and 12 in breadth, built of squared logs of wood clamped together with iron bands, and the boatmen have not the faintest idea of either sailing or steering. We just drifted down the stream at the rate of about three miles an hour, and all the energies of the boatmen were devoted to keeping us off the sandbanks, and by no means with invariable success. The Oxus, for the 40 miles of its course from Ak Kum to Karki, is very shallow and tortuous, and the scenery there, as well as beyond right down to Chaharjui, 140 miles farther, intensely uninteresting; nothing but low level sandbanks and river-flats on either side, covered with water during the floods in summer, and just the tops of the fringe of trees visible in the distance marking the line of cultivation. Not a living thing was to be seen for the greater part of the way. Two or three times we passed a ferry where a *kafilah* of laden camels was being ferried across, but the villages were rarely in sight, and the only time we really found ourselves close to habitations was where the river was changing its course, and we passed a village in rapid course of demolition. The people were all busy tearing the woodwork out of their houses, cutting down their trees, and doing their best to save what little they could before the land was washed away from under their feet. The banks were falling in in great masses every few minutes as we passed, and house after house was gradually going, and probably by this time not a trace of that village is left. Birds, too, were extraordinarily scarce all down the river, and during the four days we spent upon it I do not suppose we saw more than a few stray flocks of wild geese, and an odd duck and paddy bird or two.

We did not arrive at Karki till after midnight; but late as it was, we found a most hospitable welcome awaiting us. A small phaeton, with three ponies harnessed abreast, was waiting for us on the river-bank, with carts for our baggage; and we were driven straight off to Colonel Shorokoff the commandant's house, where we found the Colonel and his wife had prepared supper all ready for us, and that Dr Bratin, who lived next door, had kindly turned out of his house to make room for us. Our servants soon brought our baggage up; and after a hearty supper, we all turned in. The next day, Sunday, we spent quietly at Karki—dining with Colonel Shorokoff at 12 noon, and then starting again for Chaharjui later in the afternoon.

Karki is a place something like Kilif, in so far that the river is confined between two rocky points—though the river at Karki, when at full flood, must be some 1200 yards in width, or about double that at Kilif. On the north bank of the river a low range of hills comes to an abrupt end, and exactly opposite, on the southern bank, is a mound forming the site of the fort and town of Karki. The citadel of the fort rises some 50 feet or more sheer up from the river's edge; and there is a walled fort behind that again, with the bazaar and native town around it.

The Russian cantonment lies along the river-bank, about half a mile to the west of the fort; and considering that the place was only occupied in May last, it is wonderful how much has been done to make it habitable in so short a time. Both troops and officers are all comfortably housed. The barracks run in one long row, parallel to, and say 200 yards back from, the river, with the officers' houses in a parallel line close to the river-bank. The garrison consists of two squadrons of Cossacks, a battery of artillery, and a regiment of infantry. The Cossacks belong to the Astrakhan regiment on the Volga, and we hardly recognised them as Cossacks—so different were they from the Caucasian Cossacks whom we had hitherto been thrown in contact with. They wore the ordinary Russian flat cap, and trousers with an enormous yellow stripe down them—more, to our idea, like regulars than Cossacks. The artillery were a Turkistan battery, said to be a very smart one; but being Sunday, we had no chance of seeing it on parade. Russian officers seem to be very proud of their artillery, and to look upon it as the finest arm of their service; and we were sorry not to have the chance of seeing a battery on parade.

The infantry consisted of the 17th Turkistan battalion. Karki and Chaharjui, both being in Bokharan territory, belong to the Turkistan and not to the Trans-Caspian Government, and are garrisoned entirely by Turkistan troops. Colonel Shorokoff, who commands the 17th Regiment, told us that all his service had been passed in Turkistan, and that he had been almost in every part of it, from the Kuldja frontier downwards. He got the command of his battalion in eighteen years, which is quicker promotion than we get, and he had held it for the last nine years. Having been so long in Turkistan, he had settled at Tashkend, where his boys were at school—very different from us in India, who have always to send our children home to be educated, and rarely or never permanently settle in the country.

The men of the 17th Regiment were almost entirely enlisted from the valley of the Volga. They wore the usual Russian infantry dark-green blouse, a loose easy-fitting coat with a couple of pockets in front, and worn with a small black-leather belt round the waist, but instead of the ordinary trousers of the same material, they were distinguished by red or rather cherry-coloured leather trousers, which we had not seen in such use before. These trousers, we were told, were worn by all Turkistan regiments—and capital things they are: very soft and fine, cool in summer and warm in winter, and very inexpensive. They are made in Tashkend of sheep or goat skin, and cost only, I think, 1 rouble and 25 kopeks, or say two shillings to half-a-crown a pair. The 11th Hussars, I should think, would revel in them.

In Turkistan, which the Russians consider a warm country, the soldiers are given tea and sugar rations instead of spirits, and in the early morning we could see the men running off down to the river with their kettles to get the water for their morning cup. There are no such things as *bheesties* in a Russian regiment, and I did not see a single native follower or servant in the whole of Karki. The water-carts were driven down to the river and filled by soldiers; the officers' servants were all soldiers; the cooks and the very washermen were soldiers. The barracks were all built by the soldiers, as well as the officers' houses. In fact, the employment of native labour of any kind is unknown in a Russian Central Asian garrison, and therein lies the great difference between their system and ours in India. The barracks were long mud-huts, well roofed and furnished with capital doors and windows, and I must say, reflected great credit on the men's work.

Russians, as a rule, seem to be excellent carpenters, and their doors and windows were certainly capitally turned out. For the barracks the Government simply bore the cost of the material, the soldiers' labour, of course, being given free. The officers had to bear the expense of their own houses themselves, and this cost them, I believe, from 500 to 1000 roubles apiece as a rule. None of the houses or the barracks were built with verandahs as with us in India, but the officers acknowledged that in summer this would be a great improvement.

In the morning, before dining at Colonel Shorokoff's, we all walked down to the ferry to see about the change of boats to take us on to Chaharjui, and we afterwards went up into the fort to pay our visit to the Beg of Karki, as the native Bokharan governor is styled. The latter received us on the staircase clad in a most gorgeous robe of gold and many colours which he had just received as a dress of honour from the Amir of Bokhara a few days before. He was most civil and obliging, and I must say he did everything he possibly could to make us all comfortable on our journey. He had tea ready prepared for us the night before on our first arrival; and altogether, at Karki as well as at Chaharjui, both the Russian Commission and ourselves had great cause to appreciate Bokharan hospitality.

The Bokharan soldiers which formed a guard of honour at the gate were a real surprise to us, though Captain Komaroff had seen them before. Such curious figures as they were. Nothing in any native Indian State that I know of could come anywhere near them. The head-dress was a plain Astrakhan fur cap, but their coats were gorgeous in colour. The artillerymen had coats of the brightest green, and the infantry of the brightest red, both cut very short, so as to allow full display of the ample proportions of their wide yellow-leather trousers. These garments were real curiosities in their way, being worn over their top-boots, but split at the bottom and largely covered with embroidery. The effect of all this colour and embroidery surmounted by a very rusty old musket was ludicrous in the extreme.

We had a most pleasant dinner-party at Colonel Shorokoff's, and did not bid our hospitable host and hostess goodbye till well on in the afternoon. We then drove down to the ferry, and finally started, about 5 P.M. Unfortunately we could not wait to avail ourselves of the invitation of the officers of the garrison to their club in the evening, but several drove down to see us off. It is wonderful how the hackney-carriage has established itself wherever Russians are to be found in Central Asia. Even at Karki, the most forward post, only just occupied, we found the little phaeton and pair of ponies, with its Russian driver, dressed just as he would be in Russia, plying away for hire as if he had been there all his life. Good, though, as the Russians are at carriages, I must say they are just the reverse at roads. I did not see one single attempt at a road in the whole Trans-Caspian territory. At Chaharjui the roads were just the ordinary country tracks, and the bridges over the canals were simply made of brushwood laid on a few poles and covered with earth, and naturally were full of holes. Even in Ashkabad itself there was not a single metalled road, and the streets were all holes and dust, worse than the most ordinary village track in India. The telegraph line has not yet been extended to Karki, and the postal communication, I believe, is not very quick—money-orders and registered letters, &c., being only received once a-month, when an officer is sent down to Chaharjui to receive them.

On starting from Karki the boatmen lashed our two boats together, and thus, by working in relays and with the help of a full moon and a clear sky, we were able to travel day and night, and we thus accomplished our 140 miles, or whatever the distance was, in a little more than two and a half days. Lucky, indeed, it was for us that we had such fine warm weather, or those three nights in an open boat in mid-winter would have been anything but pleasant. We had some felts spread on the bottom of the boat, and there was just room for the six of us to sleep heads and tails like sardines in a tin, covered simply by our rugs and greatcoats. One man at the prow of each boat with a pole kept sounding the depth and looking out for sandbanks, and two others at the helm wielded an enormous sweep, and thus helped to guide the boat at the bowsman's direction. We drifted quietly along with the stream, disturbed by nothing but the continual sound of banks falling in on either side. The navigation seemed much easier below Karki than above it, as the river keeps more to one channel with a better depth of water.. The river seems full of sturgeon, and a fresh-caught sterlet that Captain Komaroff procured at Karki was delicious eating, and in fact lasted us all the way to Chaharjui. Some fresh caviare, too, which was given him was very good, and we feasted on it all the way down.

The Beg of Karki, thinking that we should halt each night on the way down, had sent on tents and cooks to three different places, Isan Mangli, Koraish, and Sakar Bazar, so that everything might be ready for us on our arrival. The two first places were passed at night, and we only halted for a short time at the third while waiting for the moon to rise. The Bokharan official who was deputed to accompany us in the boats rejoiced in the title of "Karawal Begi"—literally, I suppose, "the chief of the outposts;" but what his precise functions were I did not learn. No sooner, however, had we landed on the river's bank at Sakar Bazar than he sent off a boatman to the village, and in a very short time up rode the local Beg with several followers. One had a tent up behind him—not such a very big one, I confess, but of the kind we call a "Bechoba" in India. Another had a carpet; others sweets, tea, and refreshments; and in less than no time we found the tent pitched, the carpets spread, and a choice assortment of Russian and Bokharan sweets spread out before us, whilst the cook outside was busy over an enormous caldron of soup. In Turkistan everybody is so accustomed to make long journeys on horseback, and to carry everything necessary upon their saddles behind them, that the horses get trained to carry enormous weights, much more than we in India should ever think of putting on them. In Afghan-Turkistan such a thing as a cart or any wheeled conveyance is almost unknown, but directly we crossed the Bokharan frontier we found carts in common use; and now, under Russian example, their numbers will probably increase every day. All the carts I saw were drawn by ponies, not by bullocks as in India. The wheels of the carts were enormous, six feet or more in diameter, and fully five feet apart; the body of the cart looking like a little box perched up between the upper halves of the wheels. The shafts are suspended by a rope over a saddle on the pony's back—on the top of which the driver generally sits with his knees tucked up to his chin—and are fastened to a wooden yoke, resting against a piece of felt acting as a collar round the pony's neck. Chaharjui was full of these carts, as well as of the regular little phaetons, plying for hire.

We arrived at Chaharjui about 10 A.M. on the morning of the 1st of February, and suddenly found ourselves once more in the bustle of European life. We landed just under the railway bridge, a huge wooden structure on piles, in the midst of numbers of Russian workmen all hard at work. A Bokharan official, on the part of the Beg of Chaharjui, was waiting to receive us, and we all drove off to the Beg's house, recently built close to the Russian bazaar, where we were most hospitably entertained during our three days' stay. We had hardly finished breakfast before General Annenkoff's private secretary arrived with an invitation for us all to dinner. The General had just come in from his camp at the rail-head, and hearing of our arrival, at once very kindly sent over to ask us to go out again with him in the evening. After breakfast we accompanied Captain Komaroff to call upon Colonel Kazantzoff, the commandant of the garrison, consisting of the 3d Turkistan battalion, who welcomed me as an old Panjdeh acquaintance. We afterwards saw the regiment on parade, and uncommonly well they drilled. The men apparently always parade in full marching order. They have no valises, but carry their greatcoats, when not wearing them, over their shoulders, and their service-kit in a couple of large haversacks, slung one over each shoulder. These haversacks look bulky, sticking out one over each hip, but Russian officers say that they have been found by experience to be very practical, and preferable in every way to the valise.

In the afternoon we visited the two new steamers just built for service on the river. They are to be officered and manned by sailors from the navy, but have no guns, and are principally intended, we were told, to ply between Khiva and Chaharjui for the carriage of cotton. Each steamer has a large iron barge in tow for this purpose, but also capable of accommodating several hundred men if required. Curiously enough, we found a fellow-countryman belonging to a firm in St Petersburg in charge of the steamers. He it was who had brought them down in pieces from St. Petersburg, and had put them together at Chaharjui, and was then simply waiting for the arrival of the officers to hand them over.

In the evening we paid our visit to General Annenkoff, at his house near the railway bridge, and afterwards started with him in his train drawn up outside. The band of the Railway Battalion occupied the two first trucks, and the General's saloon carriage was the third. We went very slowly over the bridge, five versts an hour being the maximum speed allowed. The total distance from bank to bank is 2⅔ miles, but the actual bridge over the main channel is 2041 yards in length, and is built entirely of wood throughout, all brought down the Volga from Russia, and thence across the Caspian, and on by rail. The remainder is mostly comprised of embankments over river-flats, flooded in summer but dry in winter, with two bridges over small channels. We stopped at Farapp, the first station, five versts beyond the bridge, on the Bokhara side, and there the General took us over the train of double-storeyed waggons forming the quarters of the two companies or five hundred men of the Railway Battalion, and the gangs of Persians who were at work under him at the rail-head. All live in this train, and move on from station to station as the line advances. We entered the lower storey of one of the waggons, and this we found held twenty-four men. Two shelves or ledges across either end held six men each, while their rifles were all in racks along the roof. The colonel of the battalion had a nicely fitted-up waggon to himself, and the other officers had, I think, a truck between two or three, according to rank. The kitchen-waggon was a curious sight, the fuel being naphtha-refuse, the same as in the engines.

The General's private carriages consisted of a kitchen-waggon, a dining-saloon, and a private saloon, divided into sitting-room, bedroom, and secretary's room—all double-storeyed, with the servants' quarters above. At dinner all the officers of the Railway Battalion were present, and we sat down a party of about twenty. The General proposed our healths, and drank also to the officers both of the English and of the Indian army, which, he said, had produced such fine soldiers as Havelock, Lawrence, Roberts, and others; and with such a genial host it was little wonder that it was well past midnight before the band and ourselves got into the train that was waiting alongside to run us back to our respective quarters at Chaharjui.

Next morning we were up betimes and off by train again to the rail-head, where General Annenkoff showed us his system of platelaying. The General had sent his horses on ahead for us to ride, and we had a most pleasant morning's excursion. The men, we found, were divided into two parties, each consisting of one company of the Railway Battalion and a gang of Persian labourers. Each of these parties worked from noon one day till dusk, and then from 6 A.M. the next day till noon, when they were relieved by the other, and had their twenty-four hours off. The work was carried on entirely under the supervision of the officers of the Railway Battalion, who were all mounted. Each material train on arrival was run up to the rail-head, and the sleepers were at once thrown out and carried forward, and put down on the line by the Persians. The rails were slid along on rollers, run out on to a trolly, and linked in by the men of the Railway Battalion almost as fast as they could be brought up, being simply spiked on to the sleepers. The earthwork, of course, had all been prepared beforehand, and nothing but platelaying remained to be done, and this, the General informed us, was being laid, as a rule, at the rate of 4 versts, or $2\frac{2}{3}$ miles a-day; and though that rate could not be maintained every day, especially in sand, still he said that he hoped to run his line into Samarcand in April. In that case, all the necessary material will be over the Oxus before the next flood comes down; and even supposing any part of the bridge should give way, communication can always be kept up by boat.

The native town of Chaharjui lies some six miles to the south of the railway station on the river-bank, and the road between the two is of the worst description. We hired a phaeton, and drove out, and found an old mud-fort on an artificial mound, with the bazaar as usual below. The Beg of Chaharjui being away at Bokhara, we had no opportunity of thanking him for the kind way in which we were looked after by his officials, one of whom was with us. The bazaar was a poor one, on the whole; in fact, all business is mostly done, I fancy, in the Russian bazaar at Amu Darya, as the Russian settlement is called. The land for this was given free by the Amir of Bokhara, and the present settlement has all risen, I believe, within the last few months. The construction of the bridge, and the bringing up of such a large amount of material, brought together a large number of Russian officials and workmen, and these are now all settled down with their wives and families just as if they were in Russia. There are no buildings of any size. The troops are in long low mud-huts, and the rest of the houses are mostly of mud, or else wooden shanties. The railway station is the only conspicuous building, and that is of no particular size. The houses are scattered about around, and the only attempt at a street is in the bazaar, where the Russian, Armenian, and other shops are all in regular line. General Annenkoff has established a school for Russian children, and wonderfully well they all looked, too, when we paid them a visit one morning in company with the General's private secretary. Neither at Merv, Ashkabad, nor anywhere else, did I hear of any schools for the native population; and we in India might perhaps be better off if we took a leaf out of the Russian book, and spent a little less on high education and a little more on big battalions.

The regular passenger mail-train from Chaharjui to the Caspian runs only twice a-week; and as these trains have no first-class carriages, and only a very few apologies for second and third classes, we were indeed lucky to get an invitation from General Annenkoff to travel with him in his special train to Ashkabad, where he was going to see General Komaroff. Nothing could have exceeded General Annenkoff's kindness to us throughout our stay. The second evening he invited us to dine with him at the Chaharjui Club, and the following night to a dance at the same place, where we danced away merrily till late, and finally finished up with a supper given to us by some of the officers of the Railway Battalion, before turning in to our carriage in the special train ready for an early start in the morning. The train was made up entirely of the Boundary Commission party and General Annenkoff's private carriages. First came the Cossacks and their ponies, then Captain Komaroff, Ilyin, and Mirzaeff in a baggage-waggon, in which they rigged up their own camp-beds and made themselves very comfortable. We three followed in another, but we all spent the day in General Annenkoff's saloon. The upper storey of the latter, where we had a sort of verandah to sit in, was a very favourite resort, and gave us a capital view of all that was to be seen.

The ground between Chaharjui and Merv is densely covered with saxsal bushes, and the only real sand is a belt some 15 or 20 miles in width, running parallel to the Oxus, similar to that through which we saw the line being laid on the opposite bank of the river. Here, so General Annenkoff told us, they preserved the railway banks by putting a slight layer of clay-soil over the sand, and by laying down layers of grass along the edges; but so far as one could see, the difficulty regarding shifting sand did not seem to be anything very great. Some 17 miles from Merv we passed through old Merv, a great extent of mounds and mud-ruins stretching for several miles along either side of the railway, and now known by the name of Bahram Ali. This was the old original Merv, watered by the canals from the Band-i-Sultan, and finally destroyed when that dam was broken. The land there is excellent, but all waste at present. When the new Band-i-Sultan is finished, however, it will all be brought under cultivation again; and General Annenkoff has great schemes on hand for the colonisation of all this land, as well as of much more now lying untenanted along the banks of the Oxus between Chaharjui and Khiva, by Russian peasants. We heard that to provide funds for the new Band-i-Sultan the Emperor had advanced 1½ million roubles out of his own private purse, and in return is to receive one-sixth of the land reclaimed as his own private property.

The first sight of new Merv that we got was the walls of Kaushid Khan Kilah, a huge oblong rectangular enclosure surrounded by high thick mud-walls on three sides, but unfinished on the fourth. The railway runs through the centre of this enclosure, and inside it also are the governor's, the officer commanding, and most of the other officers' houses, and the public gardens, &c. The walls of the enclosure run along the right bank of the Murghab, here a comparatively small river, only some thirty yards in breadth, and crossed by a wooden-pile bridge. On the opposite bank, near the railway station, stand the Russian bazaar, the club-house, the hotel and *café chantant*, and other emblems of civilisation. The Turkomans to a stranger are hardly in evidence at all. Coming in by rail nothing is to be seen of them but various clusters of *kibitkas* scattered about in the distance, over a bare, arid-looking plain, without a tree or a garden, in true Turkoman fashion. Their hamlets extend for miles, I daresay, as far as the water will reach, and there they will continue to live, I presume in their old primitive fashion, for many a year to come. But one sign of improvement I noticed amongst them, and that was, that one or two of the khans or chiefs had built little enclosures and houses after the Russian pattern, in which to receive their Russian guests, though apparently they had not advanced so far as to live in the houses themselves, as I always noticed their *kibitkas* pitched outside. No Turkomans seem to be employed in Merv as servants. The latter are all either Russians or Caucasians, and such a thing as a native servant, as with us in India, seemed unknown. We arrived at Merv about 5 P.M., and just had time to drive through the bazaar, do a little shopping, see the club, and call upon Colonel Linevich, the commandant, before going on to dinner with Colonel Alikhanoff. The rapid rise of Merv has been most astonishing, I believe. We were told that a year and a half ago Colonel Alikhanoff was living in a *kibitka*, and there was not a house in the place. Now there are lots of houses and a large foreign population. By foreign I mean Russians, Armenians, Caucasians, Persians, Bokharans, and Jews, in contradistinction to the local Turkoman population. The former are almost all shopkeepers or traders of sorts, and, in fact, there seem to be so many shops that one wonders where all the customers come from.

The club-house contains some large fine rooms; and here I must say a word about Russian clubs. Wherever we went we found a club, but not like our English clubs; they were always open to ladies as well as to gentlemen. In fact, they more resembled our up-country Indian station clubs. At Chaharjui, of course, the club-house was simply a low rough building lately run up. At Merv the club-house was much better, and at Ashkabad better still, with a large ball-room, and card-rooms, &c. The ball-room and card-rooms seem to form the principal feature of all these Russian clubs, much more space and attention being devoted to them than to the dining or refreshment room, which was generally very roughly furnished. A weekly Sunday evening dance seemed to be a regular institution everywhere, and we were lucky enough to come in for one of these both at Ashkabad and at Tiflis. Newspapers, and even English illustrated journals, were taken in at all the clubs; but I saw no signs of the library that is so general in every Indian station club with us.

Colonel Alikhanoff's house is a fine one, and was erected, I believe, at Government expense as the residence for the governor, the sum of 5000 roubles having been granted for the purpose. The military officers, though, had all to build their houses at their own expense, simply receiving regimental advances, repayable by instalments, as with us in India. At Colonel Alikhanoff's I found the finest collection of Turkoman carpets that I have yet seen. Russian officers all use these carpets as hangings for their walls, and rarely or never put them down on the floor, and both Colonel Alikhanoff's and Colonel Linevich's drawing-rooms were a sight in this respect. The walls were entirely hung round with carpets, and uncommonly handsome they looked.

Our dinner-party in the evening was a pleasant one, and Colonel Alikhanoff, our host, proposed each of our healths in turn before we broke up and returned to the train to continue our journey.

The Merv troops we did not see, as they are mostly quartered some way off, the Russian officer being just as anxious as his English *confrère* to keep his men well away from the liquor-shops in the bazaar. The garrison is not a very large one, consisting only, I believe, of three battalions, two batteries, and a regiment of Cossacks. I was sorry not to have had another day in Merv, just on the chance of making the acquaintance of some more of the officers quartered there. As it was, I met one old acquaintance in the club, who came up to shake hands and remind me of our former meeting at Panjdeh, and how it was upon his *boorka* that I had sat during our final interview the evening before the attack. Otherwise I think we saw about all there was to see.

Leaving Merv at 10.30 P.M., we arrived at Ashkabad at 2.30 P.M. next day. The total length of the railway from the Caspian to the Oxus is 998 versts—say 665 miles—and this is usually run through in 54 hours, including stoppages at each station, of which there are 44 altogether, and halts of $1\frac{1}{2}$ hour at each of the three principal places—viz., Kizil Arvat, Ashkabad, and Merv, distant respectively from Uzunada 162, 136, and 215 miles—which gives an average rate for the trains of about $12\frac{1}{2}$ miles an hour. We in our special train ran somewhat quicker. The line having very slight gradients, and no sharp curves, the wear and tear of the permanent way is reduced to a minimum, and trains can travel with ease at the rate of 20 miles an hour, as our special did at times, despite the fact that the rails are simply spiked on to the sleepers, not bolted into chairs as ours are, and that the only ballast is sand, and very little of that. No money has been expended on platforms or any luxuries of that sort. Troops can climb in and out of the carriages, they say, without platforms, and one wooden ramp to each five waggons is considered ample for baggage, &c. The line is worked throughout by the two Railway Battalions. These are formed of men originally trained to railway work, and taken from their regiments after completing one year's service in the ranks, which is considered sufficient for the purely military portion of their training, and sent to complete the remaining four years of their service on the railways. Drivers, guards, pointsmen, carriage-cleaners, and all, are Russian soldiers. The station-master is an officer walking about with a sword, and so are the other officials. Repairs to the line are mostly done by Persian labourers under Russian supervision, and these Persians are the only natives of the country employed. Turkomans were engaged for a time when the line was first commenced, but as soon as the earthwork was completed they were dismissed again, and none were kept on permanently. A considerable number of men have to be kept up to watch the line, so lightly laid as this is, and for that purpose a certain number of old soldiers are retained after the completion of their service, but their pay seems to be just the same as that of the Persians—viz., 17 roubles a-month, 8 for pay and 9 for food. The rouble is now of little more value than a rupee; and as I was told by some Persians that Sunday's pay, when no work was done, was always deducted, their average earnings therefore amounted, as nearly as possible, to about 8 annas, or say 9d., a-day.

The country that we travelled through from the Tejend to Ashkabad may be briefly described as a line of snow-covered mountains along the Persian border to the south and the desert to the north. Villages were few and far between, and the different railway stations, with one or two exceptions, were little more than small Russian settlements. The Persian border lies mostly well back amongst the hills, but at one place it juts out into the plains to take in a Persian village, the only one, I believe, now remaining to them there. We stopped some little time at the railway station close by, and General Annenkoff very kindly took us over the station buildings and the quarters of the company of the railway battalion located there, a squad of recruits for which were drawn up for the General's inspection on our arrival.

The railway buildings simply consisted of a couple of blocks, containing four rooms each for the accommodation of officials and stores. The third block was the barrack, with the officers' room at one end and the men's at the other, with a row of outhouses, comprising kitchen, bakery, and storeroom behind. The first thing that caught the eye in the men's barrack-room was the company altar, surmounted by the usual embossed gilt-covered pictures, which accompanies the headquarters of each company, apparently, wherever it may go. The men's beds consisted of a wooden platform ranged down the whole length of either side of the room, upon which, apparently, they slept in one continuous row. In the kitchen we tasted the men's soup and boiled buckwheat, which seemed to form their staple food, and found it very good. It was all cooked by one of the men themselves in huge copper caldrons. The bread was black and slightly bitter, and not so much to our taste. The storeroom was well arranged, and contained the spare arms, clothing, and equipment for the whole company. In Trans-Caspia there are no such things as white ants, we were told, and the Russians are thus spared all the trouble and loss that we in India have to endure from their depredations, not to mention all the extra expense of iron telegraph poles and suchlike things.

Ashkabad is simply a collection of white houses out in the open plain, say 10 miles or so from the foot of the mountains, and very much resembles a small Indian cantonment. The houses are mostly one-storeyed, each in its own little compound and in regular rows, while the barracks are long whitewashed buildings with thatched roofs plastered over with mud, and look in the distance like low one-storeyed Indian barracks with enclosed verandahs. The railway station is on the northern side, quite on the outskirts of the town, and driving from the station we passed the fortified enclosure prepared for defence when the place was first occupied by Russian troops after the capture of Geok Tepe. It consists of a plain mud-wall and ditch, with a few small guns mounted at the angles, and a small mound or citadel in the centre; but nowadays the town has grown up all round it out in the open, just like an Indian station, and the country has been so quieted that the necessity for a fort no longer exists. An open space divides the bazaar from the cantonment proper, in the centre of which stands an obelisk erected to the memory of those who were killed in the attack on the Afghans at Panjdeh, surrounded by four of the Afghan guns captured that day. These, if I remember right, were old Cossipore smooth-bores cast some fifty years ago. The bazaar we found densely crowded with Russian soldiers, Persians, Turkomans, and Caucasians of all sorts, and the unwonted sight of British uniform made us an object of considerable interest.

We paid our visit to General Komaroff, the Governor-General, in the evening—too late, I am sorry to say, for us to be able to see his fine collection of antiquities, though we saw some of his stuffed birds and natural history specimens. The General very kindly offered us the use of his private railway carriage for our journey onwards; and though we did not get it, as it had been sent off for repair, we were given a special carriage to ourselves in its place, and we were not even allowed to pay for our railway tickets. We were treated as guests throughout by special orders, and conveyed free of all charge from one end of the line to the other.

Our last dinner with our Russian colleagues was a very pleasant one. Captain Komaroff, who on return to Ashkabad rejoined his permanent appointment on the general staff there, shared a house with Colonel Zakrchevski, the chief of the staff, my old Panjdeh acquaintance, with whom I had my interviews just before the Russian attack. He, I remember, had lunch with me on the 29th March 1885, the afternoon preceding the engagement, on the neutral ground between the two forces, the Afghan vedettes looking down upon us on one side and the Cossacks on the other; and I little thought then that the next time we should meet I should be his guest at Ashkabad; but so it was. Our party consisted of Captain Komaroff and Colonel Zakrchevski, our hosts; General Annenkoff and his secretary; Captain Ilyin and M. Mirzaeff; ourselves and another Russian officer: and after dinner Captain Komaroff, in a kind and cordial speech, gave us his final toast, and drank to our healths as brother soldiers, English gentlemen and patriots, with whom he had been living for the past two or three months, and from whom he was now sorry to part,—sentiments on our side that we cordially reciprocated and fully responded to. General Annenkoff, before leaving, presented both Major Peacocke and myself with a series of some forty or fifty photographs of the various places and points of interest on the Trans-Caspian Railway—a valuable collection, all nicely mounted, and a most pleasing memento of our visit.

Afterwards we all adjourned to the ball at the club,

where we found a large assemblage of ladies and a capital ball-room. The waltz as we dance it seems unknown in Russia, and there was not a lady in the room who had mastered the mysteries of the *troistemps;* but square dances formed the chief feature of the evening, and those we could all join in. To our surprise we met a fellow-countrywoman in the wife of a Russian railway accountant, and a true good fellow-countrywoman too, who, out of the kindness of her heart, not only did her best to entertain us at the ball, but most thoughtfully provided us the next morning with a nice hamper of cold roast-beef, white bread, good wine, and pickles, and other luxuries for our onward journey, in true English fashion.

Captain Komaroff came down early to see us off; and after a final cup of tea with General Annenkoff, we bade good-bye, and started with Captain Ilyin and Mirzaeff for Tiflis in the mail train at 9 A.M., and arrived at Kizil Arvat at sunset, and at Uzunada the following morning at sunrise.

The scenery throughout the day was just the same as that of the day before,—the same bare snow-sprinkled mountains rising like a wall to the south, and the desert plains to the north. We had expected to see a good deal of drainage from the mountains, and to find the railway crossing a succession of water-courses; but this was not the case, and there was hardly a bridge or culvert on the line. The water seemed all to run underground, and though there was no lack of it apparently when dug for, there was little or none on the surface. So easy is the water to get at, and so great is the pressure from the mountains above, that almost every station had a natural fountain continuously playing in front of it.

The second station, 28 miles from Ashkabad, was Geok Tepe, and as the railway station immediately adjoined the ruins of the old fort, we were able to have a good look at it.

At first sight one could hardly believe that this was the place from which Russian troops had twice recoiled, and that it was only taken the third time after a prolonged resistance. Imagine an open square out in the middle of a plain, a simple enclosure, say about half a mile in length and rather less in breadth, surrounded by a mud-wall about 20 feet high and from 15 to 20 feet thick. There was no large "tepe" or mound, as I had imagined from the name, nothing but a small rise in the north-west corner, and a bastion at the south-west angle, on which, I believe, the Turkomans had mounted the old guns formerly taken from the Persians, but which they did not know how to use. At the time of the final assault this enclosure was one teeming mass of *kibitkas*, men, women, and children, horses and sheep, all collected inside from far and near. During the siege the women and children, I believe, were sheltered in pits and hollows, that we could still see the marks of, dug out in the ground; and terrible indeed must have been the scene when the place was finally captured. The great fault in the work was its rectangular construction and the want of proper flanking defence; but yet with all its defects of structure, what astonished one more than anything was the little effect that the Russian artillery seemed to have had on the walls. The marks of each shot were plainly visible, but not a bit of harm had they done, and had the Russians not succeeded in mining the place, the siege might have been indefinitely prolonged. The breach through which the place was assaulted lies at the south-east angle, and just outside it is a small memorial stone marking the place where those who were killed in the assault were buried. Standing on the top of the breach, one could not help thinking what a wonderful power of resistance these mud-walls possess; and if so much could be done with a simple 20-feet wall like this, what could not be done with Herat!

At Kizil Arvat we found ourselves in a large station with

a refreshment-room, Russian ladies walking about the platform, and every sign of Western civilisation. Uzunada I described in my last letter. The railway officials were kind enough to run our carriages on from the station down to the pier, and by noon we had embarked on board the s.s. Tsesarevitch Alexander, and were at Baku by 10 A.M. the next morning. There we caught the 2.30 P.M. train, and 8 A.M. on the morning of the 9th February saw us steaming into Tiflis. General Dondukoff Korsakoff, we found, was absent at St Petersburg; but we at once called upon General Sheremetoff, his *locum tenens*, who, unfortunately, again was ill; and also upon General Zelenoy and Colonel Kuhlberg. The two latter returned our calls immediately, and were most kind and hospitable—inviting us to the ball at the club in the evening, where we did not part till after a most convivial supper-party in the early hours of the morning. 8 A.M. saw us at the railway station again, and also Colonel Kuhlberg, Captain Ilyin, and M. Mirzaeff, who kindly came to see us off; and I can only say that I hope I may always part from my Russian friends on the same cordial terms. The Black Sea is well known, and I must say no more. Our Asiatic wanderings are over for the present; and if we are destined ever to see the frontier again, the future alone can tell.

INDEX.

Ab-i-Andkhui, 230 et seq., 341 et seq.
Ab-i-Charmi, 71.
Ab-i-Kaisar, 134, 142, 213 et seq., 340 et seq., 394 et seq.
Ab-i-Kashan, 109.
Abasabad, 392.
Abdul Aziz Khan, 394.
Abdul Ghani Khan, 347, 395.
Abdul Hamid Khan, 235, 347, 395.
Abdullah Jan, 318 et seq.
Abdullah Jan Tokhi, 319.
Abdullah Khan, 100, 124.
Abdullah Khan Nasiri, 16.
Abdullah Khan Tohki, 18.
Abdur Rahman, 319.
Abdur Rahman Khan, 146, 255.
Abu Saiad, Sultan, 28.
Abu Zaid, 194.
Afghan Boundary Commission, 372 et seq.
Afghan Turkistan, 242 et seq., 338 et seq., 404 et seq.
Afghanistan, 146, 269, 342 et seq.
Afghans, 3-9, 21, 24, 53, 64, 66, 72, 90, 130, 178 et seq., 216 et seq., 265 et seq., 312 et seq., 381 et seq.
Afrasiah Khan, 275.
Afridis, 229, 294.
Aghamet, 209.
Aghaz Paz, 340 et seq.
Aimakjar, 60, 168 et seq.
Aimaks, 3, 130.
Aitchison, Dr, 10 et seq., 42, 56.
Aitchison, Lady, 377.
Ak Koprak, 239.
Ak Robat, 89 et seq., 174 et seq., 190 et seq.
Ak Robat Kotal, 239.
Ak Tepe, 186.
Akchah, 149, 226 et seq., 337 et seq., 380 et seq.

Akhal Tekes, 186 et seq.
Akkum, 397.
Ala Taimur, 157.
Alai Chalai, 161 et seq., 343 et seq.
Albury range, 255.
Ali Boghan, 369.
Ali Khan, 47, 97, 108 et seq.
Aliabad, 353 et seq.
Alikhanoff, Colonel, 149 et seq., 384 et seq., 411 et seq.
Alishahs, 125, 186.
Alizais, 218.
Allah Dad Khan, 64.
Almar, 341.
Alti Tepe, 249.
Ambia Khan, 64.
Amir Muhammad, 48.
Amir Muhammad Khan, 397.
Amir-ud-Din, 389.
Amu Daria, 229.
Amu Darya, 408.
Ananiantz, M., 206 et seq.
Anar Darah, 172.
Anderson, Mr, 370.
Andkhui, 81 et seq., 212 et seq., 334 et seq., 380 et seq.
Annenkoff, General, 404 et seq.
Aral, Sea of, 284.
Aranji, 248.
Ardewan Pass, 12, 48, 57, 145, 320.
Armalik Pass, 5.
Arsallah Khan, 161.
Asaf-ud-Daulah, 56.
Ashab-i-Kalif, 151.
Ashkabad, 323, 402 et seq.
Ashurada, 391.
Asiah Kuhnah, 260.
Askara, H.S., 343.
Asmai, 354.
Astarab, 239 et seq.

INDEX.

Astrabad, 19, 42, 323, 383 *et seq.*
Ata Khan Khojah, 230 *et seq.*
Ata Muhammad, 82, 264.
Ata Ulah Khan, Lieut.-Colonel, 331.
Au Rahak, 92, 94, 174, 176.
Awaz, 148.
Ayub Khan, 16, 218.
Azizulah Khan, 171, 206.

Baba Pass, 12.
Baba Taghi, 381.
Babulai, 180.
Bad Asiah, 314 *et seq.*
Badakshan, 160, 210 *et seq.*, 316 *et seq.*, 379 *et seq.*
Badantoo, 5.
Badghis, 4 *et seq.*, 101, 139 *et seq.*, 331 *et seq.*, 382 *et seq.*
Badghisi, 4.
Bagh-i-Babar, 358 *et seq.*
Bagh-i-Kharta, 63.
Bagh-i-Sarhang, 274 *et seq.*
Bagh-i-Shan, 392.
Baghdad, 279.
Bagran, 353.
Baha-u'-din Khan, Major, 83, 134, 144, 161, 212 *et seq.*, 317, 357.
Bahadur Ibrahim Khan, 357.
Bahaudin Khan, 62.
Bahawaldin Khan, Major, 17.
Bahawulpur, 374.
Bahram Ali, 409.
Bairach, 125, 186.
Bakshur, 101.
Baku, 19, 391, 419.
Bala Hissar, the Upper, 361.
Bala Murghab, 3 *et seq.*, 59, 98, 122 *et seq.*, 210 *et seq.*, 387 *et seq.*
Balkh, 27 *et seq.*, 82, 115, 138 *et seq.*, 194 *et seq.*, 366 *et seq.*
Balkh Ab, 239, 283 *et seq.*
Baluchistan, 58, 303, 330.
Baluchistan agency, 83.
Bamian, 51, 56, 58, 62, 239 *et seq.*
Band-i-Amir, 255 *et seq.*
Band-i-Baba, 48, 118.
Band-i-Joukar, 219.
Band-i-Kamal-Khan, 145.
Band-i-Kashan, 334 *et seq.*
Band-i-Kashka, 6.
Band-i-Kazakli, 189.
Band-i-Kilrekta, 216 *et seq.*
Band-i-Nadir, 111 *et seq.*, 175 *et seq.*
Band-i-Sultan, 390, 409 *et seq.*
Band-i-Turkistan, 104, 115 *et seq.*, 195 *et seq.*, 335 *et seq.*
Bandan, 147 *et seq.*
Bandar Abbas, 273, 333.
Bandar-i-Gaz, 392.
Bara Bagh, 65.

Barrow, Captain, 378.
Barukzais, 359 *et seq.*
Batoum, 19, 390.
Bax, Major, 3, 16 *et seq.*, 54 *et seq.*, 88, 97 *et seq.*, 200 *et seq.*, 273 *et seq.*, 326 *et seq.*, 369 *et seq.*
Bazaar, Takta, 109, 149 *et seq.*
Beg Murad Sirdar, 185.
Bel-i-Paranda, 343.
Belchiragh, 238.
Bellew, Dr, 98.
Beluch, 106, 145.
Beluchis, 146 *et seq.*
Birjand, 147 *et seq.*
Bokhara, 124, 131, 191, 240 *et seq.*, 342 *et seq.*, 379 *et seq.*
Bokharans, 242 *et seq.*, 396.
Bokun, 125, 198 *et seq.*, 210 *et seq.*, 343 *et seq.*
Boli, 84.
Bosagha, 241 *et seq.*, 351 *et seq.*, 395 *et seq.*
Boundary pillars, situation of the, 173 *et seq.*
Bratin, Dr, 398.
Brown, Sergeant, 80, 85.
Bund-i-Khinjak, 13.
Bundar Abbas, 322.
Burdalik, 346.
Burj-i-Alam Khan, 84.
Burj-i-Azaran, 256.
Burj-i-Gulwarda, 148.
Busawal, 369.
Butkak, 368 *et seq.*

Caspian, the, 19, 150, 170, 273 *et seq.*, 346, 391 *et seq.*
Chachakli, 232.
Chachaktu, 130, 157.
Chagatais, 321.
Chah Ata Murad, 232.
Chah-i-Imam-Nazar, 350.
Chah-i-Nakhash, 174.
Chah-i-Pirjik, 350 *et seq.*
Chahar Bagh, 29, 63, 251 *et seq.*
Chahar Bulak, 251.
Chahar Burjak, 83, 84, 106, 134 *et seq.*
Chahar Dar, 326 *et seq.*
Chahar Darah, 177.
Chahar Deh, 354 *et seq.*
Chahar Gazak, 19.
Chahar Jui, 170, 187, 243 *et seq.*, 322 *et seq.*, 397 *et seq.*
Chahar Shamba, 85, 98, 105 *et seq.*, 209 *et seq.*, 340 *et seq.*, 394 *et seq.*
Chahar Shangah, 242 *et seq.*
Chahar Tagao, 137.
Chaharjui, Beg of, 404 *et seq.*
Chahgazak, 17, 84.
Chaman, 49, 367.

INDEX. 423

Chaman-i-Bed, 18 et seq., 86 et seq., 100 et seq.
Chap Darah, 328 et seq.
Chap Guzar, 235, 351.
Chapman, Mr, 261.
Charakhs, 19.
Charikar, 58, 62, 262 et seq., 325 et seq.
Charles, Dr, 2, 11 et seq., 83.
Chash Baba, 346.
Chashma Sabz, 312.
Chashmah Pinhan, 164, 232.
Chashmah Shaffah, 270.
Chashmah-i-Sher, 326.
Chichli, 350.
Chihal Dukhteran, 222 et seq., 381 et seq.
Chihal Zinah, 196.
Chikislar, 391.
Chilik, 251.
Chingurak, 386.
Chitral, 268.
Chitrali coolies, 268.
Chobash, 248 et seq.
Chushka Guzar, 248 et seq.
Circassians, 295 et seq.
Clarke, Mr, 261 et seq.
Connaught, H.R.H. the Duke of, 372 et seq.
Cossack and Sepoy, 286 et seq.
Cossack drill, 291.
Cossacks, 44, 74, 77, 78, 80, 81, 90, 97, 116, 140, 205 et seq., 265 et seq., 323 et seq., 385 et seq.
Cotton, Captain, 17, 19, 48, 57, 62, 85, 98, 105 et seq., 200 et seq., 270 et seq., 323 et seq.

Daghestan, 86.
Dah Dehli, 84.
Dahan-i-Kaian, 327.
Dalli, 248.
Darah-i-Bam, 195.
Darah Yusaf, 239.
Darband Pass, 219.
Daria Band-i-Amir, 247.
Darwazah-i-Baba Koh, 259.
Dasht-i-Arzanak, 320.
Dasht-i-Bakwa, 320.
Dasht-i-Na Umed, 148.
Daulat Beg, 346.
Daulatabad, 114, 141, 213 et seq., 341 et seq.
Daulatyar, 17, 22, 51, 56.
Dawandah range, 1, 3, 5, 13, 104.
De Laessoe, Captain, 17, 19, 42, 52, 72, 79, 82, 108 et seq., 193 et seq., 273 et seq., 345 et seq.
Deh Mazang, 354 et seq.
Deh Miran, 238 et seq.

Deh Moghal, 1, 2.
Deh Shaikh, 1.
Deh Tang, 330 et seq.
Dehdadi, 250 et seq.
Dehistan, 6.
Dehzingeh Hazarah, 6.
Dengli Dagh, 90, 174 et seq.
Denisoff, Captain, 149.
Dev Kilah, 237 et seq.
Dilawar Khan, 338.
Dinkur Rao, Sir, 374.
Dizeh, 194.
Do Shakh, 170—range, 19, 23, 48.
Dondukoff Korsakoff, Prince General, 390, 419.
Dorah, 148 et seq.
Dost Mahomed Khan, 270, 318 et seq.
Drummond, Lieutenant, 2, 23 et seq., 82, 102 et seq., 149, 212 et seq., 273 et seq.
Duffadar Mir Baz, 85, 86.
Dukchi, 213 et seq., 341 et seq.
Dungez Syot, 346 et seq.
Durand, Captain, 11 et seq., 48, 55 et seq., 97 et seq., 209 et seq., 273 et seq.
Durand, Mr H. M., 372 et seq.

Ebn Haukel, 6, 26, 27, 32, 194 et seq.
Egrigeuk, 95, 174, 176, 190.
Elias, Mr Ney, 133, 151, 160, 200 et seq.
Elibir, 101.
Ersari Turkomans, 166 et seq.
Ersaris, 142, 166, 189, 231 et seq., 282 et seq.
Eshans, 152.

Faizabad, 151.
Farad Beg, 238 et seq.
Farah, 58, 148, 215, 320 et seq., 390 et seq.
Farangi, 231.
Farapp, 406.
Farash Bashi, 369.
Farinjal, 330.
Ferrier, 56.
Finn, Mr, 10, 17, 19, 42, 48.
Firozkohi country, 82, 115.
Firozkohis, 10, 22, 115, 136 et seq., 219 et seq., 387 et seq.
Fort Roberts, 367.
Foughan, 239 et seq.
Foughans, 239.

Galindo, Lieutenant, 62, 83.
Galla Chashmah, 161, 164 et seq., 350 et seq.
Galla Chashmah Shor, 197.
Gandeh Chah, 350.
Ganesh, 248.
Gang, 84.

INDEX.

Gardan Reg, 146.
Gazanfar Khan, 346.
Gazargah, 33.
Gaznigak, 314, 320.
Geok Tepe, 86, 97, 415 *et seq.*
Ghain, 146.
Ghaus-ud-Din, General, 15, 64, 215 *et seq.*, 387 *et seq.*
Ghazis, 218.
Ghazni, 367.
Ghilzai nomads, 12, 189, 217 *et seq.*,
Ghor, 42.
Ghorband, 58, 62, 262, 330 *et seq.*
Ghori, 326 *et seq.*
Ghorian, 53, 105.
Ghulam Haidar Khan, General, 319.
Gideonoff, Captain, 77, 78, 79, 91, 116 *et seq.*, 201 *et seq.*
Gilgit, 160, 268.
Girishk, 49, 58, 98.
God-i-Zireh, 145 *et seq.*
Gok Sirdar, 163, 185, 203 *et seq.*, 392.
Gondou-Bala, 1.
Gor-i-Haji, 84.
Gor-i-Mar, 314 *et seq.*
Gore, Captain, 10, 17, 19, 25, 41, 48, 61, 70, 72, 76, 79, 82, 89, 96 *et seq.*, 212 *et seq.*, 273 *et seq.*, 333 *et seq.*
Gorokh, Lieutenant, 78, 116, 149 *et seq.*, 212 *et seq.*
Gough, Sir Hugh, General, 370 *et seq.*
Griesbach, Captain, 2, 3, 16, 17, 19, 21, 42, 62, 74, 105 *et seq.*, 200 *et seq.*, 322 *et seq.*
Guchmach, 126, 188.
Gulran, 65, 68, 71, 82, 88, 119 *et seq.*, 393 *et seq.*
Gwadar, 58.

Hadjis, 249.
Hafizullah Khan, General, 319.
Haibak, 105, 272, 314 *et seq.*
Haidari, 275.
Halim Khan, 172.
Hamman, 146 *et seq.*
Hamun, Seistan, 145.
Hamun, Western, 145 *et seq.*
Harfah Guzar, 230 *et seq.*
Hari Rud, 2, 12 *et seq.*, 42, 60, 68, 75, 76, 89, 173, 175 *et seq.*, 228 *et seq.*, 383 *et seq.*
Hasan Ali Khan, 52.
Hastings, Mr, 370.
Hauz-i-Khan, 88, 96 *et seq.*, 102 *et seq.*
Hazar Sum, 322.
Hazarah Kilah, 136.
Hazarah Kudak, 350.
Hazarahjat, 52, 56, 239 *et seq.*
Hazarahs, 8 *et seq.*, 52, 109, 117 *et seq.*, 149 *et seq.*, 239 *et seq.*, 327 *et seq.*

Hazrat Imam, 60.
Heath, Captain, 17, 41 *et seq.*, 83.
Heera Singh, 42, 82, 115, 262 *et seq.*
Helmand, 83, 98, 106-134 *et seq.*, 283 *et seq.*
Herat, 1, 2, 3, 9 *et seq.*, 25 *et seq.*, 49 *et seq.*, 104 *et seq.*, 215 *et seq.*, 382 *et seq.*, 418.
Heratis, 18, 20, 21, 25, 39, 64, 72, 93.
Hindu Kush, 264 *et seq.*
Hirak, 126 *et seq.*
'History of the Russian Mission to Kabul in 1878' referred to, 249.
Hizdah Nahri regiment, 354.
Hizhdah Nahr, 267.
Holdich, Major, 17, 18, 25, 41, 48, 53, 57, 61, 70, 72, 76, 77, 79, 82, 89, 93, 96, 104 *et seq.*, 201 *et seq.*, 322 *et seq.*
Hudson, Sir John, General, 372.
Hukumat Khan, 135.
Hulu, 346.
Husain Khan, 47, 48, 338.

Ibrahim Khan, 52, 247, 273.
Ilyin, Councillor, 78, 141, 201 *et seq.*, 393 *et seq.*, 419.
Imam Ali Asgar, 7.
Imam Bakri, 247.
Imam Nazar, 395.
Imam Sharif, 82, 115 *et seq.*, 262 *et seq.*
Indian Commissariat, 312.
Irak, 25.
Isan Mangli, 403.
Isfandiar, 130.
Ishak Khan, 18, 126, 160, 234 *et seq.*, 318 *et seq.*
Isik, Bulan, 230.
Iskar, 327.
Islam, 248 *et seq.*
Islim, 24, 95, 97 *et seq.*, 174, 176 *et seq.*
Ismail Khan, 277.
Iwaz, Khan, 47.

Jagdalak, 370.
Jalaiar, 232 *et seq.*, 394.
Jamrud, 353 *et seq.*, 370 *et seq.*
Jamshidis, 3, 8, 12, 101, 104, 122, 188 *et seq.*, 303 *et seq.*
Jarkudak, 229 *et seq.*, 352, 395.
Jauz-i-Kili, 3.
Jelajin, 350.
Jeswunt Singh, 89, 273 *et seq.*
Jhind, 374.
Jui Karshasp, 145.
Juma Eshan, 184.
Juma Musjid, 27, 28, 257, 349.
Jumjuma Kilah, 233.

INDEX. 425

Kabul, 22, 29 et seq., 159, 218 et seq., 334 et seq., 385 et seq.
Kabulis, 21, 22, 46, 93.
Kafir Kilah, 51, 53, 55, 283 et seq.
"Kafirs," 331.
Kaisar, 123, 136, 195 et seq., 341 et seq.
Kaisar Rud, 81.
Kak-i-Tali, 230 et seq.
Kalat-i-Ghilzai, 218.
Kamar Kalagh gorge, 2, 65.
Kandahar, 16, 18 et seq., 40, 49, 58, 82, 196 et seq., 320 et seq., 385 et seq.
Kara Baba, 141, 161 et seq., 343 et scq.
Kara Baba Shor, 165 et seq.
Kara Bagh, 68.
Kara Bel, 141 et scq., 197 et seq., 33 et seq.
Kara Gali (Pass), 238.
Kara Jangal, 142, 195 et seq.
Kara Kamar, 249.
Kara Tepe, 24, 88, 94, 95, 103 et seq., 382 et seq.
Kara Tepe Kalan, 346.
Kara Tepe Khurd, 96, 102 et seq., 346.
Kara Turkomans, 131, 142.
Karaie, 137.
Karas, 342.
Karawal Khana, 45, 120 et seq., 173, 209 et seq., 341 et seq., 384 et seq.
Karez Dasht, 84.
Karez Elias, 61 et seq., 84 et seq.
Karki, 187, 268 et seq., 350 et scq., 401 et seq.
Karki, Beg of, 401 et seq.
Karkin, 230 et seq.
Karobar, 63.
Karujah, 248.
Karukh, 1, 2, 3, 4, 13, 14, 195 et seq.
Karukh stream, 1.
Kasawah Kilah, 230.
Kashan, 109, 110, 174 et seq., 220 et seq., 334 et seq., 381 et seq.
Kashgari Hadjis, 249.
Kashmir, 160.
Katack dance, 80, 140.
Katar Kudak, 349 et seq.
Kaurmach, 188 et seq.
Kaushid Khan Kilah, 410.
Kazaks, 246.
Kazan, 295.
Kazantoff, Colonel, 405.
Khaf, 57.
Khaibar, 369.
Khairabad (2), 233, 318 et seq., 392 et seq.
Khamiab, 160, 226 et scq., 395 et seq.
Khan Babu Khan, 17, 70, 79, 83.

Khan Bahadur Ibrahim Khan, 161, 211.
Khan Bahadur Muhammad Husain Khan, 389.
Khan Bahadur Yusuf Sharif, 389.
Khan Chahar Bagh, 236 et seq.
Khan Mullah Khan, 358.
Khan Sahib Amir Muhammad Khan, 385 et seq.
Khanabad, 133, 318.
Khanikoff, M., 172.
Khasadars, Afghan, 45, 53, 54, 216 et seq., 257 et seq., 315 et seq.
Khawak Pass, 332.
Khiva, 168, 188, 285, 405 et seq.
Khojah Ali, 335.
Khojah Salih, 226 et seq., 379 et seq.
Khojah Salih question, the, 240 et seq.
Khorasan, 27, 42, 56, 141, 191, 331, 392.
Khorasan, North-Eastern, 19, 172.
Khorasanis, 56.
Khorasanlis, 125, 186 et scq.
Khulm, 316 et seq.
Khuttucks, 229, 246.
Khwajah, 84.
Khwajah Abul Narsi Parsar, 257.
Khwajah Ali, 84.
Khwajah Altai Azizan, 152, 157.
Khwajah Gaohar, 229 et seq.
Khwajah Gogirdak, 198 et seq., 343 et seq.
Khwajah Isik Bulan, 229, 394.
Khwajah Kandu, 135, 195 et seq.
Khawjah Khairan, 281.
Khwajah Langari, 195 et scq.
Khwajah Salar, 160, 226 et seq., 378 et seq.
Khwajah Salar question, the, 336.
Kiachko, Lieutenant, 79, 116, 133 et seq., 149, 212 et seq., 229.
Kiamat Shor, 232, 343.
Kilah Kambar, 220.
Kilah Kazal, 233.
Kilah Mambar Bashi, 65.
Kilah Maur, 100, 101 et seq.
Kilah Morad Khan, 330.
Kilah Nao, 136, 195 et seq., 387 et seq.
Kilah Wali, 98, 105, 122 et seq., 210 et seq., 337 et seq.
Kilah-i-Aman Beg, 6.
Kilah-i-Dukhtar, 6.
Kilah-i-Nau, 9, 10.
Kilah-i-Nau Hazarahs, 7.
Kilah-i-Shaikh Tanai, 104.
Kilif, 242 et seq., 346 et seq., 398 et seq.
Kiliki, 48, 148.
Kin, 84.
Kipchaks, 136 et seq.

Kirman, 273.
Kizil Arvat, 412, 417 et seq.
Kizil Bulak, 65, 68, 69, 88.
Kizil Tepe, 46.
Koh-i-Baba, 331.
Koh-i-Khwajah, 147.
Koh-i-Taftan, 146.
Koh-i-Tan, 245, 252, 395.
Kohak, 98.
Kohistan, 267.
Komaroff, General, 150 et seq., 408, 415.
Komaroff, Colonel, 149.
Komaroff, Captain, 77, 78, 79, 96, 97, 109, 116, 149 et seq., 212 et seq., 267 et seq., 383 et seq., 401 et seq.
Kondratenko, Captain, 78, 116, 141, 149, 201 et seq., 383 et seq.
Koraish, 403.
Kotal, 282 et seq.
Kotal-i-Aokhurah, 5.
Kotal-i-Bargah, 327.
Kotal-i-Fazak, 327.
Krasnovodsk, 391.
Kubanski regiment, 78.
Kuchan, 19.
Kufah, 281.
Kuhlberg, Colonel, 69, 70, 73, 74, 75, 76, 77, 78, 79, 80, 81, 90, 91, 97, 102, 109, 115, 116 et seq., 198 et seq., 390 et seq., 419.
Kuhsan, 44, 45, 50, 51, 53, 54, 57, 61, 331 et seq.
Kujlak, 392.
Kuldja, 399.
Kunduz, 136, 318 et seq.
Kurban Niaz, 186.
Kurt, 16.
Kushdil Khan, 319.
Kushk, 3 et seq., 46, 53, 76, 85, 95, 100 et seq., 217 et seq., 381 et seq.
Kushk river, 5, 12.
Kushk Rud, 84.

Laghman, 354 et seq.
Lahore, 371 et seq.
Landi Baraich, 84.
Landi Khana, 370.
Landi Kotal, 369.
Langoran, 392.
Lash Jowain, 84, 172.
Leigh, Captain, 369.
Lesghin, 86.
Lesghins, 295.
Lessar, M., 70, 73, 74, 75, 77, 78, 79, 91, 97, 114, 116 et seq., 209 et seq., 322 et seq.
Linevich, Colonel, 411 et seq.
Lockhart, Colonel, 268.
Logar, 53, 225.

Lumsden, Sir Peter, 44, 111, 124, 311.
Lyttle, Conductor, 83.

MacGregor, Sir Charles, 146, 148.
M'Ivor, Major, 106.
MacLean, Colonel, 247 et seq., 392 et seq.
Machgandak, 1, 2, 4, 9, 13, 14.
Madrasah, 30, 257 et seq., 349 et seq.
Mahmud Shah, 319.
Mahomed Aslam, 17, 48.
Mahomed Aslam Khan (Sirdar), 9.
Mahomed Hassan, 229.
Maiamai, 392.
Maimanah, 57 et seq., 98, 103, 195 et seq., 318 et seq., 380 et seq.
Maimanahs, 344.
Maitland, Captain, 2, 3, 10, 17, 22, 25, 41, 51, 56, 62, 105 et seq., 200 et seq., 267 et seq.
Maiwand, 16, 218.
Malimar, 4.
Malmul, 282.
Mamezak, 62, 64, 70, 83, 84.
Mangan, 194 et seq., 224.
Manley, Sergeant, 80, 81, 85.
Marshall, Mr, 357.
Maruchak, 45 et seq., 96 et seq., 102 et seq., 209 et seq., 336 et seq., 381 et seq.
Mashhad, 10, 17, 19, 41, 42, 44, 48, 51, 52, 55, 56, 57, 118, 264 et seq., 383 et seq.
Masjid-i-Sabz, 257.
Mawar-ul-nahr, 27.
Mazar, 257 et seq., 347 et seq.
Mazar-i-Sharif, 105, 114, 160, 240 et seq.
Mazinan, 392.
Mehemetoff, M., 78, 86, 149, 212 et seq.
Mehr, 392.
Meiklejohn, Major, 11, 48, 53, 54, 83, 85, 98, 106 et seq.
Merk, Mr, 10, 19, 41, 48, 53, 62, 64, 70, 79, 81, 83, 87, 134 et seq., 200 et seq., 273 et seq., 338 et seq.
Merv, 47, 60, 111 et seq., 222 et seq., 322 et seq., 384 et seq., 408 et seq.
Merv-ul-Rud, 194 et seq., 224.
Miandasht, 392.
Ming Darakht, 231 et seq.
Mir Mortaza, 37.
Mir Sultan Murad Khan, 319.
Mirza Abdulah, 397.
Mirza Ghulam Ahmad, 17, 215.
Mirza Hasan Ali Khan, 261, 279, 356.
Mirza Hasan Khan, 79.
Mirza Khalil, 27.
Mirza Purdil Khan, 318.

INDEX. 427

Mirzaeff, M., 78, 79, 86, 116, 149 et seq., 212 et seq., 393 et seq., 419.
Mishwain nomads, 12.
Mizrab Khan, 338.
Moghor, 88, 381.
Moguls, 246.
Muhammad Afzal Khan, 86, 280, 318 et seq.
Muhammad Akbar Khan, 318 et seq.
Muhammad Akram Khan, 57.
Muhammad Alum Khan, 319 et seq.
Muhammad Amin Khan, 215.
Muhammad Amir Khan, 90.
Muhammad Aslam Khan (Kazi), 18 et seq., 70 et seq., 86, 98, 111, 240.
Muhammad Aslam Khan (Sirdar), 17 et seq., 61, 71, 86, 108 et seq., 211 et seq., 240 et seq., 355.
Muhammad Husain Khan, 83, 98, 151, 247, 357, 397.
Muhammad Husain, Ressaldar-Major, 13, 17, 19, 48, 52, 62, 212 et seq.
Muhammad Husain, Subadar, 17.
Muhammad Ishak Khan, 59.
Muhammad Khan, 274, 394.
Muhammad Sarwar Khan, 126.
Muhammad Sharif, 42.
Muhammad Taki Khan, 83.
Muhammad Umar Jan, 37.
Muhammad Yusuf Khan, 98.
Mullah Abdul Aziz Khan, 387.
Munshi Allah Baksh, 262 et seq.
Murghab, 22, 45, 60, 97, 110 et seq., 210 et seq., 337 et seq., 381 et seq.
Murray, Major-General, C.B., 372 et seq.
Musalla, 26, 30, 32, 33, 65.

Nabba, 374.
Nadali, 147.
Nadir Shah, 147, 157.
Nahun, 374.
Naib Alam Khan, 258.
Naib Kotwal, 360.
Naib Salar, 15.
Naibabad, 314 et seq.
Najaf, 279 et seq.
Naratu, 6, 11, 195 et seq.
Narin, 132.
Nasirabad, 84, 98, 147.
Natore, Rajah of, 374.
Nawab Mirza Hassan Ali Khan, 82, 88, 229.
Nazir Nurudin Khan, 394 et seq.
Neprintzeff, Councillor, 116, 149.
Neza Beg, 230.
Nihalsheni, 57.
Nimaksar, 190.
Nimlik, 255, 318 et seq.
Nishapur, 392.

Nizam-u'-Doulah, 64.
Nourozabad, 5.
Nujbudin Khan, 347.
Nujbudin Khan, General, 278.
Nushki, 58, 84.

Obeh, 2, 10, 40.
Oikal, 350.
Orbeliani, Colonel, 116, 118 et seq.
Owen, Dr, 9, 14, 17, 19, 41, 52, 62, 64, 70, 79, 82, 88, 97 et seq., 200 et seq., 273 et seq., 369 et seq.
Oxus, 114, 131, 213 et seq.; the march to the, 226 et scq., 339 et seq., 379 et seq.

Padah Khana, 247.
Pahrah, 84, 148, 390.
Paikam Daragh, 247.
Pain Guzar, 232.
Panjdeh, 9, 15, 46, 47, 60, 74, 94, 108 et seq., 178 et seq.—description of, 184, 193 et seq., 215 et seq., 334 et seq., 391 et seq.
Panjdeh Kuhnah, 1, 4, 11, 104, 124, 186, 311 et seq.
Panjdeh Sariks, 176, 179 et seq., 245 et seq., 387 et seq.
Panjdeh Turkomans, 18, 105 et seq., 302 et seq., 344 et seq., 380 et seq.
Parwanah Khan, 358, 364.
Patakesar, 247 et seq.
Pathans, 66, 162, 245, 294.
Pati Ram, 285.
Peacocke, Captain, 10, 13, 14, 17, 19, 25, 41, 48, 51, 55, 57, 60, 62, 64, 70, 72, 79, 81, 105 et seq., 200 et seq., 357 et seq., 390 et seq., 416.
Pekenna, 203 et seq., 343 et seq.
Peshawar, 52, 58, 62, 138 et seq., 248 et seq., 369 et seq.
Petroff, Captain, 149, 172.
Prinsep, Colonel, 80.
Pul-i-Khatun, 73, 75, 76, 382.
Pul-i-Khishti, 13, 17, 18, 111 et seq.
Pul-i-Malun, 26.
Pul-i-Rangar, 330.
Pusht-i-Hamwar, 167, 197.

Quetta, 43, 72, 84, 106 et seq., 218 et seq., 389 et seq.

Ramadzan, 252.
Rawal Pindi, 357 et seq.
Rawlins, Lieutenant, 48, 55, 57, 60, 62, 83.
Rawlinson, Sir Henry, 194.
Resht, 48.
Ridgeway, Colonel, 1, 3, 9, 17, 18, 19,

INDEX.

41, 48, 51, 52, 57, 60, 61, 62, 63, 64, 69, 70, 73, 75, 77, 79, 81, 82, 85, 88, 90, 102, 108, 109, 111, 112, 114 et seq., 196 et seq., 268 et seq., 325 et seq., 364 et seq., 373.
Rind, Major, 2, 3, 48, 54, 58, 83, 85.
Robat, 353.
Robat-i-Afghan, 43.
Robat-i-Baba, 194.
Robat-i-Ishmail, 194 et seq., 224 et seq.
Robat-i-Kashan, 109, 110, 171, 174 et seq., 220 et seq., 334 et seq., 382 et seq.
Robat-i-Kolari, 194.
Robat-i-Pai, 23.
Robat-i-Sargardan, 68.
Robat-i-Sir-Poshidah, 392.
Roberts, Sir Frederick, 311.
Roshan, 268, 319 et seq.
Rozabad, 369.
Rozabagh, 11, 17, 18, 19.
Rozanak, 62.
Rudbar, 84.
Rukh Mirza, Shah, 30.
Russian Commissariat establishment, 312.
Rustam Ali Khan, 63.
Rustam Khan, 15, 19.

Saad-ud-Din, 14, 74, 75, 81, 90, 97, 119 et seq., 210 et seq., 274 et seq., 354 et seq.
Sabzawar, 392.
Safed Sang, 369.
Saiadulah, 264.
Said Bai, 185.
Saighan, 318.
Sakar Bazar, 403 et seq.
Salar Gulam Haidar Khan, 354.
Salor Turkomans, 157, 221.
Salors, 189 et seq.
Samarcand, 243 et seq., 267 et seq., 407.
Sang Kotal, 65, 67, 68.
Sangalak, 341 et seq.
Sangbast, 23.
Sangbur, 84.
Sangjairak, 239.
Sarakhs, 118, 158, 170 et seq.
Sardabah, 254.
Sarhad, 146.
Sari Khojah Salih, 380.
Sari Yazi, 111 et seq., 215 et seq., 382 et seq.
Sarik Turkomans, 9, 101, 125 et seq., 232 et seq., 342 et seq.
Sariks, 18, 46 et seq., 186 et seq., 335 et seq.—Panjdeh Sariks, 170 et seq., 340 et seq.
Sariks of Panjdeh, 101, 119 et seq.
Sarimat, 350.

Sarmandal, 84 et seq.
Sarshela, 145 et scq.
Sayat, 320.
Sayeds, 153 et seq.
Sehchanche, 350.
Seistan, 58, 83, 98, 145 et seq., 331 et seq.
Seistan, Persian, 146 et seq.
Seistan, Southern, 145 et seq.
Seistanis, 72, 147.
Semmer, Dr, 78, 116, 149, 212.
Seven Sleepers, the Cave of the, 151 et seq.
Shadian, 240 et seq.
Shah Godar, 146.
Shah Jehan, 366.
Shah-Maksud, 40.
Shahghassi Sherdil Khan, 319.
Shahi Nahr, 247.
Shahr-i-Afsoz, 154 et seq.
Shahr-i-Hinduan, 257.
Shahr-i-Kishlak, 157.
Shahrud, 392.
Shahzadah, Kasim, 15.
Shaikh Ali Hazarahs, 62.
Shaikh-ul-Islam, 14.
Sharifabad, 392.
Shayak Yeuzbashi, 236.
Sher Ahmed Khan, 12, 41, 48, 59, 98, 108 et seq., 212 et seq., 316 et seq., 357 et seq.
Sher Ali, 319, 360.
Sher Ali Khan, 279, 318.
Sher Baksh, 84.
Sher Darwaza, 358.
Sher Mahomed, 229.
Sher Tepe, 382.
Sherabad, 249.
Sheremetoff, General, 419.
Sherpur, 357 et seq.
Shibarghan, 57, 200, 346 et seq.
Shignan, 268, 319 et seq.
Shirin Tagao, 230 et seq., 339 et seq.
Shor Aghaz Kin, 343.
Shor Sanam, 202.
Shorab, 95, 174, 176, 249-392.
Shorokoff, Colonel, 401 et seq.
Shukr Guzar, 125.
Shums-ud-Din Khan, 358.
Siah Ab-i-Charmgah, 353.
Siah Sang, 358 et seq.
Siahgird, 247.
Sikhs, 80, 81, 115, 270 et seq.
Silgan, 84.
Simla, 372.
Sinjao valley, 2.
Sipah Salar, 15, 19, 20, 26, 63, 64.
Sir-i-Chashma, 158.
Sirdar, the title of, 185.
Siripul, 239, 345 et scq.
Sokti settlements, 184.

INDEX. 429

Soktis, 116, 186 et seq.
Sum-i-Sangi, 322.
Sumba Karez, 92, 94, 174, 176.
Surkh Ab, 238, 326.
Swetowidoff, Councillor, 78, 97.
Syeds, 281, 348.

Tabriz, 70.
Tagao Robat, 4, 5, 11, 13, 22, 195 et seq.
Tagao-i-Jawal, 1.
Tagou-i-Jawal, 12.
Taidashti Shor, 202 et seq.
Tailan (Pass), 238.
Taimani country, 115.
Taimanis, 10, 22, 42, 48, 56.
Taiwarah, 42.
Tajiks, 3, 250 et seq., 321.
Takht-i-Khatun, 195 et seq.
Takht-i-Pul, 257 et seq., 318 et seq.
Takht-i-Rawan, 310.
Takht-i-Rustam, 2, 258 et seq., 321.
Tal-i-Bhangian, 33.
Talbot, Captain, 2, 10, 17, 22, 25, 41, 48, 51, 56, 82, 105 et seq., 212 et seq., 272 et seq., 323 et seq.
Talikan, 194 et seq., 319 et seq.
Tanur Sangi, 220.
Tarmiz, 248.
Tartars, 296.
Tash, 392.
Tashkend, 234, 270, 399 et seq.
Tashkurghan, 149, 160, 267 et seq., 366 et seq.
Taskhanoff, Lieutenant-Colonel, 215, 221, 384.
Tchaplanski, Captain, 78.
Tegend, 414.
Teheran, 19, 52, 70, 172.
Tejah Singh, 273 et seq.
Tekes, 177 et seq., 342.
Tepe Ghar, 16.
Tezakli, 350.
Tiflis, 74, 323, 390 et seq.
Tirband-i-Turkistan, 126 et seq., 216.
Tirpul, 312.
Tolmatchoff, Councillor, 78, 141, 207 et seq.
Toman Agha, 45, 51.
Toman regiment, 151.
Tomanski's Cossacks, 289.
Tope-i-Rustam, 258.
Topographical Department, Russian, 264.
Topographical Survey, Indian, 264.
Torshaikh, 194, 381 et seq.
Trakun, 145.
Trans-Caspia, 414.
Trans-Caspian Railway, 391 et seq.
Tunian ford, 12, 13, 14, 16.

Turbat-i-Haidari, 57.
Turbat-i-Shaikh Jam, 14, 17.
Turkistan, 18, 126, 210 et seq., 399 et seq.
Turkistan, Afghan, 60.
Turkoman raids, 4 et seq.
Turkomans, 21, 72, 93, 94, 105, 122 et seq., 157, 171 et seq., 244 et seq., 302 et seq., 380 et seq.—Kara Turkomans, 164.
Tutachi, 88.
Tutam Darah, 353.

Umar Jan Sahibzadah, 16.
Umbeyla, 385.
Urganj, 188 et seq.
Urush Doshan, 111 et seq.
Usbegs, 72, 106, 130 et seq., 200 et seq., 274 et seq., 344 et seq.

Varenik, Captain, 78, 116, 149 et seq.
Viceroy of India, 373 et seq.
Volkovnikoff, Captain, 137 et seq.

Wakhan, 268, 319, 379.
Waterfield, Colonel, 370.
Weir, Dr, 10, 17, 48.
Wells, Major R. E., 172.
Winnikoff, Sub-Lieutenant, 79, 116, 149, 212 et seq.
Woodhouse, Mr, 390 et seq.
Woodthorpe, Colonel, 269.
Wright, Lieutenant, 23, 41, 42, 48, 56, 57, 62, 83.

Yahud Tepe, 110.
Yakub Khan, 360.
Yalantush Khan, 64.
Yaman Kudak, 350.
Yan Chashmah, 124.
Yangi Duniya, 215.
Yarghan Chakli, 232.
Yarkand, 151, 160.
Yarkund, 133.
Yaroilan, 101.
Yate, Lieutenant, 17, 19.
Yavorski's, Dr, 'History of the Russian Mission to Kabul in 1878' referred to, 249.
Yedaram, 165.
Yedikui, 350.
Yekh Darah (Pass), 239 et seq.
Yeki-yeuzi, 381.
Yezdan, 19, 148 et seq.
Yulatan, 47, 111, 170, 181, 189 et seq., 342 et seq.
Yulatan Sariks, 189.
Yusaf Khan, 355.
Yusuf Sharif, 262 et seq.

Zaid, 346.
Zakrchevski, Colonel, 416 et seq.
Zamindawari, 22 et seq., 386.
Zarmast Pass, 4, 5, 11.
Zelenoy, General, 80, 390, 419.
Zemindawar, 16, 115, 218, 331.
Ziarat Gah, 215.
Ziarat-i-Ali Sher, 314.
Ziarat-i-Baba Furk, 68.
Ziarat-i-Baba Koh, 259.
Ziarat-i-Baba Wali, 347.
Ziarat-i-Baba Yataghan, 349.

Ziarat-i-Chahardah Ma'sum, 348.
Ziarat-i-Khwajah Salar, 241 et seq., 380 et seq.
Ziarat-i-Pistah, 122.
Ziarat-i-Shah Murdan, 230.
Zigin, 84.
Zinoview, M., 378.
Zorabad, 158, 172.
Zulfikar, 13, 43, 44, 51, 57, 60, 61, 62, 64, 69, 70, 72, 75, 76, 82, 88, 89, 94, 97, 105 et seq., 302 et seq., 393 et seq.

COMPANION VOLUME TO
MAJOR YATE'S 'NORTHERN AFGHANISTAN.'

LATELY PUBLISHED.

ENGLAND AND RUSSIA FACE TO FACE IN ASIA.

A RECORD OF TRAVEL WITH THE AFGHAN BOUNDARY COMMISSION.

By CAPTAIN A. C. YATE,

Bombay Staff Corps, Special Correspondent of the 'Pioneer,' 'Daily Telegraph,' &c., &c., with the Afghan Boundary Commission.

With Maps and Illustrations. 8vo, 21s.

"As a record of the way in which English officers and Indian soldiers can perform their duty; as a narrative of an intensely interesting episode in the history of our Indian Empire; as a story of personal adventure, not without its traits of pluck, of endurance, or its humorous or tragic incidents; as a description of places and races whose fate has become of vital interest to the British Empire—the book engages attention by the intrinsic importance of its matter, as much as by the merit of its clear and lively narrative."—*Homeward Mail.*

"The chief value of Mr Yate's volume consists, however, in the graphic description it provides of the western dominions of the Ameer of Afghanistan, and particularly of the famous town and fortress of Herat.......Mr Yate gives many important details also about the frontier positions of Lash Jowain on the Seistan frontier, and Kalah-i-Maur, now in the hands of Russia.......An extremely valuable addition to our sources of information concerning events in Afghanistan in 1884-5."—*Asiatic Quarterly Review.*

"The book is full of information on Western Afghanistan."—*United Service Gazette.*

"A book which ought to be read by any one who desires to be well informed concerning our present position on the Afghan frontier, and the prospect of an enduring concord between England and Russia in Asia."—*Morning Post.*

"A most interesting, opportune, and valuable publication."—*Civil Service Gazette.*

"A graphic and interesting book of travel, and a contribution of some importance upon one of the most obscure questions of Eastern diplomacy and Asiatic geography."—*Scotsman.*

"Is certainly the best book on Afghanistan and the Northern approaches to India that has been published for many years. As an acute and cautious observer he has let little escape him, and he has been enabled to give an admirable account of the country he passed through, its geographical and climatic characteristics, and its inhabitants."—*Army and Navy Gazette.*

WILLIAM BLACKWOOD & SONS, EDINBURGH AND LONDON.

CATALOGUE

OF

MESSRS BLACKWOOD & SONS' PUBLICATIONS.

PHILOSOPHICAL CLASSICS FOR ENGLISH READERS.
EDITED BY WILLIAM KNIGHT, LL.D.,
Professor of Moral Philosophy in the University of St Andrews.

In crown 8vo Volumes, with Portraits, price 3s. 6d.

Now ready—

DESCARTES, by Professor Mahaffy, Dublin.—BUTLER, by Rev. W. Lucas Collins, M.A.—BERKELEY, by Professor Campbell Fraser, Edinburgh.—FICHTE, by Professor Adamson, Owens College, Manchester.—KANT, by Professor Wallace, Oxford.—HAMILTON, by Professor Veitch, Glasgow.—HEGEL, by Professor Edward Caird, Glasgow.—LEIBNIZ, by J. Theodore Merz.—VICO, by Professor Flint, Edinburgh.—HOBBES, by Professor Croom Robertson, London.—HUME, by the Editor.—SPINOZA, by the Very Rev. Principal Caird, Glasgow.—BACON: Part I. The Life, by Professor Nichol, Glasgow.—BACON: Part II. Philosophy, by the same Author.—LOCKE, by Professor Campbell Fraser, Edinburgh.

In preparation.
MILL, by the Right Hon. A. J. Balfour.

FOREIGN CLASSICS FOR ENGLISH READERS.
EDITED BY MRS OLIPHANT.

In crown 8vo, 2s. 6d.

Contents of the Series.

DANTE, by the Editor.—VOLTAIRE, by General Sir E. B. Hamley, K.C.B.—PASCAL, by Principal Tulloch.—PETRARCH, by Henry Reeve, C.B.—GOETHE, By A. Hayward, Q.C.—MOLIÈRE, by the Editor and F. Tarver, M.A.—MONTAIGNE, by Rev. W. L. Collins, M.A.—RABELAIS, by Walter Besant, M.A.—CALDERON, by E. J. Hasell.—SAINT SIMON, by Clifton W. Collins, M.A.—CERVANTES, by the Editor.—CORNEILLE AND RACINE, by Henry M. Trollope.—MADAME DE SÉVIGNÉ, by Miss Thackeray.—LA FONTAINE, AND OTHER FRENCH FABULISTS, by Rev. W. Lucas Collins, M.A.—SCHILLER, by James Sime, M.A., Author of 'Lessing, his Life and Writings.'—TASSO, by E. J. Hasell.—ROUSSEAU, by Henry Grey Graham.—ALFRED DE MUSSET, by C. F. Oliphant.

In preparation.
LEOPARDI. By the Editor.

NOW COMPLETE.
ANCIENT CLASSICS FOR ENGLISH READERS.
EDITED BY THE REV. W. LUCAS COLLINS, M.A.

Complete in 28 Vols. crown 8vo, cloth, price 2s. 6d. each. And may also be had in 14 Volumes, strongly and neatly bound, with calf or vellum back, £3, 10s.

Contents of the Series.

HOMER: THE ILIAD, by the Editor.—HOMER: THE ODYSSEY, by the Editor.—HERODOTUS, by George C. Swayne, M.A.—XENOPHON, by Sir Alexander Grant, Bart., LL.D.—EURIPIDES, by W. B. Donne.—ARISTOPHANES, by the Editor.—PLATO, by Clifton W. Collins, M.A.—LUCIAN, by the Editor.—ÆSCHYLUS, by the Right Rev. the Bishop of Colombo.—SOPHOCLES, by Clifton W. Collins, M.A.—HESIOD AND THEOGNIS, by the Rev. J. Davies, M.A.—GREEK ANTHOLOGY, by Lord Neaves.—VIRGIL, by the Editor.—HORACE, by Sir Theodore Martin, K.C.B.—JUVENAL, by Edward Walford, M.A.—PLAUTUS AND TERENCE, by the Editor.—THE COMMENTARIES OF CÆSAR, by Anthony Trollope.—TACITUS, by W. B. Donne.—CICERO, by the Editor.—PLINY'S LETTERS, by the Rev. Alfred Church, M.A., and the Rev. W. J. Brodribb, M.A.—LIVY, by the Editor.—OVID, by the Rev. A. Church, M.A.—CATULLUS, TIBULLUS, AND PROPERTIUS, by the Rev. Jas. Davies, M.A.—DEMOSTHENES, by the Rev. W. J. Brodribb, M.A.—ARISTOTLE, by Sir Alexander Grant, Bart., LL.D.—THUCYDIDES, by the Editor.—LUCRETIUS, by W. H. Mallock, M.A.—PINDAR, by the Rev. F. D. Morice, M.A.

Saturday Review.—"It is difficult to estimate too highly the value of such a series as this in giving 'English readers' an insight, exact as far as it goes, into those olden times which are so remote, and yet to many of us so close."

CATALOGUE

OF

MESSRS BLACKWOOD & SONS'

PUBLICATIONS.

ALISON. History of Europe. By Sir ARCHIBALD ALISON, Bart., D.C.L.
1. From the Commencement of the French Revolution to the Battle of Waterloo.
    LIBRARY EDITION, 14 vols., with Portraits. Demy 8vo, £10, 10s.
    ANOTHER EDITION, in 20 vols. crown 8vo, £6.
    PEOPLE'S EDITION, 13 vols. crown 8vo, £2, 11s.
2. Continuation to the Accession of Louis Napoleon.
    LIBRARY EDITION, 8 vols. 8vo, £6, 7s. 6d.
    PEOPLE'S EDITION, 8 vols. crown 8vo, 34s.
3. Epitome of Alison's History of Europe. Twenty-ninth Thousand, 7s. 6d.
4. Atlas to Alison's History of Europe. By A. Keith Johnston.
    LIBRARY EDITION, demy 4to, £3, 3s.
    PEOPLE'S EDITION, 31s. 6d.

——— Life of John Duke of Marlborough. With some Account of his Contemporaries, and of the War of the Succession. Third Edition, 2 vols. 8vo. Portraits and Maps, 30s.

——— Essays: Historical, Political, and Miscellaneous. 3 vols. demy 8vo, 45s.

ACTA SANCTORUM HIBERNIÆ; Ex Codice Salmanticensi. Nunc primum integre edita opera CAROLI DE SMEDT et JOSEPHI DE BACKER, e Soc. Jesu, Hagiographorum Bollandianorum; Auctore et Sumptus Largiente JOANNE PATRICIO MARCHIONE BOTHAE. In One handsome 4to Volume, bound in half roxburghe, £2, 2s.; in paper wrapper, 31s. 6d.

AIRD. Poetical Works of Thomas Aird. Fifth Edition, with Memoir of the Author by the Rev. JARDINE WALLACE, and Portrait. Crown 8vo, 7s. 6d.

ALLARDYCE. The City of Sunshine. By ALEXANDER ALLARDYCE. Three vols. post 8vo, £1, 5s. 6d.

——— Memoir of the Honourable George Keith Elphinstone, K.B., Viscount Keith of Stonehaven, Marischal, Admiral of the Red. 8vo, with Portrait, Illustrations, and Maps, 21s.

ALMOND. Sermons by a Lay Head-master. By HELY HUTCHINSON ALMOND, M.A. Oxon., Head-master of Loretto School. Crown 8vo, 5s.

ANCIENT CLASSICS FOR ENGLISH READERS. Edited by Rev. W. LUCAS COLLINS, M.A. Price 2s. 6d. each. *For list of Vols., see page 2.*

AYTOUN. Lays of the Scottish Cavaliers, and other Poems. By W. EDMONDSTOUNE AYTOUN, D.C.L., Professor of Rhetoric and Belles-Lettres in the University of Edinburgh. New Edition. Fcap. 8vo, 3s. 6d.
Another Edition, being the Thirtieth. Fcap. 8vo, cloth extra, 7s. 6d.
Cheap Edition. Fcap. 8vo. Illustrated Cover. Price 1s. Cloth, 1s. 3d.

——— An Illustrated Edition of the Lays of the Scottish Cavaliers. From designs by Sir NOEL PATON. Small 4to, in gilt cloth, 21s.

——— Bothwell: a Poem. Third Edition. Fcap. 7s. 6d.

——— Poems and Ballads of Goethe. Translated by Professor AYTOUN and Sir THEODORE MARTIN, K.C.B. Third Edition. Fcap., 6s.

LIST OF BOOKS PUBLISHED BY

AYTOUN. Bon Gaultier's Book of Ballads. By the SAME. Fifteenth Edition. With Illustrations by Doyle, Leech, and Crowquill. Fcap. 8vo, 5s.
——— The Ballads of Scotland. Edited by Professor AYTOUN. Fourth Edition. 2 vols. fcap. 8vo, 12s.
——— Memoir of William E. Aytoun, D.C.L. By Sir THEODORE MARTIN, K.C.B. With Portrait. Post 8vo, 12s.

BACH. On Musical Education and Vocal Culture. By ALBERT B. BACH. Fourth Edition. 8vo, 7s. 6d.
——— The Principles of Singing. A Practical Guide for Vocalists and Teachers. With Course of Vocal Exercises. Crown 8vo, 6s.
——— The Art of Singing. With Musical Exercises for Young People. Crown 8vo, 3s.
——— The Art Ballad: Loewe and Schubert. With Music Illustrations. With a Portrait of LOEWE. Third Edition. Small 4to. 5s.

BALLADS AND POEMS. By MEMBERS OF THE GLASGOW BALLAD CLUB. Crown 8vo, 7s. 6d

BANNATYNE. Handbook of Republican Institutions in the United States of America. Based upon Federal and State Laws, and other reliable sources of information. By DUGALD J. BANNATYNE, Scotch Solicitor, New York; Member of the Faculty of Procurators, Glasgow. Cr. 8vo, 7s. 6d.

BELLAIRS. The Transvaal War, 1880-81. Edited by Lady BELLAIRS. With a Frontispiece and Map. 8vo, 15s.
——— Gossips with Girls and Maidens, Betrothed and Free. New Edition. Crown 8vo, 3s. 6d. Cloth, extra gilt edges, 5s.

BESANT. The Revolt of Man. By WALTER BESANT, M.A. Ninth Edition. Crown 8vo, 3s. 6d.
——— Readings in Rabelais. Crown 8vo, 7s. 6d.

BEVERIDGE. Culross and Tulliallan; or Perthshire on Forth. Its History and Antiquities. With Elucidations of Scottish Life and Character from the Burgh and Kirk-Session Records of that District. By DAVID BEVERIDGE. 2 vols. 8vo, with Illustrations, 42s.
——— Between the Ochils and the Forth; or, From Stirling Bridge to Aberdour. Crown 8vo, 6s.

BLACK. Heligoland and the Islands of the North Sea. By WILLIAM GEORGE BLACK. Crown 8vo, 4s.

BLACKIE. Lays and Legends of Ancient Greece. By JOHN STUART BLACKIE, Emeritus Professor of Greek in the University of Edinburgh. Second Edition. Fcap. 8vo. 5s.
——— The Wisdom of Goethe. Fcap. 8vo. Cloth, extra gilt, 6s.
——— Scottish Song: Its Wealth, Wisdom, and Social Significance. Crown 8vo. With Music. 7s. 6d.
——— A Song of Heroes. Crown 8vo, 6s.

BLACKWOOD'S MAGAZINE, from Commencement in 1817 to November 1891. Nos. 1 to 913, forming 148 Volumes.
——— Index to Blackwood's Magazine. Vols. 1 to 50. 8vo, 15s.

BLACKWOOD. Tales from Blackwood. Price One Shilling each, in Paper Cover. Sold separately at all Railway Bookstalls.
They may also be had bound in cloth, 18s., and in half calf, richly gilt, 30s. Or 12 volumes in 6, roxburghe, 21s., and half red morocco, 28s.
——— Tales from Blackwood. New Series. Complete in Twenty-four Shilling Parts. Handsomely bound in 12 vols., cloth, 30s. In leather back, roxburghe style, 37s. 6d. In half calf, gilt. 52s. 6d. In half morocco, 55s.
——— Tales from Blackwood. Third Series. Complete in 6 vols. Handsomely bound in cloth, 15s.; or in 12 vols. 18s. The 6 vols. bound in roxburghe, 21s. Half calf, 25s. Half morocco, 28s. Also in 12 parts, price 1s. each.
——— Travel, Adventure, and Sport. From 'Blackwood's Magazine.' Uniform with 'Tales from Blackwood.' In Twelve Parts, each price 1s. Or handsomely bound in 6 vols., 15s. Half calf, 25s.

BLACKWOOD. New Uniform Series of Three-and-Sixpenny Novels (Copyright). Crown 8vo, cloth. Now ready:—

BEGGAR MY NEIGHBOUR. By E. D. Gerard.	LADY BABY. By D. Gerard.
THE WATERS OF HERCULES. By the Same.	HURRISH. By the Hon. Emily Lawless.
SONS AND DAUGHTERS. By Mrs Oliphant.	THE BLACKSMITH OF VOE. By Paul Cushing.
FAIR TO SEE. By L. W. M. Lockhart.	
THE REVOLT OF MAN. By Walter Besant.	THE DILEMMA. By the Author of 'The Battle of Dorking.'
MINE IS THINE. By L. W. M. Lockhart.	
ALTIORA PETO. By Laurence Oliphant.	MY TRIVIAL LIFE AND MISFORTUNE. By A Plain Woman.
DOUBLES AND QUITS. By L. W. M. Lockhart.	
	PICCADILLY. By Laurence Oliphant. With Illustrations.

Others in preparation.

——— Standard Novels. Uniform in size and legibly Printed. Each Novel complete in one volume.

FLORIN SERIES, Illustrated Boards. Or in New Cloth Binding, 2s. 6d.

TOM CRINGLE'S LOG. By Michael Scott.	PEN OWEN. By Dean Hook.
THE CRUISE OF THE MIDGE. By the Same.	ADAM BLAIR. By J. G. Lockhart.
CYRIL THORNTON. By Captain Hamilton.	LADY LEE'S WIDOWHOOD. By General Sir E. B. Hamley.
ANNALS OF THE PARISH. By John Galt.	
THE PROVOST, &c. By John Galt.	SALEM CHAPEL. By Mrs Oliphant.
SIR ANDREW WYLIE. By John Galt.	THE PERPETUAL CURATE. By Mrs Oliphant.
THE ENTAIL. By John Galt.	
MISS MOLLY. By Beatrice May Butt.	MISS MARJORIBANKS. By Mrs Oliphant.
REGINALD DALTON. By J. G. Lockhart.	JOHN: A Love Story. By Mrs Oliphant.

SHILLING SERIES, Illustrated Cover. Or in New Cloth Binding, 1s. 6d.

THE RECTOR, and THE DOCTOR'S FAMILY. By Mrs Oliphant.	SIR FRIZZLE PUMPKIN, NIGHTS AT MESS, &c.
THE LIFE OF MANSIE WAUCH. By D. M. Moir.	THE SUBALTERN.
	LIFE IN THE FAR WEST. By G. F. Ruxton.
PENINSULAR SCENES AND SKETCHES. By F. Hardman.	VALERIUS: A Roman Story. By J. G. Lockhart.

BLACKMORE. The Maid of Sker. By R. D. BLACKMORE, Author of 'Lorna Doone,' &c. New Edition. Crown 8vo, 6s.

BLAIR. History of the Catholic Church of Scotland. From the Introduction of Christianity to the Present Day. By ALPHONS BELLESHEIM, D.D., Canon of Aix-la-Chapelle. Translated, with Notes and Additions, by D. OSWALD HUNTER BLAIR, O.S.B., Monk of Fort Augustus. Complete in 4 vols. demy 8vo, with Maps. Price 12s. 6d. each.

BOSCOBEL TRACTS. Relating to the Escape of Charles the Second after the Battle of Worcester, and his subsequent Adventures. Edited by J. HUGHES, Esq., A.M. A New Edition, with additional Notes and Illustrations, including Communications from the Rev. R. H. BARHAM, Author of the 'Ingoldsby Legends.' 8vo, with Engravings, 16s.

BROUGHAM. Memoirs of the Life and Times of Henry Lord Brougham. Written by HIMSELF. 3 vols. 8vo, £2, 8s. The Volumes are sold separately, price 16s. each.

BROWN. The Forester: A Practical Treatise on the Planting, Rearing, and General Management of Forest-trees. By JAMES BROWN, LL.D., Inspector of and Reporter on Woods and Forests. Fifth Edition, revised and enlarged. Royal 8vo, with Engravings, 36s.

BROWN. The Ethics of George Eliot's Works. By JOHN CROMBIE BROWN. Fourth Edition. Crown 8vo, 2s. 6d.

BROWN. A Manual of Botany, Anatomical and Physiological. For the Use of Students. By ROBERT BROWN, M.A., Ph.D. Crown 8vo, with numerous Illustrations, 12s. 6d.

BRUCE. In Clover and Heather. Poems by WALLACE BRUCE. New and Enlarged Edition. Crown 8vo, 4s. 6d.

A limited number of Copies of the First Edition, on large hand-made paper, 12s. 6d.

BRYDALL. Art in Scotland; its Origin and Progress. By ROBERT BRYDALL, Master of St George's Art School of Glasgow. 8vo, 12s. 6d.

BUCHAN. Introductory Text-Book of Meteorology. By ALEXANDER BUCHAN, M.A., F.R.S.E., Secretary of the Scottish Meteorological Society, &c. Crown 8vo, with 8 Coloured Charts and Engravings, 4s. 6d.

LIST OF BOOKS PUBLISHED BY

BUCHANAN. The Shirè Highlands (East Central Africa). By JOHN BUCHANAN, Planter at Zomba. Crown 8vo, 5s.

BURBIDGE. Domestic Floriculture, Window Gardening, and Floral Decorations. Being practical directions for the Propagation, Culture, and Arrangement of Plants and Flowers as Domestic Ornaments. By F. W. BURBIDGE. Second Edition. Crown 8vo, with numerous Illustrations, 7s. 6d.

—— Cultivated Plants: Their Propagation and Improvement. Including Natural and Artificial Hybridisation, Raising from Seed, Cuttings, and Layers, Grafting and Budding, as applied to the Families and Genera in Cultivation. Crown 8vo, with numerous Illustrations, 12s. 6d.

BURTON. The History of Scotland: From Agricola's Invasion to the Extinction of the last Jacobite Insurrection. By JOHN HILL BURTON, D.C.L., Historiographer-Royal for Scotland. New and Enlarged Edition. 8 vols., and Index. Crown 8vo, £3, 3s.

—— History of the British Empire during the Reign of Queen Anne. In 3 vols. 8vo. 36s.

—— The Scot Abroad. Third Edition. Crown 8vo, 10s. 6d.

—— The Book-Hunter. New Edition. With Portrait. Crown 8vo, 7s. 6d.

BUTE. The Roman Breviary: Reformed by Order of the Holy Œcumenical Council of Trent; Published by Order of Pope St Pius V.; and Revised by Clement VIII. and Urban VIII.; together with the Offices since granted. Translated out of Latin into English by JOHN, Marquess of Bute, K.T. In 2 vols, crown 8vo. cloth boards, edges uncut. £2, 2s.

—— The Altus of St Columba. With a Prose Paraphrase and Notes. In paper cover, 2s. 6d.

BUTLER. Pompeii: Descriptive and Picturesque. By W. BUTLER. Post 8vo, 5s.

BUTT. Miss Molly. By BEATRICE MAY BUTT. Cheap Edition, 2s.

—— Eugenie. Crown 8vo, 6s. 6d.

—— Elizabeth, and Other Sketches. Crown 8vo, 6s.

—— Novels. New and Uniform Edition. Crown 8vo, each 2s. 6d. Delicia. *Now ready.*

CAIRD. Sermons. By JOHN CAIRD, D.D., Principal of the University of Glasgow. Sixteenth Thousand. Fcap. 8vo, 5s.

—— Religion in Common Life. A Sermon preached in Crathie Church, October 14, 1855, before Her Majesty the Queen and Prince Albert. Published by Her Majesty's Command. Cheap Edition, 3d.

CAMPBELL. Critical Studies in St Luke's Gospel: Its Demonology and Ebionitism. By COLIN CAMPBELL, B.D., Minister of the Parish of Dundee, formerly Scholar and Fellow of Glasgow University. Author of the 'Three First Gospels in Greek, arranged in parallel columns. Post 8vo, 7s. 6d.

CAMPBELL. Sermons Preached before the Queen at Balmoral. By the Rev. A. A. CAMPBELL, Minister of Crathie. Published by Command of Her Majesty. Crown 8vo, 4s. 6d.

CAMPBELL. Records of Argyll. Legends, Traditions, and Recollections of Argyllshire Highlanders, collected chiefly from the Gaelic. With Notes on the Antiquity of the Dress, Clan Colours or Tartans of the Highlanders. By LORD ARCHIBALD CAMPBELL. Illustrated with Nineteen full-page Etchings. 4to, printed on hand-made paper, £3, 3s.

CANTON. A Lost Epic, and other Poems. By WILLIAM CANTON. Crown 8vo, 5s.

CARRICK. Koumiss; or, Fermented Mare's Milk: and its Uses in the Treatment and Cure of Pulmonary Consumption, and other Wasting Diseases. With an Appendix on the best Methods of Fermenting Cow's Milk. By GEORGE L. CARRICK, M.D., L.R.C.S.E. and L.R.C.P.E., Physician to the British Embassy, St Petersburg, &c. Crown 8vo, 10s. 6d.

CARSTAIRS. British Work in India. By R. CARSTAIRS. Cr. 8vo, 6s.

CAUVIN. A Treasury of the English and German Languages. Compiled from the best Authors and Lexicographers in both Languages. By JOSEPH CAUVIN, LL.D. and Ph.D., of the University of Göttingen, &c. Crown 8vo, 7s. 6d.

CAVE-BROWN. Lambeth Palace and its Associations. By J. CAVE-BROWN, M.A., Vicar of Detling, Kent, and for many years Curate of Lambeth Parish Church. With an Introduction by the Archbishop of Canterbury. Second Edition, containing an additional Chapter on Medieval Life in the Old Palaces. 8vo, with Illustrations, 21s.

CHARTERIS. Canonicity; or, Early Testimonies to the Existence and Use of the Books of the New Testament. Based on Kirchhoffer's 'Quellensammlung.' Edited by A. H. CHARTERIS, D.D., Professor of Biblical Criticism in the University of Edinburgh. 8vo, 18s.

CHRISTISON. Life of Sir Robert Christison, Bart., M.D., D.C.L. Oxon., Professor of Medical Jurisprudence in the University of Edinburgh. Edited by his SONS. In two vols. 8vo. Vol. I.—Autobiography. 16s. Vol. II. —Memoirs. 16s.

CHURCH SERVICE SOCIETY. A Book of Common Order: Being Forms of Worship issued by the Church Service Society. Sixth Edition. Crown, 8vo, 6s. Also in 2 vols, crown 8vo, 6s. 6d.

CLELAND. Too Apt a Pupil. By ROBERT CLELAND. Author of 'Barbara Allan, the Provost's Daughter.' Crown 8vo, 6s.

CLOUSTON. Popular Tales and Fictions: their Migrations and Transformations. By W. A. CLOUSTON, Editor of 'Arabian Poetry for English Readers,' &c. 2 vols. post 8vo, roxburghe binding, 25s.

COBBAN. Master of his Fate. By J. MACLAREN COBBAN, Author of 'The Cure of Souls,' 'Tinted Vapours,' &c. New and Cheaper Edition. Crown 8vo, paper cover, 1s. Cloth, bevelled boards, 3s. 6d.

COCHRAN. A Handy Text-Book of Military Law. Compiled chiefly to assist Officers preparing for Examination; also for all Officers of the Regular and Auxiliary Forces. Comprising also a Synopsis of part of the Army Act. By Major F. COCHRAN, Hampshire Regiment Garrison Instructor, North British District. Crown 8vo, 7s. 6d.

COLQUHOUN. The Moor and the Loch. Containing Minute Instructions in all Highland Sports, with Wanderings over Crag and Corrie, Flood and Fell. By JOHN COLQUHOUN. Seventh Edition. With Illustrations. 8vo, 21s.

COTTERILL. Suggested Reforms in Public Schools. By C. C. COTTERILL, M.A. Crown 8vo, 3s. 6d.

CRANSTOUN. The Elegies of Albius Tibullus. Translated into English Verse, with Life of the Poet, and Illustrative Notes. By JAMES CRANSTOUN, LL.D., Author of a Translation of 'Catullus.' Crown 8vo, 6s. 6d.

—— The Elegies of Sextus Propertius. Translated into English Verse, with Life of the Poet, and Illustrative Notes. Crown 8vo, 7s. 6d.

CRAWFORD. Saracinesca. By F. MARION CRAWFORD, Author of 'Mr Isaacs,' 'Dr Claudius,' 'Zoroaster,' &c. &c. Fifth Ed. Crown 8vo, 6s.

CRAWFORD. The Doctrine of Holy Scripture respecting the Atonement. By the late THOMAS J. CRAWFORD, D.D., Professor of Divinity in the University of Edinburgh. Fifth Edition. 8vo, 12s.

—— The Fatherhood of God, Considered in its General and Special Aspects. Third Edition, Revised and Enlarged. 8vo, 9s.

—— The Preaching of the Cross, and other Sermons. 8vo, 7s. 6d.

—— The Mysteries of Christianity. Crown 8vo, 7s. 6d.

CRAWFORD. An Atonement of East London, and other Poems. By HOWARD CRAWFORD, M.A. Crown 8vo, 5s.

CUSHING. The Blacksmith of Voe. By PAUL CUSHING, Author of 'The Bull i' th' Thorn.' Cheap Edition. Crown 8vo, 3s. 6d.

—— Cut with his own Diamond. A Novel. 3 vols. cr. 8vo, 25s. 6d.

LIST OF BOOKS PUBLISHED BY

DAVIES. Norfolk Broads and Rivers; or, The Waterways, Lagoons, and Decoys of East Anglia. By G. CHRISTOPHER DAVIES. Illustrated with Seven full-page Plates. New and Cheaper Edition. Crown 8vo, 6s.

—— Our Home in Aveyron. Sketches of Peasant Life in Aveyron and the Lot. By G. CHRISTOPHER DAVIES and Mrs BROUGHALL. Illustrated with full-page Illustrations. 8vo, 15s. Cheap Edition, 7s. 6d.

DAYNE. In the Name of the Tzar. A Novel. By J. BELFORD DAYNE. Crown 8vo, 6s.

—— Tribute to Satan. A Novel. Crown 8vo, 2s. 6d.

DE LA WARR. An Eastern Cruise in the 'Edeline.' By the Countess DE LA WARR. In Illustrated Cover. 2s.

DESCARTES. The Method, Meditations, and Principles of Philosophy of Descartes. Translated from the Original French and Latin. With a New Introductory Essay, Historical and Critical, on the Cartesian Philosophy. By Professor VEITCH, LL.D., Glasgow University. Ninth Edition. 6s. 6d.

DICKSON. Gleanings from Japan. By W. G. DICKSON, Author of 'Japan: Being a Sketch of its History, Government, and Officers of the Empire.' With Illustrations. 8vo, 16s.

DOGS, OUR DOMESTICATED: Their Treatment in reference to Food, Diseases, Habits, Punishment, Accomplishments. By 'MAGENTA.' Crown 8vo, 2s. 6d.

DOMESTIC EXPERIMENT, A. By the Author of 'Ideala: A Study from Life.' Crown 8vo, 6s.

DR HERMIONE. By the Author of 'Lady Bluebeard,' 'Zit and Xoe.' Crown 8vo, 6s.

DU CANE. The Odyssey of Homer, Books I.-XII. Translated into English Verse. By Sir CHARLES DU CANE, K.C.M.G. 8vo, 10s. 6d.

DUDGEON. History of the Edinburgh or Queen's Regiment Light Infantry Militia, now 3rd Battalion The Royal Scots; with an Account of the Origin and Progress of the Militia, and a Brief Sketch of the old Royal Scots. By Major R. C. DUDGEON, Adjutant 3rd Battalion The Royal Scots. Post 8vo, with Illustrations. 10s. 6d.

DUNCAN. Manual of the General Acts of Parliament relating to the Salmon Fisheries of Scotland from 1828 to 1882. By J. BARKER DUNCAN. Crown 8vo, 5s.

DUNSMORE. Manual of the Law of Scotland as to the Relations between Agricultural Tenants and their Landlords, Servants, Merchants, and Bowers. By W. DUNSMORE. 8vo, 7s. 6d.

DUPRÉ. Thoughts on Art, and Autobiographical Memoirs of Giovanni Dupré. Translated from the Italian by E. M. PERUZZI, with the permission of the Author. New Edition. With an Introduction by W. W. STORY. Crown 8vo, 10s. 6d.

ELIOT. George Eliot's Life, Related in her Letters and Journals. Arranged and Edited by her husband, J. W. CROSS. With Portrait and other Illustrations. Third Edition. 3 vols. post 8vo, 42s.

—— George Eliot's Life. (Cabinet Edition.) With Portrait and other Illustrations. 3 vols. crown 8vo, 15s.

—— George Eliot's Life. With Portrait and other Illustrations. New Edition, in one volume. Crown 8vo, 7s. 6d.

—— Works of George Eliot (Cabinet Edition). Handsomely printed in a new type, 21 volumes, crown 8vo, price £5, 5s. The Volumes are also sold separately, price 5s. each, viz.:—
Romola. 2 vols.—Silas Marner, The Lifted Veil, Brother Jacob. 1 vol.—Adam Bede. 2 vols.—Scenes of Clerical Life. 2 vols.—The Mill on the Floss. 2 vols.—Felix Holt. 2 vols.—Middlemarch. 3 vols.—Daniel Deronda. 3 vols.—The Spanish Gypsy. 1 vol.—Jubal, and other Poems, Old and New. 1 vol.—Theophrastus Such. 1 vol.—Essays. 1 vol.

—— Novels by GEORGE ELIOT. Cheap Edition. Adam Bede. Illustrated. 3s. 6d., cloth.—The Mill on the Floss. Illustrated. 3s. 6d., cloth.—Scenes of Clerical Life. Illustrated. 3s., cloth.—Silas Marner: the Weaver of Raveloe. Illustrated. 2s. 6d., cloth.—Felix Holt, the Radical. Illustrated. 3s. 6d., cloth.—Romola. With Vignette. 3s. 6d., cloth.

ELIOT. Middlemarch. Crown 8vo, 7s. 6d.
——— Daniel Deronda. Crown 8vo, 7s. 6d.
——— Essays. New Edition. Crown 8vo, 5s.
——— Impressions of Theophrastus Such. New Ed. Cr. 8vo, 5s.
——— The Spanish Gypsy. New Edition. Crown 8vo, 5s.
——— The Legend of Jubal, and other Poems, Old and New. New Edition. Crown 8vo, 5s.
——— Wise, Witty, and Tender Sayings, in Prose and Verse. Selected from the Works of GEORGE ELIOT. Eighth Edition. Fcap. 8vo, 6s.
——— The George Eliot Birthday Book. Printed on fine paper, with red border, and handsomely bound in cloth, gilt. Fcap. 8vo, cloth, 3s. 6d. And in French morocco or Russia, 5s.
ESSAYS ON SOCIAL SUBJECTS. Originally published in the 'Saturday Review.' New Ed. First & Second Series. 2 vols. cr. 8vo, 6s. each.
EWALD. The Crown and its Advisers; or, Queen, Ministers, Lords and Commons. By ALEXANDER CHARLES EWALD, F.S.A. Crown 8vo, 5s.
FAITHS OF THE WORLD, The. A Concise History of the Great Religious Systems of the World. By various Authors. Crown 8vo, 5s.
FARRER. A Tour in Greece in 1880. By RICHARD RIDLEY FARRER. With Twenty-seven full-page Illustrations by LORD WINDSOR. Royal 8vo, with a Map, 21s.
FERRIER. Philosophical Works of the late James F. Ferrier, B.A. Oxon., Professor of Moral Philosophy and Political Economy, St Andrews. New Edition. Edited by Sir ALEX. GRANT, Bart., D.C.L., and Professor LUSHINGTON. 3 vols. crown 8vo, 34s. 6d.
——— Institutes of Metaphysic. Third Edition. 10s. 6d.
——— Lectures on the Early Greek Philosophy. 3d Ed. 10s. 6d.
——— Philosophical Remains, including the Lectures on Early Greek Philosophy. 2 vols., 24s.
FITZROY. Dogma and the Church of England. By A. I. FITZROY. Post 8vo, 7s. 6d.
FLINT. The Philosophy of History in Europe. By ROBERT FLINT, D.D., LL.D., Professor of Divinity, University of Edinburgh. 2 vols. 8vo. [*New Edition in preparation.*
——— Theism. Being the Baird Lecture for 1876. Seventh Edition. Crown 8vo, 7s. 6d.
——— Anti-Theistic Theories. Being the Baird Lecture for 1877. Fourth Edition. Crown 8vo, 10s. 6d.
——— Agnosticism. Being the Croall Lectures for 1887-88. [*In the press.*
FORBES. Insulinde: Experiences of a Naturalist's Wife in the Eastern Archipelago. By Mrs H. O. FORBES. Crown 8vo, with a Map. 4s. 6d.
FOREIGN CLASSICS FOR ENGLISH READERS. Edited by Mrs OLIPHANT. Price 2s. 6d. *For List of Volumes published, see page 2.*
FOSTER. The Fallen City, and Other Poems. By WILL FOSTER. In 1 vol. Crown 8vo. [*Immediately.*
FULLARTON. Merlin: A Dramatic Poem. By RALPH MACLEOD FULLARTON. Crown 8vo, 5s.
GALT. Novels by JOHN GALT. Fcap. 8vo, boards, 2s.; cloth, 2s. 6d. Annals of the Parish.—The Provost.—Sir Andrew Wylie.—The Entail.
GENERAL ASSEMBLY OF THE CHURCH OF SCOTLAND.
——— Prayers for Social and Family Worship. Prepared by a Special Committee of the General Assembly of the Church of Scotland. Entirely New Edition, Revised and Enlarged. Fcap. 8vo, red edges, 2s.
——— Prayers for Family Worship. A Selection from the complete book. Fcap. 8vo, red edges, price 1s.

LIST OF BOOKS PUBLISHED BY

GENERAL ASSEMBLY OF THE CHURCH OF SCOTLAND.
—— Scottish Hymnal, with Appendix Incorporated. Published for Use in Churches by Authority of the General Assembly. 1. Large type, cloth, red edges, 2s. 6d.; French morocco, 4s. 2. Bourgeois type, limp cloth, 1s.; French morocco, 2s. 3. Nonpareil type, cloth, red edges, 6d.; French morocco, 1s. 4d. 4. Paper covers, 3d. 5. Sunday-School Edition, paper covers, 1d. No. 1, bound with the Psalms and Paraphrases, French morocco, 8s. No. 2, bound with the Psalms and Paraphrases, cloth, 2s.; French morocco, 3s.

GERARD. Reata: What's in a Name. By E. D. GERARD. New Edition. Crown 8vo, 6s.
—— Beggar my Neighbour. Cheap Edition. Crown 8vo, 3s. 6d.
—— The Waters of Hercules. Cheap Edition. Crown 8vo, 3s. 6d.
GERARD. The Land beyond the Forest. Facts, Figures, and Fancies from Transylvania. By E. GERARD. In Two Volumes. With Maps and Illustrations. 25s.
—— Bis: Some Tales Retold. Crown 8vo, 6s.
—— A Secret Mission. 2 vols. crown 8vo, 17s.
GERARD. Lady Baby. By DOROTHEA GERARD, Author of 'Orthodox.' Cheap Edition. Crown 8vo, 3s. 6d.
—— Recha. Second Edition. Crown 8vo, 6s.
GERARD. Stonyhurst Latin Grammar. By Rev. JOHN GERARD. Fcap. 8vo, 3s.
GILL. Free Trade: an Inquiry into the Nature of its Operation. By RICHARD GILL. Crown 8vo, 7s. 6d.
—— Free Trade under Protection. Crown 8vo, 7s. 6d.
GOETHE'S FAUST. Translated into English Verse by Sir THEODORE MARTIN, K.C.B. Part I. Second Edition, post 8vo, 6s. Ninth Edition, fcap., 3s. 6d. Part II. Second Edition, revised. Fcap. 8vo, 6s.
GOETHE. Poems and Ballads of Goethe. Translated by Professor AYTOUN and Sir THEODORE MARTIN, K.C.B. Third Edition, fcap. 8vo, 6s.
GOODALL. Juxta Crucem. Studies of the Love that is over us. By the late Rev. CHARLES GOODALL, B.D., Minister of Barr. With a Memoir by Rev. Dr Strong, Glasgow, and Portrait. Crown 8vo, 6s.
GORDON CUMMING. Two Happy Years in Ceylon. By C. F. GORDON CUMMING. With 15 full-page Illustrations and a Map. 2 vols. 8vo, 30s.
—— At Home in Fiji. Fourth Edition, post 8vo. With Illustrations and Map. 7s. 6d.
—— A Lady's Cruise in a French Man-of-War. New and Cheaper Edition. 8vo. With Illustrations and Map. 12s. 6d.
—— Fire-Fountains. The Kingdom of Hawaii: Its Volcanoes, and the History of its Missions. With Map and Illustrations. 2 vols. 8vo, 25s.
—— Wanderings in China. New and Cheaper Edition. 8vo, with Illustrations, 10s.
—— Granite Crags: The Yō-semité Region of California. Illustrated with 8 Engravings. New and Cheaper Edition. 8vo, 8s. 6d
GRAHAM. The Life and Work of Syed Ahmed Khan, C.S.I. By Lieut.-Colonel G. F. I. GRAHAM, B.S.C. 8vo, 14s.
GRAHAM. Manual of the Elections (Scot.) (Corrupt and Illegal Practices) Act, 1890. With Analysis, Relative Act of Sederunt, Appendix containing the Corrupt Practices Acts of 1883 and 1885, and Copious Index. By J. EDWARD GRAHAM, Advocate. 8vo, 4s. 6d.
GRANT. Bush-Life in Queensland. By A. C. GRANT. New Edition. Crown 8vo, 6s.
GRIFFITHS. Locked Up. By Major ARTHUR GRIFFITHS, Author of 'The Wrong Road,' 'Chronicles of Newgate,' &c. With Illustrations by C. J. STANILAND, R.I. Crown 8vo, 2s. 6d.
GUTHRIE-SMITH. Crispus; A Drama. By H. GUTHRIE-SMITH. In one volume. Fcap. 4to, 5s.

HAINES. Unless! A Romance. By RANDOLPH HAINES. Crown 8vo, 6s.

HALDANE. Subtropical Cultivations and Climates. A Handy Book for Planters, Colonists, and Settlers. By R. C. HALDANE. Post 8vo, 9s.

HALLETT. A Thousand Miles on an Elephant in the Shan States. By HOLT S. HALLETT, M. Inst. C.E., F.R.G.S., M.R.A.S., Hon. Member Manchester and Tyneside Geographical Societies. 8vo, with Maps and numerous Illustrations, 21s.

HAMERTON. Wenderholme: A Story of Lancashire and Yorkshire Life. By PHILIP GILBERT HAMERTON, Author of 'A Painter's Camp.' A New Edition. Crown 8vo, 6s.

HAMILTON. Lectures on Metaphysics. By Sir WILLIAM HAMILTON, Bart., Professor of Logic and Metaphysics in the University of Edinburgh. Edited by the Rev. H. L. MANSEL, B.D., LL.D., Dean of St Paul's; and JOHN VEITCH, M.A., LL.D., Professor of Logic and Rhetoric, Glasgow. Seventh Edition. 2 vols. 8vo, 24s.

—— Lectures on Logic. Edited by the SAME. Third Edition. 2 vols., 24s.

—— Discussions on Philosophy and Literature, Education and University Reform. Third Edition, 8vo, 21s.

—— Memoir of Sir William Hamilton, Bart., Professor of Logic and Metaphysics in the University of Edinburgh. By Professor VEITCH, of the University of Glasgow. 8vo, with Portrait, 18s.

—— Sir William Hamilton: The Man and his Philosophy. Two Lectures delivered before the Edinburgh Philosophical Institution, January and February 1883. By the SAME. Crown 8vo, 2s.

HAMLEY. The Operations of War Explained and Illustrated. By General Sir EDWARD BRUCE HAMLEY, K.C.B., K.C.M.G., M.P. Fifth Edition, revised throughout. 4to, with numerous Illustrations, 30s.

—— National Defence; Articles and Speeches. Post 8vo, 6s.

—— Shakespeare's Funeral, and other Papers. Post 8vo, 7s. 6d.

—— Thomas Carlyle: An Essay. Second Ed. Cr. 8vo, 2s. 6d.

—— On Outposts. Second Edition. 8vo, 2s.

—— Wellington's Career; A Military and Political Summary. Crown 8vo, 2s.

—— Lady Lee's Widowhood. Crown 8vo, 2s. 6d.

—— Our Poor Relations. A Philozoic Essay. With Illustrations, chiefly by Ernest Griset Crown 8vo, cloth gilt, 3s. 6d.

HAMLEY. Guilty, or Not Guilty? A Tale. By Major-General W. G. HAMLEY, late of the Royal Engineers. New Edition. Crown 8vo, 3s. 6d.

HARRISON. The Scot in Ulster. The Story of the Scottish Settlement in Ulster. By JOHN HARRISON, Author of 'Oure Tounis Colledge.' Crown 8vo, 2s. 6d.

HASELL. Bible Partings. By E. J. HASELL. Crown 8vo, 6s.

—— Short Family Prayers. Cloth, 1s.

HAY. The Works of the Right Rev. Dr George Hay, Bishop of Edinburgh. Edited under the Supervision of the Right Rev. Bishop STRAIN. With Memoir and Portrait of the Author. 5 vols. crown 8vo, bound in extra cloth, £1, 1s. The following Volumes may be had separately—viz.: The Devout Christian Instructed in the Law of Christ from the Written Word. 2 vols., 8s.—The Pious Christian Instructed in the Nature and Practice of the Principal Exercises of Piety. 1 vol., 3s.

HEATLEY. The Horse-Owner's Safeguard. A Handy Medical Guide for every Man who owns a Horse. By G. S. HEATLEY, M.R.C.V.S. Crown 8vo, 5s.

—— The Stock-Owner's Guide. A Handy Medical Treatise for every Man who owns an Ox or a Cow. Crown 8vo, 4s. 6d.

HEDDERWICK. Lays of Middle Age; and other Poems. By JAMES HEDDERWICK, LL.D. Price 3s. 6d.

LIST OF BOOKS PUBLISHED BY

HEDDERWICK. Backward Glances; or, Some Personal Recollections. With a Portrait. Post 8vo, 7s. 6d.

HEMANS. The Poetical Works of Mrs Hemans. Copyright Editions.—Royal 8vo, 5s.—The Same, with Engravings, cloth, gilt edges, 7s. 6d. —Six Vols. in Three, fcap., 12s. 6d.

SELECT POEMS OF MRS HEMANS. Fcap., cloth, gilt edges, 3s.

HERKLESS. Cardinal Beaton: Priest and Politician. By JOHN HERKLESS, Minister of Tannadice. With a Portrait. Post 8vo, 7s. 6d.

HOME PRAYERS. By Ministers of the Church of Scotland and Members of the Church Service Society. Second Edition. Fcap. 8vo, 3s.

HOMER. The Odyssey. Translated into English Verse in the Spenserian Stanza. By PHILIP STANHOPE WORSLEY. Third Edition, 2 vols. fcap., 12s.

—— The Iliad. Translated by P. S. WORSLEY and Professor CONINGTON. 2 vols. crown 8vo, 21s.

HUTCHINSON. Hints on the Game of Golf. By HORACE G. HUTCHINSON. Sixth Edition, Enlarged. Fcap. 8vo, cloth, 1s.

IDDESLEIGH. Lectures and Essays. By the late EARL OF IDDESLEIGH, G.C.B., D.C.L., &c. 8vo, 16s.

—— Life, Letters, and Diaries of Sir Stafford Northcote, First Earl of Iddesleigh. By ANDREW LANG. With Three Portraits and a View of Pynes. Third Edition. 2 vols. Post 8vo, 31s. 6d.

POPULAR EDITION. In one volume. With two Engravings. Post 8vo, 7s. 6d.

INDEX GEOGRAPHICUS: Being a List, alphabetically arranged, of the Principal Places on the Globe, with the Countries and Subdivisions of the Countries in which they are situated, and their Latitudes and Longitudes. Imperial 8vo, pp. 676, 21s.

JEAN JAMBON. Our Trip to Blunderland; or, Grand Excursion to Blundertown and Back. By JEAN JAMBON. With Sixty Illustrations designed by CHARLES DOYLE, engraved by DALZIEL. Fourth Thousand. Cloth, gilt edges, 6s. 6d. Cheap Edition, cloth, 3s. 6d. Boards, 2s. 6d.

JENNINGS. Mr Gladstone: A Study. By LOUIS J. JENNINGS, M.P., Author of 'Republican Government in the United States,' 'The Croker Memoirs,' &c. Popular Edition. Crown 8vo, 1s.

JERNINGHAM. Reminiscences of an Attaché. By HUBERT E. H. JERNINGHAM. Second Edition. Crown 8vo, 5s.

—— Diane de Breteuille. A Love Story. Crown 8vo, 2s. 6d.

JOHNSTON. The Chemistry of Common Life. By Professor J. F. W. JOHNSTON. New Edition, Revised, and brought down to date. By ARTHUR HERBERT CHURCH, M.A. Oxon.; Author of 'Food: its Sources, Constituents, and Uses,' &c. With Maps and 102 Engravings. Cr. 8vo, 7s. 6d.

—— Elements of Agricultural Chemistry and Geology. Revised, and brought down to date. By Sir CHARLES A. CAMERON, M.D., F.R.C.S.I., &c. Sixteenth Edition. Fcap. 8vo, 6s. 6d.

—— Catechism of Agricultural Chemistry and Geology. New Edition, revised and enlarged, by Sir C. A. CAMERON. Eighty-sixth Thousand, with numerous Illustrations, 1s.

JOHNSTON. Patrick Hamilton: a Tragedy of the Reformation in Scotland, 1528. By T. P. JOHNSTON. Crown 8vo, with Two Etchings. 5s.

KER. Short Studies on St Paul's Letter to the Philippians. By Rev. WILLIAM LEE KER, Minister of Kilwinning. Crown 8vo, 5s.

KING. The Metamorphoses of Ovid. Translated in English Blank Verse. By HENRY KING, M.A., Fellow of Wadham College, Oxford, and of the Inner Temple, Barrister-at-Law. Crown 8vo 10s. 6d.

KINGLAKE. History of the Invasion of the Crimea. By A. W. KINGLAKE. Cabinet Edition, revised. With an Index to the Complete Work. Illustrated with Maps and Plans. Complete in 9 Vols., crown 8vo, at 6s. each.

KINGLAKE. History of the Invasion of the Crimea. Demy 8vo.
Vol. VI. Winter Troubles. With a Map, 16s. Vols. VII. and VIII. From the Morrow of Inkerman to the Death of Lord Raglan. With an Index to the Whole Work. With Maps and Plans. 28s.
—— Eothen. A New Edition, uniform with the Cabinet Edition of the 'History of the Invasion of the Crimea,' price 6s.

KNEIPP. My Water-Cure. As Tested through more than Thirty Years, and Described for the Healing of Diseases and the Preservation of Health. By SEBASTIAN KNEIPP, Parish Priest of Wörishofen (Bavaria). With a Portrait and other Illustrations. Only Authorised English Translation. Translated from the Thirtieth German Edition by A. de F. Crown 8vo, 5s.

KNOLLYS. The Elements of Field-Artillery. Designed for the Use of Infantry and Cavalry Officers. By HENRY KNOLLYS, Captain Royal Artillery; Author of 'From Sedan to Saarbrück,' Editor of 'Incidents in the Sepoy War,' &c. With Engravings. Crown 8vo, 7s. 6d.

LAMINGTON. In the Days of the Dandies. By the late Lord LAMINGTON. Crown 8vo. Illustrated cover, 1s.; cloth, 1s. 6d.

LAWLESS. Hurrish: a Study. By the Hon. EMILY LAWLESS, Author of 'A Chelsea Householder,' &c. Fourth Edition, crown 8vo, 3s. 6d.

LAWSON. Spain of To-day: A Descriptive, Industrial, and Financial Survey of the Peninsula, with a full account of the Rio Tinto Mines. By W. R. LAWSON. Crown 8vo, 3s 6d.

LEES. A Handbook of Sheriff Court Styles. By J. M. LEES, M.A., LL.B., Advocate, Sheriff-Substitute of Lanarkshire. New Ed., 8vo, 21s.
—— A Handbook of the Sheriff and Justice of Peace Small Debt Courts. 8vo, 7s. 6d.

LIGHTFOOT. Studies in Philosophy. By the Rev. J. LIGHTFOOT, M.A., D.Sc., Vicar of Cross Stone, Todmorden. Crown 8vo, 4s. 6d.

LOCKHART. Novels by LAURENCE W. M. LOCKHART. See Blackwoods' New Series of Three-and-Sixpenny Novels on page 5.

LORIMER. The Institutes of Law: A Treatise of the Principles of Jurisprudence as determined by Nature. By the late JAMES LORIMER, Professor of Public Law and of the Law of Nature and Nations in the University of Edinburgh. New Edition, revised and much enlarged. 8vo, 18s.
—— The Institutes of the Law of Nations. A Treatise of the Jural Relation of Separate Political Communities. In 2 vols. 8vo. Volume I., price 16s. Volume II., price 20s.

LOVE. Scottish Church Music. Its Composers and Sources. With Musical Illustrations. By JAMES LOVE. In 1 vol. post 8vo, 7s. 6d.

M'COMBIE. Cattle and Cattle-Breeders. By WILLIAM M'COMBIE, Tillyfour. New Edition, enlarged, with Memoir of the Author. By JAMES MACDONALD, of the 'Farming World.' Crown 8vo, 3s. 6d.

MACRAE. A Handbook of Deer-Stalking. By ALEXANDER MACRAE, late Forester to Lord Henry Bentinck. With Introduction by HORATIO ROSS, Esq. Fcap. 8vo, with two Photographs from Life. 3s. 6d.

M'CRIE. Works of the Rev. Thomas M'Crie, D.D. Uniform Edition. Four vols. crown 8vo, 24s.
—— Life of John Knox. Containing Illustrations of the History of the Reformation in Scotland. Crown 8vo, 6s. Another Edition, 3s. 6d.
—— Life of Andrew Melville. Containing Illustrations of the Ecclesiastical and Literary History of Scotland in the Sixteenth and Seventeenth Centuries. Crown 8vo, 6s.
—— History of the Progress and Suppression of the Reformation in Italy in the Sixteenth Century. Crown 8vo, 4s.
—— History of the Progress and Suppression of the Reformation in Spain in the Sixteenth Century. Crown 8vo, 3s. 6d.
—— Lectures on the Book of Esther. Fcap. 8vo, 5s.

MACDONALD. A Manual of the Criminal Law (Scotland) Procedure Act, 1887. By NORMAN DORAN MACDONALD. Revised by the LORD JUSTICE-CLERK. 8vo, cloth. 10s. 6d.

MACGREGOR. Life and Opinions of Major-General Sir Charles MacGregor, K.C.B., C.S.I., C.I.E, Quartermaster-General of India. From his Letters and Diaries. Edited by LADY MACGREGOR. With Portraits and Maps to illustrate Campaigns in which he was engaged. 2 vols. 8vo, 35s.

M'INTOSH. The Book of the Garden. By CHARLES M'INTOSH, formerly Curator of the Royal Gardens of his Majesty the King of the Belgians, and lately of those of his Grace the Duke of Buccleuch, K.G., at Dalkeith Palace. 2 vols. royal 8vo, with 1350 Engravings. £4, 7s. 6d. Vol. I. On the Formation of Gardens and Construction of Garden Edifices. £2, 10s. Vol. II. Practical Gardening. £1, 17s. 6d.

MACINTYRE. Hindu-Koh: Wanderings and Wild Sports on and beyond the Himalayas. By Major-General DONALD MACINTYRE, V.C., late Prince of Wales' Own Goorkhas, F.R.G.S. Dedicated to H.R.H. The Prince of Wales. New and Cheaper Edition, revised, with numerous Illustrations, post 8vo, 7s. 6d.

MACKAY. A Sketch of the History of Fife and Kinross. A Study of Scottish History and Character. By Æ. J. G. MACKAY, Sheriff of these Counties. Crown 8vo, 6s.

MACKAY. A Manual of Modern Geography; Mathematical, Physical, and Political. By the Rev. ALEXANDER MACKAY, LL.D., F.R.G.S. 11th Thousand, revised to the present time. Crown 8vo, pp. 688. 7s. 6d.

—— Elements of Modern Geography. 53d Thousand, revised to the present time. Crown 8vo, pp. 300, 3s.

—— The Intermediate Geography. Intended as an Intermediate Book between the Author's 'Outlines of Geography' and 'Elements of Geography.' Fifteenth Edition, revised. Crown 8vo, pp. 238, 2s.

—— Outlines of Modern Geography. 188th Thousand, revised to the present time. 18mo, pp. 118, 1s.

—— First Steps in Geography. 105th Thousand. 18mo, pp. 56. Sewed, 4d.; cloth, 6d.

—— Elements of Physiography and Physical Geography. With Express Reference to the Instructions issued by the Science and Art Department. 30th Thousand, revised. Crown 8vo, 1s. 6d.

—— Facts and Dates; or, the Leading Events in Sacred and Profane History, and the Principal Facts in the various Physical Sciences. For Schools and Private Reference. New Edition. Crown 8vo, 3s. 6d.

MACKAY. An Old Scots Brigade. Being the History of Mackay's Regiment, now incorporated with the Royal Scots. With an Appendix containing many Original Documents connected with the History of the Regiment. By JOHN MACKAY (late) of HERRIESDALE. Crown 8vo, 5s.

MACKENZIE. Studies in Roman Law. With Comparative Views of the Laws of France, England, and Scotland. By LORD MACKENZIE, one of the Judges of the Court of Session in Scotland. Sixth Edition, Edited by JOHN KIRKPATRICK. Esq., M.A., LL.B., Advocate, Professor of History in the University of Edinburgh. 8vo, 12s.

M'KERLIE. Galloway: Ancient and Modern. An Account of the Historic Celtic District. By P. H. M'KERLIE, F.S.A. Scot., F.R.G.S., &c. Author of 'Lands and their Owners in Galloway.' Crown 8vo, 7s. 6d.

M'PHERSON. Summer Sundays in a Strathmore Parish. By J. GORDON M'PHERSON, Ph.D., F.R.S.E., Minister of Ruthven. Crown 8vo, 5s.

—— Golf and Golfers. Past and Present. With an Introduction by the Right Hon. A. J. BALFOUR, and a Portrait of the Author. Fcap. 8vo, 1s. 6d.

MAIN. Three Hundred English Sonnets. Chosen and Edited by DAVID M. MAIN. Fcap. 8vo, 6s.

MAIR. A Digest of Laws and Decisions, Ecclesiastical and Civil, relating to the Constitution, Practice, and Affairs of the Church of Scotland. With Notes and Forms of Procedure. By the Rev. WILLIAM MAIR, D.D. Minister of the Parish of Earlston. Crown 8vo. With Supplements, 8s.

MARMORNE. The Story is told by ADOLPHUS SEGRAVE, the youngest of three Brothers. Third Edition. Crown 8vo, 6s.

MARSHALL. French Home Life. By FREDERIC MARSHALL, Author of 'Claire Brandon.' Second Edition. 5s.

MARSHALL. It Happened Yesterday. A Novel. Crown 8vo, 6s.
MARSHMAN. History of India. From the Earliest Period to the Close of the India Company's Government; with an Epitome of Subsequent Events. By JOHN CLARK MARSHMAN, C.S.I. Abridged from the Author's larger work. Second Edition, revised. Crown 8vo, with Map, 6s. 6d.
MARTIN. Goethe's Faust. Part I. Translated by Sir THEODORE MARTIN, K.C.B. Second Ed., crown 8vo, 6s. Ninth Ed., fcap. 8vo, 3s. 6d.
—— Goethe's Faust. Part II. Translated into English Verse. Second Edition, revised. Fcap. 8vo, 6s.
—— The Works of Horace. Translated into English Verse, with Life and Notes. 2 vols. New Edition, crown 8vo, 21s.
—— Poems and Ballads of Heinrich Heine. Done into English Verse. Second Edition. Printed on *papier vergé*, crown 8vo, 8s.
—— The Song of the Bell, and other Translations from Schiller, Goethe, Uhland, and Others. Crown 8vo, 7s. 6d.
—— Catullus. With Life and Notes. Second Ed., post 8vo, 7s. 6d.
—— Aladdin : A Dramatic Poem. By ADAM OEHLENSCHLAEGER. Fcap. 8vo, 5s.
—— Correggio : A Tragedy. By OEHLENSCHLAEGER. With Notes. Fcap. 8vo, 3s.
—— King Rene's Daughter: A Danish Lyrical Drama. By HENRIK HERTZ. Second Edition, fcap., 2s. 6d.
MARTIN. On some of Shakespeare's Female Characters. In a Series of Letters. By HELENA FAUCIT, LADY MARTIN. Dedicated by permission to Her Most Gracious Majesty the Queen. New Edition, enlarged. 8vo, with Portrait by Lane, 7s. 6d.
MATHESON. Can the Old Faith Live with the New? or the Problem of Evolution and Revelation. By the Rev. GEORGE MATHESON, D.D. Third Edition. Crown 8vo, 7s. 6d.
—— The Psalmist and the Scientist; or, Modern Value of the Religious Sentiment. New and Cheaper Edition. Crown 8vo, 5s.
—— Spiritual Development of St Paul. Crown 8vo, 5s.
—— Sacred Songs. New and Cheaper Edition. Cr. 8vo, 2s. 6d.
MAURICE. The Balance of Military Power in Europe. An Examination of the War Resources of Great Britain and the Continental States. By Colonel MAURICE, R.A., Professor of Military Art and History at the Royal Staff College. Crown 8vo, with a Map. 6s
MEREDYTH. The Brief for the Government, 1886-92. A Handbook for Conservative and Unionist Writers, Speakers, &c. Second Edition. By W. H. MEREDYTH. Crown 8vo, 2s. 6d.
MICHEL. A Critical Inquiry into the Scottish Language. With the view of Illustrating the Rise and Progress of Civilisation in Scotland. By FRANCISQUE-MICHEL, F.S.A. Lond. and Scot., Correspondant de l'Institut de France, &c. 4to, printed on hand-made paper, and bound in Roxburghe, 66s.
MICHIE. The Larch : Being a Practical Treatise on its Culture and General Management. By CHRISTOPHER Y. MICHIE, Forester, Cullen House. Crown 8vo, with Illustrations. New and Cheaper Edition, enlarged, 5s.
—— The Practice of Forestry. Cr. 8vo, with Illustrations. 6s.
MIDDLETON. The Story of Alastair Bhan Comyn; or, The Tragedy of Dunphail. A Tale of Tradition and Romance. By the Lady MIDDLETON. Square 8vo 10s. Cheaper Edition, 5s.
MILLER. Landscape Geology. A Plea for the Study of Geology by Landscape Painters. By HUGH MILLER, of H.M. Geological Survey. Cr. 8vo, 3s.
MILNE. The Problem of the Churchless and Poor in our Large Towns. With special reference to the Home Mission Work of the Church of Scotland. By the Rev. ROBT. MILNE, M.A., D.D., Ardler. New and Cheaper Edition. Crown 8vo, 1s.

LIST OF BOOKS PUBLISHED BY

MILNE-HOME. Mamma's Black Nurse Stories. West Indian Folk-lore. By MARY PAMELA MILNE-HOME. With six full-page tinted Illustrations. Small 4to, 5s.

MINTO. A Manual of English Prose Literature, Biographical and Critical: designed mainly to show Characteristics of Style. By W. MINTO, M.A., Professor of Logic in the University of Aberdeen. Third Edition, revised. Crown 8vo, 7s. 6d.

―――― Characteristics of English Poets, from Chaucer to Shirley. New Edition, revised. Crown 8vo, 7s. 6d.

MOIR. Life of Mansie Wauch, Tailor in Dalkeith. By D. M. MOIR. With 8 Illustrations on Steel, by the late GEORGE CRUIKSHANK. Crown 8vo, 3s. 6d. Another Edition, fcap. 8vo, 1s. 6d.

MOMERIE. Defects of Modern Christianity, and other Sermons. By ALFRED WILLIAMS MOMERIE, M.A., D.Sc., LL.D. 4th Edition. Cr. 8vo, 5s.

―――― The Basis of Religion. Being an Examination of Natural Religion. Third Edition. Crown 8vo, 2s. 6d.

―――― The Origin of Evil, and other Sermons. Seventh Edition, enlarged. Crown 8vo, 5s.

―――― Personality. The Beginning and End of Metaphysics, and a Necessary Assumption in all Positive Philosophy. Fourth Ed. Cr. 8vo, 3s.

―――― Agnosticism. Third Edition, Revised. Crown 8vo, 5s.

―――― Preaching and Hearing; and other Sermons. Third Edition, Enlarged. Crown 8vo, 5s.

―――― Belief in God. Third Edition. Crown 8vo, 3s.

―――― Inspiration; and other Sermons. Second Ed. Cr. 8vo, 5s.

―――― Church and Creed. Second Edition. Crown 8vo, 4s. 6d.

MONTAGUE. Campaigning in South Africa. Reminiscences of an Officer in 1879. By Captain W. E. MONTAGUE, 94th Regiment, Author of 'Claude Meadowleigh,' &c. 8vo, 10s. 6d.

MONTALEMBERT. Memoir of Count de Montalembert. A Chapter of Recent French History. By Mrs OLIPHANT, Author of the 'Life of Edward Irving,' &c. 2 vols. crown 8vo, £1, 4s.

MORISON. Sordello. An Outline Analysis of Mr Browning's Poem. By JEANIE MORISON, Author of 'The Purpose of the Ages,' 'Ane Booke of Ballades,' &c. Crown 8vo, 3s.

―――― Selections from Poems. Crown 8vo, 4s. 6d.

―――― There as Here. Crown 8vo, 3s.
*** A limited impression on handmade paper, bound in vellum, 7s. 6d.

MUNRO. On Valuation of Property. By WILLIAM MUNRO, M.A., Her Majesty's Assessor of Railways and Canals for Scotland. Second Edition. Revised and enlarged. 8vo, 3s. 6d.

MURDOCH. Manual of the Law of Insolvency and Bankruptcy: Comprehending a Summary of the Law of Insolvency, Notour Bankruptcy, Composition-contracts, Trust-deeds, Cessios, and Sequestrations; and the Winding-up of Joint-Stock Companies in Scotland; with Annotations on the various Insolvency and Bankruptcy Statutes; and with Forms of Procedure applicable to these Subjects. By JAMES MURDOCH, Member of the Faculty of Procurators in Glasgow. Fifth Edition, Revised and Enlarged, 8vo, £1, 10s.

MY TRIVIAL LIFE AND MISFORTUNE: A Gossip with no Plot in Particular. By A PLAIN WOMAN. Cheap Ed., crown 8vo, 3s. 6d.

By the SAME AUTHOR.
POOR NELLIE. New Edition. Crown 8vo, 6s.

NAPIER. The Construction of the Wonderful Canon of Logarithms (Mirifici Logarithmorum Canonis Constructio). By JOHN NAPIER of Merchiston. Translated for the first time, with Notes, and a Catalogue of Napier's Works, by WILLIAM RAE MACDONALD. Small 4to, 15s. *A few large paper copies may be had, printed on Whatman paper, price 30s.*

WILLIAM BLACKWOOD AND SONS. 17

NEAVES. Songs and Verses, Social and Scientific. By an Old Contributor to 'Maga.' By the Hon. Lord NEAVES. Fifth Ed., fcap. 8vo, 4s.

——— The Greek Anthology. Being Vol. XX. of 'Ancient Classics for English Readers.' Crown 8vo, 2s. 6d.

NICHOLSON. A Manual of Zoology, for the Use of Students. With a General Introduction on the Principles of Zoology. By HENRY ALLEYNE NICHOLSON, M.D., D.Sc., F.L.S., F.G.S., Regius Professor of Natural History in the University of Aberdeen. Seventh Edition, rewritten and enlarged. Post 8vo, pp. 956, with 555 Engravings on Wood, 18s.

——— Text-Book of Zoology, for the Use of Schools. Fourth Edition, enlarged. Crown 8vo, with 188 Engravings on Wood, 7s. 6d.

——— Introductory Text-Book of Zoology, for the Use of Junior Classes. Sixth Edition, revised and enlarged, with 166 Engravings, 3s.

——— Outlines of Natural History, for Beginners; being Descriptions of a Progressive Series of Zoological Types. Third Edition, with Engravings, 1s. 6d.

——— A Manual of Palæontology, for the Use of Students. With a General Introduction on the Principles of Palæontology. By Professor H. ALLEYNE NICHOLSON and RICHARD LYDEKKER, B.A. Third Edition. Rewritten and greatly enlarged. 2 vols. 8vo, with Engravings, £3, 3s.

——— The Ancient Life-History of the Earth. An Outline of the Principles and Leading Facts of Palæontological Science. Crown 8vo, with 276 Engravings, 10s. 6d.

——— On the "Tabulate Corals" of the Palæozoic Period, with Critical Descriptions of Illustrative Species. Illustrated with 15 Lithograph Plates and numerous Engravings. Super-royal 8vo, 21s.

——— Synopsis of the Classification of the Animal Kingdom. 8vo, with 106 Illustrations, 6s.

——— On the Structure and Affinities of the Genus Monticulipora and its Sub-Genera, with Critical Descriptions of Illustrative Species. Illustrated with numerous Engravings on wood and lithographed Plates. Super-royal 8vo, 18s.

NICHOLSON. Communion with Heaven, and other Sermons. By the late MAXWELL NICHOLSON, D.D., Minister of St Stephen's, Edinburgh. Crown 8vo, 5s. 6d.

——— Rest in Jesus. Sixth Edition. Fcap. 8vo, 4s. 6d.

NICHOLSON. A Treatise on Money, and Essays on Present Monetary Problems. By JOSEPH SHIELD NICHOLSON, M.A., D.Sc., Professor of Commercial and Political Economy and Mercantile Law in the University of Edinburgh. 8vo, 10s. 6d.

——— Thoth. A Romance. Third Edition. Crown 8vo, 4s. 6d.

——— A Dreamer of Dreams. A Modern Romance. Second Edition. Crown 8vo, 6s.

NICOLSON AND MURE. A Handbook to the Local Government (Scotland) Act, 1889. With Introduction, Explanatory Notes, and Index. By J. BADENACH NICOLSON, Advocate, Counsel to the Scotch Education Department, and W. J. MURE, Advocate, Legal Secretary to the Lord Advocate for Scotland. Ninth Reprint. 8vo, 5s.

OLIPHANT. Masollam: a Problem of the Period. A Novel. By LAURENCE OLIPHANT. 3 vols. post 8vo, 25s. 6d.

——— Scientific Religion; or, Higher Possibilities of Life and Practice through the Operation of Natural Forces. Second Edition. 8vo, 16s.

——— Altiora Peto. By LAURENCE OLIPHANT. Cheap Edition. Crown 8vo, boards, 2s. 6d.; cloth, 3s. 6d. Illustrated Edition. Crown 8vo, cloth, 6s.

——— Piccadilly: A Fragment of Contemporary Biography. With Illustrations by Richard Doyle. New Edition, 3s. 6d. Cheap Edition, boards, 2s. 6d.

——— Traits and Travesties; Social and Political. Post 8vo, 10s. 6d.

OLIPHANT. The Land of Gilead. With Excursions in the Lebanon. With Illustrations and Maps. Demy 8vo, 21s.
—— Haifa: Life in Modern Palestine. 2d Edition. 8vo, 7s. 6d.
—— Episodes in a Life of Adventure; or, Moss from a Rolling Rolling Stone. Fifth Edition. Post 8vo, 6s.
—— Memoir of the Life of Laurence Oliphant, and of Alice Oliphant, his Wife. By Mrs M. O. W. OLIPHANT. Seventh Edition. In 2 vols. post 8vo, with Portraits. 21s.
OLIPHANT. Katie Stewart. By Mrs OLIPHANT. 2s. 6d.
—— The Duke's Daughter, and The Fugitives. A Novel. 3 vols. crown 8vo, 25s. 6d.
—— Two Stories of the Seen and the Unseen. The Open Door —Old Lady Mary. Paper Covers, 1s.
—— Sons and Daughters. Crown 8vo, 3s. 6d.
OLIPHANT. Notes of a Pilgrimage to Jerusalem and the Holy Land. By F. R. OLIPHANT. Crown 8vo, 3s. 6d.
ON SURREY HILLS. By "A SON OF THE MARSHES." Cr. 8vo, 6s.
OSBORN. Narratives of Voyage and Adventure. By Admiral SHERARD OSBORN, C.B. 3 vols. crown 8vo, 12s.
OSSIAN. The Poems of Ossian in the Original Gaelic. With a Literal Translation into English, and a Dissertation on the Authenticity of the Poems. By the Rev. ARCHIBALD CLERK. 2 vols. imperial 8vo, £1, 11s. 6d.
OSWALD. By Fell and Fjord; or, Scenes and Studies in Iceland. By E. J. OSWALD. Post 8vo, with Illustrations. 7s. 6d.
OWEN. Annals of a Fishing Village. Drawn from the Notes of "A Son of the Marshes." Edited by J. A. OWEN. Crown 8vo, with Illustrations. 7s. 6d.
PAGE. Introductory Text-Book of Geology. By DAVID PAGE, LL.D., Professor of Geology in the Durham University of Physical Science Newcastle, and Professor LAPWORTH of Mason Science College, Birmingham. With Engravings and Glossarial Index. Twelfth Edition. Revised and Enlarged. 3s. 6d.
—— Advanced Text-Book of Geology, Descriptive and Industrial. With Engravings, and Glossary of Scientific Terms. Sixth Edition, revised and enlarged, 7s. 6d.
—— Introductory Text-Book of Physical Geography. With Sketch-Maps and Illustrations. Edited by CHARLES LAPWORTH, LL.D., F.G.S., &c., Professor of Geology and Mineralogy in the Mason Science College, Birmingham. 12th Edition. 2s. 6d.
—— Advanced Text-Book of Physical Geography. Third Edition, Revised and Enlarged by Prof. LAPWORTH. With Engravings. 5s.
PATON. Spindrift. By Sir J. NOEL PATON. Fcap., cloth, 5s.
—— Poems by a Painter. Fcap., cloth, 5s.
PATON. Body and Soul. A Romance in Transcendental Pathology. By FREDERICK NOEL PATON. Third Edition. Crown 8vo, 1s.
PATTERSON. Essays in History and Art. By R. HOGARTH PATTERSON. 8vo, 12s.
—— The New Golden Age, and Influence of the Precious Metals upon the World. 2 vols. 8vo, 31s. 6d.
PAUL. History of the Royal Company of Archers, the Queen's Body-Guard for Scotland. By JAMES BALFOUR PAUL, Advocate of the Scottish Bar. Crown 4to, with Portraits and other Illustrations. £2, 2s.
PEILE. Lawn Tennis as a Game of Skill. With latest revised Laws as played by the Best Clubs. By Captain S. C. F. PEILE, B.S.C. Cheaper Edition, fcap. cloth, 1s.
PETTIGREW. The Handy Book of Bees, and their Profitable Management. By A. PETTIGREW. Fifth Edition, Enlarged, with Engravings. Crown 8vo, 3s. 6d.

PHILOSOPHICAL CLASSICS FOR ENGLISH READERS.
Edited by WILLIAM KNIGHT, LL.D., Professor of Moral Philosophy, University of St Andrews. In crown 8vo volumes, with portraits, price 3s. 6d.
[*For list of Volumes published, see page 2.*]

PHILIP. The Function of Labour in the Production of Wealth. By ALEXANDER PHILIP, LL.B., Edinburgh. Crown 8vo, 3s. 6d

POLLOK. The Course of Time: A Poem. By ROBERT POLLOK, A.M. Small fcap. 8vo, cloth gilt, 2s. 6d. Cottage Edition, 32mo, 8d. The Same, cloth, gilt edges, 1s. 6d. Another Edition, with Illustrations by Birket Foster and others, fcap., cloth, 3s. 6d., or with edges gilt, 4s.

PORT ROYAL LOGIC. Translated from the French; with Introduction, Notes, and Appendix. By THOMAS SPENCER BAYNES, LL.D., Professor in the University of St Andrews. Tenth Edition, 12mo, 4s.

POTTS AND DARNELL. Aditus Faciliores: An easy Latin Construing Book, with Complete Vocabulary. By the late A. W. POTTS, M.A., LL.D., and the Rev. C. DARNELL, M.A., Head-Master of Cargilfield Preparatory School, Edinburgh. Tenth Edition, fcap. 8vo, 3s. 6d.

—— Aditus Faciliores Graeci. An easy Greek Construing Book, with Complete Vocabulary. Fourth Edition, fcap. 8vo, 3s.

POTTS. School Sermons. By the late ALEXANDER WM. POTTS, LL.D., First Head-Master of Fettes College. With a Memoir and Portrait. Crown 8vo, 7s. 6d.

PRINGLE. The Live-Stock of the Farm. By ROBERT O. PRINGLE. Third Edition. Revised and Edited by JAMES MACDONALD. Cr. 8vo, 7s. 6d.

PUBLIC GENERAL STATUTES AFFECTING SCOTLAND from 1707 to 1847, with Chronological Table and Index. 3 vols. large 8vo, £3, 3s.

PUBLIC GENERAL STATUTES AFFECTING SCOTLAND, COLLECTION OF. Published Annually with General Index.

RADICAL CURE FOR IRELAND, The. A Letter to the People of England and Scotland concerning a new Plantation. With 2 Maps. 8vo, 7s. 6d.

RAMSAY. Rough Recollections of Military Service and Society. By Lieut.-Col. BALCARRES D. WARDLAW RAMSAY. Two vols. post 8vo, 21s.

RAMSAY. Scotland and Scotsmen in the Eighteenth Century. Edited from the MSS. of JOHN RAMSAY, Esq. of Ochtertyre, by ALEXANDER ALLARDYCE, Author of 'Memoir of Admiral Lord Keith, K.B.,' &c. 2 vols. 8vo, 31s. 6d.

RANKIN. A Handbook of the Church of Scotland. By JAMES RANKIN, D.D., Minister of Muthill; Author of 'Character Studies in the Old Testament,' &c. An entirely New and much Enlarged Edition. Crown 8vo, with 2 Maps, 7s. 6d.

—— The Creed in Scotland. An Exposition of the Apostles' Creed. With Extracts from Archbishop Hamilton's Catechism of 1552, John Calvin's Catechism of 1556, and a Catena of Ancient Latin and other Hymns. Post 8vo, 7s. 6d.

—— First Communion Lessons. Twenty-third Edition. Paper Cover, 2d.

RECORDS OF THE TERCENTENARY FESTIVAL OF THE UNIVERSITY OF EDINBURGH. Celebrated in April 1884. Published under the Sanction of the Senatus Academicus. Large 4to, £2, 12s. 6d.

ROBERTSON. Early Religion of Israel. Being the Baird Lecture for 1888-89. By JAMES ROBERTSON, D.D., Professor of Oriental Languages in the University of Glasgow. In one Vol. crown 8vo. [*Immediately.*]

ROBERTSON. Orellana, and other Poems. By J. LOGIE ROBERTSON, M.A. Fcap. 8vo. Printed on hand-made paper. 6s.

ROBERTSON. Our Holiday Among the Hills. By JAMES and JANET LOGIE ROBERTSON. Fcap. 8vo, 3s. 6d.

ROSCOE. Rambles with a Fishing-rod. By E. S. ROSCOE. Crown 8vo, 4s. 6d.

ROSS. Old Scottish Regimental Colours. By ANDREW ROSS, S.S.C., Hon. Secretary Old Scottish Regimental Colours Committee. Dedicated by Special Permission to Her Majesty the Queen. Folio. £2, 12s. 6d.

RUSSELL. The Haigs of Bemersyde. A Family History. By JOHN RUSSELL. Large 8vo, with Illustrations. 21s.

RUSSELL. Fragments from Many Tables. Being the Recollections of some Wise and Witty Men and Women. By GEO. RUSSELL. Cr. 8vo, 4s. 6d.

RUTLAND. Notes of an Irish Tour in 1846. By the DUKE OF RUTLAND, G.C.B. (Lord JOHN MANNERS). New Edition. Crown 8vo, 2s. 6d.

—— Correspondence between the Right Honble. William Pitt and Charles Duke of Rutland, Lord Lieutenant of Ireland, 1781-1787. With Introductory Note by John Duke of Rutland. 8vo, 7s. 6d.

RUTLAND. Gems of German Poetry. Translated by the DUCHESS OF RUTLAND (Lady JOHN MANNERS). [*New Edition in preparation.*

—— Impressions of Bad-Homburg. Comprising a Short Account of the Women's Associations of Germany under the Red Cross. Crown 8vo, 1s. 6d.

—— Some Personal Recollections of the Later Years of the Earl of Beaconsfield, K.G. Sixth Edition, 6d.

—— Employment of Women in the Public Service. 6d.

—— Some of the Advantages of Easily Accessible Reading and Recreation Rooms, and Free Libraries. With Remarks on Starting and Maintaining Them. Second Edition, crown 8vo, 1s.

—— A Sequel to Rich Men's Dwellings, and other Occasional Papers. Crown 8vo, 2s. 6d.

—— Encouraging Experiences of Reading and Recreation Rooms, Aims of Guilds, Nottingham Social Guild, Existing Institutions, &c., &c. Crown 8vo, 1s.

SCHILLER. Wallenstein. A Dramatic Poem. By FREDERICK VON SCHILLER. Translated by C. G. A. LOCKHART. Fcap. 8vo, 7s. 6d.

SCOTCH LOCH FISHING. By "Black Palmer." Crown 8vo, interleaved with blank pages, 4s.

SCOUGAL. Prisons and their Inmates; or, Scenes from a Silent World. By FRANCIS SCOUGAL. Crown 8vo, boards, 2s.

SELLAR. Manual of the Education Acts for Scotland. By the late ALEXANDER CRAIG SELLAR, M.P. Eighth Edition. Revised and in great part rewritten by J. EDWARD GRAHAM, B.A. Oxon., Advocate. With Rules for the conduct of Elections, with Notes and Cases. With a Supplement, being the Acts of 1889 in so far as affecting the Education Acts. 8vo, 12s. 6d.

[SUPPLEMENT TO SELLAR'S MANUAL OF THE EDUCATION ACTS. 8vo, 2s.]

SETH. Scottish Philosophy. A Comparison of the Scottish and German Answers to Hume. Balfour Philosophical Lectures, University of Edinburgh. By ANDREW SETH, M.A., Professor of Logic and Metaphysics in Edinburgh University. Second Edition. Crown 8vo, 5s.

—— Hegelianism and Personality. Balfour Philosophical Lectures. Second Series. Crown 8vo, 5s.

SETH. Freedom as Ethical Postulate. By JAMES SETH, M.A., George Munro Professor of Philosophy, Dalhousie College, Halifax, Canada. 8vo, 1s.

SHADWELL. The Life of Colin Campbell, Lord Clyde. Illustrated by Extracts from his Diary and Correspondence. By Lieutenant-General SHADWELL, C.B. 2 vols. 8vo. With Portrait, Maps, and Plans. 36s.

SHAND. Half a Century; or, Changes in Men and Manners. By ALEX. INNES SHAND, Author of 'Against Time,' &c. Second Edition, 8vo, 12s. 6d.

—— Letters from the West of Ireland. Reprinted from the 'Times.' Crown 8vo. 5s.

—— Kilcarra. A Novel. 3 vols. crown 8vo, 25s. 6d.

SHARPE. Letters from and to Charles Kirkpatrick Sharpe. Edited by ALEXANDER ALLARDYCE, Author of 'Memoir of Admiral Lord Keith, K.B.,' &c. With a Memoir by the Rev. W. K. R. BEDFORD. In two vols. 8vo. Illustrated with Etchings and other Engravings. £2, 12s. 6d.

SIM. Margaret Sim's Cookery. With an Introduction by L. B.
WALFORD, Author of 'Mr Smith: A Part of His Life,' &c. Crown 8vo, 5s.

SKELTON. Maitland of Lethington; and the Scotland of Mary Stuart. A History. By JOHN SKELTON, C.B., LL.D., Author of 'The Essays of Shirley.' Demy 8vo. 2 vols., 28s.

—— The Handbook of Public Health. A Complete Edition of the Public Health and other Sanitary Acts relating to Scotland. Annotated, and with the Rules, Instructions, and Decisions of the Board of Supervision brought up to date with relative forms. 8vo, with Supplement, 8s. 6d.

—— Supplement to Skelton's Handbook. The Administration of the Public Health Act in Counties. 8vo, cloth, 1s. 6d.

—— The Local Government (Scotland) Act in Relation to Public Health. A Handy Guide for County and District Councillors, Medical Officers, Sanitary Inspectors, and Members of Parochial Boards. Second Edition. With a new Preface on appointment of Sanitary Officers. Crown 8vo, 2s.

SMITH. For God and Humanity. A Romance of Mount Carmel. By HASKETT SMITH, Author of 'The Divine Epiphany,' &c. 3 vols. post 8vo, 25s. 6d.

SMITH. Thorndale; or, The Conflict of Opinions. By WILLIAM SMITH, Author of 'A Discourse on Ethics,' &c. New Edition. Cr. 8vo, 10s. 6d.

—— Gravenhurst; or, Thoughts on Good and Evil. Second Edition, with Memoir of the Author. Crown 8vo, 8s.

—— The Story of William and Lucy Smith. Edited by GEORGE MERRIAM. Large post 8vo, 12s. 6d.

SMITH. Memoir of the Families of M'Combie and Thoms, originally M'Intosh and M'Thomas. Compiled from History and Tradition. By WILLIAM M'COMBIE SMITH. With Illustrations. 8vo, 7s. 6d.

SMITH. Greek Testament Lessons for Colleges, Schools, and Private Students, consisting chiefly of the Sermon on the Mount and the Parables of our Lord. With Notes and Essays. By the Rev. J. HUNTER SMITH, M.A., King Edward's School, Birmingham. Crown 8vo, 6s.

SMITH. Writings by the Way. By JOHN CAMPBELL SMITH, M.A., Sheriff-Substitute. Crown 8vo, 9s.

SMITH. The Secretary for Scotland. Being a Statement of the Powers and Duties of the new Scottish Office. With a Short Historical Introduction and numerous references to important Administrative Documents. By W. C. SMITH, LL.B., Advocate. 8vo, 6s.

SORLEY. The Ethics of Naturalism. Being the Shaw Fellowship Lectures, 1884. By W. R. SORLEY, M.A., Fellow of Trinity College, Cambridge, Professor of Logic and Philosophy in University College of South Wales. Crown 8vo, 6s.

SPEEDY. Sport in the Highlands and Lowlands of Scotland with Rod and Gun. By TOM SPEEDY. Second Edition, Revised and Enlarged. With Illustrations by Lieut.-Gen. Hope Crealocke, C.B., C.M.G., and others. 8vo, 15s.

SPROTT. The Worship and Offices of the Church of Scotland. By GEORGE W. SPROTT, D.D., Minister of North Berwick. Crown 8vo, 6s.

STAFFORD. How I Spent my Twentieth Year. Being a Record of a Tour Round the World, 1886-87. By the MARCHIONESS OF STAFFORD. With Illustrations. Third Edition, crown 8vo, 8s. 6d.

STARFORTH. Villa Residences and Farm Architecture: A Series of Designs. By JOHN STARFORTH, Architect. 102 Engravings. Second Edition, medium 4to, £2, 17s. 6d.

STATISTICAL ACCOUNT OF SCOTLAND. Complete, with Index, 15 vols. 8vo, £16, 16s.
Each County sold separately, with Title, Index, and Map, neatly bound in cloth.

STEPHENS' BOOK OF THE FARM; detailing the Labours of the Farmer, Farm-Steward, Ploughman, Shepherd, Hedger, Farm-Labourer, Field-Worker, and Cattleman. Illustrated with numerous Portraits of Animals and Engravings of Implements, and Plans of Farm Buildings. Fourth Edition. Revised, and in great part rewritten by JAMES MACDONALD, of the 'Farming World,' &c., &c. Assisted by many of the leading agricultural authorities of the day. Complete in Six Divisional Volumes, bound in cloth, each 10s. 6d., or handsomely bound, in 3 volumes, with leather back and gilt top, £3, 3s.

STEPHENS. The Book of Farm Implements and Machines. By J. SLIGHT and R. SCOTT BURN, Engineers. Edited by HENRY STEPHENS. Large 8vo, £2, 2s.

STEVENSON. British Fungi. (Hymenomycetes.) By Rev. JOHN STEVENSON, Author of 'Mycologia Scotia,' Hon. Sec. Cryptogamic Society of Scotland. 2 vols. post 8vo, with Illustrations, price 12s. 6d. each.
Vol. I. AGARICUS—BOLBITIUS. Vol. II. CORTINARIUS—DACRYMYCES.

STEWART. Advice to Purchasers of Horses. By JOHN STEWART, V.S. New Edition. 2s. 6d.

—— Stable Economy. A Treatise on the Management of Horses in relation to Stabling, Grooming, Feeding, Watering, and Working. Seventh Edition, fcap. 8vo, 6s. 6d.

STEWART. A Hebrew Grammar, with the Pronunciation, Syllabic Division and Tone of the Words, and Quantity of the Vowels. By Rev. DUNCAN STEWART, D.D. Fourth Edition. 8vo, 3s. 6d.

STEWART. Boethius: An Essay. By HUGH FRASER STEWART, M.A., Trinity College, Cambridge. Crown 8vo, 7s. 6d.

STODDART. Angling Songs. By THOMAS TOD STODDART. New Edition, with a Memoir by ANNA M. STODDART. Crown 8vo, 7s. 6d.

STORMONTH. Etymological and Pronouncing Dictionary of the English Language. Including a very Copious Selection of Scientific Terms For Use in Schools and Colleges, and as a Book of General Reference. By the Rev. JAMES STORMONTH. The Pronunciation carefully Revised by the Rev. P. H. PHELP, M.A. Cantab. Tenth Edition, Revised throughout. Crown 8vo, pp. 800. 7s. 6d.

—— Dictionary of the English Language, Pronouncing, Etymological, and Explanatory. Revised by the Rev. P. H. PHELP. Library Edition. Imperial 8vo, handsomely bound in half morocco, 31s. 6d.

—— The School Etymological Dictionary and Word-Book. Fourth Edition. Fcap. 8vo, pp. 254. 2s.

STORY. Nero; A Historical Play. By W. W. STORY, Author of 'Roba di Roma.' Fcap. 8vo, 6s.

—— Vallombrosa. Post 8vo, 5s.

—— Poems. 2 vols. fcap., 7s. 6d.

—— Fiammetta. A Summer Idyl. Crown 8vo, 7s. 6d.

—— Conversations in a Studio. 2 vols. crown 8vo, 12s. 6d.

—— Excursions in Art and Letters. Crown 8vo, 7s. 6d.

STRICKLAND. Life of Agnes Strickland. By her SISTER. Post 8vo, with Portrait engraved on Steel, 12s. 6d.

STURGIS. John-a-Dreams. A Tale. By JULIAN STURGIS. New Edition, crown 8vo, 3s. 6d.

—— Little Comedies, Old and New. Crown 8vo, 7s. 6d.

SUTHERLAND. Handbook of Hardy Herbaceous and Alpine Flowers, for general Garden Decoration. Containing Descriptions of upwards of 1000 Species of Ornamental Hardy Perennial and Alpine Plants; along with Concise and Plain Instructions for their Propagation and Culture. By WILLIAM SUTHERLAND, Landscape Gardener; formerly Manager of the Herbaceous Department at Kew. Crown 8vo, 7s. 6d.

TAYLOR. The Story of My Life. By the late Colonel MEADOWS TAYLOR, Author of 'The Confessions of a Thug,' &c. &c. Edited by his Daughter. New and cheaper Edition, being the Fourth. Crown 8vo, 6s.

THOLUCK. Hours of Christian Devotion. Translated from the German of A. Tholuck, D.D., Professor of Theology in the University of Halle. By the Rev. ROBERT MENZIES, D.D. With a Preface written for this Translation by the Author. Second Edition, crown 8vo, 7s. 6d.

THOMSON. Handy Book of the Flower-Garden: being Practical Directions for the Propagation, Culture, and Arrangement of Plants in Flower-Gardens all the year round. With Engraved Plans. By DAVID THOMSON, Gardener to his Grace the Duke of Buccleuch, K.T., at Drumlanrig. Fourth and Cheaper Edition, crown 8vo, 5s.

THOMSON. The Handy Book of Fruit-Culture under Glass: being a series of Elaborate Practical Treatises on the Cultivation and Forcing of Pines, Vines, Peaches, Figs, Melons, Strawberries, and Cucumbers. With Engravings of Hothouses, &c. Second Ed. Cr. 8vo, 7s. 6d.

THOMSON. A Practical Treatise on the Cultivation of the Grape Vine. By WILLIAM THOMSON, Tweed Vineyards. Tenth Edition, 8vo, 5s.

THOMSON. Cookery for the Sick and Convalescent. With Directions for the Preparation of Poultices, Fomentations, &c. By BARBARA THOMSON. Fcap. 8vo, 1s. 6d.

THORNTON. Opposites. A Series of Essays on the Unpopular Sides of Popular Questions. By LEWIS THORNTON. 8vo, 12s. 6d.

TOM CRINGLE'S LOG. A New Edition, with Illustrations. Crown 8vo, cloth gilt, 5s. Cheap Edition, 2s.

TRANSACTIONS OF THE HIGHLAND AND AGRICULTURAL SOCIETY OF SCOTLAND. Published annually, price 5s.

TULLOCH. Rational Theology and Christian Philosophy in England in the Seventeenth Century. By JOHN TULLOCH, D.D., Principal of St Mary's College in the University of St Andrews; and one of her Majesty's Chaplains in Ordinary in Scotland. Second Edition. 2 vols. 8vo, 16s.

—— Modern Theories in Philosophy and Religion. 8vo, 15s.

—— Luther, and other Leaders of the Reformation. Third Edition, enlarged. Crown 8vo, 3s. 6d.

—— Memoir of Principal Tulloch, D.D., LL.D. By Mrs OLIPHANT, Author of 'Life of Edward Irving.' Third and Cheaper Edition. 8vo, with Portrait. 7s. 6d.

TWEEDIE. The Arabian Horse: his Country and People. With Portraits of Typical or Famous Arabians, and numerous other Illustrations; also a Map of the Country of the Arabian Horse, and a descriptive Glossary of Arabic words and proper names. By Colonel W. TWEEDIE, C.S.I., Bengal Staff Corps, H.B M.'s late Consul-General, Baghdad. [In the press.

VEITCH. Institutes of Logic. By JOHN VEITCH, LL.D., Professor of Logic and Rhetoric in the University of Glasgow. Post 8vo, 12s. 6d.

—— The Feeling for Nature in Scottish Poetry. From the Earliest Times to the Present Day. 2 vols. fcap. 8vo, in roxburghe binding. 15s.

—— Merlin and Other Poems. Fcap. 8vo. 4s. 6d.

—— Knowing and Being. Essays in Philosophy. First Series. Crown 8vo, 5s.

VIRGIL. The Æneid of Virgil. Translated in English Blank Verse by G. K. RICKARDS, M.A., and Lord RAVENSWORTH. 2 vols. fcap. 8vo, 10s.

WALFORD. Four Biographies from 'Blackwood': Jane Taylor, Hannah More, Elizabeth Fry, Mary Somerville. By L. B. WALFORD. Crown 8vo, 5s.

WARREN'S (SAMUEL) WORKS :—
Diary of a Late Physician. Cloth, 2s. 6d.; boards, 2s.
Ten Thousand A-Year. Cloth, 3s. 6d.; boards, 2s. 6d.
Now and Then. The Lily and the Bee. Intellectual and Moral Development of the Present Age. 4s. 6d.
Essays : Critical, Imaginative, and Juridical. 5s.

WARREN. The Five Books of the Psalms. With Marginal Notes. By Rev. SAMUEL L. WARREN, Rector of Esher, Surrey; late Fellow, Dean, and Divinity Lecturer, Wadham College, Oxford. Crown 8vo, 5s.

WEBSTER. The Angler and the Loop-Rod. By DAVID WEBSTER. Crown 8vo, with Illustrations, 7s. 6d.

WELLINGTON. Wellington Prize Essays on "the System of Field Manœuvres best adapted for enabling our Troops to meet a Continental Army." Edited by General Sir EDWARD BRUCE HAMLEY, K.C.B., K.C.M.G. 8vo, 12s. 6d.

WENLEY. Socrates and Christ: A Study in the Philosophy of Religion. By R. M. WENLEY, M.A., Lecturer on Mental and Moral Philosophy in Queen Margaret College, Glasgow; Examiner in Philosophy in the University of Glasgow. Crown 8vo, 6s.

WERNER. A Visit to Stanley's Rear-Guard at Major Barttelot's Camp on the Aruhwimi. With an Account of River-Life on the Congo. By J. R. WERNER, F.R.G.S., Engineer, late in the Service of the Etat Indépendant du Congo. With Maps, Portraits, and other Illustrations. 8vo. 16s.

WESTMINSTER ASSEMBLY. Minutes of the Westminster Assembly, while engaged in preparing their Directory for Church Government, Confession of Faith, and Catechisms (November 1644 to March 1649). Edited by the Rev. Professor ALEX. T. MITCHELL, of St Andrews, and the Rev. JOHN STRUTHERS, LL.D. With a Historical and Critical Introduction by Professor Mitchell. 8vo, 15s.

WHITE. The Eighteen Christian Centuries. By the Rev. JAMES WHITE. Seventh Edition, post 8vo, with Index, 6s.

––––––– History of France, from the Earliest Times. Sixth Thousand, post 8vo, with Index, 6s.

WHITE. Archæological Sketches in Scotland—Kintyre and Knapdale. By Colonel T. P. WHITE, R.E., of the Ordnance Survey. With numerous Illustrations. 2 vols. folio, £4, 4s. Vol. I., Kintyre, sold separately, £2, 2s.

––––––– The Ordnance Survey of the United Kingdom. A Popular Account. Crown 8vo, 5s.

WICKS. Golden Lives. The Story of a Woman's Courage. By FREDERICK WICKS. Cheap Edition, with 120 Illustrations. Illustrated Boards. 8vo, 2s. 6d.

WILLIAMSON. Poems of Nature and Life. By DAVID R. WILLIAMSON, Minister of Kirkmaiden. Fcap. 8vo, 3s.

WILLS AND GREENE. Drawing-room Dramas for Children. By W. G. WILLS and the Hon. Mrs GREENE. Crown 8vo, 6s.

WILSON. Works of Professor Wilson. Edited by his Son-in-Law, Professor FERRIER. 12 vols. crown 8vo, £2, 8s.

––––––– Christopher in his Sporting-Jacket. 2 vols., 8s.

––––––– Isle of Palms, City of the Plague, and other Poems. 4s.

––––––– Lights and Shadows of Scottish Life, and other Tales. 4s.

––––––– Essays, Critical and Imaginative. 4 vols., 16s.

––––––– The Noctes Ambrosianæ. 4 vols., 16s.

––––––– Homer and his Translators, and the Greek Drama. Crown 8vo, 4s.

WINGATE. Lily Neil. A Poem. By DAVID WINGATE. Crown 8vo, 4s. 6d.

WORDSWORTH. The Historical Plays of Shakspeare. With Introductions and Notes. By CHARLES WORDSWORTH, D.C.L., Bishop of S. Andrews. 3 vols. post 8vo, cloth, each price 7s. 6d., or handsomely bound in half-calf, each price 9s. 9d.

WORSLEY. Poems and Translations. By PHILIP STANHOPE WORSLEY, M.A. Edited by EDWARD WORSLEY. Second Edition, enlarged. Fcap. 8vo, 6s.

YATE. England and Russia Face to Face in Asia. A Record of Travel with the Afghan Boundary Commission. By Captain A. C. YATE, Bombay Staff Corps. 8vo, with Maps and Illustrations, 21s.

YATE. Northern Afghanistan; or, Letters from the Afghan Boundary Commission. By Major C. E. YATE, C.S.I., C.M.G. Bombay Staff Corps, F.R.G.S. 8vo, with Maps. 18s.

YOUNG. A Story of Active Service in Foreign Lands. Compiled from letters sent home from South Africa, India, and China, 1856-1882. By Surgeon-General A. GRAHAM YOUNG, Author of 'Crimean Cracks.' Crown 8vo, Illustrated, 7s. 6d.

YULE. Fortification: for the Use of Officers in the Army, and Readers of Military History. By Col. YULE, Bengal Engineers. 8vo. with numerous Illustrations, 10s. 6d.

ramcontent.com/pod-product-compliance
Source LLC
burg PA
115300426
300007B/716